Ill. 13. View upon the Achaemenid-period fortress of Old Kandahar, in Achaemenid Arachosia (Southeast Afghanistan). To the right, on top of the mountain, the remains of a Buddhist stupa of a later period. The citadel can be seen in the plain below. The fortress walls enclosed an area of about 1100 by 600 metres.

Ill. 14. The citadel of Old Kandahar, built during or before the Achaemenid period. Rising to a height of some thirty metres, this structure was completely man-made and still covers an area of approximately 200 by 100 metres.

A POLITICAL HISTORY
OF
THE ACHAEMENID EMPIRE

A POLITICAL HISTORY
OF
THE ACHAEMENID EMPIRE

BY

M.A. DANDAMAEV

TRANSLATED INTO ENGLISH BY W.J. VOGELSANG

E.J. BRILL
LEIDEN · NEW YORK · KØBENHAVN · KÖLN
1989

ISBN 90 04 09172 6

PRINTED IN THE NETHERLANDS BY E. J. BRILL

CONTENTS

LIST OF ILLUSTRATIONS AND MAPS

ACKNOWLEDGEMENTS

Acknowledgements are due to Prof. Dr. L. Vanden Berghe for kindly providing certain photographs (Nos. 1-2; 4; 7; 11), and to Mr A. Smeekens for the drawing of the Behistun relief (No. 10). Photographs Nos. 3 and 9 were provided by the author of the book. Photographs Nos. 12-14 are from the translator's collection. Illustrations 5 and 8 are based on drawings from Cornelis de Bruin, *Reizen over Moscovië door Perzië en Indië* (A.D. 1711).

PREFACE BY THE AUTHOR TO THE RUSSIAN EDITION
OF 1985

The Achaemenid empire originated in the sixth century B.C. and lasted for more than two hundred years. It was the first world power in history and encompassed, under the rule of the Persian kings, dozens of countries and peoples living in a huge area which stretched from Egypt in the west to northwestern India in the east. Essentially, the history of the Achaemenid realm is the history of all the Near East and West Central Asia. The Achaemenid empire represents a crucial period during which the foundations were laid for important socio-economic and political institutions and cultural traditions which were to play a vital role in world history. It is this aspect which explains the great interest in the subject shown by scholars and a wide circle of lay readers.

Although separate studies dedicated to the Achaemenid period are published almost every year, all too often the political history is discussed only superficially and commonly broken off at the fifth century B.C. After this date the authors pass on to a discussion of the campaigns of Alexander of Macedonia in the territory of the Persian kings, during the second half of the fourth century B.C. In modern times, the political history of ancient Iran was thoroughly investigated for the last time by the American orientalist A. T. Olmstead, in his *History of the Persian Empire*. Olmstead's study was concluded in 1943. After the posthumous publication of the book in 1948, archaeologists have brought to light a considerable number of written sources which frequently supplement in an essential way our information on the political events between the sixth and the fourth centuries B.C.

In the present book an attempt has been made to redraw the complete map of the Achaemenid empire's political history. This has been done with the help of all of the available information and academic literature. For an extensive survey of the written sources, and a brief discussion of the literature on the problems which will be outlined in this book, I refer the reader to a previous publication, written in collaboration with V. G. Lukonin, entitled *Kul'tura i Ekonomika Drevnego Irana* (Moscow 1980; English edition, revised and updated: *The Culture and Social Institutions of Ancient Iran*, Cambridge 1988). Information on the most important publications which have appeared since 1980 will be indicated in the course of the discussions of the relevant problems.

Iranian and other Eastern names are listed in their most common form, which is normally based on Latin and Greek tradition. References in the main text to textual sources and special studies are made in a concise manner. The full titles of the studies are listed in the bibliography. Additions which have been made in order to clarify the translation of original sources, are presented between parentheses. Reconstructions of damaged texts are put between square brackets.

During various discussions about the manuscript of this book, many valuable suggestions were made by staff members of the Leningrad Branch of the Institute of Oriental Studies of the Academy of Sciences of the USSR; Dr. V. A. Livšits offered considerable assistance in the preparation of the manuscript for publication. Work on the Russian original of the book was concluded in 1981, but later additions to the Russian text were made on the basis of the most important publications which were published subsequently.

PREFACE BY THE AUTHOR TO THE ENGLISH EDITION

The present book is a revised and updated English version of a study which was first published in Russian (Moscow 1985). Additions have been made on the basis of recent literature published until the beginning of 1988.

I should like to thank the Brill's publishing house for their acceptance of the manuscript for publication, and above all, I should like to express my sincere gratitude to Willem Vogelsang and Gillian Vogelsang-Eastwood for their comments and their tremendous, excellent and impartial work on the original Russian text.

PREFACE BY THE TRANSLATOR

During my visit to Leningrad in the spring of 1987, M. A. Dandamaev kindly presented me with a copy of his book on the political history of the Achaemenid empire, which had shortly before been published in Moscow. Back in Holland, and having read parts of the book, I asked several scholars in the field whether it would be a good idea to have Dandamaev's study translated into English, and thus ensure that the book would be easily available to Western historians, archaeologists, and all those who are interested in the history of the Persian Achaemenids. Reactions were unanimously positive. Subsequently, contact was again sought with Dandamaev, and permission was kindly granted to translate his work, and to look for a suitable publisher. Thus, in the autumn of 1987 I started with the translation; at the same time, the Brill publishing house accepted the book for publication. The first draft of the translation was completed by the end of 1987 and sent to Leningrad. In February 1988, I had the chance to meet the author again in the Soviet Union, and to discuss certain details. The final comments on the draft were received in Holland in the summer of the same year, and the translation was completed by the end of the year.

There is hardly any need to introduce Dr Dandamaev to the specialist public in the West. Being a student of famous Soviet scholars such as V. I. Abaev, V. V. Struve, and I. M. Diakonoff, Dandamaev has since 1959 been connected to the Leningrad Branch of the Institute of Eastern Studies, Academy of Sciences, USSR. His main studies include *Persien unter den ersten Achämeniden (6. Jahrhundert v. Chr.)* (1976), being a translation and revision of an original study in Russian published in 1963; *Slavery in Babylonia* (1984), original Russian edition published in 1974; and, together with V. G. Lukonin, *Culture and Social Institutions of Ancient Iran* (1988), first published in Russian, 1980.

In recent years, a number of studies have been published which discuss the history of the Achaemenid empire. These include J. M. Cook's *The Persian Empire* (1983); R. N. Frye's *The History of Ancient Iran* (1984), and *The Cambridge History of Iran. Vol. II: The Median and Achaemenian Periods* (1985). The present book constitutes an important addition to the above, since it not only discusses in detail the 'empire-building' years of the Persians, but also the last century of its existence, before the Empire was conquered by the Macedonians under Alexander. Another important aspect of the book is the use which has been made of Babylonian sources, which often seem to be neglected by historians who favour the classical information. In short, I feel sure that the present book will be an important contribution to the study of the Persian Achaemenid empire.

Willem Vogelsang, December 1988

CHAPTER ONE

THE ACHAEMENID DYNASTY IN THE EARLY PERIOD

In the transition period from the second to the first millennium B.C., Persian tribes gradually commenced to settle in a territory which at present corresponds to the Iranian province of Fars (Fārs). This name is an Arabicized form of *Pārsa*, which referred both to the land and people of the Persians, and also to its capital, Persepolis. As regards the name 'Persia', this denomination derives from Περσίς, the Greek rendering of the Old Persian word *Pārsa*. The contemporary, official name of the country, namely Iran (Irān), was attested to for the first time as Ariane, in the work of the Greek author Eratosthenes (third century B.C.). Iran, which is an abbreviation of Old Iranian *Aryānām*, '(land) of the Aryans', is thus called because the Persians and Medes, inhabiting the Iranian Plateau, referred to themselves as Aryans.

The country where the Persians settled was the native land of the Elamites. This people had built up an extremely old and original civilization, which exercised considerable influence upon the material and intellectual culture of the Persians. The penetration of the Persians into their new homeland appears to have been initially of a peaceful nature, and carried out with the permission of the Elamite rulers. It would seem, however, that at a later date a part of the local population was actually forced to yield their land to the newcomers.

The Elamites were related to the Dravidians, who lived further to the east. As a result they had no links, either ethnically, linguistically or traditionally, with the Persians. However, the land of *Pārsa* or Persis constituted only a relatively small section of Elamite territory, which included all of modern south Iran. This part of the Iranian Plateau was called Elam (written with the sign NIM meaning 'the high country') by the Sumerians. The Akkadians called it *Elamtu*, which, on the basis of popular etymology, meant 'Mountainous Land', because of the mountainous part of Elam which bordered on Babylonia. The Elamites themselves referred to their land by the name of *Hatamti*. The stretch of land between Susa and the Persian Gulf was called *Huja* by the Persians, after the Iranian name of the tribes to the east of the Elamite capital, Susa. From the word *Huja* derives the contemporary name of the province of Khuzistan, the location of which roughly corresponds to ancient Elam.

Tradition mentions Achaemenes as the founder of the oldest dynasty of Persian rulers. His period of activity, if he was not merely a mythical, eponymous figure, can be dated to the end of the eighth and the first quarter of the seventh century B.C. According to a later tradition, the confederation of Persian peoples in the period of about 675-640 B.C. was led by Chishpish, a son of Achaemenes. It has been suggested that soon after 646 B.C. Elamites and Iranian immigrants in Fars formed a kingdom which was independent of the Elamite empire with its capital at Susa. This new kingdom was ruled by the Persian kings, i.e. the Achaemenids (see de Miroschedji 1985).

According to R. Ghirshman, the main residence of Achaemenes and Chishpish was situated in a small valley among the foothills of a mountain ridge, at Masjid-i Sulaiman, among the Bakhtiari mountains, about one hundred kilometres to the northeast of Susa. Here, on a large, artificial terrace at a height of four hundred metres and approached by a stone stairway of twelve steps, are the ruins of an extensive building. Ghirshman regarded these remains as a castle of the Achaemenid rulers. In general, the terrace is reminiscent of the fortifications of a town in northwest Iran, as depicted in Assyrian reliefs. Ghirshman believed that the Persians learnt to construct these terraces while they were still residing in northwest Iran, in districts which fell under the control of Urartian rulers (Ghirshman 1950:205ff.; *idem* 1962:85ff.). On the other hand, E. Herzfeld attributed the terrace at Masjid-i Sulaiman to the Parthian period (Herzfeld 1941:303ff.). Ghirshman objected to this date by saying that the Parthians, contrary to the Achaemenids and the still earlier Urartian rulers, did not erect this type of terrace.

To support his hypothesis, Ghirshman also pointed at the so-called Achaemenid Village, which is located at a distance of one kilometre to the east of the Susa acropolis. This archaeological site was dated by Ghirshman to the turn of the eighth to the seventh century B.C. Ghirshman supported his theory by the fact that the finds from the Achaemenid Village included three Elamite tablets, which are comparable to a series of economic documents from Susa. The latter were dated by their editor, V. Scheil, to that particular period (Ghirshman 1952:18).

For several decades Ghirshman's hypothesis was accepted by most specialists. In recent years, however, his views have been rejected by many scholars who now claim that the relevant monument at Masjid-i Sulaiman is a temple complex which was built in the early Seleucid period. According to D. Stronach, the settlement at Masjid-i Sulaiman dates to the period between the fifth century B.C. and the middle of the second century A.D. (Stronach 1974:246; cf. also Wijnen 1972-1974:71, where a description of the monument is presented together with an extensive bibliography).

Ghirshman was of the opinion that at the end of the eighth century

B.C. Persians were living in the Achaemenid Village in a clan organization, inhabiting large houses with a multitude of rooms. It is difficult, however, to give an exact date to the settlement. It remains unclear whether the documents found here should be attributed to the last years of the Elamite state, namely the period between approximately 650 and 630 B.C. (this, in particular, is the opinion of H. H. Paper, the editor of the texts), or whether the composition of the texts should be dated to a much later period, when Elam had already fallen under Median supremacy, or even under the rule of the Persians, led by Cyrus II.

Whatever the case, one of the Elamite texts which were found by Ghirshman at Susa, hardly differs in its formulars from the Persepolis texts in the Elamite language which date to the Achaemenid period. Paper dated this particular tablet to c. 500 B.C. (Paper 1954; MMAI XXXVI:82). Ju. B. Jusifov attributed the relevant texts from Susa to a period between 558 and 548 B.C. (Jusifov 1958a:31f.). Such a date is perhaps closest to the truth, but the palaeographical analysis on which Jusifov based his assertions can hardly be regarded as flawless. In particular his use, for comparative purposes, of the palaeography of the Elamite version of the Behistun text needs to be questioned, as Jusifov employed the printed cuneiform writing, rather than the real shape of the signs in the text.[1]

A number of Elamite administrative texts from Susa which can be precisely dated to the seventh century B.C., refer to the ethnic term 'Persians'. These texts frequently contain Iranian personal names. Ghirshman was of the opinion that the inhabitants of the Achaemenid Village were engaged in arable and pastoral farming, and provided the royal workshops with raw materials, especially wool, and finished products such as clothing (Ghirshman 1954:71-75). According to Jusifov, however, the Persians who are mentioned in these texts never passed anything on to the warehouses, but, to the contrary, received manufactured goods from these stores, including clothing and weaponry, thus indicating that there were no craftsmen among the Persians at the Village (Jusifov 1958b:102). But it does not seem justified to state, as Jusifov has done, that at the time that the documents from Susa were written, Elam was under Persian rule, since the people who received weapons from the workshop warehouses, including the Persians, may have been in the service of the Elamite kings.

If the genealogical lists remain outside consideration, then Cyrus I is

---

[1] As a final addition to this particular discussion, it should be noted that on the basis of archaeological material, Stronach distinguished at the Achaemenid Village a series of occupation levels which he dated to the seventh and the fifth to second centuries B.C. (Stronach 1974:245ff.)

the only representative of the early Achaemenid kings who is mentioned in cuneiform records. In an inscription of the Assyrian king Assurbanipal, written in c. 640 B.C., Cyrus I is called king of the land of *Parsumash*, i.e. Fars/Persis (in other, contemporary texts the rendering *Parsuash* is found; Weidner 1931-1932:1ff.). On the Cyrus Cylinder from Babylon, Cyrus II calls himself "son of Cambyses, the great king, king of the city of Anshan, grandson of Cyrus, the great king, king of the city of Anshan, great-grandson of Chishpish, the great king, king of the city of Anshan" (Eilers 1971:162). It was therefore a logical step to presume that, at least from the time of Cyrus I, the names of Anshan and *Parsumash* indicated one and the same country. Such a suggestion was made by Herzfeld (e.g. Herzfeld 1968:170ff.). However, most specialists objected to the identification of Anshan and Persis, on the basis of the fact that the so-called Taylor Prism of Sennacherib (V 31), when summing up the allies of the Elamite king Umman-menanu, refers to both names separately.

In respect to the location of Anshan, which was the old Elamite region and city with the same name[2], until fairly recently the opinions of scholars differed considerably (for a bibliography, see Prášek 1906-1910, Vol. I, p. 189). Recent archaeological excavations, however, showed that Anshan was located on the site of the modern *tepe* of Malyan, 46 kilometres north of Shiraz. Many Middle Elamite texts (dated to between approximately the fourteenth and eleventh centuries B.C.) were found here, and significantly, apart from Anshan, no other topographical names are mentioned in these texts (Carter & Stolper 1976:38; Hansman 1972:101ff.; Reiner 1977:57ff.; Summer 1974:165ff.). It has been known for a long time from Achaemenid period texts that this area was called *Pārsa*, which is the Persis of the Greek sources, modern Fars. Consequently, it was concluded that Anshan and *Pārsa* were alternative names for one and the same country. Starting from at least the middle of the seventh century B.C., Anshan became the old, archaic and formal name, sanctified by an age-old tradition which was mainly preserved in royal titles. But the real name of the land was *Pārsa*, which was derived from the appellation of its new rulers.

Such a conclusion forces a revision of the common theory which holds that the Achaemenids were divided in two branches ruling simultaneously in Anshan and in Persis (as early as 1960, the present author

---

[2] Up to now, scholars have believed that Susa was always the capital of Elam. Recently, however, F. Vallat has brought forward the suggestion that during the years when the Elamite districts were united into one realm, its capital was Anshan, and Susa was a dependency (Vallat 1980:2ff.)

had spoken out against this theory: cf. Dandamaev 1960:3ff.; cf. now also de Miroschedji 1987:282; Stronach 1974:248).

The majority of scholars, at least until recently, were of the opinion that the information contained in the Behistun inscription of the Achaemenid king Darius I (*r.* 522-486 B.C.) attests to the fact that the ancestors of Cyrus II, the founder of the empire, did not rule in Persis. About Darius, the text reports (I 4-11): "... my father is Vishtaspa; the father of Vishtaspa is Arshama; the father of Arshama was Ariaramna; the father of Ariaramna was Chishpish; the father of Chishpish was Achaemenes ... Therefore we are called Achaemenids. From of old we are noble; from of old our lineage has been one of kings ... Eight men from our lineage were kings before. I am the ninth. We, the nine men, have been kings *duvitāparanam* (see below)."

How are these words of Darius I to be interpreted? According to F. H. Weissbach, whose opinion used to be supported by almost all the historians of ancient Iran, Chishpish ruled after Achaemenes. He divided his realm between his elder son Cyrus I, to whom the land and city of Anshan were given, and his younger son Ariaramnes, who received Persis. After Cyrus I, Anshan was ruled by Cambyses I, and subsequently, during the beginning of his reign, by Cyrus II. In Persis, Arsames succeeded Ariaramnes. After a certain period (by at least c. 547 B.C.), Cyrus II also took power in Persis, either by defeating Arsames in battle, or after the latter's death (later it became known from the inscription of Darius I concerning the construction of a palace at Susa, that Arsames was still alive in 522 B.C.).

The above hypothesis as to the course of events in Persis in the sixth century B.C. was supported by the following piece of information. In the Babylonian Chronicle for the year 550 B.C., Cyrus II is called "king of Anshan", but in the same text it is said that in the year 547 B.C. he was "king of *Pārsa*" (*Parsu*, that is, Persis) (ABC, pp. 106f., lines 1, 15). Weissbach explained this contradiction with the suggestion that in the year 550 B.C. Cyrus II was only king of Anshan, while in 547 B.C., some years after his victory over the Medes, he also ruled in Persis (Weissbach 1924: cols. 1140ff.). If this hypothesis is accepted, a number of problems occur. First of all, from the inscription of Assurbanipal referred to above (and which was published after the publication of Weissbach's article), it is known that at the time of writing of the Assyrian text, Cyrus I was king of Persis, and that he and Ariaramnes could hardly have ruled simultaneously in the same country. In addition, some inscriptions of Cyrus II have been preserved which are in the Akkadian language. These texts are dated to the period following the defeat of Media and Babylonia by the Persians (539 B.C.). It could be expected therefore that in these texts Cyrus II would call himself king of Persis, as he undoubtedly was by that time. However, none of these Babylonian texts give him the title of king of Persis. For example, an inscription from the city of Ur in Babylonia starts with the following words: "Kurash, king of all the world, king of the land of Anshan, son of Cambyses (*Kambuzija*), king of the land of Anshan" (UET, Vol. I, p. 194, lines 1-3).

In this respect, attention should also be paid to the information from Greek and Roman writers. According to these authors, the military clashes between the Median king Astyages and Cyrus II took place at Pasargadae, in Persis. It is therefore impossible that Persis was taken by Cyrus II after his victory over Astyages, as Cyrus was specifically fighting with the Median king for the independence of Persis. In the Babylonian Chronicle it is reported that Cyrus transferred booty from Ecbatana, the capital of Media, to Anshan, and according to the testimony of Ctesias, the booty was deposited at Pasargadae. As suggested by Herzfeld, both sources refer to the same land (see below). This type of anachronism can be frequently found in the Babylonian sources and is based on the extreme conservatism of the literary tradition and the conscious archaism of the ethnic and geographical nomenclature. After Cyrus II, the use of the name Anshan is lost, and none of the later Persian rulers called himself king of Anshan. Classical writers did not refer to Anshan at all, and, in all probability, knew nothing about the name. In other words, Cyrus II ruled right from the beginning over Persis, and did not conquer this land after his victory over Media in 550 B.C.

According to different sources, the ancestors of Cyrus II were insignificant rulers who owed allegiance, first to the Elamite rulers, and later to the Assyrian and Median kings. According to Herodotus (I 107), Cambyses I, the father of Cyrus II, was not king, but only a man of noble birth. Justinus (I 4.4) even calls him "a common man." According to Xenophon (*Cyropaedia* I 2.1; VII 2.24), however, who was apparently using sources which antedated Herodotus, or a reliable oral tradition of the Persians, Cambyses I was the Persian king.

Weissbach, and other scholars, in order to support the hypothesis regarding the rulership of the Achaemenids in two lineages, referred to the use of the word *duvitāparanam* in the Behistun inscription. This word was deliberately left undiscussed above. More than a century ago, J. Oppert translated this word as 'in two lineages' (Oppert 1879:163). The majority of scholars appear to have accepted this translation, in accordance with the view that the Achaemenids were divided into two branches which ruled simultaneously in two different districts: from Cyrus I to

Cambyses II on the one side, and from Ariaramnes to Darius I on the other.

Ch. Bartholomae and R. Kent sought the meaning of the disputed word in another direction, translating it as 'one after the other', 'successively': "We ... were kings one after the other" (AiWb, col. 767; Kent 1953:192). A. Meillet and E. Benveniste also accepted this translation, remarking however, that the meaning and the form of the word remained unclear (Meillet 1931, paragraphs 293, 389). Such a translation seems to be in conflict with the fact that the continuation of kingship by the Achaemenids was clearly interrupted by the rule of Gaumata, whom the composer of the Behistun text did not consider an Achaemenid. However, Gaumata was never recognized by Darius as a legitimate king. Therefore Darius could easily speak of an unbroken line of Achaemenid rulers (Vogelsang 1986:128-131).

H. Winckler and certain other scholars translated the word *duvitāparanam* as meaning 'from a very early period' (Tolman 1908:8; Winckler 1889:127).

Comparatively recently, O. Szemerényi arrived at the following conclusion. The translation 'successively', or 'following', must be rejected on the basis of grammatical aspects and historical sources (with the latter point Szemerényi referred to his hypothesis that the Achaemenids ruled in two lineages). The translation "long aforetime" could be accepted. In that case, however, Szemerényi regarded the sentence "We ... are long aforetime kings" as unusual, as the old age of the Achaemenid lineage was already mentioned in the phrase "from of old our lineage has been one of kings", which precedes the word *duvitāparanam*. Furthermore, with reference to Hittite-Luwian *tapar* ('to govern', 'to rule'), Szemerényi suggested that a solution to the problem could be found in the splitting of the Persian word into *duvi-tāpar(a)nam*, translating this as 'by double rule', 'in two royal lines' (Szemerényi 1966:209-211).

Leaving the linguists to decide whether the Hittite analogy is sufficiently close, it can be noted that the translation of *duvitāparanam* as 'from a very old time' is not at all impeded by the fact that the Behistun text has already referred to the old age of the Achaemenid lineage, because one and the same communication is often reiterated in the same text. The Elamite version of the Behistun inscription renders the word *duvitāparanam* with the word *šamakmar*. The first part of it (*šamak*) has been translated by F. Bork and W. Hinz as 'branch' (see Hinz & Koch 1987:1129). However, the word is a *hapax legomenon* and therefore its real meaning remains obscure. As to the second part of it (*mar*), it might be an affix with the meaning 'from' (cf. PF:753: 'From *šamak*', that is, perhaps, 'successively'), or the numeral 'two' instead of *ma-ir/mar-za* (see Hinz & Koch 1987:876). Finally, in the comparatively recently edited Babylonian version of the Behistun inscription (following a new reading), the corresponding Babylonian phrase means: "We are nine kings of an eternal lineage" (BID:12, line 4, and p. 54). It seems evident from this phrase that it is more akin to the translation of *duvitāparanam* as 'from a very old time', than to that of 'in two lineages'.

Thus the exact meaning of *duvitāparanam* still remains obscure. It might mean either 'in two lineages' (cf. the Old Persian *duvi-* 'two' and Elamite *mar* with the same meaning) or 'one after another', i.e. 'successively', or 'from a very old time' (cf. the Old Persian *paranam*, 'before', 'previously', the Elamite affix *-mar*, 'from', and the Babylonian translation of the phrase under consideration).

In 1930, E. Herzfeld published two inscriptions on golden plates which were found at Hamadan (ancient Ecbatana). According to the texts the inscriptions were composed by Ariaramnes and Arsames and each of these men is referred to as "great king, king of kings, king in Persis." Soon after their publication, however, H. H. Schaeder and other specialists convincingly showed, on the basis of grammatical peculiarities, that the texts must date to a period much later than the inscriptions of Darius I, and, consequently, were composed in the late Achaemenid period (see the bibliography presented by Kent 1953:107). The question also arose why these inscriptions, if they were genuine, were discovered at Hamadan while Ariaramnes and Arsames are supposed to have been kings in Persis.

According to Herzfeld, the inscription of Ariaramnes was deposited as a trophy in Ecbatana, at the time of one of the victories of the Median king over the Persian ruler (Herzfeld 1931:55; *idem* 1935:23ff.). But in that case, as it was remarked by Kent, a series of new questions arises (Kent 1946:206ff.). Why was it necessary to store an inscription of a defeated king? In what way could the son of Ariaramnes, after the total defeat of the latter, still carry the title of great king? How did the text of Arsames end up at Ecbatana? How could Ariaramnes and Arsames carry the title of 'king of kings', when they only ruled over Persis?

All the above mentioned considerations compel one to refute the hypothesis that Ariaramnes and Arsames ruled in Persis.

Another reconstruction of early Achaemenid history was suggested by G. G. Cameron. His opinion was shared by Hinz and certain other scholars. According to these scholars, Cyrus I ruled in Anshan and *Parsumash*, while Ariaramnes and Arsames ruled in *Pārsa*; these two countries were not identical (Cameron 1936:212 and 223ff.; Hinz 1971b: col. 1024). However, I. V. P'jankov rightly remarked that this theory was not convincing, because in terminological and political terms *Parsumash* and Persis were one and the same country (P'jankov 1971a:32).

As remarked above, the Behistun text reported that the royal lineage of the Achaemenids, until Darius I, included eight kings, and that Darius was the ninth ruler. Whom among his ancestors did Darius regard as being his predecessors? Starting from the last century, almost all scholars have suggested that these predecessors of Darius included Achaemenes; Chishpish; Cyrus I; Cambyses I; Cyrus II; Cambyses II; Ariaramnes; and Arsames. As was shown above however, the sources provide no real reason to suggest a period of rule by Ariaramnes and Arsames in Persis, because Cyrus II was king of Persis. It seems probable that Darius really did refer to the above mentioned men, but in that case it is necessary to infer that Ariaramnes and Arsames were princelings in some region (apparently a very small part) of Iran. In this context it should be noted that in the early Achaemenid period there were still many minor kings who ruled as tribal leaders (cf. I. M. Diakonoff 1964:180, n. 14). Apart from this, it should also be borne in mind that the Persian kings, starting from Cyrus II, carried the elaborate title of 'great king, king of Persis, king of lands', etc. The simple title of 'king' therefore should not automatically be connected with the supreme ruler. For example, Xenophon (*Oec.* 16) and Cicero (*De sen.* 17; *Ad Qu.* f. I 2.2) used the appellation of king for Cyrus the Younger, the son of Darius II. Yet it is known that Cyrus the Younger never ruled the Empire, but was the satrap of Asia Minor.

Another suggestion, based on Herodotus (VII 11), has been presented, which says that among the eight royal predecessors of Darius I there were two kings with the name of Chishpish, and two groups of three kings with the names of Cyrus and Cambyses (Herzfeld 1930a:15; Hutecker 1885:72; Nagel 1979:75; Prášek 1906-1910, Vol. I, p. 181; Winckler 1889:12). This hypothesis, however, is not supported by any cuneiform sources. Apart from that, it is not necessary to follow Herodotus strictly in this subject, because he called the father of Cambyses Teispes, while we know from the Cyrus Cylinder that Chishpish (Teispes) was the father of Cyrus I.

CHAPTER TWO

CYRUS II, KING OF PERSIS

From approximately 600 to 559 B.C., Cambyses I (*Kambūjiya*)[1] ruled the district of *Pārsa* (Persis) as a subject of the Median kings. If credence is given to the information provided by Herodotus (I 107-108, 111), Xenophon (*Cyropaedia* I 2.1), Diodorus (IX 24), and some other classical authors who refer to Persian traditions, Cambyses was married to Mandane, the daughter of the Median king Astyages. Thus, their son Cyrus (*Kŭrush*) was the grandson of Astyages. Most modern historians regard this version as reliable (Cameron 1936:224, n. 33; P'jankov 1971b:83ff.; Weissbach 1924: cols. 1128ff.). However, Hinz expressed his doubts by pointing out that Cyrus had reached his fifteenth birthday before Astyages had succeeded to the Median throne. Consequently, it was argued, Cyrus could not be the grandson of Astyages (Hinz 1971b: col. 1025). In this context, Hinz referred to a fragment from the work of Deinon, in which Cyrus is said to have become king when he was forty years old, and subsequently to have ruled for thirty years. Because the Babylonian sources have shown that Cyrus died in 530 B.C., he must therefore have been born around 600 B.C. According to Hinz, this point

---

[1] The etymologies of the names of Cambyses, Cyrus and Chishpish have given rise to many disagreements among the specialists. F. C. Andreas, R. N. Frye, A. Hoffmann-Kutschke, G. Hüsing and certain others have explained these names as being of Elamite origin (Frye 1962:87; Hoffmann-Kutschke 1907:182; Hüsing 1908:318-322). R. Zadok drew attention to the point that in a promissory note from Babylon, dated to 541 B.C. (VS III:55), amid the names of several witnesses is that of a certain *Mar-du-ú*, the son of *Ku-ur-ra-šú*. The first name may be Iranian or Elamite, but the second is the name of Cyrus (cf. the name of *Kur-raš* in an Elamite document from Susa, MDP IX:98). Starting from the fact that the relevant Babylonian document dates to two years before the fall of the city to the Persians, Zadok was inclined to regard *Kurrašu* as an Elamite name (Zadok 1976:62ff.). When attempting, however, to define the linguistic origin of the name, two points should be taken into consideration. Firstly, even before the fall of Babylon to the Persians there were people in Mesopotamia who carried Iranian names. Secondly, the Elamites also frequently bore Iranian names and apparently the name of Cyrus was one of them. W. Eilers has collected a considerable amount of material relevant to the study of the name of Cyrus, and he attempted to relate the name of Cyrus to the Iranian root *kur-*, 'blind' (Eilers 1964). This attempt has been strongly criticized by V. I. Abaev. The latter suggested that the name of Cyrus could etymologically be explained from Iranian and had the meaning of 'child', 'hero'. He explained the name of Chishpish as meaning 'strong'. As regards the name of Cambyses, Abaev accepted the opinion of J. Charpentier, namely that this name is related to the appellation of the East Iranian tribe of the *Kambojās*, who are mentioned in Indian sources and who inhabited the territory of present-day Afghanistan. This people spoke a language which was very akin to that of the Avesta (Abaev 1967:288ff.; cf. Benveniste 1958:44ff.; Eilers 1974:54).

is corroborated by information from the Book of Daniel (V 31). Here it is said that the "Mede Darius" (according to Hinz and certain other scholars, this name refers to Cyrus II) was 62 years old when he became king of Babylonia, in 539 B.C. (the date of the fall of Babylon to the Persians). But these considerations can be easily refuted, even if the information provided by Deinon is regarded as reliable (it should be noted that there are reasons to doubt this information), because Mandane could have been married to Cambyses before Astyages' accession to the Median throne. It is known from other sources, for example, that another daughter of Astyages was married to Nebuchadnezzar, the crown prince of Babylon, in 614 B.C. (see for references to the texts: Cameron 1936:216, n. 9).

A number of contradictory stories have been transmitted about the origin and early years of Cyrus. Herodotus (I 95), for instance, knew four stories about Cyrus' accession to power. According to Xenophon (*Cyropaedia* I 2.1; I 4.25), there were by the fifth to fourth century B.C. already a series of different stories about Cyrus in circulation.

According to Herodotus (I 107-121), Astyages had a dream, which was explained by court priests, or magi, as meaning that his grandson Cyrus would become king in his place. Astyages therefore summoned his pregnant daughter Mandane from Persis, and later, when Cyrus was born, Astyages ordered that the child was to be killed. The task was given to Harpagos, one of Astyages' officials. In his turn, Harpagos passed the child on to the shepherd Mitradates, one of the slaves of Astyages. The shepherd was ordered to abandon the child in the mountains, where there were many wild animals. When Mitradates took the child to his hut in the mountains, his wife Spako had just given birth to a still-born baby. They decided to raise Cyrus as their own child, and to leave the dead baby at a lonely place in the mountains, having first dressed him in the luxurious clothes of the grandson of Astyages. Following this deed, Mitradates reported to Harpagos that he had carried out his orders. Harpagos, after having sent out reliable people to inspect the corpse of Cyrus and to bury it, accepted that the king's command had been carried out.

One day, when Cyrus was ten years old and playing with other children, he was chosen by them as their king. But the son of a noble Mede refused to obey Cyrus, and the latter chastised him. The father of the boy, Artembares, complained to Astyages, stating that a slave of his was beating the children of royal dignitaries. Cyrus was sent to Astyages for punishment. The king suspected that Cyrus was his grandson when he observed certain family resemblances. Questioning Mitradates under the threat of torture, Astyages obtained the truth. He then cruelly punished Harpagos by inviting him for dinner and secretly giving him his own son to eat, who was of the same age as Cyrus. Thereafter Astyages again turned to the magi with the question whether he still needed to fear danger from the side of his grandson. They replied that the dream was already fulfilled, because Cyrus had been made king when playing with other children. Therefore there was no need to be afraid of him. Astyages then calmed down and sent his grandson to Persis and to his parents.

According to Ctesias, whose account was transmitted by Nicolaus of Damascus, Cyrus was neither the grandson of Astyages, nor even an Achaemenid, but a man of common origin, belonging to the nomad tribe of the Mardioi. His father Atradates was forced, out of poverty, to become a thief, while his mother Argoste herded goats. When she became pregnant with Cyrus, she had a prophetic dream which showed her that her son would acquire a high position in Asia. Searching for a livelihood, Cyrus found his way to the court of Astyages, where he became a servant. At first he was simply a cleaner, but later he became a torch bearer. Subsequently he was adopted by the eunuch Artembares, and he found favour with Astyages, eventually becoming the royal cup bearer. The Median king sent him out to crush a revolt by the Cadusians, but Cyrus himself revolted against Astyages and drew the rebels to his side. Later Cyrus took the throne of Media and subsequently that of Persis as well.

Ctesias' story can hardly be called reliable, even in some of the minute details, because it is known from Herodotus and cuneiform sources that Cyrus' lineage was that of the Achaemenids who ruled the Persian tribe of the Pasargadae. According to R. Kent, the version by Ctesias was concocted in the circle of courtiers around Artaxerxes II, and was devised to discredit Cyrus II. In making up such an unfavourable account, Artaxerxes II, according to Kent, was motivated by the revolt of Cyrus the Younger, whose name was hated by Artaxerxes. The name reminded Artaxerxes of the removal, by Cyrus II, of Artaxerxes' ancestor Arsames from the Persian throne (Kent 1946:211). It is difficult to agree with this hypothesis, since, even if Cyrus removed Arsames from the throne (see above), then after a lapse of more than a century this could hardly have discomforted anyone. In addition, Artaxerxes II and Cyrus the Younger were full brothers and could trace their genealogy back through the same ancestors. It is easier to accept the point of view adopted by R. Schubert, who felt that the version by Ctesias contains a Median tradition, the purpose of which was the slander of Cyrus (Schubert 1890:58). According to A. Bauer, the story of Cyrus' youth contained in the work of Ctesias is one of the many predecessors of Greek romantic literature, and only contains a few isolated, reliable details (Bauer 1882:32ff.). In addition to

Herodotus and Ctesias, Xenophon, Deinon, Diodorus, Pompeius Trogus and Nicolaus of Damascus relate the story of Cyrus' rise to power, but all of their information can be traced back to the above discussed authors (see Bauer 1882:32ff.; I. M. Diakonoff 1956:417-424; P'jankov 1971a:16ff.; *idem* 1971b:83ff.).

In 558 B.C., Cyrus II became king of the Persian sedentary tribes, a dominant place among whom was occupied by the Pasargadae. Like his father Cambyses I, Cyrus owed allegiance to the Median king. Apart from the Pasargadae, also the Maraphioi and the Maspioi formed part of the confederation of Persian tribes. In the Elamite texts from the fortification wall at Persepolis (dated to the turn of the sixth to the fifth century B.C.), reference is made to the geographical and ethnic name of *Marappiyush*. This name, as determined by E. Benveniste, corresponds to the Maraphioi of Herodotus (Old Persian *mārafya; see for references PF:773; Hinz & Koch 1987:877). According to H. Humbach, the name of the Maraphioi may have the literal meaning of 'with chariots', and the meaning of the other ethnic name (Maspioi), could be 'with horses', referring to the excellent chariots and horses of the two respective peoples (Humbach 1968:154-156).

The centre of the Persian state was located around the city of Pasargadae, the intensive building programme of which dates back to the early period of the rule of Cyrus. The Mardioi, Sagartians and some other nomadic peoples living in the mountains of Persis, and also the sedentary peoples of the Carmanians, Panthialaioi and Derousiaioi, were subjugated by Cyrus at a later date, apparently after the war with the Medes (see Herodotus I 125; Strabo XV 3.1; cf. von Gall 1972:261ff.).

Only some very general remarks can be made about the social organization of Persis during the relevant period. These observations are in the main based on possible analogies with East Iranian peoples (whose social organization is reflected in the Avesta, the holy scripture of the Zoroastrians), and on certain words and phrases in the Persian language. The basic unit of social life was the large, patriarchal family (*māna). The head of the family (*mānapati) was the *pater familias* of his line with unlimited material and spiritual power over all the members of the family. A group of families constituted a clan, the *viθ* and *taumā*. The clan, which later also became a land unit, was formed by a number of families and was led by its elder (*viθpati). Over a period of many centuries this unit remained a very significant factor. Clans were united into a tribe, *zantu*, with a *zantupati* at its head. Several tribes could form a district or a country (*dahyu*), headed by a king (*xšāyaθiya*). The population existed by means of arable farming and animal husbandry, especially of horses.

CHAPTER THREE

WAR WITH THE MEDES

When Cyrus II became king of Persis, there were four major empires in
the Near East, namely Media, Lydia, Babylonia and Egypt. At that time
Media was already preparing for an attack on Babylonia. The relationship between both countries was correspondingly tense, a fact which is
particularly attested to by the anti-Median tone of the royal Babylonian
inscriptions of that period. Indications for the worsening relationship between the two countries are also reflected in the sayings of the Hebrew
prophet Jeremiah, which were composed some decades before Cyrus'
revolt against Astyages. Jeremiah (L 9-43; LI 11-48) predicted that the
Medes, together with the Scythians and the Mannaeans (according to
him, warriors armed with bows and spears and knowing no mercy)
would conquer Babylonia, destroy her, and the land would be without
people and made into a haunt of jackals.

Babylonia, however, was temporarily saved from an attack from the
east by Cyrus' revolt against Astyages, which started in 553 B.C. Fairly
extensive stories have been transmitted by classical authors about the
revolt and the ensuing war. Important, albeit somewhat meagre information is provided by Babylonian texts.

According to Herodotus (I 123-128), the Median nobleman Harpagos,
whom Astyages had cruelly insulted, decided to take revenge upon his
master and so started a conspiracy. He drew to his side the Median
nobility, which was dissatisfied with the stern rule of Astyages, and
subsequently persuaded Cyrus to revolt. Because Cyrus was at that time
residing in Persis, and the road from Media was guarded by Median
troops, Harpagos was forced to send Cyrus a letter with the help of a
trusted servant. The letter was cleverly hidden in the insides of a hare,
with which the courier could profess himself to be a hunter. In the letter
Harpagos promised Cyrus, that, if he decided to revolt against Astyages,
he would have the guaranteed support of many noble Medes and Harpagos himself would come over to his side together with his troops. Of
course, a critical stance should be taken as regards Herodotus' story, but,
apparently, there was a group of noblemen in Media who were discontent with the policy of Astyages and who were prepared to defect to the
side of his enemies. I. M. Diakonoff and I. G. Aliev have put forward
the hypothesis that this group consisted of representatives from the tribal
nobility, against whom Astyages had fought in his endeavour to estab-

lish a strong centralized state (Aliev 1960:252ff.; I. M. Diakonoff 1956:415ff.; see also Prášek 1906-1910, Vol. I, p. 207). The dissatisfied noblemen were headed by Harpagos, whose descendants later concocted, in order to justify the disloyalty of their ancestor, certain stories about the absurd cruelty of. Astyages (as hypothesized, Herodotus received his information about the revolt of Cyrus from the descendants of Harpagos, who lived in Lycia during the fifth century B.C.). It is possible that the conspiracy of the Median nobility only took shape at the time of the war with the rebels, and that in itself it did not lead to the beginning of the rebellion, as stated by Herodotus.

When Cyrus, Herodotus continues, took notice of the contents of Harpagos' letter, he summoned a meeting of the Persian tribes of the Pasargadae, the Maraphioi and the Maspioi, and then read aloud to them an edict which he had composed, claiming that he had received it from Astyages. In this edict Cyrus stated that Astyages had appointed him as his army commander. Cyrus then dismissed his followers, ordering them to return the following morning with sickles and to clean a large tract of land from the thorny bushes. When this had been done Cyrus ordered the slaughter of some cattle which belonged to his father, and the distribution of large quantities of bread and wine, to entertain the Persians, who, the day before, had been engaged in hard labour. Addressing himself to the assembled men, Cyrus asked whether they preferred to toil with hard labour, or to spend the time at feasts and in merriment. Receiving the expected reply, he started to persuade the Persians to defect from Astyages, promising that the success of the revolt would guarantee them an easy life. The Persians, who hated the Median overlordship, willingly answered the call of their leader.

When Astyages heard about Cyrus' preparations for war, he sent a courier to summon Cyrus to the Median court. Cyrus answered that he would come sooner than expected. The refusal of Cyrus to obey Astyages was the signal for the rebellion. The outcome of the revolt was decided in two battles. At the first meeting, Astyages did not participate, and his general Harpagos defected with a large part of the troops to the other side. Astyages then ordered the impaling of the magi who had incorrectly interpreted his dream which had said that Cyrus would become the leader of Asia (it is possible that some of the magi maintained contacts with the conspirators), and that all Medes, including the old men and the youths, were to arm themselves. In spite of his advanced years, the Median king himself commanded the army in the second battle, but the Medes were defeated and the king was taken prisoner. Cyrus did not harm Astyages in any way, indeed he treated him favourably. Thus, according to Herodotus, ended the

35 year reign of Astyages, and the 128 year rule in Asia of the Medes.

An extensive account, elaborated upon with legendary motifs, is transmitted by Nicolaus of Damascus. Basically this story goes back to Ctesias. Cyrus, then in the service of Astyages in Media, came into contact with a certain groom called Oibaras, who was the slave of a Mede. Astyages cruelly punished Oibaras for some offence. As a result Oibaras conspired against the king and urged Cyrus to head a revolt of the Persians. And so war commenced. The first battle continued for two days and resulted in a complete victory for Astyages. Having been defeated so close to their border with Media, the Persians fled to Pasargadae. According to Ctesias, Cyrus defeated the Median forces near the town of Hyrba (the location of which remains unknown), but in the following fight Astyages gained the upper hand, and the Persians fled back to Pasargadae. Justinus (I 6) relates that when Astyages was beginning to lose the battle, he placed special troops behind his lines with orders to kill any defectors. The ensuing battle, according to Nicolaus of Damascus, took place near Pasargadae and also continued for two days. On the first day success was with the Median troops, but on the second day, the fleeing Persians, being shamed by their wives, started to fight in a more determined manner. The army of Cyrus achieved a crushing victory and the Persians captured the camp of the Medes. Astyages then executed his generals, on the grounds that the defeat had been their fault (Diodorus, IX 24, also reports the execution of the generals). Finding no support among his subjects, Astyages fled to Ecbatana and hid himself in the palace. Soon afterwards, however, he surrendered to Cyrus and was imprisoned.

According to Ctesias, Cyrus spared the life of Astyages and sent him as governor to one of the eastern Iranian provinces (in the land of the Barkanioi, who apparently lived in Hyrcania) (cf. Aliev 1960:254, n. 7, where the suggestion is brought forward that the Barkanioi of Ctesias are identical with the Parikanioi of Herodotus). Later Astyages was taken to the desert by the eunuch Petesacas, and at the instigation of Oibaras was there led to a certain death. It is possible that Cyrus was not directly responsible for his death, as Petesacas was later sentenced to death, and Oibaras committed suicide. If Ctesias is to be believed, Cyrus also executed Spitamas, the husband of Amytis, the daughter of Astyages. Cyrus then married Amytis, so becoming the legal successor to the Median throne. Later, according to Ctesias, the sons of Spitamas and Amytis were appointed by Cyrus as satraps of the Barkanioi and the Derbikes (Nic. Dam., frag. 66.13.46 = FGrH II A:361-370 = König 1972: 177-185; Ctesias, frag. 9 = König 1972:2-4; Justinus I 6.16).

According to Strabo (XV 3.8), Cyrus gained a decisive victory in the last battle, following which Astyages with the remnants of his troops fled to Median territory and was apprehended without difficulty. Polyaenus reported three battles in which Cyrus was defeated, while in the fourth battle he achieved a victory.

Xenophon, in his *Cyropaedia*, tells that Astyages died peacefully in his bed, as king of Media, and that the conquests by Cyrus were carried out by the latter in the capacity of general to his grandfather, the king of Media. But Xenophon must have been aware of the real turn of events, because in the *Anabasis* (III 4.8-12) he reported on the war between the Persians and the Medes, while in the *Cyropaedia* the historical facts appear to have been intentionally obscured in order to idealize Cyrus.

The information provided by the Babylonian Chronicle supports in outline the story by Herodotus. According to the Chronicle, in the sixth year of the reign of Nabonidus[1] "Ishtumegu[2] called together (his troops) and advanced against Kurash, king of Anshan, for the conquest ... The troops of Ishtumegu revolted and he was taken prisoner. They handed him over to Kurash. Kurash advanced against the capital[3] Agamtanu (that is, Ecbatana). The silver and golden (and other) goods [...], which he obtained as booty at Agamtanu, he transferred to Anshan" (ABC:106, II.1-4).[4]

---

[1] Namely in 550 B.C. This date is traditionally regarded as the year of Cyrus' victory over Astyages. Some modern scholars, however, regard this as unreliable (for references, see Drews 1969:1, n. 2). According to these specialists, there is no reason to assume that the Babylonian Chronicle dated the defeat of Media to the sixth year of the rule of Nabonidus. The preceding part of the text in the Chronicle is broken off and therefore the year in which the relevant occurrence took place is unknown. It is true that immediately following the relevant part of the Chronicle, the text continues with an account of the events in the seventh year of Nabonidus, but not every year is treated in the Chronicle. R. Drews suggested that, when exclusively using the Babylonian Chronicle, the defeat of Astyages could only be dated to a period between the first and the sixth year of the reign of Nabonidus, namely between 554 and 549 B.C., because the numbers indicating the first six years of Nabonidus' reign are broken off in the Chronicle (Drews 1969:2). Furthermore, on the basis of the Sippar Cylinder of Nabonidus, Drews was inclined to date the victory of Cyrus in the war against the Medes to the years 554-553 B.C. (Drews 1969:4). According to that particular source, the army of Astyages was in fact defeated by the Persians in 553 B.C. It is probable, however, that this defeat was only one in a long series of hostilities, and not the most decisive. Thus, the date of Astyages' defeat cannot yet be definitely determined.

[2] Namely Astyages. The real Babylonian pronunciation of the name was *Ishtuvegu*.

[3] Literally: 'The royal city'.

[4] Apparently, this treasure included a goblet of the Assyrian king Assurbanipal with an inscription bearing the name of this king; a Hittite goblet, and many other complete objects which were found at Persepolis. These items were, so it seems, taken from Nineveh to Ecbatata, and hence to the Achaemenid palace at Persepolis (Schmidt 1953-1970, Vol. II, p. 84).

Certain pieces of information about the war between the Persians and the Medes are also contained in some building inscriptions of Nabonidus. According to the Sippar Cylinder, the god Marduk sent a dream to Nabonidus, in which Marduk gave the order to restore the temple of Eḫulḫul, which was dedicated to the god Sin, at Harran (a city in northern Mesopotamia). The temple had been destroyed by Median troops in 609 B.C., at the time of the Assyrian wars, and since then it had lain in ruins. In his dream Nabonidus answered Marduk: "The Ummanmanda[5] surrounded the temple which you have ordered me to rebuild, and great is their power." Marduk replied: "Neither Ummanmanda, about whom you speak, nor their land, nor the kings who march at their side, will exist. (And indeed) when the third year came[6], he (i.e. Marduk) made rise against them Kurash, king of Anshan, his[7] young slave, and with his small army he defeated decisively the many troops of the Ummanmanda and captured Ishtumegu, king of the Ummanmanda, and brought him in chains to his (i.e. Cyrus') land" (NKI:218ff., I.8-33; see also Tadmor 1965:351). In another text of Nabonidus reference is again made to the temple of Eḫulḫul, which lay in ruins for 54 years after it was gutted and razed to the ground by the Ummanmanda (NKI:284, X.12-21).

It can be concluded in this way that Cyrus' revolt had apparently commenced in 553 B.C., and that Astyages was forced to withdraw his garrison from Harran, which after the fall of Assyria had belonged to Media. The Babylonians, taking advantage of Astyages' difficulties, occupied Harran around 552 B.C. It would also seem that at that time Nabonidus regarded Cyrus as his ally. Certain scholars also believe that an agreement was concluded between the two (Burn 1970:37; Cameron 1936:224; Lewy 1962:160), but information is lacking which would support this view.

The war between the Persians and the Medes was concluded in 550 B.C. In the same year Ecbatana became one of the Achaemenid residences. For a period Cyrus resided in the palace of the Median kings, a description of which has come down to us from the works of various classical writers. According to Herodotus (I 98), it was surrounded by seven concentric, defensive walls; one wall projected above the other to

---

[5] Concerning this ethnic name, which in the text refers to Medes, see the extensive bibliography and the various interpretations in a study by G. Komoróczy (1977).

[6] That is the third year of the reign of Nabonidus, namely, 553 B.C. In a political pamphlet directed against Nabonidus, there is also a reference to the rebuilding of the temple of Eḫulḫul in the same year.

[7] Namely of Astyages and not of Marduk as suggested by S. Langdon (NKI:221), and subsequently by many other scholars. As direct speech was used he, i.e. Marduk, would have said 'my', and not 'his' (CAD, Ṣ, p. 182; Galling 1964:13).

the height of the battlements. Each line of battlements was painted in a different colour. The inner two battlements which bordered on the palace, were covered with silver and gold respectively. According to Polybius (X 27), the circumference of the palace amounted to seven stadia (approximately one kilometre), and its roofs and porticos were made of cedar and covered with silver and gold.

The treasures which had been collected at the court of Astyages during the course of many decades were transferred to Pasargadae, and in Media taxes were levied just as in any conquered land. However, part of the Median nobility maintained its privileged position under Cyrus, and also under his successors.

Having conquered Media, Cyrus officially maintained the Median state, and he adopted the official titles of the Median kings ('great king, king of kings, king of lands'). But in practice the land was governed by a Persian governor (cf. Vogelsang 1986:131-135).

The Persians borrowed the Median system of state administration, which in its turn had borrowed much from the Assyrians. Within the empire of the Achaemenids, Media was placed in second place just after Persia itself. The Greeks, therefore, as well as the Jews, the Egyptians and other peoples of the ancient world regarded the fall of Media as a succession from Astyages to Cyrus, indeed called the Persians 'Medes', and seem to have regarded the history of the Persians as a continuation of that of the Medes (Herodotus I 206; VI 112ff.; Diog. Laert. II 5; Diod. IX 31; Plut., *Them.* 6-8; IGIDS:6). Although in the investigative parts of his work Herodotus carefully differentiated between Persians and Medes, and distinguished their customs, in the chapters which contain legends and tales he confused the two (to this point attention was drawn by A. I. Dovatur 1957:81). Theognis, Simonides and other Greek poets also called the Persians 'Medes' (see for references: Dovatur 1957:81; cf. the expression 'Medes and Persians' in the Book of Daniel, V 28; VI 8; VIII 20, and Esther, X 2). Concerning Egyptian and other sources, in which the Persians are called 'Medes', cf. E. Meyer 1939, Vol. III, p. 43, par. 24).

CHAPTER FOUR

WAR WITH LYDIA AND THE EMERGENCE
OF THE ACHAEMENID STATE

The defeat of the Medes marked the beginning of Persia's rise from a little known and peripheral district to an important contestant in the wide arena of world history. In the course of the next two hundred years, the country was to take a leading role in the political vicissitudes of the classical world and the Near East.

The chronology of Cyrus' campaigns after the war with Media is not fully clear. It is most likely that in c. 549 B.C., shortly after the victory over the Medes, all of Elam was occupied by the Persians, and that its capital Susa, according to the much later information by Strabo (XV 3.2), became one of the capitals of Cyrus' empire (cf. Carter & Stolper 1984:55; Meyer 1939, Vol. III, p. 183). Hinz and Zadok, however, were of the opinion that Elam was conquered by the Persians only after the fall of Babylon in 539 B.C. (Hinz 1964:132; Zadok 1976:61-62). To support this hypothesis, Zadok presented the following arguments. On the Cyrus Cylinder, Susa is mentioned among the cities to which the Persian king returned the idols of the gods which had been transferred to Babylonia during the rule of the Chaldaean kings. In addition, Zadok supported his theory using information provided by Strabo. According to this account, Cyrus chose Susa to be his capital because of its close position to Babylonia. This piece of information led to the supposition that Cyrus' empire already included Babylonia at the time when Susa became its capital. However, this conclusion is certainly not the only one possible. It can hardly be believed that Cyrus would delay for a full ten years the occupation of a land which lay next to Persis and which, in addition, was completely defenceless (cf. de Miroschedji 1987:305, n. 161).

Not long ago, A. K. Grayson published a Babylonian text, stored in the British Museum, which contains certain prophecies relating to the fate of the royal dynasties in Mesopotamia. In these prophecies, as in other, comparable sources, the names of the kings are not mentioned, but there is enough information to enable their identification. In one particular text it is said that "A king of Elam will attack ... (and) dislodge from the throne" the Babylonian king, who "established the dynasty of Harran" (BHLT:32, col. II.17-21). As mentioned by Grayson, the king of Elam is identical with Cyrus II, and the Babylonian king is Nabonidus (BHLT:24f.). Consequently, Elam was conquered by Cyrus before his attack on Babylonia. At the same time, it is possible to bring forward a remark by Herodotus (I 188), that at the time of Cyrus' campaign against Babylonia supplies for the army included drinking water which was transported from the river Choaspes, which flows past Susa.

In the years 549-548 B.C. the Persians occupied the countries which had belonged to the defunct Median state, including Parthia, Hyrcania and, apparently, Armenia.[1] According to Xenophon (*Cyrop.* I 1.4), the Hyrcanians voluntarily accepted Cyrus' sovereignty. Ctesias (*Persica* IX 2-3) wrote that the Hyrcanians had united with Cyrus before his victory over Astyages, while the Parthians did so after the fall of Ecbatana to the Persians. According to Justinus (I 7.2), the countries which used to be subject to the Medes, revolted against Cyrus as a result of which he was forced to wage many wars.

An extensive account about the Persian war against the Lydians is transmitted by Herodotus (I 69-91). In the middle of the sixth century B.C., Lydia, which included the northwestern part of Asia Minor, was governed by Croesus of the Mermnad dynasty. During the reigns of his predecessors Gyges and Alyattes, Lydia had become an important state, which had attempted, with success, to control the overseas and overland trade between the Greeks and the lands of the East. The economical strength of Lydia was also enhanced by its rich gold and silver mines.

At the same time that Lydia was gradually increasing its importance, large parts of the western and southern littoral of Asia Minor were occupied by Greek settlers. They formed small states which were independent of each other. The Greeks succeeded in establishing good contacts with the local people of Asia Minor, and in some countries (for example, in Caria), the local inhabitants, who spoke a Hittite-Luwian language, became mixed with the Greek new-comers. The basic means of existence of the Greeks in Asia Minor included essential crafts and trade with mainland Greece, the Black Sea littoral, and the regions of the Near East.

During the course of his fourteen year rule (from 560 B.C. onwards), Croesus subjugated and levied tribute from all of the Greek cities of Asia Minor, except Miletus. Because the Lydians could not master Miletus by force, a treaty was concluded between the two countries which provided for Miletus paying tribute and nominally recognizing the dominance of Croesus.

Croesus did not meddle in the interior affairs of the Greek city-states. He only levied a moderate tribute, and because the Lydians did not have

---

[1] N. C. Debevoise has suggested that Parthia was occupied by the Persians between 546 and 539 B.C., following the fall of Lydia (Debevoise 1938:5). It is more likely, however, that Cyrus conquered first the lands of the defunct Median empire (including Parthia), before advancing against such a mighty state as Lydia.

a fleet of their own, the overseas trade remained in the hands of the Greeks. In addition, the relations between the Greeks and Lydians were friendly, indeed for some time Lydia had become influenced by Greek culture (cf. Hanfmann 1978:25ff.). As a result of these conditions, the Greeks of Asia Minor did not feel oppressed under the rule of the Lydian king, and they maintained a favourable impression of Croesus for many centuries.

The Lydians also established intensive contacts with the inhabitants of mainland Greece. Croesus dispatched expensive offerings to Greek sanctuaries, and sometimes sent costly gifts to the inhabitants of certain Greek cities (at Delphi Croesus dedicated, for example, a golden statue of a lion which weighed ten talents (more than 260 kilo). In their turn, the Lydians received many advantages. For example, all Lydians acquired permanent citizenship of Delphi, and an exemption from customs duties on trade goods, etc.

It was not only the Asiatic Greeks, however, who were dependent on Croesus. He was able to extend his dominion over many of the remaining peoples of Asia Minor as far as the River Halys. These peoples included the Phrygians, Mysians, Paphlagonians, and the Carians. Thus, Croesus controlled all of western, central and southern Asia Minor, and the name itself of Croesus became a generic name for a possessor of fabulous riches (cf. Balcer 1984:33-58).

Croesus started to prepare for war following the subjugation of Media and subsequent military conquests by Cyrus and the Persians. Around 549 B.C., a treaty was concluded between Egypt and Lydia at the initiative of the Egyptian pharaoh Amasis. Both nations realized that sooner or later the Persians would move against them if they were not stopped by the united forces of both countries.[2] However, the two allies did not realize that immediate and decisive action was needed, as Persia was daily increasing her power.

Before commencing his military operations, Croesus decided to assure himself of the favourable prophecies of the gods. He sent his messengers to the temple of Apollo at Delphi, the sanctuary of Amon in Libya, and to other holy places. The messengers carried with them many costly gifts, a large part of which was presented to Apollo. To the question whether or not the Lydians should start a war with Cyrus the oracle of Apollo gave an ambiguous answer, namely that Croesus would destroy a mighty

---

[2] Concerning the good relations between Egypt and Lydia, there is also the evidence of Egyptian vases, figurines, etc., which have recently been found at Sardis in a collection of objects dating from the time of Croesus (Leclant 1967:219).

state if he would cross the River Halys (the eastern border of Lydia). He also advised the Lydian king to find himself a powerful ally.

When Croesus received this answer, he sent his ambassadors to Sparta with gifts and a proposal to draft a military agreement. Sparta was chosen because it was on friendly terms with Lydia. The Spartans willingly accepted the request for a treaty against a people the name of which they, in all likelihood, had never heard of before.[3]

According to Herodotus, the initiative for the war lay with Croesus, who felt too self-confident about his own victory. In the year 547 B.C. Lydian troops invaded Cappadocia, which previously had belonged to the Medes, and had since then been passed on to the Persians. Croesus established his camp near the town of Pteria, and it was to this place that Cyrus directed his troops. Cyrus' army was strengthened on the way by contingents from various peoples that lived along the route. Cyrus also turned to the Greek cities of Asia Minor with the call to defect from Croesus and to come to an agreement with him, offering the same conditions that had applied when they were subjects of the Lydians. The Greeks, however, gave a negative reply to this request, because they thought that subjugation to the Persians would be much harsher than dependence on the Lydians. Only Miletus showed some foresight and came to the side of Cyrus, drafting an agreement with the Persian king. The oracle at Didyma, near Miletus, predicted a victory by Cyrus in the coming war.

If Diodorus can be believed (IX 31), before the battle Cyrus dispatched some scouts to the main thoroughfares in Cappadocia, in order to reconnoitre the camp of Croesus. Cyrus also ordered his scouts to tell Croesus that the Persian king would forgive his former crimes and would appoint him as satrap of Lydia, if Croesus would come to him voluntarily and announce himself as his slave. To this Croesus answered that it more befitted Cyrus and the Persians, who used to be the slaves of the Medes, to call themselves the slaves of the Lydian king.

A bloody battle was fought on the banks of the Halys, but it remained inconclusive, and neither of the two parties dared risk to start another. Croesus withdrew to his capital Sardis and decided to prepare himself more thoroughly for the war and to try to receive effective help from his allies. As mentioned before, a treaty had been concluded with Amasis, the pharaoh of Egypt, even before the signing of the treaty between Lydia and Sparta. Croesus then turned towards the king of Babylon,

---

[3] Some scholars, however, have expressed doubts concerning the reliability of the information by Herodotus on the treaty between Sparta and Lydia (see the references collected by G. Bengtson 1960:126, n. 1).

Nabonidus, with the request for a military alliance. At the same time, Croesus sent messengers to Sparta with a request for troops to be dispatched in the spring (namely, after the lapse of approximately five months), in order to gain a decisive victory over the Persians. Croesus addressed his other allies (including the tyrant of the island of Samos, called Polycrates) with the same request. Finally, he dismissed, until the spring, his Greek mercenaries serving in his army.

When Cyrus was informed about Croesus' activities and intentions, he decided to surprise his adversary. He hurriedly advanced towards Sardis, over a distance of hundreds of kilometres. The inhabitants of Sardis expected no such an attack, and only recognized their danger when the Persians appeared before the city walls.

Croesus' troops consisted of armed cavalry, and these he led out of town onto the plain in front of Sardis. At the advice of his general Harpagos (the Mede who had defected to the side of the Persians at the time of the war with Astyages), Cyrus placed all the camels, which normally formed part of the army train, in front of the troops. Soldiers were also mounted on the backs of these camels. The horses in the Lydian army reacted to the unknown smell of the camels and fled (a military trick which was to be used by many later commanders). But the Lydian cavalrymen, who before were regarded as invincible, did not panic, but dismounted from their horses and started to fight on foot. A fierce battle ensued in which strength was not equally distributed. Under the pressure of Cyrus' troops the Lydians were forced to seek refuge in the citadel of Sardis, where they were besieged.

Following the view that the siege would take a long time, Croesus sent messengers to Sparta, Babylon and Egypt, with a plea for immediate help. Of the allies, only the Spartans replied in a more or less positive manner, and they prepared a expeditionary force for embarkation in ships. This was stopped, however, when they heard the news that Sardis had already fallen. As regards Egypt and Babylonia, they would have been unable to send immediate help to the Lydians, because at that time Cilicia (which at the beginning of the sixth century B.C. was still an independent country; it had fallen to the Babylonians around 559 B.C., until it again regained its independence) had gone over to the side of Cyrus, and thereby the road to Sardis was blocked to his adversaries.[4]

---

[4] According to the *Cyropaedia* (VII 4.1-3; cf. VIII 6.8) of Xenophon, at the time of Cyrus' advance against Asia Minor, the Cilicians and Cyprians were willing to extend their assistance to the Persian king. Consequently he never sent satraps to these countries. The lands remained under control of local rulers, who paid the Persian king a certain tribute, and in times of need provided the Persian army with local military contingents. Xenophon is apparently correct as regards Cilicia, but concerning Cyprian

The siege of Sardis continued for only fourteen days. An attempt to reduce the fortress by massive assault proved unsuccessful. A long siege would be impossible, however, because the Persian army did not have the disposal of large stores of supplies. One scout from the army of Cyrus, belonging to the tribe of the Mardioi, noticed a Lydian soldier descending down a steep and supposedly inaccessible rock face in search of his fallen helmet. When he found his helmet, the same Lydian climbed back to the acropolis. This part of the fortress was regarded to be completely inaccessible and it was therefore not well guarded by the Lydians. The Mardian soldier, having spent all his life in the mountains, climbed up along the cliff, and was followed by other soldiers. Thus the citadel was occupied and Croesus was taken prisoner. If Herodotus is to be believed, Sardis fell to the Persians sometime between October and December 547 B.C. (cf. Balcer 1984:95-122).

According to traditional sources, Croesus started to complain about the fact that the oracle of Apollo, in spite of generous gifts, had deceived him, predicting victory while he actually suffered a defeat. When the cunning priests of the sanctuary of Apollo at Delphi heard about these reproaches, they declared that Croesus had wrongly interpreted the prophecy, which said: if the Lydian king starts the war, he will destroy a mighty state. According to the words of the priests, this prophecy had come true, because the Lydian state had fallen, and Croesus, before commencing the war, should have asked the oracle which state was being referred to.

According to the unanimous opinion of the Greek authors, Cyrus pardoned Croesus and kept him alive. This account is plausible, when it is realized that Cyrus also showed magnanimity to other captured kings.

The Babylonian Chronicle seems to present another version of the fate of Croesus. In this source (III, 15-18; see ABC:107f.), it is said that in the ninth year of the reign of Nabonidus (547 B.C.), "in the month of Nisannu (March-April), Kurash, king of the land of Parsu, assembled his army and crossed the Tigris below Arbela.[5] In the month of Ajaru (April-May), he [marched] against the land of Ly[dia...][6], killed its king,

---

assistance to Cyrus he contradicts Herodotus (III 19). According to Herodotus the Cyprians became allies of the Persians in 525 B.C., during Cambyses' war against Egypt (Leuze 1972:164; cf. Smith 1944:41, 144, n. 106, where Smith agrees with Xenophon in suggesting that Cyprus joined the Persians under Cyrus).

[5] Thus, between Assyria and northern Syria along the Babylonian border, possibly trespassing on Babylonian territory.

[6] Certain scholars have expressed some doubt whether the word 'Lydia' should be restored at the damaged place. They are inclined to suggest that here a district of Assyria is being referred to (see, e.g., Stronach 1971:11). This hypothesis, however, is not convincing, because in the middle of the sixth century B.C. there was in the nucleus of the

took his treasures, and stationed his own garrison [...]. Thereafter the king and his garrison remained there.''

Herodotus (I 86-88) reported that Cyrus at first ordered the burning of Croesus at the stake, but at the last moment decided to pardon him and thereafter he took Croesus with him during his travels, and asked his advice on various matters. This version appears in the biography of Solon by Plutarch (*Solon* 28; see also Ctesias, *Persica* 36b.4; Diod. XIII 22.3; Xen. *Cyrop.* VII 2.9-29). It is possible that Herodotus was provided with two contradictory versions, and that he combined the two into one rational account. However, the relevant passage in the Babylonian Chronicle can also be thus explained, that Croesus suffered a complete defeat, but was not killed because the verb *dāku*, apart from the meaning 'to kill', also has the meaning of 'to inflict a defeat' (see ABC:107; Mazetti 1978:177; for an extensive bibliography: Cargill 1977:103ff.).

C. Nylander correctly suggested that the execution of the once so mighty Croesus, who was well known to the Greeks, would not have remained unnoticed by the Greek authors (Nylander 1970:117, n. 309). H. Bengtson regarded the Greek tradition about Croesus' fate as a legend. A. R. Burn also expressed some doubts, because in Iranian religious conceptions, fire was a sacred element and it was impossible to desecrate it.[7] This point, according to Burn, casts serious doubt on the story by Herodotus (Bengtson 1960:251; Burn 1970:42). Not long ago K. Mazetti drew attention to the fact that Bacchylides, a poet who lived during the

---

former Assyrian land no independent state. Comparatively recently J. Cargill thoroughly studied the relevant fragment from the Babylonian Chronicle. Cargill came to the conclusion that in the extant fragment there is no reference to the campaign by Cyrus against the Lydians, and the work of Herodotus remains, as before, our main source of information about the fall of Sardis to the Persians. Let us discuss Cargill's arguments. Part of the text of the Chronicle in the relevant line is destroyed, and of the word for the country only one sign is left, and even that sign is damaged. It is therefore very difficult to state against which country the campaign of Cyrus was directed. It is possible that the text refers to Lycia or another country in Asia Minor. In addition, the Chronicle dates the campaign to the month of Ajaru (April-May), which does not agree with Herodotus who refers to the fall of Lydia as occurring in winter. Herodotus does not give the exact year of the fall of Sardis to the Persians, which may have occurred between 545 and 540 B.C. (see Cargill 1977:97ff., for an exhaustive bibliography on this point). Cargill's arguments appear to us sufficiently strong, and until new cuneiform texts are discovered, the problem of when the Lydian state fell cannot be regarded as having been solved. However, if the restoration Ly[dia] is correct, there is no doubt that Cyrus' campaign against it took place in the ninth year of Nabonidus, i.e. in 547 B.C.

[7] Greek pottery frequently depicts Croesus at a burning stake (see Pottier 1922:201ff.). According to Nicolaus of Damascus (frag. 77), when Croesus was bound to the stake, some form of divine message came from a high mountain, and warned the Persians not to attract the wrath of the gods. Cyrus then ordered the fires to be extinguished. This, however, proved to be impossible. Apollo then listened to Croesus' plea to save him, and sent rain to douse the flames. At that moment the Persians remembered a prescription by Zoroaster prohibiting the desecration of fire.

first half of the fifth century B.C., and who wrote long before Herodotus, stated that Croesus, having been tied to the stake, was transferred by the will of Apollo to the land of the blissful Hyperboraeans (Bacchylides III 58). According to Mazetti, Herodotus gave this story a more rational aspect because he did not believe in the existence of the people of the Hyperboraeans (Mazetti 1978:177f.).

Whatever really happened, in 547 B.C. the Lydian state, to which its allies failed to give direct and effective assistance, ceased to exist. After this all the allies were defeated one by one.

As far as is known at present, the Greeks did not take any part in the main battles which determined the fate of the Lydian state. But the fall of Lydia was to remain forever an unforgettable event to the Greeks. The Greek author Xenophanes, who lived in Asia Minor and who later emigrated to Italy (c. 580-477 B.C.), wrote: "When you lie down in winter on a soft couch by the fire, cracking some nuts and drinking sweet wine after some good food, then ask yourself: Where do you come from? Tell me ... how old were you when the Mede arrived?" As suggested by R. Drews, reference is being made here to the fall of Sardis to the Persians, eye-witnesses of which were still alive during the time of Xenophanes (Drews 1973:7, 145, n. 17; see also Gentili & Prato 1979:144ff.).

Cyrus halted the looting of Sardis by his soldiers, but transferred the wealth of many rich citizens to his own treasury (Diod. IX 33.4; cf. Herodotus I 88-90).

Apparently, Cyrus split up Lydia into two provinces. According to Herodotus (III 120), in c. 525 B.C. the Persian Oroites was 'hyparch of Sardis', and Mitrobates, who was also Persian, was governor in Dascyleium. In this way, Sardis and Dascyleium, formerly both belonging to Lydia, had become, during the time of Cyrus, the centres of two different satrapies. They remained as such during the reign of Cambyses, Darius I and their successors (Leuze 1972:5). In the texts of Darius I and in the Elamite documents from Persepolis, Lydia is referred to by the name of *Sparda*, after its capital Sardis (Lydian *Sfard*; cf. the Aramaic transcription *Saparda* in the Aramaic-Lydian bilingual text from Sardis [Littmann 1916:12] and the Babylonian *Sapardu* in the Achaemenid royal inscriptions). Often also Herodotus (e.g. III 120), following Persian usage, refers to the Lydian satrapy under the name of its capital.

After the fall of Lydia it was the turn of the Greek states of Asia Minor. The Greeks sent their ambassadors to Cyrus while he was still in Sardis, to declare that they were willing to subject themselves to the Persians under the same conditions which had existed in their relationship with Croesus. But this proposition angered Cyrus, as the Greeks had earlier refused to come over to his side, but now that resistance to the Persians was proving to be dangerous, they wished to obtain favourable conditions of peace. Cyrus told the ambassadors of the Greek cities the following story: A certain flute player, when he saw in the sea a fish, started to play his flute in the hope that the fish would come out of the sea by itself. But when his waiting proved to be useless, he cast out a net and caught a large catch and thereafter told the trembling fish: "Stop your dancing; you did not want to dance when I was playing the flute." According to Diodorus (IX 35.3), the Persian general Harpagos told the Greeks that, because in the past they did not want to become Cyrus' allies, they would now become his slaves.

After receiving this answer from Cyrus, the Ionians and Aeolians surrounded their cities with walls and sent messengers to Sparta with a request for help. Danger threatened all the Greeks of Asia Minor except the people of Miletus, who had just in time subjugated themselves to Cyrus, and the Greeks of the islands, who could not be subjugated by the Persians because, as yet, the Persians did not have a fleet.

When messengers from the cities of Asia Minor arrived in Sparta and presented their request, the Spartans (or Lacedaimonians) refused to give them any help. But later they sent a ship to observe the coming events. When the ship arrived in Asia Minor the captain sent a messenger to Cyrus in Sardis with the demand that the Persians would refrain from attacking the Greek cities. Cyrus, who up to that moment had not even heard of the name of the Spartans, asked his Greek advisors who these Lacedaimonians were, and how many of them there were. When he had heard the answer, he said he could not be afraid of people who assembled at the market for buying and selling and cheating each other (Herodotus, when telling this story, indicates that the Persians did not know anything about market trade). Cyrus also threatened shortly to direct his attention towards the Lacedaimonians, and that they should not mingle in other people's business.

After this episode Cyrus appointed the Persian Tabalos as governor of Sardis, and returned to Ecbatana to plan campaigns against the Babylonians, Bactrians, as well as the Sakas and the country of Egypt. He decided to leave the conquest of the remaining part of Asia Minor to one of his generals.

Making use of the departure of Cyrus to Ecbatana, the inhabitants of Sardis rose in rebellion. They were headed by Pactyes, the guardian of the state treasury. The people of Sardis beleaguered the Persian garrison of the acropolis. The Persians were under the command of Tabalos. The Lydians then tried to persuade the Greek cities from along the sea to send their troops to the assistance of the rebels. When Cyrus heard about the insurrection, he, if we are to believe the account given by Herodotus (I 155), turned to Croesus who was in his suit, and threatened to sell all Lydians in slavery. But Croesus begged Cyrus not to destroy the famous city of Sardis, and to pardon its people. And Croesus then added that Pactyes should be punished as the instigator of the revolt, and the Lydians should be forbidden to carry weapons, so that they could never again revolt against the Persians.

Cyrus decided to follow Croesus' advice, and he dispatched an army to quench the revolt, appointing as its commander a Mede called Mazares. Mazares was also given the task of disarming the Lydians; to enslave the people of any Greek city which had given help to the rebels; and finally to send Pactyes alive to the king.

When Pactyes was told about the advance of the Persian army, he fled together with his main followers, thus ending the revolt. After many torments Pactyes eventually reached the island of Chios, but the people here handed him over to the Persians in exchange for a small gain of land on the mainland.

Persian garrisons were left behind in Lydia, and step by step the Lydians were reconciled with Persian supremacy. One of the main reasons for this seems to have been the exceptionally favourable circumstances for trade, which created many advantages for the Lydians. Apart from Herodotus (I 156), Polyaenus (*Strateg.* VII 6.4.) and Justinus (I 7) also report on the prohibition for the Lydians to carry weapons. According to A. I. Dovatur, this prohibition should not be taken literally, because at the time of the Persian campaign against Greece there were Lydian troops in the army of Xerxes. But these Lydians formed part of the infantry, and it is noticeable that the famous Lydian cavalry had ceased to exist, possibly because the social class which furnished the horsemen had been destroyed following the revolt of Pactyes (Dovatur 1957:89ff.).

Having suppressed the revolt in Lydia, Mazares commenced the subjugation of the Greek cities of Asia Minor. He conquered the valley of the Meander river, which he allowed his troops to plunder. Not long after this he died, and his place was taken by the Mede Harpagos, who during the war between the Medes and Persians had defected to the side of Cyrus. The information provided by Herodotus about this appointment of Harpagos (I 162) is supported by Lycian and Greek sources of the fifth century B.C. According to this information, descendants of Harpagos lived in Asia Minor and still carried the same name. I. M. Diakonoff has suggested that Harpagos received large estates in Asia Minor, which were passed on to his descendants (I. M. Diakonoff 1956:424, with reference to the inscription: Friedrich No. 44). In addition to this, it is clear from the account by Herodotus (VI 28-30), that a certain Harpagos commanded Persian troops in Asia Minor at the beginning of the fifth century B.C.; and in all probability, he was a grandson of the Mede Harpagos.

Harpagos started to construct high ramps against the defensive walls of the Greek cities, and subsequently reduced these places by massive attacks. The people of Phocaea, the largest Greek city in Asia after Miletus, refused to submit to the Persians and fled in their ships to Italy, to found there a new colony. Thus, without much effort, Harpagos was able to subjugate all of Ionia and subsequently the people of the Carians. Only the Lycians and Caunians (the non-Greek, autochthonous population of Asia Minor) showed resistance to the huge Persian army, meeting the Persians in open battle. The Lycians were pushed back to the town of Xanthos, where they set fire to the acropolis, but not before they had assembled all their women, children, slaves and goods in this place; the men chose to die in battle. A similar stubborn resistance was put up by the Caunians, but, essentially, they could not stop the advance of the well-armed and numerous Persian army. All of Asia Minor then fell under the force of the Persians, while the Ionians lost their hegemony in the Aegean Sea (see, extensively, Boffo 1983).

The Greek population, and other peoples of Asia Minor, were forced to pay more tribute to the Persians than they had done to Croesus. In addition they were obliged to provide contingents of troops for the Persian army. Cyrus could now have the use of Greek ships in case he decided to fight a war at sea. The Greeks, however, maintained their autonomy in internal matters, as well as their links with mainland Greece. With respect to administrative aspects, the Ionian cities were united with the Lydian satrapy with its capital at Sardis. According to a description by Pausanias (III 9.4), Sardis surpassed all towns in wealth and beauty, and the court of the Lydian satrap was built to resemble the royal palace at Susa. The Greeks living along the Hellespont belonged to the Dascyleian satrapy.

CHAPTER FIVE

THE CONQUEST OF EASTERN IRAN AND WEST CENTRAL ASIA

The chronology of Cyrus' campaigns after the conquest of Asia Minor remains unclear. As we have seen above, Cyrus entrusted the subjugation of the rest of Asia Minor to his generals, while he returned to Ecbatana in order to prepare for the conquests of Babylonia, Bactria, the land of the Sakas, and Egypt. With respect to the last mentioned country, it is well-known that it was only conquered by the Persians after the death of Cyrus.

Cyrus conquered Babylonia in 539 B.C., and it is certain that the Bactrians and the Sakas were subjugated while Cyrus was still alive. This can be shown by a reference to the Behistun inscription of Darius, which mentions among the countries subjected by the Persians, the lands of Margiana, Bactria, Chorasmia and other eastern Iranian countries, in addition to Gandhara and Sattagydia in the extreme east of Iran. It is worth noting that, according to existing sources, no wars were waged by the Persians in this area during the reign of Cambyses, who was the son of Cyrus and the predecessor of Darius. This shows that already during the time of Cyrus, Persian rule stretched to the northwestern limits of India, the southern spurs of the Hindu Kush and to the valley of the Jaxartes river. In addition, the *Naturalis Historia* of Plinius (VI 92) indicates that Cyrus destroyed the town of Capisa, which was apparently located north of present-day Kabul (Bivar 1969:20). Arrian in his *Anabasis Alexandri* (VI 24.3) gives a reference to the attack of Cyrus "on the land of the Indians" and about the loss by the Persians of a large part of their army in that area. Finally, the same writer (*idem* III 27.4) and Diodorus (XVII 81.1) mention the people of the Ariaspai along the southern borders of Drangiana (the *Zra^nka* of the Old Persian, Achaemenid sources). It was this people who provided the campaigning army of Cyrus with food and water, and who afterwards were rewarded by being relieved from the obligation of paying tribute to the Persian king.

But when were these lands conquered by the Persians? Some scholars have suggested that Cyrus occupied eastern Iran and West Central Asia only after the submission of the Babylonians (see, e.g., *Istorija Turkmenskoj SSR*, Vol. I, part 1, 1957:59). But this suggestion remains unconvincing.

Herodotus only refers to the fall of Babylonia (539 B.C.), and to

Cyrus' campaign against the Massagetae (530 B.C.), but he does not give any information about the other military activities of Cyrus following the war in Lydia. In this context, the 'Father of History' warns the reader that he deliberately does not tell anything about the majority of these campaigns, as he is only writing about those wars which cost the Persians considerable effort (*Historiae* I 177). According to Herodotus (I 177-178), while Harpagos destroyed the towns of Asia Minor, Cyrus subjugated one after the other the peoples of the Asian continent and only then advanced upon Babylonia (instead of Babylonia, Herodotus mentions Assyria, but he adds that the most important city of Assyria after the destruction of Nineveh was Babylon). From this piece of information the conclusion can be drawn that West Central Asia was occupied by Cyrus following the defeat of Lydia, but before the war with Babylonia. In this context the information which is provided by Berossus, a Babylonian historian of the third century B.C., is of particular interest. Using Babylonian sources for his account of Cyrus' campaign, he wrote that Cyrus "advanced upon Babylonia after he had conquered all the remaining parts of Asia" (FHG, Vol. II, p. 508; cf. Justinus I 7.2-3). And if it is possible to accept the information in Xenophon's *Cyropaedia* (I 1.4, etc.), it is stated that Cyrus conquered Babylon after the subjugation of the Bactrians, the Sakas and the Indians (the northwestern part of India was conquered much later by Darius I, but in Gandhara and neighbouring areas which border India to the west certain people were speaking the same Indo-Aryan dialects as in India, and others spoke Old Iranian languages). The statement by Ctesias (*Persica* 29.5) that the subjugation of Bactria and of the Amyrgaean Sakas (Ctesias called their leader Amorges; this permits the conclusion that reference is being made here to the Amyrgaean Sakas) took place before the war of Cyrus against Lydia, clearly does not inspire much confidence. Finally, it seems that two Babylonian administrative documents contain some information concerning the time when Chorasmia was conquered by the Persians. As R. Zadok has indicated, both of these texts refer to a certain Dadaparna (i.e. *Dāta-farna*), who is called 'a Chorasmian' (Zadok 1981:658). One of these tablets is UCP 9/2, No. 38, which is dated to the fifth year of Cyrus, i.e. 534 B.C., and comes from the town of Bīt-Ṣapṣap (located probably near Uruk). The same 'Chorasmian' is also mentioned in UCP 9/2, No. 39. This tablet does not contain any date, but was probably also written in 534 B.C. Both texts were discovered near Uruk and, in all probability, belong to the archives of the Eanna temple. Dadaparna is designated as a messenger and, to judge from the broken context, he was charged with the supervision of some temple property.

Zadok has already noted that, to judge from UCP 9/2, No. 38, Chorasmia was conquered by the Persians by, at the latest, 534 B.C. (Zadok 1981:658). The Chorasmian Dadaparna is referred to for that particular year as a person in royal service in Babylonia. It is evident that he could have been in Babylonia only as a subject and a soldier of the Persian king. Apparently, it took many years in order to conquer such distant countries as Chorasmia, Margiana, Bactria and other lands of West Central Asia, and to establish Persian rule, and subsequently to move the Persian army back to the Babylonian borders. There therefore can be hardly any doubt that the Chorasmian Dadaparna had been among those soldiers of the Persian army which occupied Babylonia in 539 B.C.

Based upon the above mentioned sources, the hypothesis can be brought forward that between 545 and 539 B.C. Cyrus subjugated the eastern Iranian (this term refers to the eastern provinces of Iran, and certain districts of Afghanistan, Pakistan and India) and West Central Asian domains of Drangiana, Areia, Margiana, Chorasmia, Sogdiana, Bactria, the tribes of the Sakas, Sattagydia, Arachosia, Gedrosia, and Gandhara. It was only after reaching the furthest limits of his conquests in the northeast that Cyrus advanced against Babylonia.

Unfortunately, the details of Cyrus' campaigns in the east remain completely unknown. The oldest reference to Bactria in classical sources is found in a drama by Aeschylus called 'The Persians'. In this piece reference is made to the inclusion of Bactrian troops in the Persian army of Xerxes against Greece. Ctesias wrote that Cyrus fought against the Bactrians with mixed success, but afterwards the Bactrians voluntarily submitted to the Persians when they were informed that the Median king Astyages had accepted Cyrus as his son (see König 1972:2). From this reference it is possible to conclude that, according to Ctesias, Cyrus conducted a campaign in West Central Asia immediately after the war with Media. The sources however, do not permit to accept or reject such a sequence of affairs.

What was the level of social development in the West Central Asian domains during the period of the Persian conquest?

Unfortunately, scholars do not have reliable written sources about the history of West Central Asia in the pre-Achaemenid period. It is possible that the tribes from these lands had already established relationships with the Median king Astyages (for example, Ctesias wrote that the Sakas owed allegiance to the Medes, but this statement, however, remains doubtful). Unfortunately, there are no reliable sources concerning much older contacts between the West Central Asian tribes and peoples that lived further to the west. It is true that already by the nineteenth century, certain suggestions were brought forward with regard to the siege of Bactra by the legendary Assyrian king Ninus and the fall of the same city to the not less legendary queen Semiramis. But these hypotheses were based on somewhat confused and clearly not reliable information by Diodorus (II 4) and Justinus (I 1), and also on the basis of an inscription by Tiglathpileser III (published in R II, Table 67). For instance, F. Lenormant suggested that the Assyrians had already conquered certain areas of West Central Asia (Lenormant 1870:48-55; 69-71; see also Duncker 1867, Vol. IV, p. 15). Similar suggestions were put forward by certain Russian scholars, including, for example, S. P. Tolstov (Tolstov 1938:182). However, on the basis of the existing sources, it can now be stated that the Assyrian army never penetrated further east than the Median lands.

In modern literature the opinion is often aired that certain state-like entities existed in pre-Achaemenid West Central Asia. Already by the nineteenth century, M. Duncker wrote that in the ninth century B.C. an old Bactrian kingdom had come into existence. Duncker based this statement on the discovery of an obelisk which was ascribed to the reign of the Assyrian king Salmanasar II. On the obelisk, among other objects of tribute, two-humped camels are depicted from Bactria (Duncker 1867, Vol. IV, p. 35). This suggestion was criticized by K. P. Patnakov (Patnakov 1879-1880:33ff.), but later Prášek hypothesized that there could be no serious doubt as regards the existence of an old Bactrian state, because in the Zoroastrian tradition reference is made to the Bactrian king Vishtaspa (the legendary protector of Zarathustra). According to Prášek, Bactria must have become an independent state-like entity well before the Persian occupation, with Bactra as its capital. This view was based on the idea that at the time of the Achaemenids Bactria was an important administrative unity. Prášek further suggested that also Margiana had a line of kings before the Achaemenid advance, and that the memory of these rulers was still alive even during the time of Darius I (see below). From the Behistun inscription it could be inferred that at the commencement of the rule of Darius I, Margiana was administratively linked to Bactria. Starting from this point, Prášek was of the opinion that Cyrus included Margiana in the administrative unit of Bactria (Prášek 1906-1910, Vol. I, pp. 51-54). In order to support the suggestion of an old Bactrian kingdom, scholars also refer to a piece of information by Ctesias concerning a Bactrian state, with which, according to this writer, Cyrus had to wage a war. They also draw attention to a communication by Herodotus, which stated that Bactria, next to Babylonia, Egypt and the Sakas, formed a major obstacle in the advance of the Persians towards world domination. It is also possible to refer to the opinion of

S. P. Tolstov, that ''Bactria was united with Iran, if not on equal level, then still in a privileged position as regards other political entities'' (Tolstov 1938:184). The Achaemenid inscriptions, however, include Bactria in lists of lands which paid tribute, and representatives from Bactria are illustrated in the reliefs of Persepolis, offering presents to the Achaemenid king in the company of delegates from many other subject lands. In addition, contrary to some other countries which were ruled by their own dynasties and which enjoyed local autonomy, Bactria was always ruled by satraps who were appointed by the Achaemenid king and who were usually from among his own nearest relatives.

It is evident from what has been said above that the question concerning the existence of an old Bactrian kingdom remains debatable. New material concerning the level of the growth of productive forces and social relations in West Central Asia in the pre-Achaemenid and Achaemenid periods, has been gained through the recent excavations by Soviet archaeologists. Nevertheless, the specialists do not always agree in the appreciation of the results of these excavations. According to V. M. Masson, by the first third of the first millennium B.C. an urban civilization had sprung up, based on huge irrigation systems; towns were built, and citadels were constructed on top of artificial platforms (Masson 1959:58ff., 122ff.). For instance, settlements have been brought to light in the territory of ancient Hyrcania (in the southwest of the Turkmenistan SSR), which extended over as much as 50 ha., and many of these also had citadels. Masson suggested that in the oases which were inhabited by a settled population, the first steps had been taken towards an early class system even in the pre-Achaemenid period. Furthermore, according to Masson, information in the Avesta should be taken seriously as regards the existence in West Central Asia by that period of large political entities; in the same light consideration should be given to the epic accounts about an old Bactrian kingdom, as transmitted by Ctesias (Masson 1966:335ff.).

According to M. M. Diakonoff, there were no large political entities in West Central Asia before the Persian occupation, but simply some oases with farmers, and a barbarian periphery with nomadic Sakas (both groups speaking an Iranian language). Both groups lived in the political stage of a disintegrating military democracy. In the mid-first millennium B.C., agriculture supported by irrigation in the valleys of large rivers in Chorasmia, Sogdiana, Margiana and Bactria, led to the origin of state formations whereby the primary borders of these states coincided with the borders of the irrigation systems. In particular, as suggested by M. M. Diakonoff, the Margians did not have a tradition of kingship, because the leader of the Margian revolt at the commencement of the reign of Darius I is referred to in the Behistun inscription as chief, while at the same time the leaders of the revolts in Persia, Media, Elam, Babylonia and in other countries are indicated by the title of king. Following a study of society as depicted in the Avesta, M. M. Diakonoff was of the opinion that a characteristic aspect of this society was pastoral husbandry, while arable farming played only a minor role (M. M. Diakonoff 1954:121ff.; *idem* 1961:75).

Comparatively recently, I. M. Diakonoff presented the hypothesis that during the ninth to seventh centuries B.C. significant political entities existed in West Central Asia and in eastern Iran. I. M. Diakonoff tended to regard these entities as states (I. M. Diakonoff 1982:349-350). But this suggestion is not supported by the sources and remains unconvincing.

The problem of the society as presented in the Avesta is, to date, one of the most complicated questions in the field of Iranian studies. It has long been recognized that the Avesta does not really include information about essential crafts, nor contain references to iron (but bronze, however, was already in use). The oldest parts of the Avesta describe the life and customs of settled pastoralists and farmers, living at the threshold of a class society, while still maintaining the system of clan relationships.

The land where Zarathustra commenced his proselytizing activities is known in the Avesta as *Aryānām Vaejah*. Many scholars have localized this land in Chorasmia, in the opinion that it was from here that Zoroastrianism came into existence and subsequently spread towards Sogdiana, Margiana, Bactria and other countries (Henning 1951:43; Herzfeld 1935:7ff.; Nyberg 1938:327). According to F. C. Andreas, the homeland of the Gathas (the oldest part of the Avesta) was in Sogdiana. Other scholars have located the Avestan society in Margiana (Struve 1968:29), in Bactria (Altheim & Stiehl 1961-1962:90; M. M. Diakonoff 1961:60; Meyer 1939, Vol. III, p. 97; cf. Sarianidi 1975:52). According to V. I. Abaev, Zoroastrianism originated in eastern Iran along the fringes of the settled lands bordering on the expanses occupied by Scythian nomads (Abaev 1956:55; *idem* 1974:320). J. Duchesne-Guillemin presented the opinion that the society in which Zarathustra was preaching, lived in a nomadic existence, and had not settled down. Thus, arable farming did not play a significant role (Duchesne-Guillemin 1948:12). Independently of each other, I. M. Diakonoff and G. Gnoli have suggested that the homeland of Zarathustra should be sought for in the valleys of the Helmand, Tejend and Hari Rud rivers, namely in Seistan (near the *Zra^nka* of the Old Persian, Achaemenid sources) and neighbouring districts (I. M. Diakonoff 1971:142; Gnoli 1980:129ff., with extensive bibliography on pp. 16ff.). These opinions are presented with very convincing arguments. As remarked by Gnoli, only this region is described in detail in Avestan geography, and its borders correspond approximately to Ariane, which is the name used by the Greeks from the time after the Macedonian conquests in order to indicate the eastern part of the Iranian plateau (Gnoli 1980:130ff.). The same author demonstrated that according to the finds of Italian archaeologists in the territory of Seistan there was in that region, starting from the Bronze Age until the Achaemenid period, wide-spread stock-breeding of horned cattle. This point makes an even stronger argument for the location in this district of the Gathas of Zarathustra (Gnoli 1980:153ff.).

J. Markwart presented the hypothesis that *Aryānām Vaejah* included a large, pre-Achaemenid state with Chorasmia as its centre, which was destroyed by Cyrus. This hypothesis was later supported by W. B. Henning and I. Gershevitch, and in the Soviet Union by S. P. Tolstov (Henning 1951:42ff.; Gershevitch 1959:14). Henning and Gershevitch were of the opinion that the centre of this political unity was located to the south of Chorasmia and its centre was situated in the Merv oasis (ancient Margiana) or in the Herat area (old Areia). The basis for this hypothesis about a 'Greater Chorasmia' is constituted in the main by a remark of Herodotus (III 117). Herodotus wrote that a dam across the river Akes[1] used to belong to the Chorasmians, but later was used, with permission of the Achaemenid king, by the Chorasmians themselves, the Parthians, the Sarangians, and the Thamanaeans. Elsewhere (III 93), he wrote that Chorasmia, Parthia, Areia and Sogdiana formed one satrapy in the Achaemenid period. According to the above mentioned scholars, the frontiers of this satrapy were once those of the Chorasmian state before it was conquered by the Persians (I. M. Diakonoff 1971:134-139; Gafurov 1971:15ff.; *idem* 1972:58ff.; P'jankov 1972:17). At the same time it should be noticed that, according to the tenth Yasht of the Avesta, 'Heratian Merv' belonged to a confederacy centred in Areia.

Archaeologists, however, have remarked that it was only in the sixth century B.C. that Chorasmia witnessed some progress in the development of artificial irrigation and of agriculture, and that during the eighth and seventh centuries B.C. it did not have a large population or advanced irrigation systems. The development of large settlements of the type of Kalaly-Gyr in the territory of Chorasmia should undoubtedly be dated to the Achaemenid period. On the basis of these data, Gnoli regarded the hypothesis concerning a 'Greater Chorasmia' as highly improbable (Gnoli 1980:17, 91ff.). In respect to Sogdiana of the fourth century B.C.,

---

[1] This river is generally assumed to be identical wih the modern Tejend–Hari Rud river, the valley of which bordered on Parthia and Drangiana (Masson 1967:172ff.). According to Gnoli, however, the Akes cannot be identified with any known river (Gnoli 1980:239).

Arrian and Curtius remarked that the city of Marakanda possessed a strongly fortified citadel, encircled by a wall and a moat. Both town and citadel were surrounded by a defensive wall with a circumference of approximately thirteen kilometres. As has been shown by archaeological excavations, the buildings of Marakanda covered between fifty to seventy hectares. It would appear that this large city originated in the Achaemenid period (Masson 1959:127).

It is difficult to agree with S. P. Tolstov who stated that an extensive, slave-holding state had come into existence in Chorasmia by the eighth or seventh century B.C. Tolstov added that the irrigation of the land must have been based on the labour of multitudes of prisoners of war, because, as argued by Tolstov, "in that level of historical and technical development" only slaves could build such systems of irrigation canals (Tolstov 1948:103; *idem* 1962:89-91). The only basis for this argumentation by Tolstov was that the irrigation system of Mesopotamia had been laid out by slaves, and therefore the Chorasmian canals should also have been built by using slave labour. Extensive documentary material however, testifies to the fact that for the building of the canals in Mesopotamia use was made in general of free labourers. At a level of still lowly developed production forces the application of slave labour on a massive scale was impossible; in addition, the tools with which the canals were dug were not inferior to the weapons which were found in the possession of the, supposedly, warriors and overseers of the slaves, as repeatedly remarked by I. M. Diakonoff.

The Gathas, which in a certain manner reflect the material culture and the social relationships which existed in eastern Iran and West Central Asia in the pre-Achaemenid period, indicate that there was not a developed urban life with strong state formations and a strict division of agriculture on the one hand and craft production on the other. But with the disintegration of clan ties, early class entities made their appearance. The process of class stratification also finds its reflection in the oldest parts of the Avesta. In these passages a protest is contained against the power of the nobility.

The first cities in West Central Asia only started to appear in the middle of the first millennium B.C. These included the capitals of Sogdiana, Bactria and Margiana, which were provided with citadels and covered a space of some tens of hectares. It is true, however, that by the seventh century B.C., on the territory of some above mentioned areas, a certain development of an agricultural economy took place which was based on artificial irrigation, while during the same period there would appear to have been no state formation.

CHAPTER SIX

WAR WITH BABYLONIA AND THE FALL OF SYRIA

After the death of Nebuchadnezzar II in 562 B.C., a political crisis developed in Babylonia. The roots of the problem lay in the conflict between two opposed, ethnic groups which had long before settled in Mesopotamia, namely the Chaldaeans and the Aramaeans. There were also conflicts between the priestly circles and those of the army. The priesthood started to mingle actively into politics and agitated against kings whom they did not want to accept. During the course of a few years, three kings succeeded each other, until in May 556 B.C. the 65-year old Nabonidus rose to power. Even in antiquity his character already attracted much attention, and to the present day historians continue to discuss the motives behind his political activities. Not much is known, however, about his life and it has proven difficult to distinguish between historical truth and later legends.

Nabonidus' father was called Nabu-balaṭsu-iqbi, and is referred to in the texts as 'prince' and 'governor'. In all probability, he was chief of one of the Aramaic tribes which had settled in Babylonia (Landsberger 1947:150f.). Great influence upon Nabonidus was exercised by his mother Adda-guppi, who, in the opinion of many scholars, was a priestess in the temple dedicated to the god Sin at Harran, and who after the city's conquest by Median troops fled with her son to Babylon. In the sources, however, there are no clear references to such an episode. It is possible that she lived in Babylon from childhood and did not serve as priestess of Sin, but only worshipped the god (Röllig 1964:236). At any rate, it is possible to suggest, with some certainty, that Nabonidus, contrary to the other neo-Babylonian kings, was not Chaldaean, but a leader of an Aramaic tribe which had settled in northern Mesopotamia. In one text from the year 597 B.C. (Nbk 70), reference is made to a certain Nabonidus, who served as a governor of an unspecified city. The suggestion has been put forward that this was the future king, and that he was married to a daughter of Nebuchadnezzar II (Dougherty 1932:31; Wiseman 1983:11). However, in a duplicate to the same text this person is called 'the son of the king', namely of Nebuchadnezzar II. Besides, at that time Nabonidus was only about fourteen years old (see Röllig 1964:239).

In any case, according to the words of Nabonidus himself, he became king because he was exclusively elected by the gods, who called upon him to rule the country, although he was not of royal blood (H 2, I, 7-11).

When in c. 552 B.C. Median troops retreated from the district of Harran, Nabonidus restored the temple Eḫulḫul, dedicated to the moon god Sin, and transported statues of Sin and his entourage, which had previously been kept in Babylon, to Harran. The renaissance of this sanctuary was closely linked to the important religious reforms which Nabonidus gradually introduced. Although he also worshipped the traditional gods of Babylonia, such as Marduk, Nabu, Nergal, Shamash, etc., he was inclined to address himself primarily to the moon god Sin, referred to by Nabonidus as "king of the gods in heaven and on earth" (NKI:250ff.). Nabonidus built and rebuilt temples which were dedicated to Sin, both in Babylonia itself, and beyond its borders. The problem about the activities of Nabonidus is further complicated by the fact that the god Sin who was worshipped by Nabonidus was not identical to the traditional Babylonian god Sin. His symbols and forms of worship bore a greater resemblance to that of the Aramaic gods. It is also possible that Nabonidus was planning to change the Babylonian temple of Marduk, the supreme god of the land, into a temple of Sin. These reforms brought Nabonidus into conflict with the priesthood and the population of various ancient cities, such as Babylon, Borsippa, Nippur, Larsa, Uruk, and Ur. Relations with these cities had been tense right from the beginning of Nabonidus' reign. The opposition against Nabonidus, however, was not united, and every city tried to push its own god to the first rank. According to the words of Nabonidus, people became confused, sinned against the gods, told lies and untruths and even "like dogs they devoured one another." The angered gods sent diseases and famine to the sinners, and many people died. Nabonidus, it is said, was appalled by the godlessness and lawlessness of his subjects and fled to the oasis of Tema in the northern part of central Arabia. The king was to remain there for ten years, and during this period he strengthened his position in the west. He defeated the Arabs, conquered their most important lands and founded colonies of Babylonians. In a certain inscription of Nabonidus, reference is made to his conquest of the oases of Dadanu, Padakku and Iadiḫu, which lay along a line of three to four hundred kilometres between Tema and Yatrib (Medina). If credence can be given to the words of Nabonidus, the kings from Egypt, Media and other countries sent their ambassadors to Tema to honour him (H 2, I, 20ff.). The conquest of Tema had especial significance for Babylonia, as the sea route from the Persian Gulf to southern Babylonia had become blocked due to changes in the course of the Euphrates, and it was therefore necessary to find new trade routes.

While Nabonidus was residing in the western part of his realm, the rule of Babylonia was carried on by his son Bel-shar-uṣur (the Belshazzar of the Book of Daniel).

Usually scholars regard Nabonidus as a man who was without martial qualities, estranged from life "as a pious scholar", almost an archaeologist, who, in times which were difficult for the land, was occupied with the excavation and restoration of temple buildings according to their old plans. The well-known Assyriologist, B. Landsberger, however, has presented the convincing opinion that Nabonidus strove to unify around him the many Aramaic, Sin-worshipping tribes of the Near East in order to build up a barrier against the approaching danger from Iran. In respect to the achievement of this objective, Landsberger referred to both the religious reforms[1] and the wars of Nabonidus (cf. Böhl 1939; Galling 1964:3ff.; Garelli 1958; Lewy 1962; Röllig 1964; Smith 1924:32-82; Tadmor 1965:351ff.; Wilkie 1951).

In the year 543 B.C., the age-long strife between Egypt and Babylonia came to an end; both countries had to prepare for the impending war with the Persians. At the commencement of the reign of Nabonidus, the neo-Babylonian empire included almost all of Mesopotamia, Syria, Phoenicia, Palestine, part of the Arabian peninsula, and part of eastern Cilicia. In 547 B.C. Cilicia came over to the side of the Persians. Thus, all of the lands north and east of the Babylonian realm were in the hands of the Persians. In 543 B.C. Nabonidus returned to Babylon from Tema and commenced preparations for the coming war against the Persians. Nevertheless, despite his exertions, the Babylonian troops were doomed to fail. Babylonia had no allies. Only Amasis, the pharaoh of Egypt, would have been able to lend real assistance, but he showed a lack of foresight and stayed firmly on the fence.

Even in Babylonia itself, the position of Nabonidus was difficult. He had striven to break the power and influence of the priesthood of Marduk, the most important god of Babylonia, and had neglected the religious festivals in the temple of Esagila. As a result, the influential priestly circles, who had become dissatisfied with Nabonidus' policies, were willing to help the foreign enemy. Many scholars also suggest that the priests of Marduk secretly conspired with the advancing Persians.

---

[1] As already remarked by various scholars, the religious reforms by Nabonidus took place at a time when certain definite changes occurred which led to a centralization of cults. As regards the excavations by Nabonidus of ruined temples, he did this not because of an interest in antiquity, but out of a desire to rebuild the sanctuaries according to their original plans (Goossens 1949:145f.). V. A. Jakobson presented the undoubtedly correct hypothesis, that the conflict between Nabonidus and the population of the old sacred cities reflected the traditional character of the struggle between the popular assemblies of the Babylonian cities and the Mesopotamian kings who strove to abolish the privileges of the inhabitants of Babylon, Borsippa, Uruk, etc. (for instance, the right to local autonomy; freedom from building duties, etc.).

The Persians also commanded the trade routes of Babylonia, and its merchants were therefore becoming dissatisfied with their king. They were interested in the creation of a huge empire which would guarantee them a market and safe mercantile routes to Egypt, Asia Minor and the other lands of the East. In order to achieve their aims they were prepared to defect to the side of the foreign conqueror.

In Babylonia lived tens of thousands of representatives of various foreign communities (among whom were many Jews), who had been forcibly deported from their own countries by the Chaldaean kings. These people had never lost their hope of returning to their homeland. They were prepared to help the enemy of Nabonidus and awaited the Persians as their saviours.

The social conflicts between on the one hand the peasants and the craftsmen, and the nobility (including the civil and temple servants, tradesmen, etc.) on the other, had undermined society. Farmers and craftsmen—the essential population of the country, both in number and in importance—were indifferent to Nabonidus' preparations for war and prepared to change the old rulers for new ones without remorse. Finally, the Babylonian army was worn out by numerous wars in the Arabian desert. It could hardly be expected that this army would have been capable of withstanding the pressure of the numerically superior, and better equipped forces of the enemy.

Thus, Babylonia lacked the necessary strength and vigour to show effective opposition against the Persian army. The latter, in its turn, consisted of free farmers and cattle breeders, without, as yet, an extensive social stratification. When Cyrus attacked Mesopotamia, the priests welcomed him as the appointed of Marduk; the Jewish prophets declared that he was the saviour of their people, while the other foreigners regarded him as their liberator.

In the spring of 539 B.C., the Persian army started its campaign and moved into the valley of the Diyala river. The governor of the country of Gutium, called Ugbaru, joined the Persian army together with his troops.[2] Some scholars have suggested that Ugbaru was the Babylonian

---

[2] During the first millennium B.C., the name of Gutium was an anachronism and was often mentioned together with Subartu (which was also an anachronism), or it was used instead of Subartu as a synonym of the east, or sometimes of the north (Hallo 1968-1971:717-719). Ugbaru, the governor of this province, is the very same person as the Gobryas of Xenophon's *Cyropaedia* (IV 6.1-7). According to Xenophon, Gobryas was 'an Assyrian', who defected to the side of Cyrus and surrendered to him the district which he had held as governor for the Babylonian king. The latter, in an attack of fury, had killed Gobryas' son. In this passage Xenophon apparently presents some more or less reliable information, because, contrary to Herodotus and other Greek authors, he was aware of the role played by Gobryas in the occupation of Babylon (cf. Hirsch

governor of a province to the east of the middle course of the Tigris river, appointed by Nabonidus himself, who at a critical moment decided to defect from Nabonidus and to join the forces of Cyrus (see, e.g., Hallo 1968-1971:717ff.). M. Mallowan wrote that Ugbaru, "governor of Gutium, who had been the principal general of Nebuchadnezzar, defected to the side of Cyrus" (Mallowan 1985:411). The assumption, however, that Ugbaru was a general of Nebuchadnezzar is based on an erroneous interpretation of Babylonian records and therefore cannot be accepted (see n. 2). The defection of Ugbaru to the side of the Persians is reported only by Xenophon who mentions him under the name of Gobryas (*ibid.*). According to Xenophon, Gobryas was an Assyrian. However, Xenophon, like Herodotus, makes no distinction between Assyria and Babylonia and at times gives the name of Assyrians to Babylonians. The cuneiform sources do not give any reason to suppose that Ugbaru was a Babylonian. There is also no ground to assume that Gutium was a Babylonian province located to the west of Media. As R. Zadok has suggested, Ugbaru was the governor of an Achaemenid province comprising at least part of western Media and northeastern Assyria which bordered on Babylonia. It is noteworthy that, having conquered Babylonia in 539 B.C., Cyrus returned the gods and citizens deported to Babylon at Nabonidus' order to their former abodes. According to the Cyrus Cylinder, these cities extended "until the border of Gutium." Consequently, Gutium did not belong to the Babylonian empire (see Zadok 1981-1982:138, n. 65; see also n. 2 above).

According to Herodotus (I 189), when the Persian army on its march to Babylon attempted to cross the Gyndes river (the present-day Diyala), one of the sacred white horses of Cyrus was drowned. Cyrus in his anger ordered the punishment of the river, and, postponing a further advance,

---

1985:77; Lehmann-Haupt 1902:342). I. M. Diakonoff identified Ugbaru with the Oibaras of Ctesias, suggesting that the Babylonian Chronicle when mentioning Gutium, is in fact referring to Media (Diakonoff 1956:422ff., n. 4; cf. Herzfeld 1968:201, who also regarded Ugbaru as satrap of Media). V. Scheil, on the basis of one Babylonian letter which refers to Gubaru (a variant of Ugbaru), was of the opinion that the latter during the reign of Nebuchadnezzar II occupied an important military position in southern Babylonia, and that he subsequently became governor of Gutium (Scheil 1914:165-169). This hypothesis was followed by G. B. Gray, A. T. Olmstead and many other scholars (Gray 1969:12, n. 1; Hirsch 1985:175, n. 54; Olmstead 1948:45). But in letter YOS, Vol. III, 111, on which these scholars base themselves, the text does not at all concern an army, as suggested by Scheil, but refers to escaped and deceased temple workers. In addition, already in 1921 A. T. Clay showed that the pertinent letter dates to the time of Cyrus II, and not to that of Nebuchadnezzar II (Clay 1921:466, cf. also San Nicolò 1937:12; Schwenzner 1922-1923:250). It is difficult to agree with the opinion put forward by A. T. Olmstead, H. S. Nyberg and certain other scholars, to the effect that in the Babylonian Chronicle Gutium refers to Elam and that Nebuchadnezzar II appointed Ugbaru as governor of this province (Nyberg 1954:65; Olmstead 1948:45).

commanded his troops to measure out places for 180 canals on both sides
of the river, and then to drain the river. This task occupied the Persian
army for the whole summer. G. G. Cameron suggested that, if no attention is paid to the allegorical aspect of the white horse's death,
Herodotus' account is supported by the Babylonian Chronicle. In some
badly preserved passages mention is made of certain events which took
place in the sixteenth year of the reign of Nabonidus. In particular,
reference is made to the River Tigris, and furthermore, according to
Cameron, it is said that during the month of Addaru (February/March)
"the Persian army"[3] was occupied with certain activities. Some months
later Cyrus won a battle near Opis. Nevertheless, the Persian army only
marched upon Babylon in October. In this manner, as suggested by
Cameron, both the Babylonian Chronicle and the *Historiae* of Herodotus
agree that the army of Cyrus was occupied during the whole summer in
certain activities in the region of the Diyala, near the city of Opis. According to archaeological information, there had been a drop in the
economy in this part of the Diyala basin during the course of many centuries (seventeenth to the end of the seventh century B.C.), and settled
life had disappeared completely. Subsequently, a slow resurgence and
revitalization took place in the economic life of the area. In particular,
there is information to suggest that near the city of Opis the course of the
river was altered. The process of redevelopment continued during the
whole Achaemenid period. The number of settlements of the region slowly increased from 33 to 57, and each settlement occupied a space of between 75 to 100 hectares (Adams 1965). It is evident that such a growth
was only possible because of an extension of the irrigation system. This
point, according to Cameron's hypothesis, may indicate that in the summer of 539 B.C. (even before the fall of Babylon) Cyrus started a project
to reconstruct and extend the irrigation network, thus granting a period
of prosperity to the land (Cameron 1974; cf., however, the opinion of
F. H. Weissbach, according to whom the account by Herodotus does not
contain even a grain of truth: Weissbach 1924, cols. 1150f.).

Fearing the defection of the Mesopotamian cities to the enemy during
the summer of 539 B.C., Nabonidus ordered that the idols from a
number of districts which were located outside the fortified zone, should

---

[3] *Par-[su]*. But this reading is based on a reconstruction of a damaged passage by E.
von Voigtlander, which was followed by Cameron. The reconstruction was presented in
an unpublished thesis. Usually the pertinent word is read *tam/tim]*, 'the sealand', namely
south of Babylonia (the preserved sign has, among others, the readings *par* and *tam*). The
last edition of the Babylonian Chronicle by A. K. Grayson tentatively adopts the reading
Ta/m-tim] (ABC:108; cf., however, *ibid.*:208, where Grayson writes that the reading *pa/r-
su]* is preferable).

be brought to Babylon. In doing so Nabonidus attempted to bring the cities which were threatened by a Persian attack into religious and political dependence on the capital. By depriving the cities of the protection by their local gods, Nabonidus at the same time deprived the Persians of possible assistance by these deities (Weinfeld 1964:205ff.).

About sixty kilometres to the north of Babylon stretched a long line of fortifications, which Nebuchadnezzar II had built through the valley of Mesopotamia. These defences could have delayed the victory of the Persians. The walls extended over a distance of 150 kilometres from Sippar in the west to Opis in the east. These works defended several large cities, namely Sippar, Kutha, Babylon and Borsippa. The walls still existed one and a half centuries after the fall of Babylon. Xenophon, in his *Anabasis* (II 4.12), left a description of the walls, based on his own observations. He called the walls 'Median'; they were eight metres wide and ten metres high, and built of kiln-fired bricks (for an extensive account of these walls, see Barnett 1963). In addition, if absolutely necessary, the advance of the enemy could be stopped by releasing water from an artificial lake near Sippar, which would subsequently flood the whole area to the east and northwest of Babylon.

Babylon was particularly well fortified, and indeed it was an almost unassailable fortress. The city was surrounded by a double wall which was made of mud and burnt brick, fixed with a mortar of asphalt, mixed with reed. The exterior wall had a height of 7.60–7.80 metres, a width of 3.72 metres and a total length of 8.33 kilometres.[4] The interior wall, located at a distance of twelve metres from the exterior wall, was eleven to fourteen metres high; 6.5 metres wide and with a circumference of six kilometres. On the walls, fortified towers were constructed at an intermediate distance of twenty metres. From these towers it was possible to fire arrows and other missiles onto the enemy. About twenty metres in front of the exterior wall of the defences there was a deep moat filled with water.

During those years Babylon was the most important city in the world, and housed a population of approximately 200,000 people. The city had eight gates. A third of the town was located west of the Euphrates (this was called the New City), and was linked to the rest of the city by a bridge, 123 metres in length (in our time the width of the Euphrates at

---

[4] For comparative reasons, it can be pointed out that the walls of Nineveh, the largest city in the ancient East, had a circumference of twelve kilometres. The ruins of Babylon are located 85 kilometres south of Baghdad and occupy a space in the form of an equilateral triangle. It covers more ground than the ruins of the other ancient cities in Mesopotamia, namely approximately 850 hectares (cf. for example the ruins of Nineveh cover 750 hectares; Assur: 53 hectares; Uruk: 450 hectares; Ur: 55 hectares).

Babylon is c. 150-200 metres; this helps to show how much water was absorbed in antiquity by the irrigation canals). The bridge was built on piers which were constructed out of burnt brick and placed with an intermediate distance of between seven to eleven metres (two piers were located on dry land; six in the water). The upper part of the bridge was five to six metres wide, and it was covered with wooden beams (apparently of Lebanese cedar). On one side, facing the Euphrates, stood the huge, fortified palace which was built by Nebuchadnezzar II, in which later the Persian kings would also reside. In another part of the city, on the other side of the Euphrates, was built the main religious centre of the Babylonians, the Esagila (from Sumerian, meaning 'the Temple that Raises its Head'). According to Herodotus, this was a square building, each side of which measured two stadia (c. 400 metres). The temple was built on an artificially raised terrace; it had six entrance gates, and several courts. Its main building occupied a space of 78 x 86 metres. Completely separate from Esagila, and built to the south of the temple complex, was the Etemenanki (Sumerian, 'the Temple Foundation of Heaven and Earth'), which is called the Tower of Babel in the Bible. According to tradition, the building of this complex continued for three hundred years, and it was concluded during the reign of Nebuchadnezzar II. According to Herodotus, this ziggurat included eight floors; in the cuneiform texts, however, only seven floors are reported. The information by Herodotus, however, does not contradict reality, because there was another level underground. According to the cuneiform inscriptions, Etemenanki measured 91 metres in height, width and length, i.e. approximately the height of the great Egyptian pyramids. Ascending towards the top of the ziggurat there was an external staircase, nine metres wide, with a resting place halfway up. The Holy of Holies was located at the top; this was the temple dedicated to Marduk and his wife Sarpanitu (24 x 22.5 metres). It was constructed of glazed bricks. According to Herodotus, this temple contained a golden chair and a bed which was adorned with luxurious carpets. The cuneiform texts relate that the house of Marduk "was brilliant like the sun", because the walls and ceiling were covered with gold and precious stones.

Northwards from the main entrance to the Etemenanki led a broad street for processions which took place during the New Year festival. The street widened gradually, until it was 35 metres wide (the remaining streets were narrow and curving, having a width varying between 1.6 and 6 metres). It proceeded to the Ishtar gate. This gate, covered with glazed bricks, rose up to a height of twelve metres, and has been completely excavated by archaeologists (for an extensive analysis of the cuneiform sources concerning Babylon, its walls, palaces, temples, etc.,

as well as classical references, and the results of the archaeological excavations which have continued for many years, see Koldewey 1925; see also
Unger 1970).

The strong fortifications were of little avail to Nabonidus, who lacked
the solid support from his own people. In August 539 B.C., the Persians
defeated the Babylonian army at Opis. After the fall of Opis there were
no further great battles. The Persians broke through the defences of
Nebuchadnezzar II, and then crossed the Tigris to the south of Opis, and
laid siege to Sippar. The defence of Sippar was headed by Nabonidus
himself. The Persians, however, were only confronted with minor
resistance from the garrison, and Nabonidus was forced to flee to
Babylon. On October 10, Sippar fell to the Persians. Two days later the
Persian army under Ugbaru was able to enter Babylon without hin-
drance, and Nabonidus was seized. According to the Babylonian Chronicle, the capital surrendered without struggle. This detail is corroborated
by archaeological sources, as no traces have been found of conflagrations
or violent destructions of houses, in occupation layers which date to the
fall of the city to the Persians (Reuther 1926:34-36).

On October 29, 539 B.C., Cyrus entered Babylon amid great popular
rejoicing and feasting. The Babylonian Chronicle reports the following
events for the seventeenth year of Nabonidus (III 12-23; see ABC:109ff.).

"In the month of Tashritu, when Cyrus fought a battle at Opis on [the
bank of] the Tigris, ... the army of Akkad withdrew. He (Cyrus) created
a bloodbath under the people and took away booty. On the fourteenth day
Sippar was taken without a fight. Nabonidus fled. On the sixteenth day
Ugbaru, the governor of Gutium, and the army of Kurash entered
Babylon without struggle. Thereafter, when Nabonidus withdrew, he was
captured in Babylon. To the end of the month the shieldbearers from
Gutium surrounded the gates of Esagila, (but) there was no interruption
of the rites in Esagila and (in the other) temples, and the fixed moments
for the ceremonies were not neglected. On the third day of the month of
Arahsamna, Kurash entered Babylon, and (the road) in front of him was
covered (with green branches?). Peace was installed in the city. Kurash
pronounced to all of Babylon (words of) greeting. Gubaru, his governor,
appointed the district officers in Babylon. Commencing during the month
of Kislimu, and continuing to the month of Addaru, the gods of the land
of Akkad, whom Nabonidus had ordered to be removed to Babylon,
returned to their places. On the night of the eleventh day of the month
of Arahsamna, Ugbaru died. In the month of [Arahsamna ...] the wife of
the king died. From the 27th day of Addaru to the third day of Nisannu,
[there was] general mourning in Akkad, and all people uncovered their
heads (cf. below)."

According to the account by the Babylonian historian Berossus, the attitude of Cyrus towards the conquered capital was rather hostile: ''In the seventeenth year of his (i.e. Nabonidus') reign, Cyrus, having conquered all the rest of Asia, marched from Persia on Babylonia with a great army. Nabonidus ... met him with his army and fought a battle, but, being defeated in the struggle, fled with certain others and shut himself up in Borsippa. Meanwhile Cyrus occupied Babylon and ordered to destroy the exterior walls of the city, because the city seemed very formidable to him and difficult to capture. Afterwards Cyrus marched to Borsippa, in order to organize the siege against Nabonidus. But Nabonidus did not await the end of the siege, and surrendered'' (FGrH, Vol. III C, pp. 408f.).[5]

Other sources give a completely different account of the fall of Babylon. According to Herodotus and Xenophon, the Babylonians fought with determination against Cyrus, and the city could only be taken after bitter resistance. Herodotus (I 188-191) wrote that the Babylonians had carefully prepared themselves for the siege and had collected provisions for many years. But the Persians destroyed one of the dams and directed the water of the Euphrates away from the place where it entered Babylon. Afterwards they attacked the city along the highest point of the river bed, while the people of Babylon were engaged in some festival. In this story by Herodotus, Nabonidus is called Labynetus. According to Xenophon's *Cyropaedia* (VII 5.7-32; 58), the Persians dug a huge trench around Babylon, along its outer defences, and during the night, while the inhabitants of Babylon were celebrating one of their festivals, they directed the water of the Euphrates into the trench and then entered the city along the river bed. Thereafter they quickly made their way to the palace, killing all they met. At the palace they killed the drunken guards. They then penetrated into the innermost rooms where a banquet was taking place (cf. the version in the Book of Daniel, chapter 5) and killed the Babylonian king (his name is not mentioned). Despite these events, however, the Persians still had to spend a considerable degree of energy in order to establish their control over the city and the rest of the country. Xenophon wrote that Gobryas commanded the conquest of Babylon, while Cyrus was busy occupying other Mesopotamian cities. The latter detail is corroborated by the Babylonian Chronicle.

A Jewish eye-witness to the fall of Babylon, as reported in the Book of Isaiah (XLVI 1ff.), expressed his delight with the following words: ''Bel bows down; Nebo stoops ....'' Elsewhere he stated that Babylon

---

[5] As we have seen above, however, the Chronicle states that he was arrested in Babylon, and not at Borsippa.

would never be populated again, and jackals would live in its pleasant palaces and hyenas would inhabit its towers. The youth of Babylon would be pierced with arrows, and nobody would even pity its children.

In the Book of Daniel (II-V), there is another account of the last phase of the fall of Babylon. In this account Nebuchadnezzar is brought forward as king instead of Nabonidus (the latter is completely unknown in the Bible). At the banquet, Nebuchadnezzar's son Belshazzar (that is: Bel-shar-uṣur) and the other guests in the king's palace saw a fiery hand write the following words on the wall: *mene, mene, teqel, peres* ("numbered, brought to an end, weighed and found wanting, and divided"). These enigmatic words, which predicted the approaching fall of Babylon, according to the legendary prophet Daniel, carried the following meaning: God had counted the Babylonian ruler's days, he weighed his soul, and found him wanting. God then decided to divide the state among the enemies of the king, including the Persian king, Cyrus, and the Median king, Darius. This rather unhistorical version of the happenings in Babylon is also found in the work of Josephus Flavius, who used the Book of Daniel as a source (*Ant. Jud.* X 11.2).

According to the Book of Daniel, Belshazzar was killed on the night of Babylon's fall, and authority passed to the 62-year old 'Mede Darius'. He was succeeded by a Persian called Cyrus. Many studies have been dedicated to the problem whom Daniel was referring to when he mentioned 'the Mede Darius'. A critical branch of Biblical scholars is of the opinion that he is not an historical figure, but a fictitious character who originates in an unreliable tradition. The orthodox theologians, however, on the grounds that the Biblical texts cannot contain incorrect statements, identify 'the Mede Darius' with the Median king Cyaxares, Gobryas or Cambyses (for an extensive bibliography, see Rowley 1935:5ff.).

From all of the above mentioned sources concerning the fall of Babylon, most scholars prefer to use the Babylonian Chronicle, as it is a contemporary source. Only a few scholars are of the opinion that the accounts and stories of Herodotus and Xenophon do not contradict the Chronicle, but only supplement the Babylonian source (see, e.g., Smith 1944:153).

According to Berossus, Cyrus showed magnanimity towards the old Nabonidus. Cyrus sent him out of Babylon, and appointed him governor of Carmania, to the east of Persia (FGrH, Vol. III C, pp. 394, 408).[6]

---

[6] J. V. Prášek and S. Smith regarded this piece of information as unreliable (Prášek 1906-1910, Vol. I, p. 23; Smith 1924:35). The much later writer Abydenus wrote that

According to Xenophon's *Cyropaedia* (VII 5.30), the last Babylonian king was executed. Relatively recently, however, a Babylonian text of a prophetic nature was published which states that the deposed king of Babylon would be sent by the king of Elam to a strange country. This text would, or so it appears, support Berossus' version (BHLT, p. 25, col. II, lines 19-21).

Shortly after the fall of Babylon all the country came under the control of the Persians. It is interesting to notice that the last document from Uruk which is dated according to the reign of Nabonidus (GC I, 390), was written during the day following the fall of Babylon. Apparently, at the time of writing the text the news of Babylon's fall had not yet reached the southern town of Uruk (Parker & Dubberstein 1956:13).

According to the Babylonian texts, Cyrus liberated the people of Babylonia from the oppressive rule of Nabonidus, who had been impious and disrespectful towards the gods and during whose reign people were like corpses. In a pamphlet-like poem (the so-called 'Verse Account of Nabonidus'), written in the Akkadian language and distributed for public reading, Nabonidus is accused of lawlessness; crimes against the temples and the people; the sculpturing of a monstrous statue of a foreign god, "whom nobody had ever seen before", and building this god a temple at Harran; the squandering of other people's property; the oppression of the people of the land; a long sojourn abroad; the building of a palace at Tema which was comparable to the palace at Babylon; and, finally, he was accused of blasphemy, ignorance and stupidity. "Justice was ignored by him, he killed with weapons [the strong] and the weak ... he deprived merchants of their trade routes ... he ruined the land; there were no songs in the land, nobody was happy ... an evil demon possessed him, [only] evil demons walked on [his] side ... he had no sacred feelings ... nobody in the land saw him ... He handed part of the army to his eldest son, and he himself led the greatest part of his forces to [many] countries. He gave him the kingdom, and himself started on a long journey ... In an assembly he boasted: "I am wise, intelligent, and I see what is hidden, (although) I do not know how to write (with the stylus)" (for the latest edition, see Landsberger & Bauer 1927:88-94). It is stated in the Chronicle that starting from the seventh year of his reign, the king did not reside in Babylon, and as a result for many years the annual New Year festival could not be celebrated in the temple of Esagila, as the personal participation of the king was necessary. According to the above

---

subsequently Darius took from Nabonidus a part of Carmania (Burstein 1978:28). But when Darius acceded to the throne, the aged Nabonidus was in all probability not more among the living.

mentioned pamphlet, Nabonidus said that, until the reconstruction of the temple of Eḫulḫul was completed, "I will omit (all) festivals, I will stop the celebrations of the New Year." In the above mentioned prophetic text a prediction is included (in fact the text was written *post factum*), "A rebellious king will rise [... and install] a dynasty of Harran. For seven-, teen years [he will be king]. He will oppress the land and [stop] the festival at Esagila ... He will plan evil against Akkad" (BHLT p. 32, col. II, lines 11-16).

According to the pamphlet, Cyrus "restored the statues of the Babylonian gods in their sanctuaries, and satisfied their hearts ... [daily] he presented the gods with food ... Happiness returned to the people of Babylon. He liberated them from prison ...." In the Chronicle it is said that Cyrus returned peace to the people of Babylon and kept the army from the temples. In one inscription from the temple of Eanna at Uruk Cyrus declares: "I am Kurash, king of lands, caretaker of the temples of Esagila and Ezida (temple in Borsippa), son of Cambyses, a mighty king" (Schott 1929:63, Table 31, No. 1, 2). The following inscription of Cyrus has been preserved from Ur: "I am Kurash, king of the universe, king of Anshan ... The great gods have delivered all the countries into my hands. I restored prosperity in the land." (UET I: No. 194; concerning the restoration by Cyrus of the temple at Ur, see Woolley 1955:244ff.).

In spirit and content these texts are comparable to the Cyrus Cylinder, in which, in particular, the following is stated: "He (i.e. Nabonidus) took away the images of the gods ... In an hostile manner he stopped the daily offerings (to the gods). He consigned the worship of Marduk, the king of the gods, to complete oblivion. He always directed his anger towards his (i.e. Marduk's) city ... Because of the people's complaint, the lord of the gods (namely, Marduk) became angered ... He started to search and he looked through all countries, trying to find a just ruler ... He commanded Kurash, king of Anshan, to become the ruler of the whole world. He made the land of Gutium and all of Ummanmanda bow to Cyrus' feet.[7] And he (Cyrus) treated the 'black-headed' (the Babylonians) with justice, whom he (Marduk) urged Kurash to conquer."

"Marduk, the great god, protector of his people, being satisfied with his (Cyrus') good deeds and his upright mind, ordered him to advance against his city Babylon ... Marduk went with him as a friend, permitting him to enter his city Babylon without any battle, without inflicting any damage to the city. He handed him Nabonidus, the king who did

---

[7] Namely, Media. As remarked by G. Komoróczy, it is hard to say whether the addition concerning Ummanmanda refers to the district of Gutium, or whether in this case it points out another people, not identical with the Medes (Komoróczy 1977:50ff.).

not worship him. All the people of Babylon and of the entire country of Sumer and Akkad, and the kings and governors bowed before him and kissed his feet, beaming with pleasure because the kingdom was his. They greeted him with joy as the king of the world, with whose help they had returned from death to life ... and they blessed his name ...."

"I am Kurash, whose rule is beloved by the gods Bel and Nabu, whom they wanted as king, to satisfy their hearts ... My numerous soldiers entered Babylon in peace and I did not allow anyone to frighten the inhabitants ... I established peace in Babylon and in all sacred cities ... I relieved them of their yoke ... I brought back peace to their disrupted houses and made an end to their grievings. Marduk, the great lord, was satisfied with my deeds and sent down his blessing upon me, Kurash, the king, who worships him, and on Cambyses, my son, and on all my soldiers ...."

"All the kings of the universe, from the Upper Sea to the Lower Sea[8], they, who live in royal palaces ... all kings of the western lands, who live in tents, brought their heavy tribute to me in Babylon and kissed my feet ...."

"In Assur and Susa, Agade, Eshnunna, Zamban, Me-Turnu, Der, until the border of Gutium, I brought the gods back to their former places in their sacred cities on the other side of the Tigris, to their sanctuaries, which in the course of many years had fallen to ruins. I gathered all their inhabitants and returned (to them) their houses. At the command of Marduk, the great lord, all the gods of Sumer and Akkad whom Nabonidus had carried to Babylon to the anger of the lord of the gods, these I all returned unharmed to their former sanctuaries, their abodes, with which they were satisfied. May all the gods whom I returned to their sacred cities, pray to Bel and Nabu for my long life ...." (for the last edition: KZ).

Comparatively recently, P.-R. Berger concluded that a fragment of a cuneiform text which is kept in the Babylonian collection of Yale University (BIN II, 32), forms part of the Cyrus Cylinder. In this fragment mention is made of the institution by Cyrus of new offerings in the temple of Marduk and of the reconstruction of the city's fortifications. Cyrus continues by saying: "I saw the written name of my predecessor Assurbanipal." Here, apparently, he refers to a particular building inscription of Assurbanipal which was found in Babylon during reconstruction works. The conclusion by Berger was anticipated by J. Harmatta, who already prior to the identification of the relevant fragment had remarked on the similarity in style between the Cyrus Cylinder and the inscriptions

---

[8] Namely, from the Mediterranean Sea to the Persian Gulf.

of Assurbanipal (Harmatta 1971). In this connection, C. B. F. Walker correctly remarked that the Cyrus Cylinder is a normal building inscription within the Assyrian-Babylonian tradition, and can certainly not be regarded as some declaration of human rights (Walker 1972:159; see also Kuhrt 1983; Van der Spek 1982).

The hostile tradition against Nabonidus, and the favours extended to Cyrus, are also reflected in Biblical literature. Nabonidus is referred to in the Old Testament as "the mad king", although in this work his person as the last Babylonian king is swopped for the much better known Nebuchadnezzar II. The writer of the Book of Isaiah, a witness to the fall of Babylon, apparently knew about the general political attitudes of Cyrus. Large sections of his writing are in spirit reminiscent of Babylonian texts which emphasize the praise of Cyrus and condemn Nabonidus. Josephus Flavius wrote that passages from the Book of Isaiah, relating to the time of Babylon's fall to Cyrus, were read before Cyrus (Bickerman 1967:62). In a later legend, transmitted in the manuscripts from Qumran dating to the first century B.C., it is said that Nabonidus lived at Tema for seven years, suffering from leprosy which was inflicted by God for his idol worship (Amusin 1958:104-117; *idem* 1971:326ff.; Meyer 1962:7ff.; Milik 1956:407-417).

In Xenophon's *Cyropaedia* (V 4.35; VII 5.32), the last Babylonian king is called a "dishonest" man, and an "enemy of the gods and of the people."

Almost all the texts, however, which praise Cyrus, have the character of propagandistic writings and demand a very critical approach, as they were composed by Babylonian priests at a time subsequent to the fall of their country to the Persians, at the command, either of their new king, or of some of his following. In addition, the texts were written in conformity to the much earlier Babylonian inscriptions of Assurbanipal. The account by Herodotus about the fall of Babylon, and also the communication by Berossus, make us think, not without some reason, that by accepting everything said in the texts which were composed by Babylonian priests, we ourselves become the victims of Cyrus' propaganda. In this context it is necessary to refer to a Babylonian prophetic text, in which mention is made of a "bad" reign of some king, who, in all probability, is identical with Cyrus (BHLT, p. 25, col. II, lines 22-24).

In his inscriptions, Nabonidus declared that during his reign Babylonia was prosperous, and her enemies smashed. Approximately four thousand economic and legal documents from the time of Nabonidus show that the economy of the land continued to prosper, and that the contents of Babylonian texts dating from the time of Cyrus which report Nabonidus' impoverishment of the people, carry a clear tendentious character. It is true that one document has been preserved which testifies to the fact that during the year of 544 B.C. the country was stricken by famine and a certain widow was forced to hand two of her young sons as slaves to the temple of Eanna at Uruk, in order to save the boys from starvation (YOS, Vol. VI, 154). According to an inscription of Nabonidus, after a drought the god Adad sent rain following the instructions of Sin, thus creating prosperity, and 234 *qa* (about 230 lbs) of barley, or 270 *qa* of dates cost one shekel of silver, which is approximately one third of the normal price (BBS, 37; about the date, see Landsberger 1947:118, n. 2). There is also a text which is not completely preserved (the name of the king is broken off), but which was dated by W. G. Lambert to the time of Nebuchadnezzar II, and which W. von Soden, with much more grounds, regarded as a text of Nabonidus. In this document the justice of the ruler of Babylon is praised, and also his success in internal and external policies. Finally, the text mentions the prosperity in the land (Lambert 1965; von Soden 1975:283; see also *idem* 1983).

Within this context it is necessary to emphasize that, while Cyrus trod in the footsteps of ancient Babylonian traditions, his policy towards subjugated nations in some aspects differed from that of the Assyrian and Babylonian rulers. They strove to collect a maximum of tribute from the conquered lands and in doing so used excessive violence towards the unwilling, or applied deportations of sometimes whole groups of the population. Under Cyrus, the idols which Nabonidus had ordered to be carried to Babylon, were now re-installed in their proper places. The statues of alien gods, formerly carried away from Susa and from the cities of northern Mesopotamia, were also returned to their former sanctuaries. The ruined temples of Babylonia, Elam, and what used to be Assyria were reconstructed. Cyrus also ordered the rebuilding of the temple of Jerusalem, which had been destroyed long before by Nebuchadnezzar II. Ugbaru was ordered by Cyrus to protect Babylon and its temples from plunder. Esagila, the main religious centre of Babylon, was protected by a special guard of soldiers from Gutium, to prevent the remaining army from plundering it. In addition, Cyrus ordered special offerings to Marduk, as was expected and traditional to the Babylonian lords.

Cyrus permitted the return of the foreigners who had been forcibly settled in Babylonia at the command of the Babylonian kings, to their own countries. Amongst these people were Phoenicians, Elamites, etc. Most notable, perhaps, were the Jews, who obtained permission to return to their land and to rebuild their temple. This was only one of many examples of the general principles of Cyrus' reign (Diodorus XIII 22.3; Cameron 1955:77ff.).

After the conquest of Babylon, Cyrus gave his power the character of a personal union with the Babylonians. He formally maintained the Babylonian kingdom and nothing was changed in the social structure of the land. Babylon was made into one of the royal residences. Apparently no alterations occurred in the economic life of the land until the end of the sixth century B.C. The interval between the date of the last documents of the reign of Nabonidus, and the first economic texts related to the reign of Cyrus, amount to only fourteen days. As far as can be concluded from the legal documents, the majority of the officials (possibly, all of them) maintained their position in the state administration, in spite of the fall of the country to the Persians. These people included judges, governors, etc. And as is shown by hundreds of documents from many cities of Babylonia, prices for various commodities, including those for food, remained basically at the same level as before. Cyrus tried to reinstate normal conditions for the economic life of the country; for a flourishing of transit trade, as well as for the maintenance of the traditional methods of administrating the land. The priesthood was given the chance to revive its ancient cults under the protection of Cyrus. Of greater significance, perhaps, was the fact that Cyrus' rule in Babylon was not regarded as foreign domination, as he had received his right to rule from the hands of Marduk, and because he carried out the sacred old rites. Cyrus adopted the official title of 'king of Babylon, king of the lands' (only in a small number of texts the simpler title of 'king of the lands' was used). This title was also carried by his successors up to the time of Xerxes.[9] People also started to invoke the name of Cyrus in judicial affairs.

---

[9] The founder of the neo-Babylonian state, Nabopolasser, carried the ancient title of "king of Babylon, king of Sumer and Akkad." Nebuchadnezzar II, however, together with his Chaldaean successors, called himself "king of Babylon." In Iran the Achaemenids usually carried the title "king of kings, king of the lands." The title "king of the lands" was in certain cases also used by the Assyrian king Assurbanipal and the Babylonian king Nebuchadnezzar II (TMH II/III, 36, 37; ABL, 266, 272 etc.; YOS, vol. XVII, 162; cf. ibid. p. XXII; cf. San Nicolò 1937:43, n. 2). In all probability, the Achaemenids adopted this title from the Assyrians, with the Medians as intermediaries. It is difficult to agree with R. N. Frye, who wrote that the title 'king of kings' reflects an Iranian concept, and in those cases when the title was used by other peoples, he regards this as a product of derivation (Frye 1964:36ff.; cf. Griffiths 1953:148). In one particular text from Babylon, Cyrus is called "king of the lands, king of kings" (BE, Vol. VIII, 58), and in another, "king of the Persians" (YOS, Vol. VII, 8). It appears as if at the commencement of his reign in Babylonia there was as yet no uniform title which had been approved from above, and the scribes used various variants. The Greeks rendered the title of the Persian king with the words "the great king". Compare also the Phoenician title of the Achaemenid kings as "lord of kings" (personal communication by I. Sh. Shifman).

Yet, in spite of all these points, Babylonia had turned from an independent state into a satrapy of the Achaemenid empire and had lost every vestige of independence in its foreign policy. Even within the country, the highest administrative power now lay with the Achaemenid governor.

Ugbaru was appointed as the first governor of Babylon. In his hands lay the factual power over the capital and country. In the Babylonian Chronicle (III 15, 20) mention is made of Ugbaru, "the governor of Gutium" and the general of Cyrus, and to Gubaru, "the governor" of Cyrus in Babylon. In all probability, they are one and the same person (Röllig 1971:671; San Nicolò 1937:63ff.; cf. Smith 1944:153, n. 144, where the opinion is put forward that they were different people; see n. 15).

Ugbaru died three weeks after the fall of Babylon. It would seem likely that he was an old man, as seems confirmed by Xenophon's *Cyropaedia* (IV 6.1-7). As seen from the Babylonian Chronicle, soon after the death of Ugbaru "the king's wife died." Then there was a public mourning in Babylonia from the 27th of the month Addaru to the 3rd of the month Nisannu, i.e. March 21-26, 538 B.C. (see ABC:111, III:23). This queen could only be Cassandane, the wife of Cyrus II and the mother of Cambyses. M. Boyce has suggested that she was buried in the Zindan-i Sulaiman tower at Pasargadae (see M. Boyce 1984).

In 538 B.C. Cyrus appointed his son Cambyses as king of Babylon. In order to give this appointment a legitimate character, Cambyses participated in the religious New Year festival. Thus he became king of Babylon by receiving his authority from the hands of the supreme god Marduk in his temple of Esagila. Following Babylonian ideas, the New Year ceremonies should also ensure fertility for the land and victories for the king for the ensuing year. The festival took place during the first eleven or twelve days of the month of Nisannu (the first month of the Babylonian cyclic calendar, corresponding to March or April). The statues of gods from other cities of the country were collected in Babylon, with the statue of Nabu from Borsippa in the foremost place in order to greet his father Marduk. Subsequently the procession of gods left the temple of Esagila and went along the sacred road to the Gate of Ishtar, which was decorated with depictions of mythical animals, executed in brightly coloured tiles. Within the proximity of this gate a barque was moored, in which all the statues, as well as the king, proceeded along the canal of Araḫtu to 'The Temple of the New Year Festival'. The statue of Marduk was installed on a high pedestal in this building for the duration of the ceremonies (see Falkenstein 1959b:147ff.; cf. Berger 1970:155ff.).

It is known from a certain text that during this festival the king wore a linen cloak, a linen turban, as well as golden bracelets (Falkenstein 1959a:40ff.). According to the opinion of A. L. Oppenheim, Cambyses discontinued this Babylonian custom. A fragment has been preserved from the Babylonian Chronicle, which has been published comparatively recently by this scholar. He translated it as follows: "When on the fourth day[10], Cambyses, son of C[yrus], went to the temple ... the priest [gave him] the sceptre of Nabu ... [They did not allow him] to accompany the image of Nabu on account of (his, namely Cambyses') Elamite dress; [only when they removed] from [him] his spears and quivers [did ...], the son of the king [go] to the ser[vice ... (when?)] Nabu returned (with the procession) to the temple of Esagila, [he, i.e. Cambyses, performed] the sacrifice in front of Bel and the son of Bel" (Oppenheim 1974:3500; ABC:111, col. III, lines 24-28).

This text has been badly preserved and apparently not all of the reconstructions are reliable. Oppenheim has suggested that Cambyses entered the temple while dressed in his normal Elamite garb and fully armed, despite the fact that priests must have previously told him how he, the king, was supposed to approach the gods. At first the priests did not allow him to play a role in the rituals. They eventually convinced him that he should at least lay down his weapons. According to Oppenheim, Cambyses complied with this demand, but did not change his clothes. He was nevertheless allowed to offer the sacrifices to the gods, and receive the royal sceptre. From this reconstructed text Oppenheim came to the conclusion that Cambyses had intended to demonstrate his rejection of a foreign religion and to insult it (Oppenheim 1974:3501). The same author also wrote that Cambyses, contrary to the famous tolerance of Cyrus, had "a deep-seated religious conviction outweighing political considerations" (Oppenheim 1985:557). However, neither Cyrus nor Cambyses thought about such notions as tolerance or religious freedom. These ideas did not exist at all in their empire and there was no need for them: one can tolerate only what one does not like. And there are no grounds to indicate any essential difference in religious or political actions of Cyrus and Cambyses. They both worshipped all the Persian and foreign deities of their empire, they believed in their power and tried to gain their favours. As to the above mentioned reconstruction of the passage of the Babylonian Chronicle, M. Boyce has correctly stated that "the passage has been restored and interpreted in the light of Perso-Egyptian propaganda against Cambyses ... rather than providing independent corroboration for it" (Boyce 1982:73, n. 15a).

---

[10] The event occurred in the month of Nisannu, that is, on March 15, 538 B.C.

Cambyses, however, was only king of the city of Babylon and the northern part of the land. The central and southern parts of Babylonia remained under control of Cyrus or his officials (San Nicolò 1937:51-54). Eight documents from this period are dated to "the first year of Cambyses, king of Babylon, the son of Cyrus, king of the lands", or carry the formula "the first year of Cambyses, king of Babylon, while Cyrus, his father, is king of the lands" (Camb., 42, 46, 72, 81, 98, etc.). All of these texts date to a period between the second and ninth month of the year 538 B.C. Twenty other documents date to the "first year of Cambyses, king of Babylon" without reference to Cyrus (see Camb., 28, 39, 40, 45, etc.). All the above mentioned documents, or at least most of them, relate to the period in which Cambyses had not yet become king of the Achaemenid empire, namely, prior to the time that he took the title "king of Babylon, king of the lands."

W. H. Dubberstein has suggested that Cambyses was not appointed as king of Babylon in 538 B.C., but in 530 B.C., namely before Cyrus' last campaign against the Massagetae, when Cyrus kept the title of 'king of the lands' for himself (Dubberstein 1938:418). The majority of documents which date to the first year of Cambyses as king of Babylon should therefore be dated, following the opinion of Dubberstein, to the year 530 B.C. Dubberstein based this assertion on information provided by Greek authors who communicate that Cyrus appointed his eldest son as regent before he started on his campaign against the Massagetae (Herodotus I 208; Xenophon, *Cyropaedia* VIII 7.11). One document, however, is dated to "the first year of Cyrus, king of the lands, and of Cambyses, king of Babylon" (Cyr., 16). Because this document is undoubtedly dated to the year 538 B.C., it is completely clear that by that date Cambyses was king of Babylon. Concerning southern and central Babylonia, the documents from Nippur and Uruk are exclusively dated to the first year of Cyrus, king of the lands. It is thus evident that the jurisdiction of Cambyses did not extend to these regions.

The last clay tablet which relates to the rule of Cambyses in Babylon, is dated to the twentieth day of the month of Tebetu in the year 537 B.C. (Camb., 89). Cambyses thus ruled in Babylon for about nine months. Cyrus removed him from office in 537 B.C. The reasons for this action remain obscure (San Nicolò 1937:51ff.).

Recently, W. H. Shea has attempted to revise the current opinion about the rule of Cambyses in Babylon during the first years after Cyrus' conquest of Mesopotamia. He regarded with unbelief the hypothesis that Cambyses would have been appointed as king of Babylon in 538 B.C.; that he was shortly afterwards removed from office, to be reinstated just before the death of Cyrus. Following Dubberstein, Shea suggested that

Cambyses did not commence his rule in Babylon at the beginning of Cyrus' rule in Mesopotamia, but rather at the end (Shea 1971/1972, part II, pp. 104ff.). According to Shea, Cyrus officially became king of Babylon approximately fourteen months after his subjugation of the city, and before that time he bore the title 'king of the lands' (*idem*:123ff.). This point automatically raises the question as to who was the official king of Babylon, following the fall of the city to the Persians until the end of the first year of Cyrus' domination as 'king of the lands'. Shea is of the opinion that Cyrus' general Ugbaru was king in Babylon. According to the Babylonian Chronicle, however, Ugbaru died three weeks after his entrance into Babylon. In this context Shea suggested that the composer of the Chronicle has not placed the information about the death of Ugbaru in chronological order, and the death of Ugbaru must have taken place, not in the month of Araḫsamna in 539 B.C., but in the same month of the year 538 B.C. Thus, according to Shea, from the spring of 538 B.C. until his death in October of the same year Ugbaru was the vassal king of Babylon, and after his death the title of 'king of Babylon' was added to that of 'king of the lands' (Shea 1971/1972, part III, pp. 99ff.). On this basis, Shea is of the opinion that Cyrus' general Ugbaru was the same person as the Babylonian governor Gubaru (Shea 1971/1972, part IV, pp. 163ff.).

If the hypothesis is accepted that Ugbaru was the vassal king of Babylon, it becomes impossible to explain certain references in the texts. For example, not once in the Chronicle is Ugbaru called king; besides, there are no documents which are dated to his rule. In addition, as we have seen above, one of the texts which have survived is dated to "the first year of Cyrus, king of the lands, and of Cambyses, king of Babylon'. This document indicates without any doubt that soon after the fall of Babylonia, Cyrus appointed Cambyses, rather than Ugbaru, as king of Babylon, while retaining for himself the title of 'king of the lands'.

After the fall of Babylonia, all of the lands which were located to the west as far as the frontiers of Egypt appear to have submitted voluntarily. The people from the mercantile ports of Phoenicia, together with the traders from Babylonia and Asia Minor, were in favour of the creation of a large empire with safe trade routes, where all transit commerce could be kept securely in their own hands.

In all probability, the Persians during the same time gained control over the various districts of the Arabian peninsula which had been previously conquered by Nabonidus, and even expanded their influence in that area. In the Cyrus Cylinder the mention of 'kings in tents' who sent tribute to the Achaemenid king, probably refers to the chiefs of Arabic tribes, while at the same time the mention of 'kings in palaces' refers to Phoenician, Syrian and other rulers. R. P. Dougherty and S. Smith were inclined to suggest that the Persians conquered Arabia and Syria from Nabonidus, attacking these countries from Asia Minor in about 540 B.C., and only afterwards encroached upon Babylonia (Dougherty 1929:161-166; *idem* 1932:120; S. Smith 1924:82, 102; *idem* 1944:41ff.). But the only argument in favour of this hypothesis is a reference in Xenophon's *Cyropaedia* (VII 4.16). In this instance it is stated that Cyrus defeated the Phrygians, the Cappadocians and the Arabians, before the subjugation of the Babylonians. Unfortunately, it is difficult to accept the theory that in this particular statement Xenophon provides some reliable information. The majority of specialists are of the opinion that Syria and Palestine submitted in 539 B.C., immediately following the fall of Babylon. The Persian administration retained the local Phoenician kings, because they had voluntarily recognized the authority of Cyrus. For example, King Hiram of Tyre, who ascended the throne of Tyre in 552 B.C., remained in office until his death in 532 B.C.

K. Galling suggested, however, that the above mentioned lands were only subjugated in 526 B.C., just before Cambyses' attack on Egypt. This hypothesis is based on the following arguments. Amidst the cuneiform texts from Neirab (in Syria) there are no documents which can be dated to the period between the sixteenth year of Nabonidus (540 B.C.) and the second year of Cambyses (528 B.C.). From this information, or rather lack of it, Galling has drawn the conclusion that relations between Babylonia and the lands to the west of the Euphrates were broken off in 539 B.C., and were only re-established ten years later. Furthermore, in 539 B.C., Cyrus had permitted the Jews to rebuild their temple in Jerusalem, and had ordered that local functionaries should, in all possible manners, cooperate in this undertaking. However, in 538 B.C., when Sheshbazzar, the governor of Judah, laid the foundations of the temple, he did not receive any political or financial support from the rulers in Samaria. As a result, further rebuilding of the temple had to be postponed until 520 B.C. This point, according to Galling, testifies to the fact that Samaria was still "relatively independent" of the Persians (Galling 1964:39-41). Finally, Galling also supported his theory by using information provided by Herodotus (see below).

Let us discuss the above mentioned arguments. In the first place, Herodotus does not say that the Phoenician cities submitted to the Persians under Cambyses. Herodotus only says (III 19) that the Phoenicians submitted voluntarily to the Persians, but refused to follow the command of Cambyses to campaign against the Carthaginians, because they were related to them. Furthermore, the quantity of cuneiform texts from Neirab is very small (27 texts in the aggregate), and they cover a long period of time, from Nebuchadnezzar II to the reign of Darius I. Among these texts there are no tablets which date to the reign of Amel-Marduk and Labashi-Marduk, although during that time Syria still formed part of the Babylonian empire. In a comparable manner, the absence of documents from the period of Cyrus can easily be explained by the limited quantity of the tablets from Neirab. In this context, I. Eph'al has convincingly argued that the cuneiform tablets from Neirab were not written at that place, but were stored there as a family archive by people who used to live in Babylon (Eph'al 1978:84-87). As regards the unwillingness of the governor of Samaria to help in the rebuilding of the Jerusalem temple, it should be noted that analogies are known from a much later period when Samaria and Judah undoubtedly formed part of the Achaemenid empire. In addition, it is not very likely that after the fall of Babylon the Persians would wait thirteen years to extend their rule over countries which previously used to belong to Babylonia and which at that moment could put up no resistance in any form. Cyrus declared in the Cylinder that "all kings ... from the Upper to the Lower Sea ... and all kings from the western lands" brought tribute to him in Babylon. It is evident that here particular reference is being made to the lands west of the Euphrates river. Finally we may note in anticipation of further discussions that during the fourth year of the rule of Cyrus in Babylonia (535 B.C.), a united province was created consisting of Babylonia and 'Across-the-River', and that this contained Mesopotamia and the lands to the west of the Euphrates. It follows therefore that by 535 B.C., at the latest, all of these lands had recognized the authority of the Persian king.

The question as regards the date of the conquest of Jerusalem by the Persians demands a much more extensive discussion. It is known that in the years 598 and 587 B.C., following a long struggle by Judah to remain independent of Babylonia, Nebuchadnezzar II forcibly deported 12,000 inhabitants of Jerusalem, without counting the women and children, to Mesopotamia (in total, the number of people moved must have amounted to about 30,000. Previously, in 722 and 701 B.C., approximately 30,000 Israelites had been deported to Mesopotamia by the Assyrian kings). The Jews were settled in Mesopotamia in special districts, and were divided up into semi-autonomous groups which were headed by their elders (for instance, in the settlement of Tell Abib, near Nippur).

The Jewish prophets encouraged their compatriots in captivity by predicting the impending fall of Babylon and the ensuing return of the Jews to their homeland. By the beginning of the sixth century B.C., the prophet Jeremiah had predicted that the multitudinous Medes together with the people of Urartu (Ararat); the Mannaeans (Minni) and the

Scythians (Ashkenaz) would carry out the vengeance of Yahweh and destroy Babylon. Jeremiah exclaimed with joy (LI 11ff.): "Sharpen the arrows, take up the shields. The Lord has stirred up the spirit of the kings of the Medes, because his purpose concerning Babylon is to destroy it ... One runner runs to meet another, and one messenger to meet another, to tell the king of Babylon that his city is taken on every side." Somewhat later, Isaiah predicted (XIII 17-22) that the Medes, "who have no regard for silver and do not delight in gold", would move against Babylon, and the prophet expressed the hope that Babylon would be completely destroyed and that on its territory shepherds would not even pasture their sheep. When the Persians started to stir themselves, Isaiah exclaimed (XXII 6): "And Elam bore the quiver ... and Cyrus uncovered the shield."

The enemies of the Babylonian kings, however, waited for more than sixty years. Only when Media, and subsequently Lydia, were defeated by the Persians did the prophets regain their former optimism. This point is reflected in the Book of Isaiah (Deutero Isaiah), in chapters 40-48 (and apparently also in chapters 49-55), the composition of which dates to the period between the fall of Lydia and that of Babylonia to the Persians (Jenni 1954:241). Certain passages in these chapters are so similar, both in spirit and in content, to contemporary cuneiform documents (in particular the Cyrus Cylinder), that it is possible that the writer of the Book of Isaiah (Deutero Isaiah) knew about the Babylonian texts (see Cameron 1955:85; Olmstead 1948:55). In particular, Isaiah (e.g. XLV, 1ff.) several times mentions Cyrus by name, calling him the anointed (Messiah) of the Lord Yahweh. The latter says about Cyrus: "He is my shepherd, and he shall fulfil all my purposes." And about Jerusalem: "She shall be inhabited", and about the temple: "Your foundation shall be laid" (XLIV 28). "Thus says the Lord to his anointed, to Cyrus, whose right hand I have grasped, to subdue the nations before him and ungird the loins of kings, to open doors before him that gates may not be closed. I will go before you and level the mountains, I will break in pieces the doors of bronze and cut asunder the bars of iron" (XLV 1-2).

According to traditional Jewish sources, however, the anointed by Yahweh could only be a Jew of the lineage of David, and he had to be chosen by God to reinstate the Jewish state. Consequently the question is raised as to why Isaiah should call a foreigner the anointed by Yahweh. Ch. C. Torrey suggested that all references in the Book of Isaiah to Cyrus and Babylon are later interpolations (Torrey 1928:40ff.). This theory is unanimously refuted by all Biblical specialists. Following a suggestion by S. Smith, the Jewish prophet in fact regarded Cyrus as the anointed and as the legal successor of David; in the eyes of his contemporaries he therefore obtained, later on, the reputation of a traitor (S. Smith 1944:74). Finally, another hypothesis has been put forward, saying that the word 'anointed', used in relation to Cyrus, has the meaning of 'governor' (Jenni 1954:255). For instance, the late I. D. Amusin presented the idea that originally the word *Messiah* ('anointed') indicated those people who by the favour of Yahweh were called to kingship or high priesthood, and that the word only obtained its eschatological meaning during the Hellenistic period (personal communication).

As was said previously, in 538 B.C. Cyrus allowed the Jews to return from Babylonian captivity to their homeland and to rebuild the temple of Jerusalem. In addition, Cyrus appointed Sheshbazzar, the leader of the Jews in captivity and descendant of the line of David, as governor of Judah.

Cyrus' edict is transmitted in the Book of Ezra in two versions, one of which is written in Hebrew, the other in Aramaic. In content the two versions are not identical. Scholars have long polemized as regards the question which of the two versions is authentic. Many specialists are inclined to prefer the Aramaic version, while certain scholars regard both variants as much later falsifications. E. J. Bickerman, however, has convincingly shown that we are dealing with two documents which were drafted independently of each other and which are thus both genuine: the Aramaic version was the official decree of the royal chancellery, while the Hebrew text was composed with due observance of its purpose, namely its oral proclamation in Jerusalem, and therefore in conformity to traditional and local phraseology (Bickerman 1976:72ff.; with regard to the historical background of the edict, see H. Tadmor 1964:450ff.).

The Hebrew version (Ezra I 1-8) of the edict runs as follows: Cyrus "made a proclamation throughout his kingdom, and also put it in writing. Thus says Cyrus king of Persia: Yahweh, the God of Heaven, has given me all the kingdoms of the earth, and he has charged me to build him a house at Jerusalem ... Whoever among you[11] so wishes ..., let him go up to Jerusalem ... and Cyrus brought out the vessels[12] in charge of Mithredath the treasurer ..., and gave them to Sheshbazzar."[13]

The Aramaic version (Ezra VI 1-5) reads thus: "Then Darius[14], the king, issued a decree, and search was made in Babylon, in the archives of the treasuries. And in Ecbatana, the capital which is in the province

---

[11] Namely, the Jews in Babylonian captivity.
[12] Reference is made to the vessels from the temple at Jerusalem, which were kept in Babylon.
[13] See also: II Chronicles XXXVI 22-23; Nehemiah VII 6; Josephus, *Ant. Jud.* X 10; XI 1-6.
[14] Namely, Darius I.

of Media, a scroll was found on which this was written: In the first year of Cyrus the king, Cyrus the king issued a decree: Concerning the house of God at Jerusalem, let the house be rebuilt, the place where sacrifices are offered ... let the cost be paid from the royal treasury. And also let the gold and silver vessels of the house of God, which Nebuchadnezzar took out of the temple that is in Jerusalem and brought to Babylon, be restored and brought back to the temple which is in Jerusalem ....''

Cyrus also ordered that the Syrian and Phoenician governors should finance the rebuilding of the temple and other needs of the temple from their provincial treasuries, and that they should also contribute towards the purchase of economic and domestic necessities by those who returned, such as building timber; money; horned cattle; wine; flour, etc. (Ezra III 7). In the Book of Ezra it is stated: ''And they gave money to the masons and carpenters, and food, drink, and oil to the Sidonians and the Tyrians, to bring cedar trees from Lebanon to the sea ..., according to the grant which they had from Cyrus, king of Persia.''

Thus the above decree of Cyrus forms the basis of the autonomous temple community of Jerusalem. Cyrus' edict, however, was not followed by the immediate return by the Jews from Babylonia, where they had gradually settled as if it was their own land. Josephus Flavius in his 'Jewish Antiquities' (XI 1.3) tells that many Jews preferred to remain behind in Babylonia, rather than leave their possessions. In addition, life in Judah was difficult because the local population was hostile towards those who returned. By the commencement of Darius' reign only 42,000 people at Jerusalem (not including the women and children), went from Babylonia to Jerusalem, and after some time, in 458 B.C., some 50,000 more.

It is difficult to agree with K. Galling, who suggested that Cyrus permitted the rebuilding of the temple only to those who were still living at Jerusalem, and that the majority of the Jews who returned from Babylon only arrived there in the years between 523 and 521 B.C.; some small groups had arrived there previously without permission (Galling 1937:29ff.; idem 1964:56). The realization of Cyrus' decree concerning the reconstruction of the Jerusalem temple was met with many near insuperable problems, brought about by the historical situation. The construction works were therefore not started during the reign of Cyrus. If we can believe the information which is provided by Josephus Flavius in his 'Jewish Antiquities' (II 249, 315), it was Cambyses, when he had become king, who even forbade the rebuilding of the temple. The building was only started at the commencement of Darius' reign.

After the fall of Babylon, Cyrus at first maintained the governor of northern Mesopotamia, the Babylonian Nabu-ahhe-bulliṭ, in office. This functionary had occupied the position from the time of Nabonidus onwards. After four years, however (possibly after the death of Nabu-ahhe-bulliṭ), in 535 B.C., he made Mesopotamia and the lands to the west of the Euphrates into one province, and appointed the Persian Gubaru (Gobryas)[15] as its satrap. Numerous cuneiform texts refer to the administrative details. The province contained almost all the former territory of the former neo-Babylonian empire. It was called Babylonia and 'Across-the-River' (Aramaic *Abar-Nahara*; Akkadian *Ebir-Nari*). Gubaru continued in the function of satrap for at least ten years, namely until 525 B.C. (possibly even to the beginning of 520 B.C., see San Nicolò 1937:53ff.).

---

[15] Certain scholars are of the opinion that this Gubaru was the same person as the Ugbaru of the Babylonian Chronicle. It is impossible to agree with this suggestion, because Ugbaru died soon after the fall of Babylon to the Persians. W. Schwenzner goes even further, in presenting the hypothesis that Ugbaru (the governor of Gutium), Gubaru (district governor of Babylon), and Gubaru, the accomplice of Darius in the murder of Gaumata, and finally the lance bearer of Darius, who is depicted in the Naqsh-i Rustam relief and who carries the same name, are all one and the same person (Schwenzner 1922-1923:48).

CHAPTER SEVEN

THE CAMPAIGN AGAINST THE MASSAGETAE
AND CYRUS' DEATH

There is no doubt that Cyrus had begun to make preparations for the conquest of Egypt. He decided first, however, to safeguard the northeastern borders of his empire against inroads by the nomadic tribes of the Massagetae from Central Asia. These raids brought considerable losses and damage to the sedentary Iranian peoples who had been incorporated into the Achaemenid empire.

In order to avert the danger from the Massagetae, Cyrus established along the extreme northeastern limits of his realm a series of fortified frontier posts, which were generally referred to as cities by classical writers. One of these settlements, founded in the valley of the Jaxartes (Syr Darya) in Sogdiana, was apparently located at the site of modern Ura-Tjube. It was still inhabited at the time of the Macedonian invasion. Classical authors gave this fortification the name of Cyropolis or Kyreskhata.[1] R. T. Hallock was initially inclined to believe that the fortified town of Kurishtish, referred to in the Persepolis Elamite texts, is identical with Kyreskhata. Later, however, he refuted his previous ideas (PF:29, n. 26; see also Hinz & Koch 1987:522). Cyropolis was taken by the Macedonian army by merely breaching the walls with siege engines.

In 530 B.C. Cyrus started his campaign against the Massagetae. This war brought Cyrus to a fateful end. According to I. V. P'jankov, the campaign was directed against a nomadic tribe which resided in the plains to the north of Hyrcania and to the east of the Hyrcanian Sea (P'jankov 1964:128). During the battle which took place east of the Amu Darya, Cyrus not only suffered a complete defeat, but was also mortally wounded and eventually he died. The battle, in all probability, took place at the very end of 530 B.C. (see below).

A number of different versions have been transmitted concerning the death of Cyrus. His defeat remained a dark spot in classical literature. If we believe the ancient Greek authors, Cyrus lost 200,000 men in the war against the Massagetae. Of course, this number must be vastly exaggerated. One version which was very popular in ancient times was exten-

---

[1] Amm. Marc. XXIII 6.59f.; Arrian, *Anab. Alex.* IV 3.1; Curtius, *Hist. Alex.* VII 6.16, 19, 20; Strabo XI 11.4; cf. Metzler (1977:277ff.) who, in particular with reference to E. Benveniste, suggests that the origin of this name lies in a Persian toponym, namely *Kurushkatha*, 'town of Cyrus'.

sively reported by Herodotus (I 201-214). This version, which, with certain variations, is followed by the majority of the classical writers[2], states that Cyrus attacked a camp of the Massagetae using subterfuge, and killed all the people therein. Afterwards, however, the main forces of the Massagetae under command of Queen Tomyris inflicted a heavy defeat on the Persians, and Cyrus was killed. The decapitated head of Cyrus was put into a skin with human blood so that he could quench his thirst for blood. Herodotus writes that this battle was the most bloody of all those fought by the 'barbarians'.[3]

In their account of this event, Berossus and Ctesias sketch a somewhat different course of events. According to Berossus, Cyrus died in a battle with the Daai (Dahae), a Scythian tribe of West Central Asia (FHG, Vol. II, p. 505). According to Ctesias (*Persica* 29.6-7), Cyrus' last battle was fought against the Derbikes, who were assisted by Indian troops with their war elephants. During this battle a certain Indian wounded Cyrus with his spear in the liver, and Cyrus died from this wound on the third day. When Amorges, king of the Scythians, was informed about this battle, he and 20,000 of his tribesmen came to the rescue of Cyrus. After a stubborn resistance the Derbikes were finally defeated (cf. Francfort 1985). It would appear that Ctesias' version originates from the official Persian tradition. In any case, all the surviving accounts agree on the outcome of the war, namely the defeat which was inflicted on Cyrus by his enemies, and Cyrus' death. Ctesias is incorrect, also when he says that the Derbikes lived along the Indian border. In reality they lived in proximity to the Hyrcanians (Henning 1951:26).

There is a contradiction in certain classical sources as regards the question of which tribes actually managed to defeat Cyrus. It is possible to explain the contradictory statements by suggesting that the Derbikes formed part of a confederacy of Massagetian tribes who inhabited the steppes between the Caspian and the Aral Sea. At the time of Ctesias the Derbikes were better known than the remaining Massagetian tribes. But long before Berossus, who lived at the commencement of the third century B.C., the Dahae had taken the former place of the Massagetae in the historical arena. Therefore Berossus mentions them as the adversaries of Cyrus.

---

[2] Amm. Marc., XXIII 6.7f.; Arrian, *Anab. Alex.* IV 11.9; V 4.5; Diodorus II 44.2; Frontinus, *Strat.* II 5.5; Josephus, *Ant. Jud.* XI 2.1; Just. I 8; Polyaenus VIII 28; Strabo XI 6.2; XI 8.6.

[3] As is known, Herodotus uses this term to indicate these people as non-Greeks, without adding any derogatory connotations to the word. According to Strabo (XIV 2.28), the name 'barbarian' was first given to the Carians, who of old had lived within the sphere of influence of Greek culture, but when speaking Greek, they sounded as though they said *bar-bar*.

It is true that Xenophon wrote that Cyrus had died a natural death in his own capital, after ordering that his corpse should be buried in the earth, rather than being encased in silver or gold (*Cyropaedia* VIII 7). Xenophon, however, in his endeavour to depict in the person of Cyrus an ideal ruler, did not shrink away from a direct perversion of the facts. At the same time it is also known that Cyrus was buried at Pasargadae, and this forces a critical attitude towards the details about Cyrus' death (which also have a novelistic character and are evidently not according to the real turn of events) as reported by Herodotus (cf. Sancisi-Weerdenburg 1985). It is possible that the corpse of Cyrus was brought back from the Massagetae. Ctesias reports (*Persica* 29.9; see König 1972:5) that Cambyses sent his courtier Bagapates with Cyrus' corpse to Persia for funeral. If credence is given to Cicero (*De Divin.* I 23.46), who based his assertions on much older Greek sources, Cyrus died at the age of seventy.

Cyrus was the most popular Persian king, and the founder of a world empire. He was regarded by the priests of Babylon as the appointed by Marduk; the Jews thought he was the anointed by Yahweh, and the Greeks saw him as a great statesman. He was, as noted above, buried at Pasargadae. His tomb, which has been preserved to the present day, is surprising in its noble beauty. It is distinguished by the novelty of its architecture and is perhaps the most remarkable monument of Pasargadae. Since the early Islamic period the tomb of Cyrus has become known as 'the tomb of the mother of Solomon'. The identification of the monument by Western travellers was considerably facilitated by the description given by classical writers, which in turn were based in the main on accounts left by the companions of Alexander the Great.

Cyrus' tomb rests on a high platform made up of large slabs of sandstone. On top of the platform rises the funerary chamber. This room has a height of 2.10 m; a width of 2.10 m and a length of 3.17 m. The entrance to the chamber is via a low and narrow doorway. The tomb is covered by a gabled roof. The complete height of the structure is about eleven metres. Not long ago British archaeologists discovered on the façade of the building the depiction of a sun disk. According to D. Stronach, this disk is the early symbol of the god Ahura Mazda, who, in the opinion of Stronach, was worshipped by Cyrus (Boyce 1982:54-57; Stronach 1978).

The works of the classical authors also contain a description of the inner view of the tomb. Arrian (*Anab. Alex.* VI 29.4-11) and Strabo (XV 3.7) wrote that the tomb was located in a park (*paradeisos*), in a thick copse of wood. In the room stood a golden coffin which contained the body of Cyrus. There was also a couch with golden feet and covered with hides adorned with a purple colour. On these hides were placed the royal robe and other clothes, in addition to bracelets, daggers, etc. Next to Cyrus' tomb stood a small building for the magi who guarded the monument. Arrian also told that Alexander of Macedonia visited the tomb on two occasions, first in 330 B.C., and then in 325 B.C. By the time of his second visit, however, the tomb had been plundered.

As stated by C. Nylander, whatever the origins of the architectural form and the structure of Cyrus' tomb, all the components of the building are fused together into an organic, Iranian structure, which was adapted to the new empire, its ideology and the ideas of Cyrus' realm. The gabled roof of the tomb is traditional for the ancient Iranian houses, while its stepped platform, apparently, finds its origin in the Babylonian ziggurat. Just like other structures at Pasargadae, the tomb of Cyrus clearly reflects the ideological and political concepts of the ruler of the Persians, who had subjugated numerous tribes and nations (cf. Nylander 1970:138-146).

CHAPTER EIGHT

THE CONQUEST OF EGYPT

From the time of the Persian entry into Babylon onwards, it seems that Cambyses spent most of his time in Mesopotamia. In particular, one of his houses was located in the city of Sippar (NRV, 17). At first an inexperienced countryman, who in 538 B.C. appeared at the Babylonian New Year festival in Elamite garb, Cambyses soon adapted to the business life of his new subjects and did not refrain from instructing his agents to invest his money. Thus, in 535 B.C., "the scribe of the crown prince Cambyses" lent out "1 and 1/3 minas of silver, property of the crown prince Cambyses" with a house as security (Cyr., 177). In the texts there are certain references to stewards of Cambyses (Cyr., 199, 270, 335; NRV, 17), and also to his slave, a craftsman in the manufacture of seals, who instructed other men in this trade (Cyr., 325).

According to Herodotus (I 208), Cambyses joined Cyrus in the expedition against the Massagetae, but was sent back to Persis as the successor to the throne before the decisive battle in which Cyrus was killed.[1] It is possible that Cyrus appointed Cambyses as his co-regent before his last campaign against the Massagetae in 530 B.C. Until now it has been considered that the documents BE, Vol. VIII, 74 and VS, Vol. V, 42 were the last texts dated to Cyrus' reign. The first of them was drafted at Nippur on the thirteenth day of the month Abu (the fifth month of the Babylonian calendar) of the ninth year of Cyrus, i.e. on August 2, 530 B.C. The second document was written at Borsippa on the twenty-third day of the month Abu of the same year, i.e. on August 12, 530 B.C. If the date of the first document is beyond any doubt, the sign for the month in VS, Vol. V, 42 is written indistinctly. M. San Nicolò and A. Ungnad have read the sign under consideration in this text as Ululu (the sixth month of the Babylonian calendar) with a question mark (see NRV:29). Indeed, the sign for the month in the hand-copy of the tablet reads rather like Ululu and certainly cannot be read as Abu. However, Parker and Dubberstein have supposed that this sign could not be read as Ululu since a text has been preserved which is dated to the twelfth day of the month Ululu of the accession year of Cambyses, king of Babylon, king of the lands (August 31, 530 B.C.). This text was drafted at Babylon (Camb.,

---

[1] See also Ctesias, *Persica* 29.8 (König 1972:5), and Xenophon, *Cyropaedia* VIII 7.11.

1). The next text (Camb., 2) dated to Cambyses also comes from Babylon and was written on the sixteenth day of the month Ululu of the accession year of Cambyses (September 4, 530 B.C.). If we read the name of the month in VS, Vol. V, 42 as Ululu, we have to assume that on September 12, 530 B.C., Cyrus was still considered to be king of Babylon, king of the lands, despite of the fact that, according to document Camb., 1, Cambyses was already ruling with the same title by August 31 of the same year. Therefore Parker and Dubberstein have declined the possibility to date VS, Vol. V, 42 to the month Ululu, and such an opinion has been accepted by all scholars (see Parker & Dubberstein 1956:14). However, it seems to me that this opinion should be reconsidered in view of document OECT 10, 123, which provides the latest date for the end of the reign of Cyrus. The text has been discovered in the city of Kish but does not contain any indication to the place where it was drafted. It is a promissory note dated to the nineteenth day of the month Araḫsamna (the eighth month) of the ninth year of Cyrus, king of Babylon, king of the lands. Thus, this document was written almost three months later than VS, Vol. V, 42, if we are to read the month's name in the latter as Abu. However, taking into account OECT 10, 123, written on December 4, 530 B.C., and nevertheless dated to the reign of Cyrus, the sign for the month in VS, Vol. V, 42 can be read as Ululu with much more probability. Thus, to judge from OECT 10, 123, Cyrus and Cambyses simultaneously bore the title 'king of Babylon, king of the lands' at least for three months (cf. also CT, Vol. LVI, 142, drafted on the second day of the month Du'uzu of the first regnal year of Cambyses, king of the lands, son of Cyrus, king of the lands; in other words, Cyrus and Cambyses here bear the same title of king of the Achaemenid empire).

It is possible that following his father's death Cambyses attempted to safeguard the northeastern frontiers of his realm against inroads by the Sakas, but the sources remain silent on this point. In any case, Cambyses commenced his campaign against Egypt after a lapse of five years.

In the meantime, the Egyptians, who realized the growing danger, prepared for war. In 654 B.C., after the Assyrians had been ousted from Egypt, the throne was occupied by Psammetichus I, the founder of the 26th dynasty. This dynasty is also called the Saite dynasty, after the religious and political centre of the land, which shifted to the city of Sais in the Delta. Following these events, Egypt witnessed a period of renaissance; its economic and political life prospered. At the same time, many ancient traditions were revived. Instead of the Theban deity Amon, who for centuries had been foremost within the Egyptian pantheon, the gods of the Delta came to the foreground. Among these were the goddess

Neith, the protectress of Sais, and the god Ptah of Memphis. The ancient god Osiris also received more attention, while worship of animals was carried to the extreme, as is shown by the numerous animal cemeteries.

Psammetichus died in 610 B.C., and power was passed to Necho II, who ruled until 595 B.C. The two subsequent pharaohs, Psammetichus II and Apries, ruled from 595-589 B.C. and 589-570 B.C. respectively. Thereafter commenced the long reign of Amasis.

While preparing for the inevitable war with the Persians, Amasis established friendly relations with the tyrant of Samos, Polycrates; with the Lydian and Babylonian kings, and also with Cyrene, a Greek city-state to the west of Egypt, along the African littoral of the Mediterranean. Contacts with the Greek world were also deliberately strengthened. By the seventh century B.C., Greek mercenaries were already assisting the Egyptian pharaohs, whose military strength increasingly became dependent upon a large number of foreign soldiers. During the reign of Amasis, whom the Greeks regarded as their benefactor and as a philhellene, Greek mercenaries started to spread all over Egypt. The Greek factory of Naucratis in the western part of the Delta, which was founded during the seventh century B.C., started to grow into a large city with purely Greek interior institutions and sanctuaries for the Greek gods. New Greek factories also began to appear along the banks of the Nile. When, however, the number of Hellenes and other foreigners in Egypt had risen to a very high level, conflicts broke out between the foreigners and the Egyptians. There are grounds to suggest that the Egyptians behaved much more hostilely towards the Greeks than towards the Phoenicians, Jews and other Semitic peoples, because the Greeks were more inclined to keep themselves aloof from the native population. There was a considerable difference between Egyptian and Greek customs, while the Semitic foreigners in Egypt had many traits in common with the native population. To diminish the antagonism, Amasis started to build special, isolated residences for the Greeks, Carians and other foreigners, and to centralize his mercenary troops at Memphis. There was also a stop to the free trade by the Greeks in Egypt. However, Naucratis received the monopoly on Graeco-Egyptian trade. These mercantile contacts were very important for the Egyptians, as they provided Egypt with Greek silver which was necessary for the upkeep of the foreign mercenaries. Amasis also sent rich dedications to temples on the Greek mainland and on the islands.

During the reign of Amasis, Egypt witnessed its greatest economic prosperity. According to Herodotus, there were 20,000 towns in Egypt, a figure which is, of course, exaggerated. In all probability the population of Egypt amounted to between 7 and 7.5 million people, a number which in modern history was only surpassed at the beginning of the twentieth century (Kienitz 1967:274).

The international political situation, however, developed very unfavourably. By the middle of the reign of Amasis, Egypt had lost almost all its allies, only Polycrates of Samos remained outside Persian bondage. When at the end of 526 B.C. tension with Persia was growing to a climax, Amasis suddenly died.[2] His successor Psammetichus III only ruled for six months. He was destined to be the last Saite pharaoh.

Cambyses started his campaign after long military and diplomatic preparations which left Egypt completely isolated. Egyptian sources depict the Persian attack as an invasion by people from many strange countries ("people of all the lands"), who attacked Egypt together with Cambyses (Posener 1936:16, 167, with references to the relevant texts). Herodotus also states (III 1) that all subject peoples accompanied Cambyses against Egypt. In some way this picture is reflected by a document from Babylon, according to which in 524 B.C. a certain Iddina-Nabu sold "an Egyptian woman from the booty of his bow", together with her three-months old daughter (Camb., 334). It seems evident that this woman was captured during the campaign by Cambyses in Egypt, because the war, as can be deduced from the sources, also involved Babylonian troops. The Persian army was also augmented by contingents from other subject peoples, including Greeks from Asia Minor (Herodotus III 7, 25).

The Persian army on land received help from the Phoenician fleet (cf. Wallinga 1987:68ff.). The former ally of Amasis, Polycrates of Samos, with a strong fleet, also went over to the side of Cambyses and sent forty ships to support him. This small fleet, however, never reached the scene of the war, because Polycrates had included certain people whom he wanted to be rid of, and they turned the ships around in order to dethrone their tyrant. In addition, the Cyprians, who under Amasis had become dependent on Egypt, chose the side of Cambyses and sent him their ships.

The army was assembled in Palestine, while the fleet was concentrated at Akko. According to the information provided by Herodotus (III 7, 88), Cambyses sent ambassadors to the king of the Arabs, asking for a safe passage to Egypt. Apparently, reference is made to the Arab tribes that herded their flocks in the steppes and deserts between Egypt and southern Palestine. The Arab king agreed to Cambyses' proposition and

---

[2] The majority of Egyptologists used to be of the opinion that Amasis died in 527 B.C. R. A. Parker, however, has shown that Amasis ruled for 44 years and died in 526 B.C. He based his argument on a particular document which contained a double date based on the Egyptian and the lunar calendars (Parker 1957:208-212).

concluded a treaty with him. He then provided the Persian army with food and water for its march to Egypt, driving camels packed with water bags to the Persians. On the basis of this assistance the Arabs were subsequently regarded, not as subjects, but rather as allies of the Achaemenid king.

Cambyses' army reached the Egyptian frontier town of Pelusium (c. forty kilometres from present-day Port Said) without meeting any serious problems.[3] The subsequent course of events is strongly reminiscent of the conquest of Babylonia by Cyrus. The commander of the Egyptian fleet (at the same time he was also the high priest of the goddess Neith at Sais), Udjahorresne, apparently had no intention of showing any resistance to the foreigners and only waited for the right opportunity to defect. Phanes of Halicarnassus, the commander of the Greek and Carian mercenaries, was appointed to his post by the Egyptians during the reign of Amasis. He quarrelled with his Egyptian paymasters about wages, and defected to Cambyses.[4] Having gone over to the side of the Persians, he gave them valuable information about the military preparations by the Egyptians and showed them how to bypass the fortifications which lay along the route of the Persian army.

The Egyptian army awaited the enemy near Pelusium. The army of Cambyses camped nearby. At that decisive moment the Greek and Carian mercenaries did not panic nor lose heart. It is generally believed that mercenaries cannot be trusted in times of military danger, and that they easily defect to the other side. The mercenaries of Psammetichus III (just like the Greek contingents which later served the Persian kings), however, never lacked a feeling of military duty and honour. In their anger towards their former commander, Phanes, who had defected to the Persians, the Greeks killed his sons in front of the ranks and mixed their blood with wine. After having drunk this mixture they commenced the fight. Their martial spirit is also attested to by the fact that the foreigners constituted the main support for the pharaoh.

The sole great battle was fought in the spring of 525 B.C., near the city of Pelusium. This was a bloody event in which both sides suffered heavy losses. According to Polyaenus (*Strat.* III 9), the Persians assaulted the fortress many times, while the Egyptians put up a desperate resis-

---

[3] During the fifth century B.C., the Persian army used ships in order to crush other revolts in Egypt, thus avoiding the Sinai desert. During the time of Cambyses, however, the Persians were not sufficiently familiar with this mode of transportation to use the sea effectively.

[4] A coin has been found at Halicarnassus, which contains a legend with the name of Phanes (How & Wells 1928, Vol. I, p. 236). In addition, a statue fragment has been discovered in the temple of Apollo at Naucratis, Egypt, which was dedicated by "Phanes, son of Glaucus" (Petrie 1886:55).

tance, throwing burning wood and stones at the enemy, and shooting arrows. The information provided by Polyaenus, however, saying that Cambyses reduced the fortress of Pelusium by positioning in front of his army a number of cats, dogs and ibises, which were considered sacred by the Egyptians, thus forcing them to stop shooting, is certainly of an apocryphal character.

The battle at Pelusium resulted in a victory for the Persians. Remnants of the Egyptian army and of the foreign mercenary contingents fled in disorder to Memphis. Herodotus, who approximately seventy years later visited the battlefield, wrote that it was still possible to see the skeletons of the soldiers, which had been collected in a heap (*Historiae* III 12).

The victors moved deeper into Egypt, both over land and water, without meeting any resistance. The commander of the fleet, Udjahorresne, did not put up any resistance to the advancing Persians. He surrendered Sais and the fleet without a fight.

Cambyses sent a ship with an ambassador to Memphis, demanding its complete surrender. But the Egyptians attacked the ship and butchered its crew and the royal messenger. When Memphis was besieged, the Egyptians surrendered. Two thousand captives, including the son of Psammetichus III, were executed for the murder of the ambassador. Psammetichus himself, however, was kept alive and detained at the court of Cambyses.

It should be noted that many possessions of the pharaoh were confiscated. Various objects of this booty, inscribed with the names of Necho, Amasis and Psammetichus III, were found by archaeologists in the treasury of Persepolis. In addition, some figurines of the gods Bes and Isis, Egyptian ivories, and alabaster vases were found, either at Persepolis or at Susa (MDP, Vol. I. pp. 117ff.; Posener 1936:190; Schmidt 1953-1970, Vol. I, pp. 25, 182; Vol. II, pp. 68, 81-83). Diodorus (I 46.4) wrote that Cambyses robbed gold, silver, and ivory from the Egyptian temples, and sent the craftsmen of Egypt as captives to Persepolis, Susa and Media in order to build his palaces. Ctesias (*Persica* 13.30 = FGrH, Vol. III, pp. 459f.) reported about the deportation to Persis, on command of Cambyses, of the Pharaoh Amyrtaeus (should be: Psammetichus) and of six thousand Egyptians to Susa. Ctesias also wrote that 50,000 Egyptians were killed during the conquest of the country, with 7,000 killed on the Persian side, but these numbers can hardly have been based on accurate sources.

A Coptic account has been transmitted about Cambyses' conquest of Egypt. The text, however, does not contain any valuable information, because in it the Persian king is confused with Nebuchadnezzar II, and two completely different campaigns were united into one (Jansen 1950; Spalinger 1977:239).

By the summer of 525 B.C., all of Egypt was in the hands of the Persians. The period from 525 B.C. to approximately 401 B.C., when the Egyptians rebelled against the Persians, is generally called the first period of Persian domination in Egypt.

The Libyans, who lived to the west of Egypt, and also the Greek people of Cyrene and the city of Barka, voluntarily submitted to Cambyses, and as a sign of their subjugation sent tribute.

Towards the end of August[5] 525 B.C., Cambyses was officially installed as king of Egypt. To judge from certain Demotic texts, Cambyses did not accept Psammetichus III as his legal predecessor (the last three documents which are dated according to Psammetichus' reign were drafted in March 525 B.C.), and he added the six months of Psammetichus to his own reign, regarding himself as the successor of Amasis to the Egyptian throne (Gyles 1959:98ff.; Parker 1957:209ff.). One Egyptian document is even dated to the eighth year of Cambyses, although the latter died three years after his conquest of Egypt. This particular text seems to indicate that Cambyses regarded himself as the pharaoh of Egypt from the time that he ascended the Persian throne in 530 B.C.

Cambyses founded the new, 27th dynasty of Egypt. As the Egyptian sources indicate, he gave his conquest the character of a legitimate union with the Egyptians. He was enthroned according to local customs; he used the traditional Egyptian dating system; and he adopted the title 'king of Egypt, king of (foreign) countries', and other titles, such as 'descendant of (the gods) Ra, Horus, Osiris'. He went to Sais in order to participate personally at the religious ceremonies at the temple of Neith, and he worshipped this goddess on his knees. He offered sacrifices to the Egyptian gods and showed them other signs of respect (for references to the texts, see Posener 1936:170ff.). Two seals of Cambyses which were made in the traditional Egyptian style have been preserved. One of them contains the following inscription in hieroglyphics: "The king of Upper and Lower Egypt Cambyses, beloved of (the goddess) Wadjet, lady of (the city of) Imet, the great, the mistress of the heaven, the Eye of the Sun, mistress of gods (to whom) life is given like the sun" (see Hodjache & Berlev 1977). The Egyptian texts indicate that Cambyses continued the

---

[5] The earliest record of Cambyses' stay in Egypt dates from that time, and not to May 29, as was suggested earlier (Atkinson 1956:170, n. 30a). Posener was of the opinion that the conquest of Egypt could not be dated later than the month of June, because Psammetichus III ruled for six months, and classical writers refer to the end of his reign as taking place in the month of June (Posener 1936:173, n. 2).

policy of the preceding 26th dynasty and made an effort to draw the people of Egypt to his side. On reliefs he is depicted in local costume (not in Elamite garb!), kneeling in front of the gods (Gunn 1926:85ff.).

In order to give the conquest of Egypt a legitimate character, certain stories were made up and propagated about supposedly matrimonial relations between the Egyptian princesses and the Achaemenids, and in particular about Cambyses' descent from the marriage of Cyrus with an Egyptian woman called Nitetis, the daughter of Pharaoh Apries, while the successor to the last Amasis was depicted as an usurper (three versions of this story have been transmitted: Athenaeus XIII 10; Ctesias, *Persica*, frag. 13a; Herodotus III 1-3). In this context Herodotus remarked that "the Egyptians regard Cambyses as their own", and do not see him as a foreign king. It is well known, however, that Cassandane was the mother of Cambyses. She belonged to the Achaemenid clan. In all probability, the source of the legend about the links between Cyrus and the Egyptian princesses is not Egyptian in origin, but Persian or derives from Asia Minor (Gyles 1959:155; von Hoffmann & Vorbichler 1980:87ff.; Meulenaere 1951:176).

After the war, life in Egypt returned very quickly to normal. Legal and administrative texts from the time of Cambyses attest to the fact that the first years of Persian rule did not inflict any significant damage to the economic life of the country (Gyles 1959:69; Posener 1936:169). It is true that soon after the fall of Egypt the Persian army committed some pillaging, and it is possible that a school of the Sais temple was plundered. Cambyses, however, who was apparently not personally responsible for this violence, is known to have ordered his troops to stop their rampage and to leave the temple precinct (at least, at Sais). He recompensed the damage inflicted upon the temples (Posener 1936:11-16).

These events are related by an inscription of Udjahorresne on a *Naophoros* statue (that is, a statue of someone holding a replica of Osiris in his hands). The text is dated to the fourth year of Darius I's reign. Next to the *Historiae* of Herodotus this text is one of the most important sources on the first six years of Persian rule in Egypt. In essence the work is an *apologia pro vita sua*, which attempts to explain the defection of the author to the side of the Persians. The various events of the period are selected and presented in a tendentious manner (in particular, there is no reference to a decree by Cambyses to reduce the income of the temples, including the temple of Neith at Sais). Udjahorresne depicts himself as the right hand of Cambyses and Darius, who, according to him, were pious pharaohs. He also writes that due to his influence on the Persian kings he was able to provide the greatest favours to the city of Sais, its gods and to his family. G. Posener, who thoroughly studied the text, remarked that the inscription, because it was exhibited in a public place and could be read by passers-by, could hardly be expected to contain a significant distortion of the facts (Posener 1936:166; for the text, a French translation and a commentary, see *idem*:1-26). In particular, Udjahorresne wrote about himself: ''Honoured by the great Neith ... treasurer of the king ... scribe ... steward of the palace, commander of the royal fleet ... Udjahorresne says: The great king of all the foreign countries, Cambyses, came to Egypt, and the foreigners of all the foreign lands were with him. He ruled the whole land, and they settled in the land, and he became the great king of Egypt, and the great ruler of all the foreign countries. His Majesty appointed me as head physician; he wanted me to be near him as his friend, to administer the palace, and to compile for him his titles ... I showed His Majesty the Highness of Sais ... I turned towards the king of Upper and Lower Egypt with the request that all foreigners who had settled in the temple of Neith should be recalled; that the temple of Neith would be given its former glory. His Majesty ordered the recall of all foreigners... to destroy their houses, and all of their uncleanliness in the temple... His Majesty ordered to purify the temple, and commanded that all its people should return to the temple... His Majesty ordered to bring offerings to the great Neith... and the gods who were in Sais, as it was done of old... Cambyses, king of Upper and Lower Egypt came to Sais. When His Majesty came to the temple of Neith, he bowed on his knees before her, just as it was done by all the kings, and he sacrificed in a grand manner of all that was good to Great Neith ... and the gods who are at Sais, such as was done by the preceding kings ... His Majesty performed all that was useful at the temple of Neith ... I established eternal sacrifices to the Great Neith ..., in accordance with the commands of His Majesty'' (translation by O. D. Berlev).

Following the policy of his father, Cambyses allowed the Egyptians their freedom in religious and private matters. The Egyptians, just like the representatives from other nations, continued to carry out their functions in the state machinery and passed these posts on in an hereditary fashion. Thus, during the reigns of Cambyses and Darius I, the above mentioned Saite priest and army commander Udjahorresne not only kept all his state functions (except that of admiral of the fleet), which he had fulfilled during the reigns of the Egyptian pharaohs Amasis and Psammetichus III[6], but he was also appointed to other positions (such as chief

---

[6] It should be noted that G. Posener was of the opinion that Udjahorresne, the son of a Saite priest who remains unknown from other sources, is not identical with someone of the same name who was an important official at the court of the Saite kings (Posener 1936:164f.). In the above mentioned inscription, however, Ujahorresne calls himself: ''commander of the king's fleet.''

of the physicians). Ensuing his defection to the Persians, he was generously recompensed and became their counsellor for Egyptian affairs (on his activities, see Bresciani 1985). It was he who devised the titles for the Persian kings on the basis of the traditional forms of address of the preceding pharaohs. Apparently, he was also included within the number of royal 'benefactors'.

Amidst other functionaries who kept their position during the reign of Cambyses, there was Khnumibre, the son of the supervisor of the stone quarries at Wadi Hammamat. He occupied the position of his father as early as 526 B.C., during the reign of Amasis, and continued to work for the Persians. In one of his inscriptions the name of Cambyses is referred to (Posener 1936:95; cf. Gauthier 1907-1917:136-139, where references are made to all Egyptian documents which contain the name of Cambyses). Finally attention should be drawn to the fact that for over fifty years (until 473 B.C.), the quarrying of stones in the Wadi Hammamat was continued under the general management of a Persian director (Goyon 1957:116ff.).

It should not be forgotten, however, that the decrease of temple income; the heavy royal taxes which had to be paid in silver and natural products, and the deportation of Egyptian craftsmen for the construction of royal palaces in Iran evoked strong dissatisfaction with foreign rule, both among the priests and the people themselves.

After the conquest of Egypt, Cambyses reflected upon the subjugation of the rest of Africa, about the extent of which he had no more than a vague idea. The realization of these plans would have given the Persians dominance over the western part of the Mediterranean. Very soon, however, plans to conquer Carthage had to be abandoned, because the Phoenicians strongly opposed the idea of participating in a war against a settlement which they themselves had founded (see Elayi 1981:20). Without the Phoenician fleet Cambyses could not carry out his intentions for a huge naval enterprise. Thus, it remained to occupy the Oasis of Amon to the west of Egypt in the Libyan desert, and Nubia (according to Herodotus the land of the Ethiopians, or Kush as it is called in the Achaemenid inscriptions).

Preparing his campaign against Nubia, Cambyses sent spies to the land and founded several fortified towns in Upper Egypt.[7] The army of Cambyses split up at Thebes. One section, with Cambyses as commander, headed south; the other section moved up towards the Oasis of

---

[7] Compare the information which is provided by various classical authors: Plinius, *Nat. Hist.* VI 181; Ptolemaeus, *Geogr.* IV 7; Josephus Flavius, *Ant. Jud.* XI 4.4; cf. also II 15.1, with an unlikely account that Cambyses was responsible for the foundation of the town called Babylon, near Memphis.

Amon. En route Cambyses apparently visited the fortresses at Elephantine and incorporated Semitic settlers from the time of the Saite kings into his army.

According to Herodotus (III 17, 25), Cambyses marched to Nubia without sufficient preparations and without enough provisions, and subsequently his soldiers had to resort to cannibalism. Cambyses was eventually forced to withdraw, thus losing a large part of his army. Diodorus (III 3.1) wrote that, according to the Ethiopians, Cambyses attacked them with a huge army, but was completely defeated. E. Meyer was of the opinion that this war is reflected in an inscription of the Ethiopian king Nastasen, in which he boasts that he forced a certain Kambasuden to withdraw (Meyer 1939, Vol. III, p. 191). It was later ascertained, however, that the text dates from the end of the fourth century B.C. (Posener 1936:269, n. 3).

Indeed, certain historians assume, not without grounds, that the account about the defeat of Cambyses contains a considerable degree of exaggeration. According to A. R. Burn, it is not likely that Cambyses would have advanced against the Ethiopians without previous preparations, especially when it is realized how extensive were his provisions for crossing the Sinai. In addition, the 'long-living Ethiopians', against whom Cambyses would have campaigned, according to Herodotus, appear to be a legendary people, the name of which is already reflected in the works of Homerus (Burn 1970:87). In any case, Cambyses conquered the northern part of Nubia along the borders with Egypt (beyond the First Cataract). This area used to be a dependency of the pharaohs. The occupation of this area is recorded by Herodotus at a second instance (III 97). It can be surmised that Cambyses advanced to the Second Cataract. There are certain references (although they are not very reliable), which may point out that the Persians advanced a considerable distance up the Nile. Classical authors report about a place called the 'Storehouse of Cambyses' near the Third Cataract, still carrying this name in the Roman period.[8] It is possible, however, that these classical authors have mistaken a certain similarly sounding place-name for the name of Cambyses (Burn 1970:87; cf. Posener 1936:169, n. 4). The opinion of some ancient historians[9] that Cambyses reached Meroe and called this town after his sister, is evidently incorrect. The country of Kush (Nubia) is not mentioned among the subject lands listed in the Behistun inscription, although it does appear in much later texts of

---

[8] Ptolemaeus, *Geogr.* IV 7.16; cf. Plinius, *Hist. Nat.* VI 55.
[9] Diodorus I 33.1; Josephus Flavius, *Ant. Jud.* II 10.2; Strabo XVII 1.5.

Darius I from Persepolis. This point may indicate that Kush was only included within the Achaemenid empire during the reign of Darius I.

According to Herodotus (III 26; cf. Diodorus IX 14.3), the Persian army which was sent to the Oàsis of Amon in Libya, completely perished in a sand storm. This piece of information is doubted by certain historians who are inclined to assume that Cambyses in fact conquered Libya (Prášek 1906-1910, Vol. I, p. 42, n. 1; Schmidt 1953-1970, Vol. I, p. 25; cf. Burn 1922:87). In that case, however, the name of Put (Libya) would have been included in the list of subject lands in the Behistun inscription, and not only in the much later texts. The conquest of Libya by the Persians should therefore be dated to the reign of Darius I.

Cambyses resided in Nubia for a considerable period of time. During his absence the Egyptians, knowing his lack of success and apparently convinced that he would not come back, rose up in revolt against Persian rule. When, however, Cambyses returned to the capital Memphis, at the end of 524 B.C., he dealt with the rebels in a severe manner. Direct information on what happened is scarce. Herodotus (III 15) tells that the former Pharaoh Psammetichus III, residing at Memphis, used all sorts of tricks to rouse the Egyptians to rebellion. When his deeds were exposed, Cambyses ordered him to commit suicide. According to V. V. Struve, the rebellion is reflected in a passage from the Udjahorresne inscription (Struve 1954:11). G. G. Cameron and other scholars, however, are of the opinion that the revolt which is referred to in the text took place during the first year of the reign of Darius (Cameron 1943:307ff.; Kent 1943:105). This, in my opinion, does not seem likely.

In spite of his loyalty to Cambyses, whose continuation of former traditions he describes, Udjahorresne tells about the start of chaotic times; disturbances and riots the likes of which had never occurred before, either at Sais or in the rest of Egypt. In his own words: "I saved the people when in a great misery that ruled over all the earth, the like of which had not been seen in this world. I protected the weak from the strong; I saved the frightened when wrong was done to them. I did for them useful deeds ... For them (namely, for his brothers) I established the posts as servants of the god, I gave them splendid fields according to what His Majesty forever provided me with ... I fed all their children ... I did for them what was useful, such as what a father would do for his children, when evil befell the nome at a time of great evil, which spread over all the world" (translation by O. D. Berlev).

Scholars have often linked this passage in the inscription to the account by classical writers about Cambyses' mockery of the Egyptian temples (cf., however, the work of Posener, where such a link is refuted: Posener

1936:168). These authors unanimously describe Cambyses' reign in Egypt as a period of violence, of pillaging of temples and mockery of the gods.[10] In particular, these sources say that Cambyses killed the sacred bull (Apis). But the Egyptologists have long since refuted this idea. As indicated by Egyptian texts, the bull which was born in the 27th year of the reign of Amasis, died a natural death during the sixth year of the rule of Cambyses, and was solemnly buried. The official epitaph has been found, which says that Cambyses offered a beautiful sarcophagus for the burial of this Apis. The succeeding Apis only appears during the first year of the reign of Darius I; consequently, it cannot have been killed by Cambyses (Atkinson 1956:170; Bresciani 1965:311f.; Gyles 1959:39; Parker 1941b:286; Posener 1936:30-33, 171-175). The stories about the death of the Apis bull, therefore, do not reflect the truth and in all probability were made up by Egyptian priests after the death of Cambyses (cf. Von Hoffmann & Vorbichler 1980:105).

According to Herodotus (III 16), Cambyses moved from Memphis to Sais, and ordered the removal of the mummy of Amasis from his tomb; he flogged the mummy and finally burnt it. Herodotus writes that this was blasphemous both to the Persians and the Egyptians, because the Persians regarded the fire as sacred, while the Egyptians believed that a man would lose his future life if his corpse were destroyed. E. Bresciani was of the opinion that in this case Cambyses acted in accordance with Egyptian attitudes when he attempted to destroy all trace of a man whose reign he regarded as illegitimate (Bresciani 1965:313f.; see also Atkinson 1956:171). The story of Herodotus, however, can hardly be linked to the account given by Udjahorresne as regards the information that Cambyses sojourned at Sais for another reason, namely for the worship of the goddess Neith. Herodotus' account is apparently a much later malicious concoction by Egyptian priests. The suggestion by certain scholars, therefore, namely that Cambyses mocked the religious feelings of the Egyptian people, by showing his 'Eastern barbarism' (Lewy 1949:98ff.; Scharff & Moortgat 1950:186), appears to be without foundation. It can only be said that at the time of the revolt certain Egyptian temples were plundered. But the reason for these attacks was not the hostile attitude of Cambyses towards the Egyptian sanctuaries, but the disloyalty of the Egyptians towards the Persian king.

---

[10] Diodorus I 44.3; I 49.5; X 14.3; Herodotus III 27-38; Justinus I 9; Plinius, *Hist. Nat.* XXVI 66; Plutarch, *Mor.* 368 F; Strabo XVII 1.27.

CHAPTER NINE

COUP D'ETAT IN IRAN

During the three years that Cambyses resided in Egypt without returning to Iran, unrest started in his own country. In March (or perhaps in April) 522 B.C., he received the news that his younger brother Bardiya had revolted in Persia and had become king. According to Herodotus (III 62), Cambyses was in Syria on his way to Persia when a royal herald arrived with the news of the palace revolution. Cambyses hastened towards Persia, but died during the journey under mysterious circumstances without having regained his authority (for the relevant literature, see Balcer 1987:52, 95ff.; Walser 1983:8ff.). Not much later Bardiya (or, following the official version, the magus Gaumata, who impersonated the long dead Bardiya) was killed by Darius who then ascended the Persian throne. This is basically the course of events in 522-521 B.C. For many hundreds of years these events appealed to the imagination of the classical writers.

Apart from the official version, as recounted in the Behistun text, other accounts also refer to the revolution in Persia. These were presented by Aeschylus; Ctesias; Herodotus; Plato; Plutarch; Polyaenus; Pompeius Trogus; Strabo, and Xenophon.[1] The question whether Darius killed the impostor or the real son of Cyrus has for a long time been a moot point. Even the late classical and early medieval authors such as Agathias; Ammianus Marcellinus; Johannus of Antiochia; Orosius and Porphyrius from Tyre wrote about this problem.[2]

Historians strongly disagree concerning the place, time, manner, and the circumstances of the death of Bardiya, the youngest son of Cyrus.

According to the Behistun text (I 26-33), Bardiya was killed by Cambyses before his war against Egypt: "Says Darius the king ... The son of Cyrus, Cambyses, of our family, was king here. Cambyses had a brother called Bardiya, of the same mother and father as Cambyses. Afterwards, Cambyses killed Bardiya. When Cambyses killed Bardiya, the people did not know that Bardiya was dead. Then Cambyses left for Egypt."

---

[1] Herodotus III 61-79; Plato, *Leg.* III 694-695; *Epist.* VII 332 A; Plutarch, *Moral.* 490 A; Polyaenus VII 11.2; Strabo XV 3,24.
[2] Amm. Marc., *Hist.* XXIII 6.36; FHG, Vol. IV, 552; Orosius II.8; FGrH, Vol. II, 1222.

According to Herodotus (III 61-79), Smerdis (this is how he calls Bardiya)[3] was with the troops in Egypt. Cambyses sent his brother from Egypt back to Persia out of jealousy, because only Smerdis was capable of drawing a special bow with a breadth of two fingers, which was sent by the king of the Ethiopians. Subsequently Smerdis was killed by a Persian called Prexaspes, on the instructions of Cambyses who feared that Smerdis was involved in a conspiracy. Herodotus presents two versions of Smerdis' death. The first account states that he was killed near Susa during a hunt. The second version relates how Smerdis was drowned in the Erythraean Sea. The reason for this murder was, according to Herodotus (III 30), a dream of Cambyses which told him that Smerdis would become king. Apart from Cambyses and Prexaspes, only the magus Patizeithes[4] knew about the murder. The latter was appointed by Cambyses to supervise the palace. Patizeithes convinced his brother who was also called Smerdis to take the place of Cyrus' son.

Although the information provided by Ctesias in general has a legendary character and is often unreliable, it cannot be left out in a study of what happened during the period of Darius' accession. We know from the work of Ctesias (*Persica* 29.8-14; see König 1972:6-7), what exactly was said at the Persian court about the mysterious disappearance of Cyrus' son and about the accession to the throne by Darius.

In certain cases Ctesias was undoubtedly better informed about the official Persian traditions than Herodotus and the other writers. For instance, Ctesias is the only Greek author who knew the official date of the death of Cyrus' son Bardiya. The other Greek writers, following Herodotus, date his death to the period of Cambyses' residence in Egypt, or later. Ctesias is also the only Greek source who, just like the Behistun text, refers to a magus usurper. The other classical writers refer to two persons. It is therefore difficult to agree with the hypothesis, first brought forward by J. Markwart, that Ctesias based his account about the death of Bardiya on the events during the reign of Artaxerxes II, when Cyrus the Younger revolted against him (Markwart 1891:619-620). Markwart

---

[3] Bardiya (Behistun inscription); Smerdis (Herodotus); Mardos (Aeschylus); Merdis (Nicolaus of Damascus); Mergis (Pompeius Trogus). These renderings all reflect one and the same name. Compare also the name of Smerdes, which is used by Aristoteles (*Polit.* V 8.13) for a Greek from Asia Minor (cf. Schmitt 1978:28f.). In the Akkadian version of the Behistun text, and in legal documents from Babylonia, usually the Median rendering is used: Barziya. Only in two Babylonian documents this name is spelled as Bardiya (see Leichty & Grayson 1987:387, nos. 7409 and 7514).

[4] As was shown by J. Markwart, this was not his real name, but a title with the meaning 'superintendent of the royal house' (Markwart 1896:213ff.; see also extensively, J. Wiesehöfer 1978:49-50). According to E. Herzfeld, Patizeithes was the title of Bardiya, the son of Cyrus (Herzfeld 1947b:205).

suggested that Tanyoxarkes[5] (this is how Bardiya is called by Ctesias) was an image of Cyrus the Younger, but they had little in common. Tanyoxarkes, according to Ctesias, was the governor (it is said: 'lord') of the Bactrians, Choramnians (that is, the Chorasmians), the Parthians and the Carmanians. He had a magus called Sphendadates[6] flogged for some crime. The magus went up to Cambyses and slandered Tanyoxarkes. Tanyoxarkes was killed on the orders of Cambyses: they gave him bull's blood to drink. And Sphendadates, who very much resembled the deceased, became the governor instead.[7] Reading this account it is difficult to see an analogy with the rebellion by Cyrus the Younger, and as such there are no grounds to suggest that Ctesias transposed the scenery of events at the end of the fifth century B.C. to a much earlier period by using the stories which were circulating at the court of Susa at his time. Ctesias tells what he heard at the Persian court. It is true that many times he distorts the facts, but the reason for this is often the unreliability of the historical tradition at the Persian court about events which happened more than a hundred years previously.

Ctesias writes that before his death Cyrus appointed Tanyoxarkes as governor of some eastern provinces, including Bactria and Parthia. It is known that Achaemenids or their closest relatives used to govern Bactria as satraps. During the reign of Cambyses, according to Ctesias, Tanyoxarkes was replaced by the magus Sphendadates. Certain scholars are inclined to regard this piece of information by Ctesias as reliable (Herzfeld 1929:117; Junge 1944b:38; König 1938a:213; Prášek 1912:28). According to the Behistun inscription, however, Dadarshish was satrap in Bactria when Darius ascended the Persian throne, and Vishtaspa, the father

---

[5] In translation the name means '(having) a large (or strong) body' (for references, see Dandamaev 1976:110, n. 452). The name of Bardiya literally means 'high (or exalted)', and, apparently, also refers to his great physical strength. In Herodotus Bardiya appears as a giant, as the seven conspirators could only kill the two magi (Patizeithes and Smerdis) with the greatest of efforts (cf. Struve 1949b:19ff.). J. Prášek suggested that initially the son of Cyrus was called Tanyoxarkes, and subsequently took the title of Bardiya (Prášek 1913:4). It is more likely to assume, however, that Bardiya was his real name as he is referred to under this name in the Behistun inscription, while Tanyoxarkes is a nickname given to him because of his great strength.

[6] Ctesias, *Persica* 29.8. The name of Sphendadates (in the Avesta: Spentodata) is not fictitious, but genuinely Iranian. The name is mentioned in the Avesta and means 'created by the sacred spirit'. J. Oppert (1851:262) and Markwart (1891:620) suggested that Sphendadates was the second Bardiya referred to in the Behistun text with the name of Vahyazdata. According to F. Justi, Sphendadates is a nickname of Gaumata (Justi 1895:308).

[7] The later writer Cedrenus also refers to the magus Sphendadates: "They were brothers, the magi Sphendanes and Kimerdios, and they ruled for seven months" (Cedrenus, *Georgius*, ed. Im. Bekker, Vol. I, Bonn, 1838:252). It is difficult to determine which source was used by Cedrenus. The name of Kimerdios is reminiscent of Bardiya.

of Darius, was governing in Parthia and Hyrcania. It cannot be excluded therefore that Xenophon was correct (*Cyropaedia* VIII 7.11) when he referred to Tanaoxares (this is the name of Bardiya in the work of Xenophon)[8] as the satrap of Media, Armenia and the tribe of the Cadusians (Meyer 1939, Vol. IV, p. 64; Olmstead 1948:92; cf. Struve 1949b:27f.). It is true that the suggestion can be made that Dadarshish and Vishtaspa were appointed later, during the reign of Gaumata or Darius.[9] It should be taken into account, however, that Dadarshish, immediately after Darius came to power, went over to his side, and therefore would hardly be a protégé of Gaumata. In addition, at the beginning of his reign Darius did not have any real power in the far-away districts of Parthia, Hyrcania and Bactria, and therefore could not appoint satraps for those provinces.

The version which is told by Pompeius Trogus is again different from that of Herodotus and Ctesias. First of all, the magus impostor is called Cometes, which seems to be a perfect Latin rendering of the Iranian name of Gaumata, as the Old Persian diphthong 'au' was pronounced 'ō'. This indicates that Trogus reproduced a reliable and oral historical tradition of the Persians, which was unknown to Herodotus. But this tradition must have been meagre, because for further details Trogus turned to information provided by Herodotus.

In the work of Trogus, as in that of Herodotus, two magi appear, although with different names. Cometes makes his brother Oropastes[10] the new king. In this manner, Patizeithes of Herodotus corresponds to the Cometes of Trogus, and Smerdis is identical to Oropastes. But contrary to Herodotus, Trogus does not refer to Prexaspes, and Cometes himself fulfills his role, namely killing Bardiya (whom he calls Mergis). According to Trogus, the death of Mergis occurred after that of Cambyses (Just. I 9).

During the nineteenth century attempts were already being made to link the information of Herodotus concerning the rule of the false Smerdis with certain data from the Avesta. These attempts are also often found in modern literature. A group of scholars, on the basis of the Avestan Yasna 53, suggested that the events which surrounded the rule of Gaumata, find direct reflection in the Avesta (Hertel 1924a:79ff.; *idem*

---

[8] J. Markwart and A. T. Olmstead suggested that in his account about Tanaoxares, Xenophon based himself on Ctesias (Markwart 1891:618, n. 397). Xenophon, however, also had other sources at his disposal. According to K. Lehmann-Haupt, in this case Xenophon followed Dionysius of Miletus (Lehmann-Haupt 1921: paragraph 5).

[9] For instance, F. W. König suggested that Dadarshish and Vivana, the satrap in Arachosia, were appointed to their positions by Darius or Vishtaspa (König 1938a:334).

[10] An Iranian name, which testifies to the fact that Trogus not only used Herodotus' *Historiae*, but also had recourse to other sources.

1924b:44-47; Herzfeld 1933:141f.; *idem* 1935:43; Hoffmann & Kutschke 1907:188; Lehmann-Haupt 1933:272ff.). In this Yasna it is said that Ahura Mazda had to bring death and a bloody punishment to the advocates of evil. And further it is said about someone, without any obvious context, that he had to endure much hardship but soon afterwards rose to power. From this passage, according to some scholars, the following conclusion can be drawn: Vishtaspa decided not to dethrone Gaumata; but Darius followed the advice of Zarathustra and thus realized the prophecy of the latter, and became king. This hypothesis, however, only rests on the opinion that Darius was a follower of Zarathustra, and saved the religion created by the prophet from persecution by Gaumata. It is, however, impossible to find any information in the sources to support this hypothesis.[11]

Let us now turn to the question of the relationship between Gaumata and Cyrus' son Bardiya. Above we have seen that the information about Bardiya's death is contradictory. According to Herodotus, he participated in the Egyptian campaign of Cambyses and subsequently was sent back to Persis where he was murdered. In the Behistun inscription it is said that Bardiya was killed before the start of the Egyptian war, and that the people remained unaware of this deed. Also Ctesias writes that the murder was committed before Cambyses' war against Egypt. For the rest, contemporary scholarly opinion is unanimous: Gaumata became king with the name of Bardiya, the son of Cyrus, in order to reinstate Median hegemony. Influential Persians headed by Darius heard about this, and killed the false son of Cyrus, thereby re-establishing Persian

---

[11] E. Herzfeld attempted to reconstruct the genealogy of Zarathustra. His starting point was the communication by Ctesias that the Mede Spitamas was married to Amytis, the daughter of the Median king Astyages. Their son was called Spitakes. According to Herzfeld, Spitakes means 'the younger Spitamas' and he would have been no other than Zarathustra, because Spitamas was the family name of the prophet, as reported in the Avesta. If this is correct, then Astyages was the grandfather of Zarathustra. Subsequently, when Cyrus married Amytis, their daughter Atossa became the halfsister of Zarathustra; in other words, Zarathustra was the brother-in-law of Cambyses and Darius, who were subsequently married to Atossa. Herzfeld suggested that Zarathustra, when informed by Prexaspes about the murder of Bardiya, persuaded Darius to dethrone the impostor, and he also asked Darius, in his modesty, not to mention him in the Behistun text (Herzfeld 1947b:46-66); compare the criticism towards this hypothesis by W. B. Henning (1951:7f.), where, in particular, it is indicated that Zarathustra was the son of Pourushaspa and a woman by the name of Dugdova. In addition, Spitamas was a common name with Iranians, which is also recorded by Ctesias during the time of Artaxerxes I (FGrH, Vol. I, p. 467). A. T. Olmstead also suggested that Darius had many meetings and discussions with Zarathustra. The latter was killed, according to Olmstead, by the hands of Frada, the leader of the insurgents in Margiana, in 522 B.C. (Olmstead 1948:113).

dominance over the Medes. Yet, a careful analysis of the sources casts some doubt upon the correctness of such an hypothesis.

Herodotus (III 61) calls the son of Cyrus by the name of Smerdis. The magus, who managed to ascend the throne as Cyrus' son, carried the same name, and they strongly resembled each other.[12] Ctesias agrees: "This magus was to the highest degree resembling Tanyoxarkes ... He did everything similarly to Tanyoxarkes."

The magus, according to Ctesias, so resembled Cyrus' son, that even those who were the closest to them both, could not distinguish one from the other. When Tanyoxarkes was killed, Cambyses summoned his eunuchs and showed them the magus Sphendadates, dressed in the robe of the murdered prince. Cambyses asked the eunuchs: Is this man Tanyoxarkes? They, greatly surprised, answered: Who else, if it is not him? This piece of information by Ctesias apparently originates in a Persian tradition. Here Ctesias supports Herodotus, whom normally he continuously and naggingly tries to correct. It is apparent that the Persian tradition was known to both Herodotus and Ctesias. The tradition identified Bardiya with the person whom Darius called Gaumata. Also Trogus told about the likeness of the magus with Cyrus' son. On the basis of this point, many contemporary scholars have concluded that the magus did in fact strongly resemble Bardiya, and that this helped him to become king, by impersonating the latter (see, e.g., Justi 1879:50; Keiper 1877:45; Sykes 1921, Vol. I, p. 158). Such an explanation of the sources, however, seems to me to be a simplification.

It is not without grounds that historians have given pre-eminence to the information about Bardiya's death provided by the Behistun text, and not to the account presented by Herodotus. Evidently, this choice cannot be questioned, because there was no point for Darius, being a contemporary to the events, to date the death of Bardiya to a much earlier time, if it actually happened after the Egyptian campaign. Egypt was conquered no later than June 525 B.C., while the death of Bardiya, according to the Behistun inscription (I 48-61) and Herodotus (III 68), was only known by September 522 B.C. But because not much time can have elapsed between the death of Bardiya and the conquest of Egypt, Bardiya must have died, following the Behistun text, thus no later than 526 B.C. In that case four years passed between Bardiya's death and the

---

[12] Herodotus, however, wrote that the magus Smerdis had no ears. But this is a distortion, based on a play with words. The word 'magus', in particular, has the connotation of a priest who follows a literary tradition, and would therefore be without ears (Darmesteter 1880-1883, Vol. II, p. 4; Bertin 1890:821f.). The legend that Smerdis had no ears is apparently a Greek concoction (Demandt 1972:95ff.). In any case, in the Behistun relief Gaumata is depicted with his ears.

moment that this became widely known. This suggestion, surprisingly enough, agrees with the information which is provided by Ctesias, who writes that the deceit only became known after five years, and Amytis, the mother of Tanyoxarkes, heard about the true state of affairs from a eunuch.[13] It is evident that the information of Ctesias originates from the official Persian tradition. The indicated date for the murder of Bardiya does not raise any doubts and is accepted by all scholars. Yet they do not consider the question how the death of Bardiya, a prominent satrap of certain important lands, son of Cyrus, could have remained unknown for five years. How could his sisters, his mother, daughter and other relatives, his friends and servants, have remained ignorant about his death for so long? How could they only have discovered about this five years later, when they heard about it from Darius who had just killed his predecessor on the throne and became king himself? How could the death of Bardiya for so long have been known only to the two magi?[14] Certain scholars, using the information of Xenophon (*Cyropaedia* VIII 8.2; see also Plato, *Leg.* III 695 B), are inclined to believe that Bardiya was already dead in 530 B.C.[15] (Elwell-Sutton 1952:113; Prášek 1906-1910, Vol. I, p. 177). In that case it must be accepted that the death of Bardiya remained a secret for eight years. Who took Bardiya's place as satrap? Ctesias writes that Cambyses appointed the magus Sphendadates as satrap, in the disguise of Tanyoxarkes, and that it was this magus who played the role of Cyrus' younger son for five years, and even became king, still under the name of Tanyoxarkes. Certain scholars regard this piece of information by Ctesias as completely reliable (König 1938a:217, 340). For example, E. Herzfeld suggested that Gaumata had become

---

[13] According to Ctesias, Astyages had no sons, only a daughter called Amytis. As reported, she was married to Spitamas. Cyrus killed the latter and became the husband of Amytis; Cambyses and Tanyoxarkes were their sons. According to Herodotus (II 1; III 2), however, who deserves much more credence than Ctesias, the mother of Cambyses and Smerdis was Cassandane, the daughter of Pharnaspes, from the clan of the Achaemenids. According to Hellanicus (FGrH, Vol. I, p. 149), Cambyses had two brothers, Maraphis and Merphis. This piece of information is contained in the scholias to Aeschylus' 'The Persians'. The contents of the corresponding passage in the work of Hellanicus have perhaps not correctly been transmitted by the scholiasts. In all probability, Maraphis and Merphis are different variants of the name of Bardiya.

[14] According to Herodotus (III 66-67), the death of Smerdis was only known to Cambyses, Prexaspes, and the two magi. At the same time the Persians were convinced that they were ruled by the son of Cyrus. According to Ctesias (*Persica* 29.10), the murder was known to Cambyses, the magus Sphendadates, and the courtiers Artasyras, Bagapates and Izabates.

[15] Xenophon reports that Tanaoxares rose up in revolt against Cambyses. Herodotus and Ctesias, however, agree in saying that the younger son of Cyrus did not undertake any action against Cambyses and was therefore falsely accused.

satrap instead of Bardiya by 529 B.C., and, consequently, seven years passed before he was discovered to be an impostor (Herzfeld 1930a:47).

As is known from the work of Herodotus (III 68), the sister of Cambyses and Bardiya, called Atossa, and the wives of Cambyses, were contained in the royal harem from the commencement of Gaumata's coup, and consequently had ample opportunity to discover the deceit. But this did not happen. The source which was used by Herodotus makes pains to overcome this problem by stating that the women in Smerdis' harem were isolated. But it is clear from Herodotus (III 68-69) that this isolation was not complete, for example Phaidyme, the daughter of Otanes, who lived in the harem of Smerdis, communicated with the outside world on more than one occasion. Nor was the palace of Smerdis isolated; at the crucial moment the seven conspirators could enter without obstacle, without anyone of the palace guard stopping them. The guard did not even ask the conspirators their reasons for entering the palace.

Prexaspes, who was officially regarded as the murderer of Smerdis, frequently and very clearly denied it. It is true that Herodotus writes that Prexaspes feared punishment for the murder. According to the account presented by Herodotus, the magi decided to try to win Prexaspes over to their cause. They persuaded him to climb on a tower and declare to the Persians that they were governed by the son of Cyrus. Prexaspes, according to Herodotus (III 75), agreed to that procedure, but having addressed the Persians he disclosed the deceit and jumped from the tower. In reality, however, this cannot have happened, as already remarked by M. Duncker (Duncker 1867, Vol. II, p. 813). For it is Herodotus himself who writes that subsequent to the death of Cambyses, only Prexaspes knew about the murder of Smerdis, and that he categorically denied this deed.[16] Therefore, the magi had no reason whatsoever to urge Prexaspes to tell the Persians about the murder. It is clear from the Behistun inscription (I 35-43), Herodotus (III 66-67) and Ctesias, that the people were convinced they were ruled by Cyrus' son. In all probability Prexaspes was killed by the co-conspirators of Darius because he continued to deny that he had killed Bardiya.

The Behistun text does not present information about all the enigmatic events which are described in the works of Herodotus and Ctesias. In his inscription Darius gives extensive information about many of his adversaries, whom he had to fight immediately after his accession to the Persian throne. Darius indicates who the various rebels were by descent, and

---

[16] In the *Persica* of Ctesias (29.13; see König 1972:7), the role of Prexaspes is played in an analogous manner by the eunuch Izabates. He tells the troops about a different course of events, and thereafter seeks refuge in a temple. He was, however, decapitated in the temple.

where they started their revolts; how their ancestors were called, etc. But the most dangerous adversary of Darius is constantly called "the magus Gaumata." Such a sign of despise towards Gaumata is hardly fortuitous.

Now we turn towards the information which is transmitted in a drama by Aeschylus, called 'The Persians' (774-777). Aeschylus writes, through the lips of the ghost of Darius, while listing the Median and Persian kings: "Fifth to rule was Mardos, a disgrace to the fatherland and the ancient throne. The noble Artaphrenes killed him with treachery in the palace, together with his friends, whose task this was." This makes clear that Aeschylus did not regard Mardos as a usurper and impostor (cf. Olmstead 1948:109). The negative description of Mardos is here in its place, because it is presented by Darius.

All circumstances which are described above force us to doubt the truth of Darius' statement that he killed a false Smerdis. Although we will never really know who was the predecessor of Darius on the Persian throne, it is possible to suggest that Bardiya, Mardos, Smerdis, Tanyoxarkes and the person whom Darius called "the magus Gaumata", were one and the same person, namely the younger son of Cyrus. This opinion was already aired by A. T. Olmstead and certain other scholars (Burn 1970:91ff.; Nyberg 1954:75; Olmstead 1948:92f.; Rost 1897:107-109; Winckler 1898:38ff.; cf. also Balcer 1987:101ff.; Bickerman & Tadmor 1978:240ff.; Cook 1983:52; Gershevitch 1979; Sancisi-Weerdenburg 1980:84-93).

In the Behistun inscription all those who oppose Darius are called "liars". At the same time its author repeatedly talks about his own love for the truth. But in order to achieve his ambitions, Darius was prepared to do anything. Herodotus, who can hardly be accused of hostility towards Darius, tells about Darius' readiness to lie when it was to his advantage. The Father of History (III 72) attributes the following sentence to Darius: "When necessary one should lie, for we all strive after the same goal, those who lie and those who stick to the truth." These words, according to Herodotus, were spoken by Darius when the seven Persian conspirators came together immediately before their planned attack on Smerdis.

In the Behistun inscription the tendentious character of the account of the events related to Darius' coming to power is evident. Its author had to seek his refuge in a conscious distortion of the facts. Essentially, the Behistun text does not refer to any defeats suffered by Darius in his wars against the rebellious peoples of the Achaemenid empire. According to Darius, he was always and everywhere the victor. The composer of the Behistun text (IV 52-59) realized very well that his account could be labelled as unreliable by anyone reading it. But he still urged all to believe his text, and to distribute its contents as the true account of events. It is clear that Darius' contemporaries contested the official version of events. This made Darius doubt whether future generations, for whom the text was principally engraved in the Behistun cliff, would believe him any more than his contemporaries. Therefore he laid such stress on his sense of justice.

According to the Behistun inscription (I 32-43), when Cambyses had gone to Egypt and Bardiya was dead, "the people became rebellious, and there was much lying in the country, in Persia, in Media, and in the other countries ... Then there was one man, a magus with the name of Gaumata ... he rose up ... Subsequently all the people became rebellious and defected from Cambyses to his side, in Persia, Media and the other lands." In this manner, the coming to power of Gaumata was preceded by unrest in Persia and other lands, directed against Cambyses. This turbulence brought Gaumata to power and it stopped with his accession. He rose up on March 11, 522 B.C., and was known in Babylonia within a month. From Babylonia we have, commencing in April, business documents which are dated to his reign. They are mainly legal contracts from Babylon, Sippar, Uruk and other cities (for a list of these documents, see Dandamaev 1984:14, to which now the following texts should be added: Leichty 1986:284, no. 59425; Leichty & Grayson 1987:387, s.v. 'Bardiya' and 'Barziya'). With the drafting of various contracts in Babylonia, the following gods and Barziya were called upon: "Bel, Nabu and Barziya, the king of Babylon, and the king of the lands" (Sm, 7). In April, 522 B.C., Cambyses was still alive and in certain places of Babylonia he was still mentioned. Thus, from April 18, 522 B.C., we have the last document which is dated to Cambyses' reign (Camb., 409). It was found at Shahrinu, a suburb of Babylon.

Two Babylonian contracts, which can be dated to the reign of Bardiya, call him "king of the lands"; the other documents give him the titles: "king of Babylon, king of the lands." Four documents from Babylonia are dated to the "accession year" (in fact: "the year of the commencement of the reign") of Bardiya. But the very same year is called in the remaining contracts: "the first year of the rule" of Bardiya.[17]

---

[17] In the Babylonian cyclic lunar calendar the new year started in the month of Nisannu (March-April). The lapse of time between the actual accession to the throne and the first day of the month of Nisannu is referred to as the 'accession year', while the first year of the new king started on the first of Nisannu. Gaumata rose in rebellion on the fourteenth day of the month of Addaru (the twelfth month of the Babylonian calendar), and, thus, the beginning of his reign did not coincide with the beginning of the new year. The first seventeen days of the rule of Bardiya should therefore be considered as 'his accession year', while documents, drafted after the first of Nisannu, were to be dated to the first year. The scribes, however, showed some inconsistency in this particular case.

By July 1, 522 B.C., Gaumata had received general recognition and was apparently crowned at Pasargadae according to ancient rites, and thus became king of an empire which had been originally created by Cyrus and Cambyses.

There was no unrest during the whole of Gaumata's reign. All sources unanimously report that his rule covered a period of peace. The widespread opinion that many countries of the Persian empire were in a state of continuous rebellion during the whole period that Gaumata was in power, is not supported by the sources. The Behistun inscription clearly shows that the rebellions in Elam, Media, Persia, Babylonia and many other countries only started after the death of Gaumata and were directed against Darius: "When I killed the magus Gaumata, then one man with the name of Açina ... rose up in Elam" (I 73-75). Consequently, the revolt of Açina occurred after the accession to the Persian throne by Darius. After Açina, Nidintu-bel in Babylonia revolted. While Darius quenched the revolt of Nidintu-bel, Vahyazdata rose in Persia; Fravartish in Media; Ciçantakhma in Sagartia; Frada in Margiana, etc. Thus, all these revolts occurred after September 29, 522 B.C., when Gaumata was killed, and at the moment that his death and Darius' accession were made public.

The fact that there was no turbulence before the death of Gaumata is also evident from the introductory part of the Behistun inscription (I 12-17), according to which Ahura Mazda presented Darius with the kingship of 23 countries after he had ascended the throne. Consequently, at the moment when Darius came to power in Persia the 23 lands listed in the text still formed part of the empire. From that date onwards, however, turbulences broke out in most of these lands. According to F. W. König, the revolt of Nidintu-bel in Babylonia took place in August, 522 B.C., that is when Gaumata was still alive, and was directed against him (König 1938a:38). But, without even referring to the Behistun inscription, such an hypothesis is also contradicted by Babylonian legal documents. Gaumata was killed on September 29, 522 B.C., and from September 20 of the same year there is a document from Babylon which is dated to his rule (Sm., 9).[18] And the first document dated to the reign

[18] According to Leichty (1986:284), the document BM 59425 is dated to the twentieth day of the month Araḫsamna of the first regnal year of Barziya (November 9, 522 B.C.). This document, in all probability, comes from Sippar. So far the latest known document dated to Barziya has been the above mentioned Sm. 9 written in Babylon on September 20, 522 B.C. The date of the tablet BM 59425 is in obvious contradiction with the fact that three documents dated to the 14th, 17th and the 20th day of the month of Tashritu of the accession year of Nebuchadnezzar III (October 3, 6, 9, 522 B.C., respectively) have been preserved from Sippar and Babylon. Barziya could therefore hardly be at the same time, or even a month later, king of Babylon. Moreover, to judge from the Behistun

of Nidintu-bel (Nebuchadnezzar III), comes from Sippar and dates from October 3, 522 (Nbk, 1; cf. Parker & Dubberstein 1956:15), that is on the fifth day after Darius' accession to the throne. In all probability, Nidintu-bel occupied the throne of Babylon just after the death of Gaumata.

According to Herodotus (III 67), Smerdis ruled for seven months "in peace", and it was because of his death that all the subject peoples rebelled.

---

inscription, Barziya (or Gaumata) was assassinated by Darius on September 29, 522 B.C. I can only suggest that the sign for the month in BM 59425 should be emended to Nisannu. In that case the tablet was written on April 15, 522 B.C., which is in full accordance with some other documents dated to Barziya.

CHAPTER TEN

THE POLICY OF GAUMATA

As early as the middle of the nineteenth century, various scholars put forward the suggestion that Gaumata's coup reflected a response by the Median nobility to Persian supremacy, and that Gaumata strove to restore Median domination over the Persians and consequently to reinstate the Median empire (Duncker 1867, Vol. II, pp. 816ff.; Gray 1969:174; Niebuhr 1847:156ff.; Nyberg 1938:375, 395; Prášek 1906-1910, Vol. I, p. 261; *Vsemirnaja Istorija* 1956, Vol. II, p. 24). Such an hypothesis, however, simplifies the complicated and unique historical situation which unfolded itself in Persia by the end of the 520's.

First of all, the coup by Gaumata did not take place in Media, but at *Paišiyā^huvādā*, which was situated in Persia. The location of this place is evident from a report in the Behistun inscription about a later revolt by a man called Vahyazdata, who also found support at that place.[1] In addition, the Behistun inscription (IV 9-10) makes it clear that Gaumata carried out his coup in Persia. The same inscription (III 23-24) also says that Vahyazdata "made the second uprising in Persia." Thus, according to the Behistun inscription, Gaumata's coup took place in Persia.

The pertinent sources, however, provide no information which indicates that Gaumata was planning to give Media, or any other land, a more privileged position than Persia. The information provided by Herodotus (III 67) regarding the point that Smerdis exempted the subject peoples from tribute and military duties for a period of three years is sometimes regarded as a reflection of the privileged position of the Medes during the reign of Gaumata. All subject peoples of the Persian empire, however, were exempted, not just the Medes. The temporary exemption of tribute, contrary to the opinion of certain scholars, could also, incorrectly, be regarded as a demagogic stunt (I. M. Diakonoff 1956:432; Struve 1949b:20ff.). In fact the situation was far more complicated. Heavy taxes and military duties had evoked a strong feeling of discontent among the subject peoples. The position of Persia as regards the conquered lands at the end of Cambyses' reign was very weak. It was amidst such circumstances that a declaration was issued which exempted the subject lands from tribute and military duties. It is clear that these

---

[1] According to J. Hansman, *Paišiyā^huvādā* was located in southern Persia, to the west of Yautiya (Hansman 1975:304; see also Wiesehöfer 1978:51-54).

measures were taken in order to keep the subject peoples within the Empire, rather than in the interest of the Medes. In addition, the exemption from tribute was not without precedent in Persian policy. According to Herodotus (VI 59), the Persian kings remitted any arrears from the preceding years when they came to power. At the commencement of Gaumata's reign, however, the simple remission of arrears was not sufficient to assuage the subject peoples. To maintain the unity of the Achaemenid empire it was necessary to forego the arbitrary gifts and to change the whole financial system.

Scholars who are of the opinion that the measures by Gaumata were directed against the Persian people, base their hypothesis on a certain piece of information in the Behistun inscription (I 50-51), namely that "the people feared" Gaumata. But even from the official version, contained in this text, it is evident that when Gaumata became king, the majority of the Persian people unanimously came over to his side, while the accession of Darius was attended by a serious and long enduring revolt against him in Persia itself. It is evident from the work of Herodotus that the Persians were not less sympathetic towards the reforms of Smerdis than were the subject peoples.

Many scholars, as stated above, have regarded the possibility of describing Gaumata's coup as being Median in character. In doing so they base themselves on the fact that Gaumata was killed in Media, in the district of Nisaya, at the fortress of *Sikaya^huvatiš*. They have suggested that he moved his capital to Media because he was afraid of remaining in Persia (Duncker 1867, Vol. II, pp. 553, 816; König 1938a:196; Prášek 1906-1910, Vol. I, p. 265). However, also this hypothesis can hardly be accepted. Herodotus (III 70) and Ctesias (*Persica* 29.14) wrote that the magus lived and was subsequently killed in his own capital, namely at Susa. At first glance it would appear that both classical authors were incorrect, because the Behistun inscription (I 57-59) reports that he was killed in Media. The remarks by Herodotus and Ctesias, however, attest to the fact that Susa remained the capital of the Empire during the reign of Gaumata. His residence in Media must have been based on other reasons. It is known that Cyrus II and the succeeding Persian kings used to live in different cities of their Empire, in accordance with the season of the year.[2] Gaumata was killed at the end of September, that is during the period of the year when the Achaemenid kings used to live at the capital of Media, Ecbatana, where the summer was usually comparatively cool. It is not surprising, therefore, that

---

[2] Arrian, *Anabasis Alexandri* III 16.7; Daniel 8.2; Esther I 2.5; II 3.5; Plutarch, *Moral.* 78 D; Strabo XI 13.5; Xenophon, *Cyropaedia* VIII 6.22; *idem*, *Anabasis* III 5.15.

Gaumata spent the summer and the commencement of the autumn not far from Ecbatana, in the famous district of Nisaya, the fertility and favourable climate of which were praised by many classical authors.[3]

The coup by Gaumata is also sometimes regarded as the establishment of a theocracy by Median magi (Henning 1944:133f.; Hutecker 1885:61; Junge 1944a:43; G. Rawlinson 1875-1880, Vol. II, pp. 549-553; Widengren 1968:532). Adherents of this theory support their ideas on a piece of information given by Herodotus (III 79) and Ctesias (29.15) on the murder of the magi (the Magophonia) at the time of the accession of Darius I, and the establishment of a national festival during which the magi were molested. As indicated by J. Markwart, however, the origin of the idea of a national day for molesting the magi can be related to an incorrect interpretation of the Old Persian name of one of the months, namely *Bāgayādiš*, and of the festival which was celebrated during this month (Markwart 1896:234-236; see also Boyce 1982:86ff.; Christensen 1933:130; Duncker 1867, Vol. II, p. 821; *idem*, Vol. IV, p. 462; Frye 1984:99; Messina 1930:88). This was a festival in honour of one of the gods of the Iranian pantheon (in all probability, Mithra), which coincided with the death of Gaumata. Apparently, the conspirators chose this day in order to catch Gaumata and his court unawares.

W. B. Henning, basing himself on the expression 'murder of the magi', which he found in a Sogdian-Manichaean text, suggested that the festival dedicated to the physical abusing of the magi was indeed instituted by Darius I (Henning 1944:133-136; see also Nock 1949:282). In the pertinent fragment, however, reference is made to the murder of magi by Alexander of Macedonia. As is known, the Zoroastrian tradition accused the latter of burning the Avesta and murdering the magi. It is difficult to agree with Henning, when he states that the magi tried to obliterate the memory of the true origin of the Magophonia, by accusing Alexander instead of Darius. Even the classical philosopher Hermodoros, who is quoted by Diogenes Laertius, knew that it was not Darius, but Alexander of Macedonia who punished the magi (Altheim 1951:192). After a lapse of many centuries following the death of Darius, when very few people, if any at all, would still have been interested in the coup by Gaumata, why would the magi have tried to hide the fact that once, a long time ago, they fought for political power? In addition, in the district of Nisaya where Gaumata was killed, there cannot have been many Persians able to carry out a massive slaughter of magi. There

---

[3] Arrian, *Anabasis Alexandri* VII 13.1; Herodotus, VII 40; Strabo XI 13.7; XI 14.9. The locality of Nisaya is already mentioned in Assyrian sources as Niššaya (see Parpola 1970:269).

is also another indisputable fact, namely that the magi continued to act
as the court priests of the Achaemenids. Finally, it may be worthy of note
that the Behistun inscription, which extensively reports on the death and
execution of the enemies of Darius, does not describe the murder of any
magi.

Even when it is accepted that the strange custom of molesting the magi
did exist, then there is still no foundation for the hypothesis that
Gaumata was the advocate of Median supremacy over the Persians. If
Gaumata had reinstalled Median privileges, Darius would not have
hesitated to report in his Behistun text that Gaumata had taken authority
away from the Persians, and that he, Darius, accorded the Persians the
greatest of favours by giving them back their former power.

Describing the events which were related to the reign of Gaumata, the
Behistun inscription does not say anything about a pro-Median character
of the king.[4] This is all the more worthy of attention, because in the description of the revolts by Nidintu-bel, Fravartish, Frada, Arakha, etc.,
there are clear references to their anti-Persian character. When, however, the text is referring to Gaumata, Persia occupies the first place, and
not Media. Persia in particular plays a prominent role in the coup by
Gaumata, for example at the commencement of the revolt "all the Persian people" chose his side, and only subsequently did the Medes and
other subject peoples follow suit. Darius declares in the Behistun inscription (I 48-53): "There was no man, neither a Persian, a Mede, neither
one of our lineage, who would remove the magus Gaumata from
kingship." Official propaganda was not depicting Gaumata as a liberator
of the Medes from the Persian yoke, but as a symbol of evil, the per-
sonification of the Lie. It should not be forgotten that, whoever he may
have been in reality, he was king with the name of Bardiya, son of Cyrus,
the founder of the Persian empire.

It is true that, in passing, Herodotus reports (III 67) that all the nations bar the Persians deplored the death of Smerdis. He does not say,
however, that only the Medes lamented his death. Nowhere does
Herodotus write that during the reign of Gaumata the Medes received
extra privileges. The statement by Herodotus, therefore, that the Persians did not deplore the death of Smerdis, probably does not reflect a
Persian tradition.

The incorrectness of the opinion that Gaumata supported the Median
cause is also evident from the Behistun text. The text says that after the

---

[4] It is true that in the Babylonian version of the Behistun text, Gaumata is called "the
Median (by name) Gaumata, a magus" (BID, 1.15), while in the other versions he is
simply called "the magus Gaumata."

murder of Gaumata, Darius did not receive support from Persis, where Vahyazdata, who called himself Bardiya, assumed kingship.

In an attempt to understand Gaumata's policies, it is necessary to review the social policy of Cambyses. Many historians regard Cambyses as a mad despot, without any rational goals and apt to commit absurd crimes. Greek tradition, which explicitly reported on the boundless despotism and sickly cruelty of Cambyses, is based, in all probability, on a Persian source. A whole series of facts demonstrates the hostility of Darius and his fellow conspirators towards Cambyses. According to Herodotus (III 80), the Persian nobleman Otanes complained about the arbitrariness of Cambyses towards the Persian nobility. He turned towards his companions in the conspiracy against Smerdis with the following words: "You have all seen yourselves to what degree the debauchery of Cambyses had advanced." Otanes also accused Cambyses of the execution without trial of Persian noblemen and described him as a despot who broke with ancestral traditions. Here clearly we hear the disapproval by the Persian nobility of Cambyses' policy. The above words of Otanes, according to Herodotus, were spoken in the discussion of the seven Persians about the most preferable form of government (see below). Herodotus tells that he is sorry to state that the Greeks did not believe that this discussion ever really took place. This led V. V. Struve to the conclusion that in this case a Persian tradition was used as a source. The story may have been made known to Herodotus by Zopyrus, the great-grandson of Megabyzus, who was one of the murderers of Smerdis (Struve 1943:15).

The hostile attitude of the official Persian tradition towards Cambyses can also be noted in the following. While the tomb of Cyrus was guarded as a state sanctuary by specially appointed magi, Cambyses did not even receive an official grave. According to Ctesias (29.13; see König 1972:7), the corpse of Cambyses was buried in Persia. Gaumata, apparently, did not prevent this from happening. E. Herzfeld and W. Kleiss suggested that the unfinished tomb at Takht-i Rustam, near Persepolis, which because of its steps is reminiscent of the tomb of Cyrus, was intended for Cambyses (Herzfeld 1935:36; *idem* 1941:214; Kleiss 1971:157ff.). If this is correct, then its construction was apparently carried out during the lifetime of Cambyses, and remained unfinished after his death.[5] Herodotus (III 64) writes that Cambyses had hoped to die, at an advanced age, at Median Ecbatana, as he thought it was predicted, but it was

---

[5] In that case the transfer of the capital from Pasargadae to Persepolis, realized by Darius I, was already planned during the reign of Cambyses (Schmidt 1953-1970, Vol. I, p. 25).

destined that he would end his life at Syrian Ecbatana. The geography
of ancient Syria, however, is sufficiently well known and such a city in
Syria did not exist. J. C. Greenfield has presented a convincing
hypothesis, namely that in mentioning Syrian Ecbatana reference is
being made to the important town of Hama. Its pronunciation in Greek
is very similar to that of the Median capital (personal communication).
According to Josephus Flavius (*Ant. Jud.* XI 2.2), Cambyses died at
Damascus. Of great interest in this respect is the reference in the
Demotic Chronicle from Egypt about Cambyses' death. According to the
Chronicle, Cambyses died en route, "when he had not yet reached his
country" (DC:30, cols. C.6).

The classical tradition idealizes Cyrus for his humanitarian attitude
towards his subjects. In the work of Herodotus, the figure of Cyrus
receives a morally abstract character (Avery 1972). As discussed above,
according to Herodotus none other than the Persian nobleman Otanes
stepped forward to accuse Cambyses. The opposition between Cyrus and
Cambyses which is sketched in the classical sources is a reflection of the
official Persian tradition. Historians have often used flowery phrases to
describe the extent to which Cyrus embodied "a high moral character",
"the wisdom of a statesman", or "a sharp political vision." During an
international congress at Shiraz in 1971, which was organized to
celebrate the 2,500 year jubilee of the Iranian state, many papers were
presented in which the Cyrus Cylinder was characterized as the first
'Charter of Freedom' in history (see, e.g., Nyberg 1974). Certain con-
tributors particularly emphasized the point that Cyrus, contrary to the
successors of Muhammad, did not enforce his religion on the subject
peoples (see, e.g., Ben-Gurion 1974:127ff.). Such considerations, however, do not take into account the singular characteristics of the ideology
of ancient societies. First of all, ancient religions before the rise of Chris-
tianity were generally not dogmatic and intolerant. It was, therefore,
neither desirable for Cyrus, nor expected of him to persecute the religions
of the subject nations. Just like other Persian kings, he could therefore
seriously and voluntarily worship his own, Iranian gods, and those of the
Greeks, Babylonians and other subjects, and ask their support. In addition, he did not consider some sort of 'Charter of Freedom' for his
Cylinder, which to the contrary is composed in the traditional style of the
Assyrian royal inscriptions; he did not grant his subjects any freedom,
bar the repatriation to their homeland of those who had been forcibly
deported by the Babylonian kings. Their repatriation, however, was to
the benefit of Cyrus' policies.

The question arises as to which social group in Persia would idealize
Cyrus and slander Cambyses. To answer this question, it is necessary to

take into account that the Persian state, which had only shortly before emerged during the reign of Cyrus II, had become a world empire in literally two decades, and that it was still not free from the influence of tribal relations. Persia therefore did not pass through that historical phase which characterized the majority of other ancient states. This historical phase involved a long struggle between the royal power on the one hand, which attempted to establish an unlimited rule, and, on the other hand, the tribal nobility, attempting to retain its traditional privileges.

During the rule of Cyrus this struggle was not really noticeable, because the Persians were subjecting numerous nations, one after the other. The attention of Cyrus was focussed on further conquests which would give the tribal nobility the possibility to enrich themselves and to extend their influence (cf. Briant 1984:114f.). The privileges of the seven most prominent representatives of the Persian nobility, which Herodotus (III 84) related to the dethronement of Smerdis, in fact dated back, as noted long ago, to the reign of Cyrus II (Duncker, Vol. II, 1867, p. 811; Floigl 1881:13, n. 2; Prášek, 1906-1910, Vol. 1, p. 204). From the work of Herodotus it is evident that these privileges were acquired long before the time of Darius, and that the latter only reinforced them. The privileges included the following: the king could only marry a woman who belonged to one of the seven noble families; representatives of these families had the right to enter into the presence of the king unannounced; they had the right to an hereditary governorship in their domains and the right to counsel the king. Finally, they had the privilege to wear the upright tiara.

During the reign of Cyrus these privileges were strictly observed. There was no specific necessity to infringe upon these rights. The Persian state, however, developed further and broke away from the limitations of tribal-patriarchal relationships; many new countries were conquered, but the social base of the state remained, at first, very small. During the reign of Cambyses the opposition between the clan nobility and the royal power, which attempted to abolish the old privileges of the first, came to the surface. The policy of Cambyses was also directed towards this objective. Herodotus (III 89), Diodorus (IX 24) and other classical authors tell that, according to the appreciation by the Persians, Cambyses was strict and arrogant, traits which led them to give him the nickname 'despot'. Cyrus, on the other hand, was called 'father', because of his humanity and his paternal care and love for the Persians.

In respect to the Persians, it is the nobility which should be taken into account when Herodotus tells that the people did not favour the severe character of Cambyses. It should be realized that Herodotus most likely received much of his information about Persian matters from Zopyrus, a representative of the nobility. Cambyses is depicted as a cruel despot, although his deeds, which the tribal nobility regarded as senseless crimes, were directed towards the organization of a strong and centralized state. The movement towards a strong royal power and the abolishment of the privileges of the clan nobility, which are so clearly reflected during the reign of Cambyses, must have had their influence on the course of history both during and after his death.

CHAPTER ELEVEN

THE ACCESSION OF DARIUS I

At the end of the Behistun text (IV 80-88) the names are given of those who, together with Darius, participated in the murder of Gaumata. "Says Darius the king: These are the men who were there when I slew Gaumata the magus ... the men cooperated as my followers: Vindafarna, son of Vayaspara, a Persian; Utana, son of Thukhra, a Persian; Gaubaruva, son of Marduniya, a Persian; Vidarna, son of Bagabigna, a Persian; Bagabukhsha, son of Datuvahya, a Persian; Ardumanish, son of Vahauka, a Persian. Says Darius the king: You who shall be king hereafter, protect well the family of these men."

A much more extensive account of the murder of Smerdis (as Gaumata is called by Herodotus) is presented in Herodotus' *Historiae* (III 70-79). In his report the names of the conspirators, bar one, agree with the list in the Behistun text. In Herodotus' list, Ardumanish is not mentioned at all; in his place, we read the name of Aspathines. The latter was apparently included by Herodotus because he occupied a high position at Darius' court. He is depicted in the reliefs of Naqsh-i Rustam next to the throne of Darius. In his left hand he holds a quiver and bow, in his right a battle axe. Another depiction of Aspathines, but without any inscription, is to be found among the reliefs in the throne hall at Persepolis where he is shown holding a short sword, a bow and a battle axe. At Persepolis a seal impression was found with the legend: Aspathines, the son of Prexaspes. Apparently, he was the son of Prexaspes whom Herodotus named as a trusted courtier of Cambyses. According to W. Hinz, Aspathines was of Median origin and charged with the responsibility of Darius' wardrobe and weaponry (Hinz 1971a:270; *idem* 1973:59). The hypothesis, however, about his ethnic origin could be incorrect, because it is only based on the circumstance that Aspathines is depicted in the reliefs wearing a costume which, according to Hinz, is of the Median type.

In his account of the murder of the magus, Ctesias deviates considerably from both the report by Herodotus and the Behistun version. In Ctesias' list of conspirators only three names are correctly presented. The remaining names are those of representatives of the families which played an important role at the court of Artaxerxes II, where Ctesias himself stayed for a considerable period of time.

The sources describe the circumstances of Gaumata's (Smerdis') death in different ways. But they are unanimous in the report that the murder was committed following a surprise attack by seven Persian noblemen. Ctesias (29.14; König 1972:7-8) adds that Artasyras and Bagapates joined the seven conspirators. They were courtiers of the magus Sphendadates (who is identical with the Gaumata of the Behistun inscription) and they used to be counsellors of Cambyses. Previously Bagapates had carried the weaponry out of the palace. He was able to do this without being noticed because he had the keys of the palace. The magus Sphendadates, Ctesias continues, defended himself against the conspirators with the help of a chair, but he was finally overwhelmed. According to Herodotus (III 78-79), Smerdis (Gaumata) and his brother stubbornly resisted the conspirators, although they were in an extremely unfavourable position. And, although forces were evidently divided in an unequal manner, they killed two Persians. The report by Ammianus Marcellinus (XXIII 6.36), who wrote about the occupation of the throne by seven magi, differs from that by Herodotus. The remaining sources follow Herodotus in their description of the events.

Of particular significance is the question to which social group the six men belonged who, together with Darius, killed Gaumata.

If we believe the *Cyropaedia* of Xenophon (VIII 3.21), Intaphernes (Vindafarna) belonged to a noble family which even by the reign of Cyrus II had attempted to attain independence from royal power. Otanes (Utana), according to Herodotus (III 2, 68), belonged to the clan of the Achaemenids. He and his family were remunerated by Darius with extensive domains in Cappadocia. Strabo (XII 3.15) refers to their residence, called Gaziura, as an old, royal residence. The family of Otanes was related to that of the Persian kings via marital relationships. According to Herodotus (II 1; III 68-69), his sister Cassandane was married to Cyrus II, while his daughter was a wife of Cambyses. Each year the descendants of Otanes received from the king Median clothes and other precious gifts. In addition, Otanes and his family were not compelled to obey the king as long as they did not infringe Persian laws.

Gaubaruva (in Greek transcription: Gobryas) descended from the noble family of the Patischorians. Herodotus (VII 2, 5, 97) stated that his daughter was a wife of Darius and that he was married to a sister of the latter. During the reign of Darius, Gobryas appears to have been the foreman of the royal spearbearers and he is depicted in the reliefs of Naqsh-i Rustam to the left of Darius' throne. As a reward for his participation in the conspiracy, Vidarna (Hydarnes) received an hereditary governorship in Armenia, where his family, according to Strabo (IX 14.15), remained until the time of Antiochus the Great. In the Persepolis Fortification tablets several men are mentioned by this name (in Elamite rendering: Mitarna). D. M. Lewis is inclined to believe that the Mitarna who directed the redeployment of large groups of labourers of the royal household was the same person as the Vidarna of the Behistun text (Lewis 1977:84, n. 14). Bagabukhsha (Megabyzus), if we can believe the *Cyropaedia* of Xenophon (VIII 6.7), was a Persian nobleman, who by the reign of Cyrus II already occupied an important position. As regards Ardumanish, nothing is known about him apart from the information given in the Behistun text. It is possible that he was killed during the fight with the magi. The seventh participant to the conspiracy, Darius, came, as is known, from the clan of the Achaemenids (for an extensive discussion of the seven conspirators, see e.g. Boyce 1982:91ff.; Gschnitzer 1977; Wiesehöfer 1978:170ff.).

It can thus be surmised that the murderers of Gaumata (or at least the majority of them) were representatives of the tribal nobility. It would appear that Darius did not play the main, decisive role in the conspiracy, as he later claims to have done in his Behistun text. According to Herodotus (III 67-72), Otanes was the organizer of the conspiracy, and it was he who won over Gobryas to his plans. Subsequently Intaphernes, Megabyzus and the others joined Otanes. Also Pompeius Trogus states that Otanes played a leading role in the conspiracy. Ctesias says that Darius did not play an important role in the murder of the magus Sphendadates, and it is noticeable that in the list of conspirators his name is given last.

Aeschylus regarded Intaphernes, whom he called Artaphrenes, as the murderer of Mardos (Gaumata). In the Behistun text, Darius himself puts Intaphernes in the foremost place amidst the conspirators. As far as it is possible to judge on the basis of the scholias to Aeschylus' 'The Persians', Hellanicus also regarded Intaphernes as the murderer of Mardos. Apparently, when Aeschylus refers to the murder of Mardos by Artaphrenes and his men "whose lot this was", Darius and the remaining conspirators should be included among the latter. It seems that in the historical tradition, which was known to Aeschylus, Intaphernes was regarded as the main force behind the conspiracy.

In this manner, it is apparent that there is no source, apart from the Behistun text of which the tendentious character is obvious, which indicates a decisive role of Darius in the struggle against Gaumata.

After the murder of Gaumata, the conspirators started to discuss the form of government which they preferred. Herodotus (III 80-84) extensively reports about these talks. The majority of contemporary historians are disinclined to believe that this discussion could have taken place in the Persia of the sixth century B.C. They are of the opinion that the arguments reflect fabrications by Greek authors, made up on the basis of sophistic discussions popular at that time at Athens (see, for example, Duncker 1867, Vol. II, p. 456; Lur'e 1947:63; Margules 1960:21ff.; Prášek 1906-1910, Vol. I, p. 281). According to F. Gschnitzer, the discussion, as presented by Herodotus, is based exclusively on Greek tradition and is presented with an eye on Greek readers (Gschnitzer 1977:31-35). V. V. Struve, however, disputed this opinion by referring to a certain passage in a text from Naqsh-i Rustam (text DNb), which indirectly reflects, according to Struve, the main arguments in the political discussion reported by Herodotus (Struve 1943:12ff.). A. I. Dovatur and I. M. Diakonoff also came to the conclusion that the report by Herodotus originated in a Persian tradition (I. M. Diakonoff 1964:182; Dovatur 1957:138ff., 195ff.). In their recent works certain Western scholars have also hypothesized that the political discussion of the Persian noblemen in its essence reflects historical facts and that it is not a complete fabrication (Apffel 1957; Brannan 1963; Schmitt 1977).

If the concrete historical situation is taken as a starting point, there is not one single point which contradicts a discussion about the political organization. During the reign of Cyrus II the nobility held a series of privileges. During the reign of Cambyses, however, an historically irreversible development commenced towards a more centralized royal authority and towards more independence of the state from the tribal nobility. During the reign of Gaumata the strive between tribal nobility and royal power continued. A clear reflection of this struggle is found in the speech of Otanes, who argues against monarchy. After reminding his noble accomplices to which excesses the insolence of Cambyses had led, Otanes continued: ''And you yourselves suffered from the insolence of the magus.'' This passage from the work of Herodotus (III 80) does not leave any doubt against whom Gaumata was directing his policies. And when Herodotus writes that the magus Smerdis, after he had become king, did not invite the Persian noblemen, this should be seen as him deliberately ignoring the right of the representatives of the tribal nobility to unimpeded access to the king.

It is evident from Otanes' speech that in general the activities of the magus were not without precedents, and that to some degree his policy was a continuation of that conducted by Cambyses. It is significant that Persian tradition, as presented by Otanes, places Cambyses on the same level as the magus Smerdis.

Following the dethronement of Gaumata, Persian tribal nobility ceased to believe that royal power would guarantee their privileges, and they wanted to keep all their power in their own hands. The tribal nobility wanted to install an oligarchy. In the description by Herodotus, however, of the political discussion between the seven conspirators, Otanes is represented as an advocate of democracy. But in reality reference was made to a reinstallation of the traditional tribal democracy, where, under the conditions of community-tribal relations, the popular assembly would inevitably fall under the influence of the nobility. Thus, while the tribal nobility advocated with complete unanimity against the hated Gaumata, they subsequently disagreed as to the form of government following his death.

Finally, however, the following compromise was apparently reached: (1) one of the seven conspirators would be appointed as king by a portent; (2) the new king would uphold the privileges of the tribal nobility, which were established at the time of Cyrus II; (3) in its turn, the nobility would support the king. According to Herodotus, all the conspirators against Smerdis, bar Otanes, wanted to become king. Otanes, who refuted all claims to the throne, demanded for himself and his family a series of additional privileges, which were still maintained at the time of Herodotus.

All classical authors seem to agree as to the manner in which Darius became king. The report by Herodotus (III 85-86) is confirmed even by the quarrelsome criticism of Ctesias. The six pretenders to the throne agreed that the one among their group would become king whose horse at sunrise would neigh before the others. Such a manner of selecting a king, which is attested to by all historical sources except for the Behistun text, is apparently not without precedent. In another passage in his *Historiae* (III 83), Herodotus writes that in Persia the king is either appointed by a portent, or on the basis of a decision of the people (apparently, of the popular assembly). According to the statement provided by Strabo (XV 3.24), the seven Persian families chose Darius as their king. As hypothesized by G. Widengren, the kings of ancient Iran were chosen from amidst certain families. He continues by arguing that the pertinent account by Herodotus is supported by Indian analogies (Widengren 1969:102ff.; *idem* 1974:84ff.; see also Bongard-Levin & Grantovskij 1974:78ff.; Huart & Delaporte 1952:250; von der Osten 1956:70). There is also a Sasanian text from Paikuli which refers to a selection of a king by the nobility. According to Herodotus, a subtle trick by the groom Oibares elevated Darius to royal power.

Darius did not become king according to the rights of succession, but as a representative of the noble conspirators. It is true that in the Behistun text and in other inscriptions he repeatedly points out that royal power belonged to his family. But in that case his father Hystaspes (Vishtaspa) or his grandfather Arsames should have become king, rather than Darius. It is difficult to accept the opinion which is often presented in literature, namely that Vishtaspa refused the throne because of his age (see, e.g., Nöldeke 1887:30; Sykes 1921, Vol. I, p. 160). In 522 B.C., he commanded the suppression of the revolt in Parthia and Hyrcania, and at that time Vishtaspa's father, Arshama (Arsames), was still alive. In 530 B.C., when Cyrus set off for his campaign against the Massagetae, Darius was approximately twenty years old. Consequently, when Darius became king, he was not much older than 27 or 28. In addition, as is evident from the work of Herodotus (I 209), Darius was the eldest son of Vishtaspa, thus in 522 B.C. the latter cannot have been much older than 55, which is not a very advanced age. None of the classical writers mentions anything about the royal origin of Darius. In fact, all sources emphatically report that Darius, until his accession to the throne, was a man with an insignificant position. For instance, according to Herodotus (III 139), Darius "was of no particular importance" before he became king. The fact that Darius in almost all of his inscriptions is forced to write that he was a legitimate king, testifies to the strong political struggle which coincided with his accession. And everywhere Darius presents, as the first and major argument for the fact that he is a legitimate king, the point that Ahura Mazda had expressed the wish that "kingship came" to him. Darius says: "This was the wish of Ahuramazda: he chose me as (his sole) man on all the earth (and) he made me king in all the earth" (DSf text from Susa). It is true that Darius was born in the royal clan of the Achaemenids, but to this clan also belonged, for instance, Otanes, who thus had the same rights to the throne as Darius.

In order to legitimize his power, Darius married Atossa, a daughter of Cyrus, and all the other women from the harem of Cambyses and Gaumata (previously Darius had married a daughter of Gobryas, who gave him three sons). The crafty and power loving Atossa obtained a very influential position at Darius' court, and became all powerful. On the accession of Darius to the throne it would appear that she played a not insignificant role.

The majority of the representatives of the nobility agreed to the accession of Darius. Intaphernes, however, did not intend to give up his claims to the throne. Herodotus (III 118-19) reports his tragic death and that of his family, after he had forcibly tried to enter into the royal quarters. Darius was at first afraid that Intaphernes' deed indicated another plot by the six remaining conspirators against Gaumata. Summoning each of them, one after the other, and finding out that the activities of Intaphernes were not agreed upon by the others, Darius acquiesced, and only then ordered the arrest of Intaphernes and his subsequent execution. He was apparently of the opinion that the latter had infringed the agreement which had been made between the nobility and the royal authority, and therefore deserved a severe punishment. According to V. V. Struve, Megabyzus also did not agree to the accession to the throne by Darius and did not shrink away from a struggle with the king (Struve 1943:15). However, in spite of an attempt by certain representatives of the tribal nobility to win, via a palace coup, the throne which had been taken by Darius, the nobility were in general faithful to their new monarch. The subject peoples and the masses of the Persian people, however, reacted in a very different manner to Darius' accession.

In paragraph 14 of the Behistun inscription (I 67-71), there is a summary of the negative policies of Gaumata, from the point of view of the composer of the text, and a survey of the positive policies of Darius himself. The study of this particular passage has a history of more than a hundred years. The first student of the text, H. Rawlinson, noted the exceptional difficulty in the interpretation of the passage (Rawlinson 1847:206). To date the Iranists and Assyriologists have at length studied this fragment, but there are still disagreements concerning its translation, not to mention the many differences in interpretation. In the Persian version of the text, paragraph 14 is preserved completely; in the Elamite version it is almost complete, while in the Akkadian text the paragraph is partly destroyed. The Aramaic version of the relevant paragraph only contains two words.

It is here impossible to present an analysis of the pertinent passage, and we will only give a translation (see for literature: Dandamaev 1976:186-198; M. M. Diakonoff 1961:368-372; see also Boroljubov 1974:110; Hinz 1963:234; *idem* 1973:52ff.; Klima 1967:37ff.; Schmitt 1967:57). In the Persian version of the text Darius states: "The kingdom which had been taken away from our family, this I restored at its proper place. I restored it at the place where it was before. The sanctuaries which the magus Gaumata had destroyed, I restored. I returned the fields, herds, slaves and goods (which belonged) to the people-army. These had been taken away by the magus Gaumata. I re-established the land, both Persia, Media and the other lands, as before. I re-established what had been taken away. I did this by the favour of Ahuramazda. I strove to re-establish our house at its former place. By the favour of Ahuramazda I strove, so that the magus Gaumata did not remove our house." According to the Elamite version, Darius "restored the pastures, herds, slaves and goods which belonged to the people ..." In the Aramaic version only the words are preserved which are translated "their goods and their houses." On the basis of the new edition of the Akkadian text of the Behistun text, prepared on the basis of squeezes made by G. G. Cameron, and which have not been published earlier, the relevant passage can be thus read: "I gave back to the people-army [cattle, sheep, fields, hired labourers, allotments of the] bow[1], which this magus Gaumata had taken away'' (BID, 1.26). Within the square brackets a number of words are given, the Akkadian equivalents of which are badly preserved and do not allow an undisputed reading. If the new reading of the pertinent passage in the Akkadian version is accepted, it is evidently necessary to hypothesize that in this case the Babylonian translator presented a somewhat different report of events than presented in the Old Persian and Elamite versions. But, while it was possible to take away herds and fields from the people or the army, it is difficult to understand how people could be deprived of hired labourers, who worked according to contract and for wages. Of course, it was possible to deprive soldiers of their fiefs. It is still difficult to understand, however, for what purposes Gaumata would have executed such a policy in Babylonia during the time of his short reign.

In any case, it is clear from the Aramaic version of the text that Gaumata took away from 'the people' their movables and houses and that Darius restored these to their former owners. Further finds and research can add additional support to this hypothesis, but they can hardly alter it.

The question arises as to whom Darius returned the goods which Gaumata had previously confiscated.

It would be erroneous to regard Gaumata as some sort of revolutionary, a predecessor of Mazdak, the leader of the revolting masses in Sasanian Iran, and as an advocate of the interests of the suppressed lowest classes of society, an enemy of the feudal property owners and the Achaemenid state itself, as supposed by E. Herzfeld, F. W. König and certain other scholars. According to them, the Persian state at the time of Gaumata was ruled by ''chaos, death and the rule of the fist'', because Gaumata, in order to win the lowest classes of society for his cause, strove towards a radical rearrangement of the old social order. The above mentioned scholars were of the opinion that paragraph 14 of the Behistun text, and the reports by Herodotus regarding the temporary exemption from tax-paying and military duties, indicate that Gaumata confiscated the land and feudal entourage of the nobility (which the authors identify with the Old Persian word $k\bar{a}ra$), and also that Gaumata abolished the natural levies provided by the serfs to their feudal lords in the form of animals, wine, grain, etc. (Herzfeld 1933:138ff.; *idem* 1938:52; *idem* 1947a, Vol. I, p. 209; Junge 1944:43, 48, 166; König 1938a:52ff., 71ff.).

According to E. Herzfeld, common folk did not play any role in the revolts of the year 522-521 B.C., and were only passive onlookers. This

---

[1] The allotments which the Achaemenid administration granted to its soldiers for their services as bowmen in the army.

situation, according to Herzfeld, not only occurred in Persia, but also in Babylonia where common people did not revolt against Darius. It was the army and the nobility who rebelled (Herzfeld 1930a:34ff.). The question arises, however, as to which group gave its support to Darius, if the common people remained indolent onlookers, and the army and nobility rose against him. If Gaumata stepped forward towards the defence of the suppressed masses and against the feudal landlords, why did the common people fail to revolt against Darius, the enemy of Gaumata?

In reality the word *kāra* is a general term, which covers not only the nobility, but also the agriculturalists, village dwellers and soldiers, which means all those who were free members of society in which family and clan relationships were of great significance². It is therefore difficult to agree with those scholars who take the word *kāra* as only referring to the masses of serfs, thus suggesting that Gaumata deprived the Persian farmers of their goods, while Darius restored them to their owners. According to these scholars, Gaumata exercised a policy which was to the benefit of the nobility and Median priesthood, but went against the interests of the Persian people, destroying their temples, confiscating their pastures and herds, pillaging their houses, taking away from the villagers their wives and children, in order to make them work in the royal household (Galling 1937:37; Hermes 1938:443; Hertel 1924b:42; King and Thompson 1907:xl; V. O. Tjurin 1951:31ff.; *idem* 1956:521).

Some scholars seek the motive for Gaumata's coup in a religious struggle between the Persians and Median magi. They regard the usurpation as a reflection of the stubborn resistance of the priesthood against Zoroastrianism, deservedly punished by Darius, who, according to these scholars, was a pupil of Zarathustra (Bertin 1890:821; Hertel 1924b:3ff.; Herzfeld 1930b:1-11; Thumb 1902:392). To support this hypothesis the assumption is brought forward that Achaemenid kings carried two names, one of which was of a religious nature, and the other a throne name. In the Zoroastrian 'Bundahishn', and in Yasht 13 of the Avesta, reference is made to *Spentōdāta*, the son of Vishtaspa (the protector of Zarathustra), and as a result, therefore, the above mentioned scholars identify *Spentōdāta* with Darius and regard this as his religious name which he carried as a 'Mazdayasnian' believer. These scholars are of the

---

² W. Widengren, on the basis of an hypothesis by W. Eilers which was presented at a congress of German Orientalists, suggested that the word *kāra* is the Old Persian equivalent of Median *spāda* (Widengren 1968:533). In my opinion, however, the difference between both terms is not merely dialectical: *spāda* referred to the professional army, while *kāra* denoted the militia. It may be important to draw attention to the fact that amidst the Iranian languages there is at least one in which the two pertinent words, Old Persian *kāra* and Median *spāda*, are reflected, namely Sogdian. In Sogdian there is the word *sp'd*, 'army', and the word *k'r*, 'people' (information provided by V. A. Livšits).

opinion that the magus Sphendadates in Ctesias' *Persica* is in fact Darius, whom the Greek author called a magus by mistake (Herzfeld 1947a, Vol. I, p. 95; Hoffmann-Kutschke 1907:187ff.; Hüsing 1933:59; König 1938a:278, 334). It remains difficult, however, to find any convincing argument to support this hypothesis[3].

If we accept the widely accepted opinion that Gaumata persecuted the religious customs of the land and destroyed its social institutions, while Darius restored the old order, then the official version of events, as

---

[3] Some Achaemenid kings did in fact adopt new names after their coronation. R. Schmitt recently reviewed all these cases. Josephus Flavius (*Ant. Jud.* XI 6.1) wrote that "when Xerxes died, royal power was transferred to his son Cyrus, whom the Greeks call Artaxerxes" (he refers to Artaxerxes I). According to Ctesias (*Persica* XV 50, 55), the satrap Ochus (*Vahuka* in Old Persian) of Hyrcania was crowned under the name of Darius II, and Arsaces (in another rendering he is called Arses) adopted the name of Artaxerxes II when he succeeded to the throne. These changes of name are also reflected in the Babylonian texts. In LBAT 1426, reference is made to "Umakush, called Darius." The date formula of the Babylonian astronomical text LBAT 162, mentions "Arshu called Artakshatsu the king." The text here refers to Artaxerxes II. Diodorus (XV 93.1) writes that Ochus changed his name into Artaxerxes III when he succeeded to the throne. Babylonian astronomical tablets (LBAT 1394, etc.) say about him: "Umakush (that is, Vahuka, Ochus) called Artakshatsu." It is clear from the work of Curtius Rufus (IV 1.10) that Darius III carried another name before he was crowned king. According to the above mentioned astronomical texts (LBAT 193-194), he was called Artashatu ("Artashatu called Darius the king") before his coronation. In this connection R. Schmitt correctly remarked that despite Justinus' remarks (X 3.3-5), Codomannus was his sobricquet, and not his real name. Finally, it is well known that Bessus declared himself the new king with the name of Artaxerxes (IV). On the basis of all these data, R. Schmitt came to the following conclusions: the adoption of a crown name by the Persian kings is well attested for the period from Artaxerxes I to Darius III. And although there is no direct evidence for a change of name by the Achaemenid kings before Artaxerxes I, it can be suggested that the names of Darius I and Xerxes were also throne names; in all likelihood, the custom to adopt a throne name dates back to Darius I (Schmitt 1982:92-93; cf. Frye 1984:106). This hypothesis seems somewhat categorical. First of all, there is no direct evidence to suggest that the names of Darius and Xerxes were in fact throne names. Xerxes was succeeded by his son Artaxerxes, who, if Josephus Flavius can be believed, used to be called Cyrus. It is difficult to say which sources were used by Josephus Flavius when he stated this point. As is known, he basically used Biblical sources in which the Achaemenid chronology is often unreliable. In any case, the Greek authors were much better acquainted with Persian affairs than Josephus Flavius. These Greeks, who were contemporaries of the Achaemenids, do not refer to the point that Artaxerxes carried the name of Cyrus before he became king. The adoption of throne names by Darius II, Artaxerxes III, Darius III and Bessus may have been isolated phenomena, based on exceptional circumstances, and not indicative of the custom that every king should choose a new name at his coronation (cf. Hertel 1924:64). None of them was the legitimate successor to the throne; Darius II was the son of a Babylonian concubine; Artaxerxes III was not the eldest of the royal princes; while Darius III and Bessus were only distantly related to the royal family. It should be admitted, however, that Artaxerxes II, who was the legitimate successor to the throne, as pointed out above, carried another name before his coronation. It is possible that a future edition of the extensive collection of Babylonian astronomical texts, kept in the British Museum, will clarify this point, because their date formulas include considerable information about the rule of the Achaemenid kings (see the preliminary study by Sachs, 1977:129ff.).

reported in the Behistun text, remains incomprehensible. In this text it is unequivocally stated that after the coup by Gaumata "all the people became rebellious against Cambyses, and defected to his (that is, Gaumata's) side, both in Persia, and Media, and the other lands." If Darius returned the confiscated goods to the commoners, it remains in-comprehensible why this benevolent deed should have been met with widespread revolts all over the Empire.

We should not be surprised that the composer of the Behistun text in his report of the negative measures by Gaumata and of his own positive activities limits himself to general remarks, without trying to be more concrete about which social group had their goods confiscated by Gaumata and to whom Darius returned these goods. Instead of shedding more light upon this cardinal question, the Behistun text sketches Darius as a protector of the whole community, and not of some specific social group. Darius laid claim to the fact that he put an end to political, social and religious anarchy and reinstated the just principles of state rule. As remarked by I. M. Diakonoff, the representatives of the tribal nobility were the victims of the reforms by Gaumata (I. M. Diakonoff 1956:433). Namely it was from the latter that Gaumata confiscated their goods, although the Behistun text sketches him as an enemy not so much of the nobility, rather than the population as a whole. The Persian commoners supported Gaumata, because his reforms were to the benefit of the ma-jority of the population, as the abolishment of the privileges of the tribal nobility led to the emancipation of the masses from the domination by this nobility.

CHAPTER TWELVE

REVOLTS IN PERSIA AND OTHER COUNTRIES

Immediately after Darius had come to power the Elamites and Babylonians started a revolt (for the chronology of these revolts, see Balcer 1987:133ff.; Borger 1982:113ff.; Nagel 1983:175ff.; Vogelsang 1986:127-131). The revolt in Elam did not apparently involve the large masses of the population, and was therefore easily suppressed. Darius reports in the Behistun inscription (I 72-83): "After that I had killed the magus Gaumata, one man by name of Açina, the son of Upadarma, he rose up in Elam. To the people he thus spoke: I am king in Elam. Afterwards the Elamites became rebellious, and went over to Açina. He became king in Elam ... After that I sent a messenger[1] to Elam. Açina was led to me bound; I slew him."

However, the revolt in Mesopotamia, in the centre of the Empire, was much more dangerous. Herodotus (III 150) writes that the Babylonians rose against Darius immediately after he had deposed Smerdis. If we believe the Old Persian and Elamite versions of the Behistun text, a certain Nidintu-bel, son of Ainaira, pretended to be the son of the last Babylonian king, Nabonidus, and began to rule under the name of Nebuchadnezzar (III). It cannot be excluded that he really was a son of Nabonidus, only seventeen years having elapsed after the latter's overthrow. In the Behistun relief Nidintu-bel is depicted as a man at an advanced age. It is interesting also to note that Darius refrained from showing Nidintu-bel, after his arrest, to the people, as he was used to do with those who pretended to belong to ancient dynasties.

An unexpected piece of information about Nidintu-bel is contained in the newly edited Akkadian version of the Behistun text. There (line 31) the following is said about him: "Nidintu-bel, the son of Kin-zēr [...], the *zazakku*[2]." E. von Voigtlander, the editor of the Akkadian version, writes that the word *hānara* (cf. the *Ainaira* of the Old Persian variant) in Elamite is possibly an occupational term (BID:20). It remains difficult to comprehend, however, why in the Elamite and Old Persian versions it is clearly stated that Ainaira was the father of Nidintu-bel.

---

[1] As reported in the Elamite and Akkadian versions of the text. The Old Persian version remains silent about the dispatch of a messenger.

[2] A highly placed official of the fiscal apparatus.

According to Darius, "the whole Babylonian people went over to Nidintu-bel. Babylon became rebellious; he seized the kingdom in Babylon" (DB I 79-81). By October 3, 522 B.C., Nidintu-bel had been proclaimed king, as is attested to by a document from Sippar (Nbk, 1). Other documents which date to his reign come from Babylon and Borsippa. They give Nidintu-bel the title of "king of Babylon, king of the lands."

Darius personally led the campaign against the insurgents. The first battle took place on December 13, 522 B.C., on the banks of the River Tigris. In the Old Persian and Elamite versions of the Behistun inscription (I 84-89) it is stated: "The army of Nidintu-bel held the Tigris ... The river was navigable. Thereupon I put my army on inflated skins, others on camels, and for the remaining I sent horses. Ahuramazda bore me aid. By the favour of Ahuramazda we crossed the Tigris. There I decisively defeated the army of Nidintu-bel." The Akkadian variant of the text, as presented in the new edition, contains an interesting deviation: "I embarked the army upon leather boats. Together with horses and camels we crossed the Tigris" (line 35). In other words, the horsemen were also transported to the other side of the river with the help of boats. The editors of the Old Persian and Elamite versions of the text apparently did not clearly comprehend the military activities in Babylonia, and were of the opinion that the army had crossed the river on inflated skins and camel back.

Five days later, on December 18, Darius won another victory at the site of Zazana along the Euphrates. Part of the Babylonian army was "thrown into the water, (and) the water carried them away" (DB I 91-92). Contrary to the Old Persian and Elamite versions of the text, the Babylonian variant (line 38), drawing up the results of Darius' campaign against Babylonia, says that: "we killed all of them (namely, those on the side of Nidintu-bel), and none of them was taken prisoner."

Nidintu-bel fled to Babylon "with a few horsemen", but he was soon captured by the Persians. In the Old Persian and Elamite versions of the Behistun text it is stated, at the end of the report on the revolt in Babylon, that "subsequently I executed this Nidintu-bel in Babylon." The Babylonian version (line 40) is more informative: "Afterwards in Babylon I impaled this Nidintu-bel, and the men who were with him. In total I executed 49 people. This is what I did in Babylon."

While Darius was engaged in the punitive expedition in Babylonia and subsequently spent about three months, until the beginning of February, 521 B.C., in all probability in the palace of Nebuchadnezzar II in Babylon, messengers arrived from all corners of the Empire with disquieting news. Persia, Media, Elam, Margiana, Parthia, Sattagydia, the

Saka tribes of West Central Asia, and finally Egypt had risen in rebellion against him. What followed was a long and bloody strife in order to bring the Achaemenid empire back to its former position.

In Persia itself, a certain Vahyazdata rose as a competitor to Darius, under the name of Bardiya, son of Cyrus. He found widespread support among the population, and he succeeded in winning the southern and southeastern lands of the Iranian Plateau as far as Arachosia in modern southeast Afghanistan.

The Behistun inscription does not give any clear information as regards the commencement of Vahyazdata's uprising. However, it is evident from this source that the Persians rose between October and December of the year 522 B.C., when the main forces of Darius were engaged in Babylonia. Towards the second half of December 522 B.C. the rebellion had grown to such an extent, that the soldiers of Vahyazdata fought battles in Arachosia, at a distance of hundreds of kilometres from Persia.

On December 29, 522 B.C., the forces of Vahyazdata joined in battle with the army of Darius, at the fortress of Kapishakanish. Darius' army was commanded by Vivana, a Persian. The battle, in which 303 supporters of Vahyazdata were killed, did not prove to be decisive for either party, in spite of the statement in the Behistun inscription that the rebels were totally defeated. Vivana only won a decisive victory on February 21, 521 B.C., in the region of Gandutava in Arachosia. In this battle a number of 4579 rebels were killed. "Thereupon the man, who was the chief of the army which was sent by Vahyazdata against Vivana, fled together with a few horsemen. He fled towards the fortress of Arshada in Arachosia. Subsequently Vivana with his forces followed and captured him and the men who were his foremost followers, (and) executed (them)" (DB III 69-75).

In Persia itself, however, Vahyazdata still held a dominant position. On May 24, 521 B.C., the rebels joined in battle at the town of Rakha in Persia with the army of Darius, which was commanded by Artavardiya. During this battle Vahyazdata lost 4,404 of his men. But in spite of Darius' usual statement about his victory, the battle proved to be inconclusive. Artavardiya achieved a better result with a victory near the mountain of Parga, as late as July 15, 521 B.C. Of the rebels, 6,246 were killed and 4,464 were captured. Vahyazdata himself was also arrested. Together with 52 of his closest followers he was impaled at the town of Uvadaicaja[3] in Persia. Thus, the revolt which started approximately at

---

[3] This was apparently an important settlement, because the Behistun text does not relate its location, as it tends to do with little known towns. In the Elamite version the

the same time as the two other great popular uprisings, namely in Margiana and Media, was crushed after a period of eight months.

In historical literature the opinion is widely held that in these difficult times for Darius, the Persians remained loyal to him and did their utmost to help him to victory, while Vahyazdata was supported by the Utians and other nomadic peoples, who were later excluded from the confederacy of Persia and regarded as mere subjects and obliged to pay royal taxes (Junge 1944:173, n. 38; Markwart 1901:30; Prášek 1906-1910, Vol. I, pp. 201ff.; *idem*, Vol. II, p. 52). This hypothesis is presented in the following manner: it is said in the Behistun text that before his uprising Vahyazdata was living in the district of Yautiya in Persia. In the work of Herodotus (III 93) it is stated that the Utians, together with the Sagartians, Mukoi, and a series of other peoples were incorporated into the fourteenth tax paying unit of the Achaemenid empire. On the basis of this point the conclusion was drawn that until the uprising by Vahyazdata, Yautiya belonged to Persia, and that subsequently it was set apart because of the rebellion.

The suggestion, however, that Vahyazdata was only supported by the Utians is contradicted by the data contained in the Behistun inscription. "Vahyazdata lived in the town of Tarava[4], in the district of Yautiya in Persia. He made the second uprising in Persia ... Thereafter the Persian people ... became rebellious, and defected to Vahyazdata. He became king in Persia ... (and) made Persia rebellious" (III 22-27; IV 28). When Darius' general Artavardiya arrived in Persia, Vahyazdata "went with his army to the town of Rakha in Persia", to join battle (III 34-35). Subsequently Vahyazdata marched towards Paishiyauvada, where one year previously Gaumata had risen. "From there he assembled an army (and) again directed himself to join in battle with Artavardiya" (III 42-44). In the conclusion to his report on the quelling of Vahyazdata's rebellion, Darius states: "This is what was done by me in Persia" (III 53). The discussed passages leave no doubt that the uprising by Vahyazdata is described in the Behistun text as a revolt which took place in Persia.

Old Persian *Uvādaicaya* corresponds to Matezziš, which is often referred to in the Fortification Tablets from Persepolis (PF 741, 760 etc.). According to these texts, also the king went there sometimes. Hallock states that it was "the most important site, after Persepolis, in the Persepolis area" (Hallock 1985:595). R. Zadok has proposed that the name of *Uvādaicaya* is also attested to in nine Babylonian documents from the early Achaemenid period, namely in the Babylonian transcription of *Ḫumadēšu* (Zadok 1976:69-70; see also Stolper 1984:306).

[4] This must be the town of Taruana in Carmania, referred to by Ptolemaeus (Poebel 1938:286).

In the Behistun text special attention is drawn to the fact that the revolt by Vahyazdata spread beyond the borders of Persia. Vahyazdata not only managed to extend his control over Persia, but also over Carmania, Drangiana, Gedrosia, and certain parts of Media, Arachosia and Sattagydia.

Concerning Vahyazdata's revolt, the Old Persian and Elamite versions of the Behistun text (III 25-28) tell in particular that "subsequently the Persian people-army, which (resided) in (their) houses and (which) previously had come from Yada, became rebellious from me (and) defected to Vahyazdata." The Babylonian version (line 72) contains the following phrase: "Thereupon the Persian people, as much as there were at the palace of Babylon (and which) before had come to me from Anshan, turned against me and defected to the side of Vahyazdata." If this reading is correct, the question arises as to how the Persian army, garrisoned at the Babylonian palace, could choose the side of a rebel who had his stronghold in Persia. Further, Darius states in the Old Persian version (III 28-29): "Subsequently I sent (against Vahyazdata) the Persian and Median army which was with me." The Elamite version says: "Then I sent the small Persian army which was in the palace (?) and which had not defected from me and the Median army which was with me." The Babylonian text (lines 72-73) relates: "Thereupon I sent to Persia another, small Persian army which had not risen against me, and a Median army which (was) with me." There are more differences between the various variants of the report on Vahyazdata's revolt in the Behistun text. For instance, in the Persian variant the district of Gandutava, where one of the battles between the adherents of Vahyazdata and the army of Darius was fought, is not further specified. According to the Elamite text, however, the district was situated in Arachosia, while the Babylonian version (line 81) tells that it was located in Sattagydia (cf. Vogelsang 1985:79-81; *idem* 1987:186). At the end of the report on the suppression of the revolt by Vahyazdata in the regions outside Persia, Darius tells in the Old Persian and Elamite versions of the text: "This is what was done by me in Arachosia", while in the Babylonian variant he says: "This is what was done by me in Sattagydia and Arachosia."

In any case, the Persian people showed strong support for Vahyazdata. A. T. Olmstead wrote that Vahyazdata was not an 'Aryan', because in the Behistun relief he is depicted with a low, flat nose, a round head and a chin without beard (Olmstead 1948:111). The Behistun text, however (cf. the Babylonian variant, line 71), makes it very clear that he was a Persian[5], and his name has a well-established Iranian etymology

---

[5] According to K. Hoffmann, Vahyazdata was a Persian, to whom Persia was much obliged for the spread on its territory of Zoroastrianism. Vahyazdata sent his troops to

('created by the best among the gods', according to V. A. Livšits). Apparently, Vahyazdata adopted to some degree the political programme of his predecessor, Gaumata, because both stepped forward under the name of Bardiya.

As regards the Utians, it still remains unclear whether they participated in the uprising by Vahyazdata or not. According to the Behistun text, Vahyazdata resided prior to his revolt in the district of Yautiya, but commenced his uprising, so it seems, at the town of Uvadaicaya, where he was also, much later, executed. Evidently, it would have been easier to proclaim himself a son of Cyrus in a strange town, rather than in his own land, where he would have been known. In addition, the identification itself of Yautiya with the Utians is disputed. According to E. A. Grantovskij, this identification is without foundation, because the Utians were not an Iranian people, while Yautiya was inhabited by Iranians (Grantovskij 1962:239ff.). E. Herzfeld also suggested that the Utians were of non-Iranian origin (Herzfeld 1968:301).

The crushing of Vahyazdata's revolt constituted a major victory for Darius, and resulted in all of Persia coming into his hands. But in other lands the uprisings continued. A certain Martiya, a Persian, and a son of Cincikhri, who used to live in the Persian town of Kuganaka, had risen in Elam and told the people: "I am Imanish[6], king in Elam." According to the Behistun text, the Elamites became afraid when they heard that Darius at that time was not far from Elam, and "they seized Martiya, who was their chief, and killed him" (DB II 11-13).

At the time when the authority of Darius in Elam was re-established, almost all of Media fell into the hands of Fravartish. He rose under the name of Khshathrita, from the old family of the Median king Cyaxares. Fravartish managed to extend his control, in addition to Media, over the territories of former Assyria, Armenia, Parthia and Hyrcania. Contrary to the opinion of certain scholars who regard the uprising of Fravartish as a revolt by the Median aristocracy, this was a massive popular movement (I. M. Diakonoff 1956:436-440). According to the Behistun text (II 17ff.), "the Median people who were in (their) houses (?), turned against me (namely, Darius), and defected to the side of Fravartish. He became king in Media."

Darius sent his general Vidarna against the insurgents: "Thereupon this Vidarna with his army marched off. When he arrived in Media, he joined battle with the Medes near the town of Marush, in Media. He

---

Arachosia against Vivana, because he regarded Arachosia as his "religious homeland" (Hoffmann 1979:92; see also Gnoli 1983:124-125).

[6] In the Elamite version Imanish is called Ummanish, which is apparently the name of an earlier Elamite king, Humban-nikash (cf. I. M. Diakonoff 1956:276, 456).

who was chief of the Medes, he at that time was not there'' (DB II 23-24).
This battle was fought on January 12, 521 B.C. Following the words of
Darius, his ''army heavily defeated the rebellious army'', killing 3,827
people and seizing 4,329 men. But in reality the battle was indecisive, a
point shown by the fact that for a number of months Vidarna refrained
from further skirmishes, that is, until Darius arrived from Babylon in
Media with the main forces. Concerning this point it is stated in the Old
Persian version of the Behistun text (II 27-29): ''Thereafter my army
waited for me in the district of Kampanda in Media, until I arrived in
Media.'' At this passage the Elamite version states: ''Thereupon my army remained inactive, and waited for me in the district of Kampanda in
Media.'' The Babylonian version (line 47) here reports the following:
''Thereupon Vidarna did not undertake another campaign against
Media. At the town of Kampanda, which lies in Media, they waited for
me until I arrived in Media. Subsequently they came to me in Ecbatana.''
    Darius decided to lead the crushing of the dangerous Median revolt
personally. At the same time, Median troops which had remained loyal
to Darius, were sent to Persia to take part in the struggle against
Vahyazdata.
    On May 8, 521 B.C., the decisive battle took place at the place of Kun-
durush, in Media. The rebels were defeated. Of the Medes, some 34,425
men were killed and 18,000 were taken prisoner.
    Fravartish, however, succeeded in making his escape, together with
some of his adherents, and they fled to the district of Raga in the extreme
east of Media. But at some point during the month of June of the same
year he was seized and led to Darius, who dealt most severely with him,
by cutting off his nose, his ears and tongue and then putting out one of
his eyes. Afterwards they led Fravartish in chains to Ecbatana where he
was impaled. Thence were also sent his closest adherents, who were imprisoned in the fortress. Subsequently they were flayed and their skins
were filled with straw. These were exposed on the wall of the fortress, as
a warning. The severeness directed towards the leaders of the revolt, and
the full description of the details of their execution, combined with the
great number of Medes killed and captured, testify to the fact that this
revolt was one of the biggest, and most dangerous for Darius. This point
is also attested to by the fact that of the many revolts which broke out at
the commencement of Darius' reign, Herodotus (I 130) only knew about
the uprisings in Media and in Babylonia. After the crushing of the revolt,
which had lasted for more than seven months, Media gradually lost her
position as a privileged satrapy.
    Related to Fravartish' uprising was another revolt, namely by the
people of Sagartia in western Media and in the former lands of Assyria,

with its centre at Arbela (the Zikirtu of the Assyrian sources (Grantovskij 1962:250; Herzfeld 1968:301; Nagel 1975:364). Sometimes Sagartia is located to the east of Media, but it seems to me that the Behistun text refers to a revolt in a district with Arbela as its centre (cf. Eilers 1987:701). Darius states: "One man by name Çiçantakhma, a Sagartian, became rebellious towards me. He thus addressed the people: I am king in Sagartia, of the family of Cyaxares. Thereupon I dispatched a Persian and Median army. I appointed a Mede by name Takhmaspada, my servant, as their commander ... Thereupon Takhmaspada marched off with the army and joined battle with Çiçantakhma. Ahuramazda bore me aid. By the favour of Ahuramazda my army defeated the rebellious army, seized Çiçantakhma (and) led (him) to me. Subsequently I cut off his nose and ears, and put out one of his eyes. He was kept in chains at the gates of my residence. All the people saw him. Thereupon I impaled him at Arbela ... This is what was done by me in Media" (DB II 78-92). According to the Babylonian version, this battle was fought on Tashritu 5 (i.e. October 10), 521 B.C.

Meanwhile, Darius' father Vishtaspa, who probably was governor in Parthia and Hyrcania which together formed one satrapy, had, for several months, refrained from joining battle with the rebels in these lands who had gone over to the side of Fravartish. Darius tells: "Parthia and Hyrcania became rebellious from me and defected to the side of Fravartish. Vishtaspa, my father, was in Parthia. The people abandoned him, (and) became rebellious" (DB II 92-94). A battle at the place of Vishpauzatish in Parthia, on March 8, 521 B.C., brought neither of the two contesting parties a decisive victory, in spite of the assurance by Darius about a full victory of his army over the rebels. In this battle, 6,346 rebels were killed and 4,336 were captured. Vishtaspa had to wait three months, until the summer of 521 B.C., for assistance from the side of Darius. On July 11, 521 B.C., the revolt was finally crushed at the place of Patigrabana, in Parthia. Of the rebels, 6,570 men were killed, and 4,192 were taken prisoner. Eighty men, together with the leader of the revolt (his name is not mentioned in the text), were executed.

Another revolt, in Armenia, also caused Darius much trouble. Darius' generals, the Armenian Dadarshish and the Persian Vaumisa, had attempted, without success, to crush the revolt. A large battle was fought as early as December 31, 522 B.C., at the place of Izala, in the former territory of Assyria, where the rebels had also established their control. Darius' army was apparently defeated, although the Behistun text relates that the rebels were totally beaten. Subsequently the generals of Darius refrained from further military activities until May 20, 521 B.C., when they joined battle with their adversaries at the place of Zuzu in Armenia.

Ten days later, at the stronghold of Tigra in Armenia, another battle was fought. Darius' army, however, did not succeed in completely breaking the resistance of the rebels. As a result, Darius sent new reinforcements to his army in Armenia. On June 20, 521 B.C., at the fortress of Uyama in Armenia, the rebels were conclusively defeated by the troops of Dadarshish, while some days previously, on June 11, Vaumisa had won a decisive victory over the rebels in a battle in the district of Autiyara. In all, Armenia was only subjected after seven months of fighting. In this period, five major battles occurred which cost the Armenians 5,097 people dead, and 2,203 men captured.

The scholarly world has presented different opinions as regards the uprising in Armenia. V. V. Struve suggested that the insurgents were not Armenians, but Scythian tribes that had invaded the country. I. M. Diakonoff, however, considered that the insurgents were Armenians. According to G. A. Kapantsjan, the revolt in Armenia was a movement of the Ḫaia tribes (I. M. Diakonoff 1956:359; Kapantsjan 1956:155ff.; Struve 1946a:31ff.). The reason for the dispute is the fact that the Behistun text does not name the insurgent people by name, nor does it present the name of their leader. The continuing and stubborn resistance of the rebels, however, testifies to the fact that this revolt was supported by a large segment of the local population, namely the Armenians. When the Behistun text relates that Armenia was seized by revolt, then it is likely that the composer of the text did not consider it necessary to mention specially the ethnic identity of the rebels, because this must have been self-evident.

While Darius was engaged in crushing the revolts in Armenia and other countries, the Babylonians made another attempt to gain independence. This time the insurgence was led by a certain Arakha, the son of Haldita, who claimed to be Nebuchadnezzar (IV), son of Nabonidus. In the Old Persian and Elamite versions of the Behistun text he is called an Armenian, while in the Akkadian version he is referred to as an Urartian. In the Old Persian variant (III 79-83) it is said: "From the district of Dubala he thus lied to the people." Subsequently: "the Babylonian people went over to the side of Arakha. He seized Babylon and became king in Babylon." The Elamite text specifies that Dubala was a town in Babylonia. Instead of mentioning the town of Dubala, the Babylonian text (line 85) tells, rather unexpectedly, that Arakha "arose in (the town) by name of Ur, in Babylonia."

Commencing on August 23, 521 B.C., the Babylonian documents are dated to the first year of the reign of Nebuchadnezzar (IV). He managed to control the whole land, as is testified by documents from Babylon, Sippar and Borsippa to the north and Uruk to the south (cf. Bühl

1968:151ff.; to the texts which are referred to should be added the following: YOS, Vol. XVII, 301-302; OECT 10, 406, and Nbk 13).

It is difficult to agree with the hypothesis of K. Galling, namely that the insurrection by Arakha and by his predecessor, the rebel Nidintu-bel, was not followed by the people, rather than by the army (Galling 1954:21). It will suffice to say that after the occupation of the country by Cyrus, there was no Babylonian army in the land, and it remains hard to understand why some of the Persian garrisons would rebel against Darius, while residing amidst a hostile population in a strange country. In addition, the Behistun text clearly states that the Babylonians went over to the side of Arakha.

The opinions differ as regards the person of Arakha. The name of his father is theophoric, linked with the name of the Urartian god Haldi. I. M. Diakonoff suggested that Arakha was an Urartian, and the name of his father can be translated as 'Haldi is great'. In that case he is simply called an Armenian in the Behistun text because he lived in the land of Armenia (I. M. Diakonoff 1968:235, n. 116). In the Behistun relief, the depiction of Arakha shows certain anthropological features which are typical for the Armenians. The name of Arakha is also met in Babylonian business documents of the Achaemenid period (Eilers 1955:233). Consequently, at that time Babylonians could also have carried the name of Arakha.

G. A. Kapantsjan suggested that Arakha was the Persian governor in Babylon. When the Armenians revolted against Darius, he decided to assist his compatriots (Kapantsjan 1947:211). Cuneiform texts, however, do not support this hypothesis, and it would be unlikely that an Armenian (and not a Persian, or at least a Mede) would have been appointed satrap in Babylonia. It also proves difficult to find support for a hypothesis by F. H. Weissbach, namely that Arakha had joined the Armenian insurrection, and after that it was crushed by the Persians, fled to Babylon and headed a new revolt against Darius (Weissbach 1908:638ff.).

According to G. Brunner, Arakha is identical with the Nebuchadnezzar who is mentioned in the Book of Judith (Brunner 1959). An even more far-reaching hypothesis is presented by C. Schedl. He suggested, also on the basis of the book of Judith, that Arakha was not his personal name, but an Armenian title with the meaning of 'crown-prince'. The real name of Arakha, according to Schedl, was Nebuchadnezzar. He was the son of the dethroned Nabonidus and went to Babylon to claim the throne of Babylon for himself (Schedl 1965:245). These attempts, however, to find more information about Arakha (about whom all more or less reliable information is limited to a few lines in the Behistun text) in the Book of Judith, which dates to the Seleucid period, are without firm foundations. As has been established a long time ago, the Nebuchadnez-zar of the Book of Judith is Antiochus IV (I. M. Diakonoff 1956:41; cf. Greenfield 1961:298).

To subdue the Babylonians, Darius dispatched an army which was headed by the Persian general Vindafarna (Intaphernes), one of his ac-complices in the conspiracy against Gaumata. On November 27, 521 B.C., the army of Arakha, which counted, according to the Akkadian version of the Behistun text, 2,497 men, was crushed, and Arakha and his closest adherents were impaled in Babylon.

Herodotus also reports on the insurrection by the Babylonians against Darius (III 150-160). According to the Greek historian, the besieged Babylonians held out for twenty months against the Persian army which was commanded by Darius himself. When the siege at first proved un-successful, the Persian general Zopyrus mutilated himself and went to the Babylonians telling that Darius had thus treated him. In addition he told the Babylonians that he was prepared to show them the military plans of the Persian king.[7] Shortly afterwards he was appointed by the Babylo-nians to the post of commander of the fortress, immediately following which Zopyrus opened the city gates to the Persians. This story, how-ever, which includes some very unlikely details (for instance, the Babylo-nians, after having prepared themselves for a long siege, should have strangled many of their women, in order to save food), is difficult to reconcile with the information which is provided by the Behistun text. It remains unclear, therefore, which insurrection Herodotus is referring to. According to some historians, this was the revolt by Nidintu-bel, who called himself Nebuchadnezzar (III) (see, for instance, Wells 1907:45ff.; cf. de Kuyper 1983:24). It cannot be excluded, however, that Herodotus was using information about both revolts and mistakenly treated them as one insurrection by the Babylonians.

Herodotus tells that once Darius had taken Babylon, he ordered the death of 3,000 noble inhabitants of the city and the levelling of the city walls. Archaeological excavations have shown that the external walls of Babylon were indeed levelled, but the inner walls are still reported to be standing in various documents a long time after the crushing of the

---

[7] See also Frontin., *Strat.* III 3; Just. I 10. These writers refer to the same event, but relate it to the time of Cyrus II. According to Ctesias, when the Babylonians revolted against Xerxes, they killed their governor Zopyrus. In order to avenge his father, his son Megabyzus mutilated himself and told the Babylonians that the king had ordered his punishment. Thus obtaining the confidence of the Babylonians, he deceived them. Much later a grandson of Zopyrus, also called Zopyrus, fled to Athens. As suggested by certain scholars, he there came into contact with Herodotus. It is significant that, according to Herodotus, the revolt of Babylon was quelled by Zopyrus, although such a statement is completely at odds with the information contained in the Behistun text.

revolts (Wetzel & Schmidt & Mallwitz 1957:70; cf. Ravn 1942:31, 36). Another opinion has been presented, to the effect that following the insurrection by Nebuchadnezzar IV the temple of Eanna in Uruk was destroyed (Woolley 1962:49). The sole foundation for this hypothesis was the fact that the latest texts from Eanna were dated to the second year of the reign of Darius (519 B.C.). Not very long ago, however, archaeologists at Uruk found new archives of Eanna, which, in particular, contained documents dated to as late as the reign of Darius II.

In the northeastern parts of the Empire, another revolt had broken out. This was the insurrection of the Margians under Frada. In the Behistun inscription (DB III 10-19), Darius reports the following: "A land by name Margiana became rebellious to me. One man by name Frada, a Margian, him they made chief (in the Elamite and Babylonian versions he is called king). Subsequently I sent (a messenger) to Dadarshish, a Persian, my servant, the satrap in Bactria, and I told him the following: Go, and defeat the army which does not call itself mine. Thereupon Dadarshish marched out with an army, and joined battle with the Margians." The date of Frada's revolt is not quite certain. According to the Behistun inscription, Frada lost his battle to Dadarshish on the 23rd day of the month Kislimu. However, we do not know whether the battle occurred in the accession year of Darius I or in his first regnal year, and depending on this problem Frada's revolt was quelled on December 10, 522 B.C. or December 28, 521 B.C. In contrast to all other scholars, Weissbach was in favour of the latter date (Weissbach 1908:639f.). In 1960, Hallock also assumed that Frada was defeated on December 28, 521 B.C., since, as argued by Hallock, at the beginning of his reign Darius could not have been in the position to send to Dadarshish, satrap in Bactria, orders to slay the rebellious troops in Margiana. Besides, according to Hallock, in 522 B.C. no one could guess whether Darius would succeed and Dadarshish would choose to await the issue of events. But at the end of 521 B.C., "Darius obviously was in a position to send orders to the satrap of Bactria, and the satrap obeyed" (Hallock 1960:37f.). This opinion has also been accepted by Hinz and Borger (Borger 1982:118-122; Hinz 1976-1979, I, pp. 160f.). Borger refers to the Behistun inscription, according to which a number of countries, including Margiana, revolted while Darius was in Babylonia. Darius won his victory over Nidintu-bel on December 13, 522 B.C., and, according to Borger, would not have been able before that time to send orders to Dadarshish. However, these arguments are not decisive. Nidintu-bel revolted on October 3, 522 B.C. (if not earlier), and Darius soon went to Babylonia to quash the rebellion. From Babylonia he sent messengers to his satraps and generals ordering them to suppress the insurrections.

Dadarshish, being a Persian, had no alternative whether Darius would succeed or not. The revolt in Margiana was directed against Persian domination and could spread into neighbouring nations. Thus, the choice between the above mentioned dates is not easy. However, following Nagel, the decisive fact may be that Frada is depicted on the Behistun relief at the last place among the 'impostors' who revolted in 522-521 B.C. Thus, his defeat might be considered the last event described in the columns I-IV of the inscription and, in all probability, it occurred on December 28, 521 B.C. (see Borger 1982:124; Nagel 1983:175-179).[8]

In any case, Frada and his Margians were defeated. Subsequently there was a massacre, in which 55,243 rebels were killed and 6,972 were captured.[9] The numbers alone attest to the fact that the revolt in Margiana was one of the largest popular uprisings in antiquity. J. Junge suggested that the number of 55,243 killed for such a small region as Margiana was excessively high, and that among the number of fallen there were included representatives from the Saka tribes who may have participated in the revolt (Junge 1944:182). V. M. Masson, however, held the opinion that, on the basis of archaeological data, the Margian oasis was densely populated in antiquity. After crushing the revolt, life in Margiana declined and the agricultural areas along the three branches of the Murghab river were deserted (V. M. Masson 1959:142ff.). It is possible that some of the captured Margians were later sold into slavery. For instance, in 512 B.C. a "Bactrian woman" was sold into slavery at the Babylonian city of Sippar (Pinches, RP IV:104) (after the suppressing of the revolt Margiana was probably united with Bactria).

The insurrection by Frada was the last great popular revolt in the Persian empire. Concluding his report on the crushing of all uprisings, Darius laconically states in the Old Persian and Elamite versions of the Behistun text that: "I seized these nine kings in nineteen battles." The Babylonian version is more explicit: "These are the nine kings who were defeated by my army (and those who survived) were captured and executed. My army defeated their forces in these battles" (lines 95-96).

---

[8] For Frada's rebellion, and for a different interpretation of Frada's place in the Behistun relief, namely as being determined by aesthetic considerations, rather than the exact date of events, see Vogelsang 1986:124-127.

[9] These figures are contained in the Aramaic version of the text; the Babylonian version mentions 6,572 captured and 55,200 killed (the last number is damaged); see BID:31, line 70; BIDAV:34, line 34. The Babylonian version, in contrast to all other texts, also reports that Frada was executed. It must be noted that numbers of fallen and captured rebels are only referred to in the Babylonian and Aramaic versions of the Behistun inscription. When the Elamite and Persian texts were drafted, these figures were apparently not yet known. Thus, the Babylonian and Aramaic texts were composed at a later date than the other two versions.

Thus it was only fifteen months after his accession to the throne that Darius could start to strengthen his position and fully re-establish Achaemenid power within its former borders.[10]

But to do so, more time was needed. According to the report by Herodotus (III 127), the unrest in the Empire continued into 519 B.C. Darius, being unable to send troops against Oroites, was forced to use a trick in order to remove him. Oroites was the satrap of Lydia, Phrygia and Ionia, and had refrained from supporting Darius in the crushing of the various insurrections. At the same time Oroites had attempted to spread his own influence in the western part of Asia Minor (for an extensive account of his actions, see Boffo 1979). Although the Behistun text does not report anything about disturbances in Asia Minor, the return by the Persians to Ionia, Dascyleium and Lydia is not only reported by Herodotus, but also by Diodorus (X 38) and Athenaeus (XII 522 B).

In the list of insurrections, the Behistun text does not report on events in Sogdiana, Areia, Drangiana and Arabia. However, the Arabs were regarded as allies, and not as subjects, and the other lands possibly rose against Darius in a coalition with Margiana (cf. Olmstead 1938:398).

Darius' text does not report on unrest among the Jews. According to certain scholars, however, the words of the prophets Haggai and Zechariah describe the political situation at the commencement of Darius' reign and contain calls for a revolt against the Persians and the establishment of an independent state. These scholars suggest that at the time of Nidintu-bel's and Arakha's insurrections, Haggai, Zechariah and the provincial governor of Judah called Zerubbabel, were linked with the Babylonian rebels. Subsequently, Persian administration should have deprived Zerubbabel of his authority (Meyer 1923:17; *idem* 1939, Vol. III, p. 127, n. 1; Olmstead 1931:560ff.; Waterman 1954:73ff.). According to A. T. Olmstead, Zerubbabel must have been executed as a rebel, as his name is not mentioned in historical sources later than 519 B.C. (Olmstead 1948:142).[11] More correct, perhaps, is P. R. Ackroyd,

---

[10] Darius also repeatedly states that all battles were fought within a period of one year. For an attempt to fit the military events reported in the Behistun text into approximately one year, see Vogelsang 1986:127-131.

[11] On February 15, 519 B.C., Zerubbabel and the High Priest Joshuah laid the foundation for the Temple of Jerusalem. Very soon afterwards, however, the provincial Persian administrators and the governor of Samaria started to hinder the building activities. The satrap of Across-the-River, Tattenai, who was the immediate superior of the governor of Judah, went to Jerusalem and asked who had given permission for the building. The Jewish leaders answered by referring to Cyrus' decree, a copy of which they could, however, not show. Tattenai reported to Darius that the people of Jerusalem were building a temple, on the basis of a decree by Cyrus. In his letter Tattenai also suggested that the construction activities should be stopped because the temple may in future be used as a centre for insurgents. Darius ordered a search for Cyrus' decree in the royal

who is of the opinion that the calls for an independent state in the pro-phecies of Haggai and Zechariah are not oriented towards a concrete political situation, but are general remarks (Ackroyd 1958:13-27).

Thus, when Darius ascended the throne, only Bactria remained loyal to him (its governor, Dadarshish, was possibly related to Darius), and so did the peoples who lived to the west of the Euphrates, who had generally been treated with some respect by the Persians, in comparison with the previous regimes of Egyptians, Assyrians and Babylonians. Almost all the remaining peoples were involved in insurrections. The Behistun text describes nineteen battles, in which more than 100,000 rebels were killed (cf. Schmitt 1980:108).

In Persia and Media, commoners "who lived in their houses" revolted against Darius (the Babylonian version of the Behistun text says: "the Median people, as many as were at home"). But who were those who sup-ported Darius in 522-521 B.C., when his position was almost hopeless? Darius states that he dispatched against the rebels "the people-army, which was with me." The people-army, which was with Darius, evidently differed from the people who were "at home" and who joined the revolt.

As is known, the permanent army of the Persian kings consisted of the ten thousand 'immortals'; the garrisoned troops of the satraps, and those of the fortress commanders. It is completely clear that at the time of the crushing of the popular revolts, Darius was supported by the ten thousand immortals; the troops of the satraps who had remained loyal, and the tribal nobility with their numerous followers. The regular army had only been organized in Persia by the time of Cyrus II. These troops were com-pletely dependent upon the king and therefore constituted a solid support for his power. The remaining Persians formed a reserve army which was only conscripted when required for large campaigns. It is not surprising that thirty years after the start of Persia's rise to power, the regular army had become detached from its roots. These years had been filled with uninterrupted military campaigns which demanded much from the well trained, disciplined army. It is essential that we see this army, during the time of the insurrections in 522 and 521 B.C., as fighting on the side of Darius. This regular army, which consisted of Persian and Median soldiers, was comparatively small. Darius reports about these troops: "the Persian and Median army which was with me, was small" (DB II

---

archives at Babylon. Searches at that place, however, proved unsuccessful, but the docu-ment was eventually found at Ecbatana, where Cyrus resided at the time that he issued the decree, in 538 B.C. Thereupon Darius sanctioned the completion of the building ac-tivities and ordered the satrap of Across-the-River to give every cooperation to the building (Ezra VI 7-9). The building of the Temple was completed after five years (519-515 B.C.).

18-19). Although forming a comparatively small group, the soldiers who had been attracted towards military life were hardened in repeated campaigns, they were disciplined and obedient. Darius made use of his army in a very astute manner. He recognized his most dangerous enemies without error and defeated them at the first opportunity. He was, however, not capable of directing simultaneous punitive expeditions because of the relatively small numbers of troops.

The majority of Darius' army consisted of Persians, but there were also Median troops, Elamites, Sakas and representatives of other peoples. The Medes who served in Darius' army were for the greater part representatives of the nobility, such as we can see in the figure of Takhmaspada, a general of Darius, who helped to quash the revolt of his own people. Darius' army also consisted of garrison troops, residing in Bactria, Arachosia and other countries. These troops were widely used for the crushing of local revolts. Of course, the well-being of the garrisons was based on tribute from the subject peoples. These troops lived amidst a hostile population and therefore had to remain loyal to Darius when the central government was threatened. Finally, at the time of the unrest of 522-521 B.C., Darius' side was strengthened by the Persian and Median tribal nobility. Gobryas, Intaphernes, Takhmaspada and other representatives of this nobility commanded contingents of Darius' army at the most important battles in Babylonia, Persia, Elam, Media and other lands.

According to the Behistun text (I 34) and other inscriptions of Darius, it was the Lie which made his subject lands rebellious. Darius could state: "what was wrong, I did well." He claims that he re-established order which was based on justice and the law. Darius says: "Much which was ill-done, that I made good. Provinces were in commotion, one man was smiting the other" (DSe 30-33). The subjects of the Persians, however, accepted the 'order' which was established by Darius only after a stubborn and continued resistance. He managed to apply all forces at his disposal, and, what was even more important, he knew how to use them. According to Plutarch (*Moral.* 172F), Darius was proud of the fact that he remained quiet and calm in battles, even when·opposing the most pressing dangers. Very much the same is said by Darius in his tomb inscription at Naqsh-i Rustam: "I am not hot-tempered. What things develop in my anger I hold firmly under control by my thinking power. I am firmly ruling over my own (impulses) ... I have a strong body. As a soldier, I am a good soldier ... I see, who will rebel and who will not ... First I will think, then I will act" (DNb 13-40).[12]

---

[12] Strabo (XV 3.8) is fairly correct, although in a general manner, in his rendering of this inscription: "I was a friend to my friends; the best horse rider and bowman, and

The privileges of the tribal nobility, which had been annulled by Cambyses and Gaumata, were all reinstated by Darius. He took all possible measures to bring the nobility to his side and to assure himself of their loyalty. Plato (*Leg.* III, 695 B-E) writes that Darius divided his empire into seven parts and gave it to his accomplices against Smerdis. This piece of information, although not reflecting an actual situation, can only have originated in the exclusive position which the Persian tribal nobility occupied during the reign of Darius. The first Greek author who was well acquainted with Persian affairs was Aeschylus. He referred to six hereditary princes who in importance and honours were close to the king (*Persai* 956-960). In addition, it is stated in the Book of Esther (I 14) that those closest to the Persian king were "the seven princes of Persia and Media, who could see the face of the king (and) sat first in the kingdom", and also gave advice to the king. It is not surprising therefore that Persian official tradition has idealized Darius. He left many inscriptions in which he declared himself the enemy of the Lie; an advocate of justice; an exemplary ruler, and the representative on earth of Ahura Mazda. In Persepolis, relief scenes have been preserved which depict victorious fights of the Persian kings with composite monsters with the body of a lion; the horns of a bull; the claws of an eagle, and the tail of a scorpion, personifying the Lie and Evil. These depictions, symbolizing the victory of order during the reign of Darius, are often also found in Old Persian seals.[13]

On the basis of contemporary Persian traditions, Aeschylus (*Persai* 645) wrote that in Persia there were no people equal to Darius, and, remaining silent about Darius' defeat in Greece, he compared him to a god. Plato also idealized Darius (*Leg.* 694 A-C). According to him, Cyrus gave his subjects a great deal of freedom, but this situation was put to an end by Cambyses. During the reign of Darius, Plato continues, freedom was almost completely returned to the Persians and Darius dealt with the people in a friendly manner.

---

an eminent hunter. I could do everything." Compare a special rendering of the text in the work of Athenaeus (*Deipnos.* X 434 D): "I could drink a lot of wine, and still stand it well." Relatively recently an inscription of Xerxes was found which is an exact copy of the tomb inscription of Darius I. According to W. Hinz, the inscription of Xerxes was copied from a document in the royal chancellery, and not from the Darius inscription itself (Hinz 1969:45ff.). Of course, the contemporaries of Alexander the Great, whose work was used by Strabo, also did not read the text from the rock face, but had the opportunity to see a copy in a probably Aramaic translation, deposited in the archives (cf. Herzfeld 1938:13).

[13] See photographs of such seals (Schmidt 1953-1970, Vol. II, pp. 7ff., 29ff., etc.). On a number of seals there are also trilingual inscriptions with the name of Darius and Xerxes. Many such seal impressions have been found during excavations at Dascyleium, the residence of the Persian satrap in the northwestern part of Asia Minor (Balkan 1959:124ff.), and also in Achaemenid Egypt (Kraeling 1953:123f.; cf. Root 1979).

It appears that Darius attempted to maintain the masses of common Persians as a military reserve and to protect them from excessive exploitation by the nobility. At the same time, however, he protected the influence and wealth of the Persian nobility from popular demands (Struve 1943:24). According to Darius, he achieved a situation whereby ''people did not kill each other, and every man was in his place ... the strong did not smite the weak and did not kill (him)'' (DSe, 37-41).

CHAPTER THIRTEEN

THE VICTORY PROCLAMATION OF DARIUS

Having crushed, by the end of 521 B.C., the main centres of rebellion, Darius started work on his majestic memorial at the rock cliffs of Behistun. In this memorial he addressed the coming generations with an account of the many victories which he achieved. In the rock face a trilingual inscription was carved which contains about a thousand lines, each generally two metres in length.

The text is written in the Old Persian, Elamite and Akkadian (Babylonian) languages. The three versions present three variants which in the main are identical, although the Akkadian variant, contrary to the Old Persian and Elamite ones, includes certain significant divergences. The composition of the inscription in various languages was to a certain degree determined by tradition, as Akkadian and Elamite had been written languages since at least the third millennium B.C. In addition, Darius tried to make the contents of his inscription known to all the subjects of the Empire.

The text was translated into many languages and distributed in "all the lands", as it is said in the text itself. The text is inscribed in the rock face at a great height, 105 metres above the road, too high to be approached for reading. At the commencement of this century some badly preserved papyri were found with a translation of the Behistun text into Aramaic (AP:249ff.; BIDAV). The Aramaic text, written in the official royal chancellery, was destined for distribution in the western parts of the Empire. The Aramaic text is for the greater part identical with the Akkadian variant; only these two versions, contrary to the Old Persian and Elamite texts, contain information about the number of rebels being killed and arrested. Finally, during excavations in the northern part of Babylon, in 1899, in the former palace of Nebuchadnezzar II, a section of a stone slab was found with a fragment of the Akkadian version of the Behistun text. In the same palace archaeologists have found a fragment of a relief, in subject and style reminiscent of the Behistun relief. The relief was apparently attached to the wall of the building for public viewing (Seidl 1976:125 and Fig. 34).

The text comprises an introduction, which contains a genealogy of Darius; a completely historical part, in which the events are described during the years which led to Darius' firm occupation of the Persian throne, and a conclusion. In the latter part Darius calls for the favour of

Ahura Mazda to those who will preserve the inscription, and he calls for the curse of the god on those who will damage the memorial.

The historical part of the main text commences with a report on the campaign by Cambyses to Egypt and concludes with a description of the victory by the troops of Darius over Arakha. The report is presented in a geographical, rather than in a chronological sequence. In other words, the text presents a description of the military campaigns in the different countries. In this sequence, the military activities which were commanded directly by Darius are presented in the first place, whenever this was possible without a disruption of the logical links in the presentation of events.

The text presents many precise dates and places of battles, and also (in the Akkadian and Aramaic versions) the precise number of rebels killed and taken prisoner. On the basis of this point it is possible to conclude that reports on the important battles were drafted immediately after the fight. This is a strong indication for the accuracy of many pieces of information contained in the text. Nevertheless, the Behistun inscription is evidently an official document with a propagandistic character, and as such a typical royal document with a tendentious, subjective report of the events, which was drafted in order to please Darius. He states that he killed and arrested tens of thousands of adversaries, but he does not spend one word about the defeats he suffered.

According to the text (IV 2ff.), all events which were related to the struggle for power by Darius, and which are described in the first four columns of the inscription, occurred within the lapse of one year. "Says Darius the king: This is what I have done by the favour of Ahuramazda in one and the same year after that I became king. I fought nineteen battles ... I smote them (the rebels) ... and captured nine kings." An explanation of these words has aroused much controversy among the historians, because from the moment of the death of Gaumata (September 29, 522 B.C.) until the crushing of the insurrection of the Margians (December 28, 521 B.C.), a period of some fifteen months elapsed. It should be taken into account, however, that the accession year of Darius included an intercalary, thirteenth month. In other words, all the deeds of Darius which are recorded in the main part of the Behistun text, were completed within the course of one year and some two months instead of the alleged one year.[1] In all probability this point reflects the

---

[1] But see Vogelsang 1986:121-131, in which an attempt is made to date Frada's revolt in Margiana to the accession year of Darius, and Frada's defeat to December 10, 522 B.C. This would limit the 'one year' of Darius to a period of one year and six weeks (when taking into account the intercalary month of the Babylonian calendar). See also note 10, Chapter Twelve.

style of the Urartian royal inscriptions, which contain the traditional phrase: "By the favour of the god Haldi I completed these heroic deeds within the course of one year" (Struve 1968:50; I. M. Diakonoff 1970:121).

Darius says: "You who will later read this inscription, believe that what was done by me, do not think it is a lie ... Much else was done by me, that has not been written down in this inscription. It was not written down, in order that he who will later read this text, will not think that (too) much was done by me, and will not believe it, but think it is false ... Those who were kings before, (in the course of their life) did not do as much as was done by me with the favour of Ahura Mazda in the course of one and the same year" (DB IV 42-52). These words, however, are the common statements of kings in the ancient East (cf., for instance, an inscription by Nebuchadnezzar II (NKI:186).

Above the inscription rises a relief with a height of 3 metres and a length of 5.48 metres. The god Ahura Mazda, who floats above all figures, stretches his left hand holding a ring towards Darius, symbolically handing him the royal power and blessing him with his raised, right hand. The height of the figure of Ahura Mazda is 1.27 metres. Darius is depicted, to his natural scale, in a standing position and wearing a royal crown. His height on the relief is 1.72 metres. Darius' right hand is raised in a gesture of worship towards Ahura Mazda, while in his left hand he holds a bow. Below the left foot of Darius lies Gaumata, with one leg and both hands raised in agony. To the left, behind Darius, stand two of his courtiers, Gobryas his lance bearer, and apparently his bow carrier Aspathines. In stature they are shorter than Darius (1.47 metres), but they rise above the rebels, who hardly exceed above the chest of Darius (1.17 metres). These eight rebel leaders are depicted immediately behind Gaumata. Behind them stands the ninth prisoner, the chief of the Saka people of the Tigraxauda, whose figure rises eight centimetres above that of Darius, because of the Saka's tall, pointed cap. The hands of the rebels are bound behind their backs, and in addition, they are chained one behind the other in a long line.[2] The whole relief is worked in situ rather than being prefabricated, bar eight inserted details (the bow of Darius; the crown of Ahura Mazda, etc.) (Cameron 1960:60, n. 4).

In spite of autumnal storms and rains, and sharp frosts of the winter season, the monument and the inscription were finished within a comparatively short time, between November 521 and March 518 B.C. After the conclusion of the work, the height of the rock as far as the inscription

---

[2] For a discussion of the basic concept behind the sequence of the captives, see Vogelsang 1986:121-127.

was smoothed; as a result the text area forms some sort of recess. Starting from the promontory, to which it is possible to climb up from below, there are still about 35 metres to go in order to reach the inscription, along a completely smooth and steep rock face. The path which originally led upwards was destroyed by the workers in order to make the monument inaccessible, and to keep it from wilful destruction.

CHAPTER FOURTEEN

THE CAMPAIGN AGAINST THE *SAKĀ TIGRAXAUDĀ*

In 520 B.C. the Elamites rose against the Persians for the third time. The fifth column of the Behistun text contains the following laconic report: "The land by name Elam became rebellious. An Elamite by name Atamaita, him they made chief. Subsequently I sent an army. A Persian by name Gaubaruva, my servant, him I made commander of them. Thereupon Gaubaruva marched off with his army to Elam. He joined battle with the Elamites. Thereupon Gaubaruva smote and crushed the Elamites. He captured their chief, and brought him to me, and I executed him. After this the country became mine."

In the same column of the Behistun inscription, the story is told of Darius' campaign against the *Sakā tigraxaudā*. This campaign, according to the text, was carried out during the third year of the king's reign, namely in 519 B.C.[1] "Says Darius the king: Thereupon I marched with my army to the land of the Saka. Thereupon the Saka who wear pointed caps, came out to join battle. When I came to the river, I crossed with the whole army to the other side.[2] Thereupon I smote part of the Saka exceedingly, and the other (part) was captured ... Their leader, by name Skunkha, was taken prisoner and led to me. Then I appointed another leader (for them), as was my wish. Thereupon the land became mine."

---

[1] L. Trümpelmann has suggested that, because Gaumata was killed on September 29, 522 B.C., that date should be taken as the first day of Darius' first year, and consequently his third year would end in October 519 B.C. (Trümpelmann 1967:297). Such a date, however, is disputable, because, as said above, on the basis of the Babylonian texts from the Achaemenid period the interval between someone's accession to the throne and the beginning of the new year at the first day of the month of Nisannu (March-April), is regarded as the accession year of the king, and his first regnal year starts in the month of Nisannu. Consequently, the interval between September 29, 522 B.C., and April 14, 521, is the accession year of Darius, while his first regnal year started on the first of Nisannu, which is April 14, of the following year, 521 B.C. Therefore, the third year of Darius covered the period between March 23, 519 and March 12, 518 B.C. It should be added that E. J. Bickerman was inclined to believe that in Iran itself the Achaemenids did not follow the Babylonian system of dating (pers. comm.).

[2] Cf. the translation of this passage by J. Harmatta: "I arrived at the sea. A river by name Araxšā, I crossed it with all equipment." According to Harmatta, Darius advanced as far as the Aral Sea to the mouth of the river Araxšā, which Harmatta identified with the Araxes of Herodotus and the Oxus of the Hellenistic period, namely the Amu Darya (Harmatta 1979:23ff.; cf. also the translation by W. Hinz 1972:243f.; Shahbazi 1982:191f.).

Scholars have located the *Sakā tigraxaudā*, 'the Sakas who wear pointed caps' in different locations (for relevant literature, see Dandamaev 1963b:177ff.). In particular, it was J. Oppert who wanted to identify the battle mentioned in the fifth column with the well-known campaign of Darius against the Scythians of the Black Sea (Oppert 1851, Vol. 18, pp. 364ff.). An extensive account of the latter campaign is presented by Herodotus. This hypothesis was accepted by many historians. According to E. Herzfeld, the headdress and clothing of the 'Sakas with the pointed cap' differ from the headgear and costume of the *Sakā haumavargā*, but closely resemble the headdress and attire of the Black Sea Scythians (*Sakā paradrayā*). With this as a starting point, Herzfeld suggested that the account in the fifth column of the Behistun text refers to a campaign against the Black Sea Scythians. In the Persepolis reliefs a particular delegation is depicted which shows the same high headdress as Skunkha in the Behistun relief; this delegation is probably identical with that of the *Sakā tigraxaudā*. The high headdress was probably made of felt.

Comparatively recently, J. M. Balcer attempted to give a firmer footing to the hypothesis that the Greek sources concerning Darius' Scythian campaign, and the information contained in the fifth column of the Behistun text, describe one and the same event, namely the campaign against the Scythians of the Black Sea (Balcer 1972a). This hypothesis was supported by G. G. Cameron (1975).

Scholars usually date Darius' military campaign to the west and north of the Black Sea to the years between 514 and 510 B.C. They base this date on a Greek text, known under the name of the *Tabula Capitolina*. Balcer suggested that this date was conditional, and perhaps not precise. J. Harmatta, however, decisively refuted Balcer's suggestion, stating that the *Tabula Capitolina* should in all probability be dated to between 515 and 513 B.C. Harmatta does not agree with Balcer in relating Polyaenus' account about the Sakas to the Black Sea Scythians (Harmatta 1979:21ff.). In addition, because the Achaemenid empire by 519 B.C. was still unsettled following the unrest of the previous years, it would seem unlikely that Darius would start a war against the Black Sea Scythians. Also, at that time, long before the military preparations against Greece, a campaign in that direction had no strategic significance (E. V. Černenko has drawn attention to this point). And between the events which are described by Herodotus and the information contained in the fifth column of the Behistun text, it is difficult to find parallels. A conclusive argument against the identification discussed above is the fact that in the Achaemenid inscriptions which give a list of the subject lands in geographical order, the *Sakā tigraxaudā* are always mentioned together with the peoples of Central Asia. It should also be noted that more recently, in private correspondence, Balcer has refuted his opinion and he now dates the campaign against the Black Sea Scythians to the years 514-511 B.C., and the war with the *Sakā tigraxaudā* to the year 519 B.C.

Where did the *Sakā tigraxaudā* live? To answer this question, attention should be drawn to the lists which are contained in the Achaemenid inscriptions, of peoples who were subject to the Persians. In the Behistun inscription (I 16-17), the Sakas are mentioned amidst the peoples of Central Asia who were subject to Persia in 522-521. They are listed without a more concrete indication of the name of the people. In the fifth column of the same inscription, however, as discussed above, reference is made to the "Sakas who wear the pointed cap." In an inscription of Darius from Persepolis (DPe), the Sakas are mentioned in the 25th place, without further indications. But they are listed amid Central Asian satrapies in a geographical order. The inscription of Darius from Susa (DSe) reports respectively on the 15th and 16th place the names of the *Sakā haumavargā* and the *Sakā tigraxaudā*. In an inscription of Darius from Naqsh-i Rustam (DNa), both names are reported in the 14th and 15th place, while in the 25th place the name is presented of the *Sakā paradrayā* ('those across the sea'). In another inscription of Darius, from Hamadan, reference is made to 'the Sakas beyond Sogdiana', in order to indicate the easternmost border of the Empire. In an inscription of Xerxes from Persepolis (XPh), the *Sakā haumavargā* and the *Sakā tigraxaudā* are listed in the 26th and 27th place respectively.

Thus, in all pertinent inscriptions, the *Sakā haumavargā* and the *Sakā tigraxaudā* are mentioned within the same context as the Central Asian satrapies, and the *Sakā paradrayā* are placed between Ionia and Thrace. It follows that the *Sakā haumavargā* and the *Sakā tigraxaudā* used to live in Central Asia[3], while the *Sakā paradrayā* resided beyond the Black Sea. It is therefore difficult to agree with the opinion of certain scholars who think that the Black Sea Scythians are not mentioned in the Achaemenid texts, and that the *Sakā paradrayā* indicate the Sakas who lived near the Aral Sea (Konow 1933:220ff.; Nagel 1983:171; Struve 1949:25ff.).

Comparative studies of the mention of Saka peoples in the Achaemenid inscriptions thus permit the following statement: In the early texts, when the Persians had only come into contact with one Saka people, they called them simply the Sakas. In other words, with the collective name of 'the Sakas' (the Scythians), the Persians referred to a specific Saka people. Later, when the Persians had also subjected other Saka tribes, they started to differentiate between them. In particular,

---

[3] The area in which the *Sakā haumavargā* were living extended as far as the Eastern Pamir (Litvinskij 1969:115ff.).

attention may be drawn to the long reference to the *Sakā tigraxaudā* in the fifth column of the Behistun text, namely "the Sakas who wear a pointed cap." In the inscription of Darius from Naqsh-i Rustam, the general name for all Saka peoples, 'the Sakas', disappears, and is replaced by concrete references to the *Sakā haumavargā*, *tigraxaudā* and *paradrayā*. The *Sakā haumavargā* were the first Sakas that came into contact with the Persians, apparently during the reign of Cyrus. They were known to the Greeks under the name of the Amyrgaean Sakas.

Many scholars identify the Sakas which rebelled at the commencement of Darius' reign with the *Sakā tigraxaudā* of the fifth column of the Behistun inscription. They do so on the basis of the idea that these Sakas had already been subjugated by Cyrus (Hinz 1939:371; Junge 1944:50; Weissbach 1940:65, 77). According to R. G. Kent, Skunkha, the leader of the rebellious Sakas, headed the insurrection of his people from the commencement of Darius' reign, and remained undefeated until 519 B.C. (Kent 1953:161). The *Sakā tigraxaudā*, however, were independent until the advent of Darius, and the campaign against them was not a punitive expedition following an insurrection. This is clear from the following: it is stated in the Behistun text that all rebel leaders against Darius were executed. In addition, their death is generally described in detail. There is, however, in the Behistun text no reference to the execution of Skunkha.[4] The minor inscriptions which contain information about the depictions of the pretenders, describe their crime, accusing them all of adhering the Lie and of revolting against Darius. The minor inscription, however, which is the label to the depiction of Skunkha, shortly states: "Skunkha, the Saka." It should be taken into account that in the Achaemenid inscriptions the word 'Lie' is used in a certain religious-political meaning for a description of an insurrection against 'legitimate' authority.

In the Behistun relief all rebel kings are depicted without their headdress; their remaining, ethnographical characteristics, however, are presented in all possible manners. Skunkha, however, is depicted with a tall, pointed cap with a height of about 80 centimetres[5], which is half of

---

[4] The opinion, therefore, of E. Schmidt and A. T. Olmstead, to the effect that Skunkha was executed, is without foundation (Olmstead 1948:141; Schmidt 1953-1970, Vol. I, p. 38).

[5] This tall hat must be the origin of their name, *tigraxauda* ('pointed cap'). The Greek name for this people was Orthokorybantioi, referred to by Herodotus (III 92; VII 64). This Greek name seems to be a Greek translation of the Persian name (Kiessling 1901:16ff.). From the remaining Central Asian Scythians, and also from the people of Chorasmia and Bactria, the *Sakā tigraxaudā* differentiated themselves with their headgear, at the time when the remaining outfit of all these peoples was identical and consisted of a short tunic with a broad belt and narrow trousers. Herodotus (VII 64) erroneously connects the pointed cap with the Amyrgaean Sakas, and not with the Orthokorybantioi.

the height of Skunkha himself. In addition, the *Sakā tigraxaudā* in the Behistun inscription are never described as rebellious, contrary to the Elamites, Babylonians and other peoples who revolted against Darius. This point is confirmed by the fact that Skunkha was pardoned, although he was removed from his position as leader. In his place Darius appointed someone else from among the Sakas as their new leader. This was necessary because it was impossible for a Persian governor, who was not a representative of the population itself, to rule the nomadic peoples who lived along the borders of the Empire (see Frejman 1948:235ff.; Struve 1946b:249).

The triumph of Darius over the *Sakā tigraxaudā* also found its reflection in a seal which, according to its style, dates from the time of Darius I. On this seal the king is depicted in combat with a Saka, who is characterized by his tall cap. The king seizes him with his left arm, while his right hand raises a short sword for a stroke. A second Saka has already been defeated and lies on the ground (Ward 1910, No. 1052).

CHAPTER FIFTEEN

DARIUS IN EGYPT

The Behistun inscription reports on a large number of insurrections which started when Darius ascended the Persian throne. The text also alludes to revolts by the Egyptians, Sakas and Sattagydians. The Behistun text, however, does not give any information about the crushing of these uprisings. As a result, many scholars are of the opinion that Egypt, together with the land of the Sakas and Sattagydia, were only brought back within the folds of the Achaemenid empire after 518 B.C., when Darius' campaign against the *Sakā tigraxaudā* was concluded and the work on the monument of Behistun had been completed. Thus, it would have been impossible to add a report on the most recent events (Cameron 1943:309-311; Herzfeld 1947a:184; Hinz 1939:372; Kent 1953:163; Weissbach 1940:74; Wiedemann 1880:236). It is, however, difficult to agree with this opinion, because a demotic text has been preserved, dated to December 30, 518 B.C., which contains an order by Darius to the Egyptian satrap (his name is not preserved), to dispatch to the royal court at Susa a number of Egyptian experts in local laws. In addition, there is a demotic text which is dated to the third year of Darius' reign (519 B.C.) (CDP, Vol. III, pp. 25ff.). It can be concluded from these texts that the revolt in Egypt was crushed, at the latest, in 519 B.C. As regards the land of the Sakas and the land of Sattagydia, they were, in all probability, already subjugated in 521 B.C., but the Behistun inscription does not report about these events because the insurrection in Sattagydia was suppressed following the victory of Darius' forces in neighbouring Arachosia. In any case, as observed above, the district of Gandutava, where a battle took place between the forces of Vahyazdata and those of Darius, is located by the Elamite version of the Behistun text in Arachosia, and by the Babylonian version in Sattagydia. The insurrection of the Sakas was apparently related to that of some neighbouring region in Central Asia (cf. Struve 1954:8).

V. V. Struve has drawn attention to the point that the historical sections in the Behistun inscription start in the 27th line of the first column, and the reference to the insurrection in Egypt is only referred to at the beginning of the second column. In the passage between the 14th to the 17th line of the first column, however, which was composed during the second year of Darius' reign when he had crushed the revolts and had ordered the construction of the Behistun monument, Egypt, together with the land of the Sakas, Sattagydia, and other countries, was counted among the lands that recognized the rule of Darius. In other words, the Egyptian insurrection, and the revolts of other peoples, were crushed no later than in the second year of Darius' rule (Struve 1954:7ff.).

The sources do not permit to give a decisive answer to the question whether the insurrection in Egypt was supported by broad strata of the population. G. G. Cameron, on the basis of an inscription of the high Egyptian official Udjahorresne, was of the opinion that the crushing of this revolt took considerable bloodshed (Cameron 1943:309-311). V. V. Struve, however, held the opinion that the unrest reported upon in the inscription of Udjahorresne dates to the time of Cambyses' return to Egypt from Nubia. The revolt against Darius, on the other hand, was, still according to Struve, an insignificant event which remained unknown to Herodotus (Struve 1954:7ff.). J. V. Prášek suggested that Egypt did not revolt at all at the commencement of Darius' reign, instead Egypt's satrap, Aryandes, acted independently from the new king Darius (Prášek 1906-1910, Vol. II, p. 41). E. Bickerman presented the hypothesis that, following the report by Herodotus, there was at the commencement of Darius' reign no insurrection whatsoever in Egypt, if the revolt in Libya is not included. The latter country was independent at that time, if only for a short period (pers. comm.).

It is possible that Aryandes, whom Cambyses had appointed as satrap of Egypt, Libya and Cyrene, did not hurry in showing his loyalty to Darius, and that he did not help Darius in the reconstruction of the Achaemenid empire. According to Herodotus (IV 166), Aryandes issued silver coinage, the purity of which was not inferior to the royal coinage. This was regarded as high treason and served as an argument for his eventual execution. It is difficult to say how far this piece of information is a reflection of reality. According to Herodotus, the coins of Aryandes were still in circulation when he visited Egypt, but to date none have been found. It is also possible that Darius executed Aryandes on the basis of another charge which remains unknown to us.

The sources do not contain any indication as to when the death of Aryandes took place. Sometime after the decease of Cambyses, Aryandes crushed a revolt in Libya. He may, however, not have acted in the interest of Darius. According to Herodotus (IV 200, 204), the Persians under Aryandes beleaguered Barka and started to undermine the walls of the town. Thereupon Barka surrendered on the condition that the Persians would not destroy it. Nevertheless the people from Barka were enslaved and deported to Persia. The precise date when the siege of Barka occurred, however, remains unknown. J. Yoyotte dated this event to 513-512 B.C. (Yoyotte 1972:266). F. K. Kienitz suggested that

Aryandes was executed between 510 (which according to Kienitz is the date of the campaign against Barka) and 492 B.C., when Pherendates was mentioned as satrap of Egypt (Kienitz 1953:64f., n. 7). A similar opinion was adhered to by A. T. Olmstead (Olmstead 1948:225).

At the end of the summer of 518 B.C., Darius travelled to Egypt and eventually arrived at the capital Memphis. It is possible that at that time Aryandes was discharged and a new satrap, by name Pherendates, appointed (Cameron 1943:311ff.; Wiedemann 1880:236; cf. Parker 1941a:376f., where various dates concerning Darius' sojourn in Egypt, from 519 to 515 B.C., are listed). Olmstead suggested that Darius crushed a revolt of the Egyptians, restored Aryandes to the position of satrap and almost immediately returned to Persia, after having received information about a conspiracy by Intaphernes, one of his accomplices in the murder of Gaumata (Olmstead 1948:142f.). The sources, however, contain no support for this hypothesis.

If we believe Polyaenus (VII 11.7), the Egyptians, not being able to tolerate the cruelty of Aryandes (whom Polyaenus calls Oryandros), rose in revolt and forced the satrap to leave the country. Darius therefore marched to Memphis to defeat the rebels. At that time the death occurred of Apis, the sacred bull which was worshipped by the Egyptians. Darius paid one hundred silver talents for the search of a new sacred bull. The Egyptians, being surprised by the magnanimity of the king, voluntarily stopped the revolt. It is difficult to say whether there is a kernel of truth in Polyaenus' story. According to Egyptian sources, Apis died on August 31, 518 (see Posener 1936, text No. 5).

While he was in Egypt, Darius ordered the construction of a canal from the Nile to the Red Sea. The canal was needed to establish a direct link between Egypt and Persia which avoided the journey through the desert of the Sinai. The latter route had become unreliable because of the inroads made by nomadic tribesmen. Classical information about the canal is contradictory. According to Herodotus (II 158; IV 39), the Egyptian pharaoh Necho was the first to start the digging of the canal, and the work was continued much later by Darius, as Necho did not complete the work because of an unfavourable pronouncement of an oracle. According to Herodotus, the canal could be sailed from beginning to end in four days, and two triremes (ships with three lines of rowers) could pass each other. The canal started at the eastern branch of the Nile, near the city of Bubastis, proceeded through the Wadi Tumilat and finally ended in the Red Sea near the modern city of Suez. Contrary to the modern Suez canal, which enables ships to sail from Europe to the Indian Ocean, the ancient canal was dug in order to facilitate connections between the Nile Valley and the Red Sea littoral.

Three stelae of Darius present information on the digging of the canal.[1] They are composed in Egyptian (hieroglyphic script); Old Persian, Elamite and Akkadian. It should be added that the Egyptian version is not a translation of the cuneiform texts, as its style and phraseology are purely Egyptian. B. A. Turaev suggested that the composer of the Egyptian version was the high priest of Sais, Udjahorresne (Turaev 1911:360). One of the stelae dedicated to the construction of the canal was found in 1864 by a French employee of the Companie du Canal de Suez and then re-excavated in 1889 by W. S. Golénischeff, near Tell el-Maskhuta at a former crossing of the canal (see Roaf 1974:79). This stela could have been seen from a ship sailing through the canal. Another stela was found about 33 kilometres to the north of Suez, at Shallufa. The third stela, from Suez, contains the titles of Darius: "King of Upper and Lower Egypt, long live the eternal great king, king of kings, son of Vishtaspa, the Achaemenid." In the hieroglyphic text of all three stelae, comparable depictions are presented in which both halves of Egypt are symbolically united with a cartouche which contains the name of Darius (*Intrjwš*). Furthermore, the hieroglyphic text of the Suez stela contains references to 24 subjects from Darius' empire, including men from Persia and Media. The representatives from each of the lands are depicted in different fortress ovals. The faces of the men are directed towards the cartouche with the name of Darius. This list is very similar to the one of subject lands which is contained in inscriptions from Naqsh-i Rustam. Contrary to the Behistun inscription, the Suez stela includes three new provinces: India (Hindush); Libya (Put) and Nubia (Kush). Consequently, it can be concluded that by the time of the digging of the canal, these three lands had been conquered by the Persians (apparently around 517 B.C.).

According to Egyptian texts, the canal had a length of 84 kilometres. A certain, badly preserved Egyptian inscription states that a fleet of 24 (or 32?) ships sailed from Egypt to Persia (Posener 1936:180ff.; all the available information about the canal has been collected and studied by G. Posener 1936:48-87; 1938:259ff.).

The most extensive of the cuneiform inscriptions, from the Suez crossing, has the following content: "A great god is Ahuramazda, who created yonder heaven and who created this earth, who created man, who created prosperity for mankind, who made Darius king, who gave King Darius a large kingdom, with good horses and good people. I am Darius, great king, king of kings, king of lands with many people, king of this

---

[1] Fragments of another stela were found, in 1799 and 1884, at the wrongly named site of 'Serapaeum'; these fragments were subsequently lost in Paris: see Roaf 1974:79.

great (and) wide land, son of Vishtaspa, an Achaemenid. Says Darius the king: I am a Persian; from Persia I conquered Egypt (*Mudrāya*). I ordered to dig this canal from the River Nile (*Pirāva*) which flows in Egypt, to the sea, which borders Persia. Thereupon this canal was dug, as I ordered, and ships sailed from Egypt to Persia through this canal, as it had been my wish.''

According to Egyptian texts, Darius as successor to the traditions of the old pharaohs behaved benevolently towards local culture and religion. Diodorus (I 95.4-5) wrote that Darius studied theology with Egyptian priests and imitated the pharaohs who reigned before him, therefore the Egyptians behaved towards him with the greatest of respect, and following his death granted him divine honours. This, of course, is an exaggeration. But in accordance with an order by Darius, a temple dedicated to the God Ptah, in Memphis, was restored, and a large sanctuary for the God Amon was built to the west of Thebes, in the oasis of El Kharga in the Libyan desert. The ruins of this building, the construction of which continued for twenty years (510-490 B.C.), have been preserved to the present day. In an inscription at this temple it is said: "King Darius built (this as a memorial) to his father Amon-Re ...." (translation by O. D. Berlev; see the edition: Brugsch 1878, Table XII; see also Gauthier 1907-1917:140). Darius also presented the Egyptian temples with rich donations. In one of the texts from the Serapaeum at Memphis, he is called: "King of the South and North, may he live eternally, the Beloved by Apis." This text is written on a vase which was dedicated by Darius to the Apis of that time (Vercoutter 1962:56ff.). It is stated in the Demotic Chronicle that the Egyptians were obedient to Darius because of the superiority of his heart (DC:31, column C 8). Darius was proclaimed to be the son of the goddess Neith at Sais and her temple acquired a privileged position. Darius ordered the High Priest Udjahorresne, who at some time had resided at Susa, to return to his native city, namely Sais, and to re-establish the school (academy?) of the temple which was destroyed during the period of unrest in the nome of Sais (Posener 1936:175-190; see also Capart 1946:18f.; Chassinat 1897-1934, No. 7, pp. 219, 248). In the inscription of Udjahorresne it is stated: "The ruler, prince, treasurer of the king of Lower Egypt ... the great healer Udjahorresne ... says: The king of Upper and Lower Egypt, Darius, may he live in eternity, summoned me to return to Egypt, when His Highness was in Elam, he is the great king of all and the great ruler of Egypt, to build mansions of the living, when they had fallen into ruins. The strangers brought me from country to country, to Egypt according to the order of the Lord of Both Lands. I did in accordance with the orders of His Majesty. I provided them (the mansions) with personnel, all boys, none of them from the masses. His Majesty ordered to give them all good things, so that they could do all their good works ... His Majesty did this, because he realized the use of this craftsmanship, in order to revive all sufferers, in order to establish the names of all gods, their temples, their sacrifices, and the execution of their festivities for ever'' (translation O. D. Berlev).

The name of Darius I is found in the Egyptian monuments more frequently than the names of all the other Persian kings taken together. The building activities of Darius in Egypt are also attested to by inscriptions in the quarries of the Wadi Hammamat. According to G. Posener, among the 250 inscriptions which were found at the quarries, 17 are dated to the 27th, Persian dynasty. Work at this place continued uninterruptedly from 524 to 477 B.C., while there was peace in Egypt. The name of Darius is also preserved on stone blocks in the Fayum, at Memphis, etc. (Gauthier 1907-1917:146-155; Posener 1936:88).

CHAPTER SIXTEEN

THE CONQUEST OF HINDUSH AND MACEDONIA AND THE SCYTHIAN CAMPAIGN OF DARIUS

Having crushed the various revolts against his accession to the throne and having firmly established his authority, Darius decided upon new conquests. It would seem that by 517 B.C. the Persians subjected the northwestern part of India[1], which prior to that time had consisted of many minor political entities. The conquest of these lands was preceded by an expedition under the command of the Carian pilot Scylax. The voyage took the explorers along the Indus river to its debouchure into the Indian Ocean, and hence back to the west. The exploration provided information about the Indians along the route, which was needed by the Persians prior to their conquest of the region.

The new satrapy, which received the name of Hindush, extended from the centre to the lower part of the Indus Valley, in present-day Pakistan. It was the most eastern province of the Achaemenid empire, and according to Herodotus (III 106; IV 40) and his contemporaries, it was regarded as the most eastern land of the world, behind which stretched an empty and unknown desert. Herodotus' concepts about India were rather vague. He tells about huge beasts and raw cotton from which the Indians made clothes, and about large quantities of gold dust which was dug up by ants. Thus, the geographical horizon of the subjects of the Achaemenid empire was extended considerably. Strabo (XV 1.10) writes, on the basis of the work by Eratosthenes, that immediately prior to the time of the Indian campaigns by Alexander of Macedonia, the River Indus served as the border between India to the east and (Persian) Ariane to the west.

At the same time the Achaemenid conquest continued of the Aegean coast, where the island of Samos had remained as the last, major independent state. The rulers of the island possessed a strong war navy. Around 522 B.C., the important tyrant of Samos, Polycrates, was treacherously murdered by the Persian satrap in Lydia, Oroites, and as a result the island came under the administration of Polycrates' secretary, Meandrius. In about 517 B.C. a Persian army, commanded

---

[1] E. Herzfeld dated this conquest to 519-518 B.C. A. T. Olmstead preferred a date sometime before 513 B.C. (Herzfeld 1928:2; Olmstead 1948:145).

by Otanes, one of the seven conspirators who participated in the murder of Gaumata, occupied Samos after an unexpected attack. The island was plundered and incorporated into the Achaemenid empire. Syloson was appointed as its vassal ruler. He was a brother of Polycrates, and prior to Darius' rise to power he had become known to the Persian king when he helped Darius in a minor matter. One of the inhabitants of Samos, Lykaretos, had also defected to the Persian side and he was shortly afterwards appointed as governor of the island of Lemnos which had also been recently conquered by the Persians. At approximately the same time, Chios recognized Persian hegemony.

Around 516 B.C., Darius assembled a large fleet consisting of ships from the Greek cities of Asia Minor. These he dispatched to the littoral of the Black Sea. Local people of those regions, as far north as the mouth of the Ister (Danube), together with the Greek settlers, submitted without resistance. An experienced Greek engineer called Mandrokles constructed a bridge from boats at the most narrow place of the Bosphorus, and as a result Europe and Asia were for the first time united. Along the coasts of the Bosphorus two marble memorial stelae were set up with an inscription in Greek and also, according to Herodotus (IV 87), with "Assyrian characters", which probably refers to Old Persian, Elamite and Akkadian. Herodotus (IV 87), whose Achilles' heel is almost always his reference to numbers, wrote that 700,000 men, including cavalry, were assembled near the bridge (this is an undoubtedly fantastic number), together with 600 ships. The Persian army crossed the bridge and arrived in Thrace. Subsequently, without meeting any resistance, they continued to the lower course of the Ister.

Darius had decided to organize a military campaign against the Black Sea Scythians. He probably did so in order to prevent a growing interest from Scythian side into the rich lands of Thrace. Earlier, the satrap of Cappadocia, Ariaramnes, had made a voyage into the Black Sea with a small fleet and had taken some captives in order to obtain the necessary information prior to the planned campaign. A pontoon bridge was constructed across the Danube. Once across the river, Darius started to manoeuvre in the south Russian steppes. Darius also left behind a contingent of Ionian soldiers who had accompanied him to the Danube, in order to guard the bridge. According to Darius' instructions, the Greeks had to guard the bridge for sixty days. If the Persian army had not returned by that time, they were to destroy it and return home.

When precisely the Scythian campaign took place is unknown, but it is possible to date this event, more or less accurately, to the years between 516 and 512 B.C. (Beloch 1912-1927, Vol. II, part 2, p. 60ff.; Bengtson 1960:136; Cameron 1943:313; Harmatta 1979:19ff.). The most important source on Darius' Scythian campaign is the fourth book of the *Historiae* of Herodotus.

The Scythians did not dare risk a decisive battle against the huge army of their adversaries. They therefore resorted to their beloved scorched earth tactic. They retreated, taking with them their livestock, burning the grass and filling in the water pits. In addition, Scythian cavalry repeatedly attacked and destroyed small Persian hunting parties. The Persians were worn out by their protracted pursuit of the Scythians deep into their own territory. While Darius was looking for a way out of this predicament, the Scythian leaders in response to his demand that they would either come out for an open battle or submit voluntarily, sent a messenger to the Persian camp. Subsequently, if Herodotus is to be believed, Darius was presented by the messenger with a bird, a mouse, a frog, and five arrows. Darius thought that the Scythians thus announced their submission. Gobryas, however, one of the seven conspirators against Smerdis, gave a completely different explanation: If the Persians could not fly in the sky like birds, could not burrow into the ground like mice, or jump into the lakes like frogs, then they should expect to die by arrows.

In the meantime, a group of Scythians that had gone around the Persians approached the bridge across the Danube and turned towards the Ionian guardsmen with the demand that the bridge should be destroyed as soon as the required sixty days had elapsed. In return, the Ionians could go home and regain their freedom. They owed nothing to Darius, the Scythians argued, for he himself had commanded them to return after the sixty days had passed. The Ionians promised to fulfil this demand and the Scythians returned to their main forces.

Because of a lack of provisions required to continue the war and missing possibilities of joining into open battle with the Scythians, Darius decided to withdraw. The Persians started in the middle of the night for their secret retreat, leaving behind the sick soldiers and part of the army train, and illuminating the camp with blazing campfires in order to hide their sudden withdrawal.[2] On the following day the Scythians went to

---

[2] According to Polyaenus (VII 11), a certain Scythian with the name of Syrakes, mutilated himself and went to the camp of Darius. He told the king that the Scythian leaders had done this to him. Promising to show the Persians a special route, Syrakes led them to a completely barren desert. Thereupon Darius, placing his tiara, sceptre and crown on a high hill top, prayed to his god to send rain. Darius' request was answered and the Persian army was saved. This legend has a clearly legendary character. It is possible, however, that Polyaenus' report relates to Darius' campaign against the Sakas of Central Asia. The name Syrakes is characteristic for this area (pers. comm. by V. A. Livšits).

look for the Persians. When they could not find them they started in pursuit. They missed them, however, and arrived much earlier than the Persians at the bridge along the Danube. Finding the bridge still complete, they again turned towards the Ionians with the demand that the bridge should be destroyed. The leaders of the Ionians considered their reply. Some participants at the council were of the opinion that the Scythian request should be heeded and that at the same time they should liberate Ionia from the Persian oppressors. The tyrant of Miletus, however, Histiaeus by name, opposed this suggestion, reminding all the tyrants present at the council that they ruled their towns by the favour of Darius and that they would lose their power at Darius' death because the cities would then refuse to accept their authority. Having almost decided to destroy the bridge, the Ionians eventually decided to follow Histiaeus' advice. To pacify the Scythians, Histiaeus told them that the Ionians would accept their demand. They commenced to destroy the bridge, starting at the further, Scythian side of the river. Subsequently the Scythians left. After the lapse of some time the Persian army arrived at the bridge and the troops safely crossed towards Thrace (see extensively the work by E. V. Černenko 1984; see also Mazetti 1982:106ff.).

This campaign, which clearly ended unsuccessfully, should not be studied in isolation from the foreign policy of the Achaemenids as regards the peoples that surrounded the Achaemenid empire to the north and northeast. Darius, just like Cyrus, attempted to liquidate the danger imposed by the predatory inroads by Scythian tribes into the lands of the Achaemenid empire. Just like Cyrus, who at an advanced age campaigned against the Massagetae, Darius personally participated in two campaigns against Scythian tribes. This point attests to the significance that the Achaemenids adhered to the subjugation of their northern and eastern neighbours. In instructing the Ionians to destroy the bridge after the lapse of two months, Darius may have given a sign that he planned to march along the whole Scythian steppe belt, from the lands to the north of the Black Sea, all the way towards the Caucasus or even Central Asia, and to return to Persia by way of some of their subject lands (Meyer 1939, Vol. IV, pp. 104ff.; Rostovtzeff 1918:41; see, however, also Burn 1970:131, where some doubts are cast on the concept that Darius would have imagined such a huge undertaking). Darius could hardly have grasped the sheer distances involved between the lands north of the Black Sea and Central Asia, or the difficulties in crossing the large rivers, or the endless steppes.

Although Darius' Scythian campaign remained without success, Darius had marched deep into Scythian territory in pursuit of his ever retreating adversaries. This justified Darius in including the Black Sea

Scythians into the list of subject peoples[3] with the name of the 'Scythians across the sea' (*Sakā paradrayā*). By the time of Xerxes, however, these people were already omitted from the inscriptions.

From Thrace Darius returned to Iran, leaving his general Megabyzus behind with the order to complete the conquest of the districts along the Hellespont and in Thrace (for an extensive account, see Balcer 1972b). Soon Persian supremacy was established along both sides of the sea lanes between Europe and Asia. In this manner the Persians could deprive the Greeks (and notably the Athenians) of the possibility of receiving grain from the coastal regions of the Black Sea and shipwright's timber from Thrace. Megabyzus also conquered several Greek cities along the northern coast of the Aegean, the inhabitants of which, among other subject peoples, were mentioned in the Achaemenid inscriptions under the name of 'the petasos-wearing Ionians'.

Thrace was inhabited by many tribes, which were, however, continuously at war with each other. It was therefore an easy prey for the Persians. They conquered a land with silver and gold mines and with fertile lands, especially in the valley of the river Strymon. Several thousands of its inhabitants, belonging to the people of the Paeonians, were forcibly resettled in Asia Minor. The reason for this extreme measure should apparently be sought in the resistance of the Paeonians against their new masters, although Herodotus states that Darius ordered the deportation of the Paeonians because he had been surprised by the hard-working nature of their women.

When the Persian army reached the borders of Macedonia, the king of this land, who was called Alexander, hastened to offer his submission. He also gave his sister in marriage to a Persian nobleman. It should be noted that Herodotus reports that Alexander killed the Persian ambassadors, but this version was concocted at a later date when the Persians in their war with the Greeks were on the defensive (Burn 1970:134). Persian garrisons were stationed in Macedonia and Thrace, and by 512 B.C. both of these lands constituted a satrapy under the name of Skudra (cf., however, Szemerényi 1980, who suggested that *Skudra* is a Scythian tribe which, according to him, lived in Macedonia and Thrace).

---

[3] F. H. Weissbach suggested that, because Herodotus' description of Darius' campaign against the Scythians indicates a Persian defeat, while in the Achaemenid texts the Scythians are indicated as a subject people, Darius may have invaded the Scythian lands for a second time, with more success (Weissbach 1940:80). In support of this hypothesis the information provided by Ctesias is used, to the extent that Darius ordered Ariaramnes, his satrap in Cappadocia, to make an inroad into the northern littoral of the Black Sea to collect information. As indicated above, however, this inroad predated Darius' campaign against the Scythians (see Athen. XII 522; Ctesias, *Pers.* XIII; see König 1972:8, paragraph 16; Strabo, VII 3.14).

Approximately at the same time Darius appointed his half-brother Artaphrenes (Old Persian: *Artafarna*, 'with truthful sacredness') as satrap of Lydia. The command over the fleet in the northern part of Asia Minor was given to the Persian Otanes, the son of Sisamnes. His residence was located at Dascyleium. He was, apparently, placed under Artaphrenes (Burn 1970:136).

Histiaeus, the tyrant of Miletus, who had extended considerable assistance to Darius at the time of the Scythian campaign, received as recompense extensive lands in Thrace, where he subsequently started to build fortifications. In the eyes of Megabyzus this constituted a danger to Persian hegemony, and he complained to Darius. The latter summoned Histiaeus to his court and detained him at Susa on the pretext that he wanted a trustworthy counsellor at hand. On the recommendation of Histiaeus, his brother-in-law and cousin, Aristagoras, was appointed as the ruler of Miletus. The Greek Coes, who had also shown assistance to Darius, was appointed as tyrant of his native town Mytilene on the island of Lesbos.

The end of the sixth century B.C. was the period of the largest expansion of Achaemenid power. The Empire included more than eighty peoples and its borders stretched from the Indus river in the east to the Aegean Sea in the west, and from Armenia in the north to Nubia in the south. Darius also sent three ships with spies to Italy and Sicily, where a war was impending between the Greek and Phoenician colonists. The latter were in principle allies of the Persians in the expected war with the Greeks, and Darius followed with great attention the course of events in the whole of the Mediterranean region, the eastern part of which was already controlled by the Persians. By that time the Persians commanded a mighty fleet which consisted of ships from the Phoenicians, Carians, Ionians and other maritime peoples.

In the inscriptions of Darius from Persepolis and Ecbatana this period of Persian power is characterized by the following words: "Darius, great king, king of kings, king of lands, son of Vishtaspa, the Achaemenid. Darius the king says: This kingdom, which I rule, (it stretches) from the Sakas that live beyond Sogdiana to Nubia; from India to Lydia. Ahuramazda, the greatest of the gods, bestowed (it) on me. May Ahuramazda[4] protect me and my house" (DPh/DH inscriptions).

---

[4] In the Akkadian version it says: "Ahuramazda with the (other) gods."

CHAPTER SEVENTEEN

THE IONIAN REVOLT

During the sixth century B.C., the leading role in cultural and economic developments in the Hellenic world was not played by the Greeks from the Balkan peninsula, but by colonists (especially the Ionians) who had settled along the western coastal regions of Asia Minor. This area included important settlements such as Miletus and Ephesus (cf. Sealey 1976:170). These cities were located in wide, fertile lands. They had a highly developed craft production and had access to trade markets in the Near East. Even in the eighth century B.C., Greek merchants from Asia Minor were trading with the cities of the Assyrian empire. In doing so, they were successfully competing with the Phoenicians. The Persian conquest of Asia Minor enlarged the Ionian trade possibilities with neighbouring and distant lands. The Ionian merchants, and especially those from Miletus, not only traded with the lands of the Near East, but also with the mainland Greeks and the coastal regions of the Black Sea.

Having conquered the Greek cities of Asia Minor, the Persians did not change the traditional institutions of local autonomy, nor did they impede in any way the economic and cultural development of these settlements. During the period of Achaemenid rule in Miletus, which was the most important city of Ionia, there lived the eminent philosopher Anaximander and the geographer and historian Hecataeus. The famous mathematician Pythagoras was born and lived part of his life on the island of Samos, which was also subject to the Persians. The 'Father of History', Herodotus, was born at Halicarnassus, and before his emigration to mainland Greece was a subject of the Persian empire. There are also indications that the Greek alphabet developed in Miletus.

Apparently, Darius held the opinion that he had no reason to be afraid of any challenge to the strength and continuity of his power in Asia Minor. By the time of his reign the Ionians had been under Persian rule for several decades. The Greeks had become accustomed to live with the Persians, and the prosperity of many groups within the Hellenic towns had become dependent on the Persians. Subsequent events, however, ruined these peaceful prospects.

In 500 B.C., a sudden change of power took place on the island of Naxos, which is located in the centre of the Cyclades and at that time was still independent of the Persians. The power of the aristocracy was broken in favour of that of a democracy. The banished 'bellied ones', as the representatives of the aristocracy were called on Naxos, fled to Miletus and turned for help to the local ruler, the tyrant Aristagoras. The latter, in a desire to extend his influence, suggested that the satrap of Lydia, Artaphrenes, should organize a combined campaign against Naxos in order to subject the island to the Persians and return it to aristocratic rule. Artaphrenes counselled his brother, King Darius, about this plan. In the spring of 499 B.C. he received Darius' approbation. He fitted out a fleet of 200 ships. It would seem likely that by that time the Persians not only planned to conquer Naxos, but also the other Cycladic islands. The Achaemenid Megabates was appointed as the commander of the fleet, while Aristagoras, who had hoped to receive the overall command of the expedition, had to subject himself and his troops to Persian leadership. Megabates wanted to attack Naxos surreptitiously in order to surprise the people of the island. He therefore ordered the fleet to sail first in the direction of the Black Sea. Thereupon he turned around towards the island, trying to remain unobserved. Someone, however, managed to warn the Naxians who subsequently prepared to offer resistance. For four months the fleet of the Persians and the Milesians besieged Naxos. The siege, however, remained unsuccessful. This was partly caused by the rivalry between Megabates and Aristagoras. At the end of four months the funds which had been reserved for the campaign, began to dry up and the ships were ordered to leave the coast of Naxos and to return to the mainland of Asia Minor.

If we can believe Herodotus (V 35), Aristagoras feared punishment for the failure of the campaign and therefore decided to revolt against the Persians. While he contemplated his plans, a secret messenger arrived from his father-in-law Histiaeus, who had been detained by Darius at Susa. As already mentioned, Histiaeus used to be the tyrant of Miletus, but Darius suspected him of planning to revolt against the Persians and therefore ordered Histiaeus to hand over his authority to Aristagoras. Darius did not punish Histiaeus, because he remembered Histiaeus' assistance in the past, namely when he refused to destroy the bridge across the Danube during the Scythian campaign, which meant that the Persian army could escape unhurt from the Scythians. Now Histiaeus turned to Aristagoras, via a messenger, with the call to organize a revolt against the king.

Aristagoras assembled the citizens of Miletus and persuaded the majority of those present to support his call for rebellion. The logographer Hecataeus attempted to change the mind of his fellow citizens by describing the military strength of the Persians, which was formed by the levies from numerous peoples. Hecataeus' admonitions, however, were drowned in the chorus of those who wanted action. Thus, in the autumn of 499 B.C., the Ionian revolt broke out.

Aristagoras laid down his authority as tyrant and passed all his powers to the council, the leading role in which was played by the merchants and craftsmen of Miletus. According to Herodotus (V 37), Aristagoras laid down his office in order to urge the people to his side. Aristagoras was chosen as the military leader of the revolt. The people's assembly declared its freedom and called for all the Greeks to join in the war against Persian domination.

When a messenger announced the revolt to the sailors of the fleet which had just returned from Naxos and which was anchored not far off from Miletus, they received the call for freedom with enthusiasm. Following the Milesians, and with their support, the Greeks from many other cities in Asia Minor deposed their tyrants. Some of the tyrants were stoned to death, but the majority managed to escape and were forced into exile. Thus many Greek districts in northern and southern Asia Minor joined the revolt and representatives from the various towns selected a united military command. A start was made with the minting of coins in electrum with a generally accepted standard, instead of the old coins from different mints. As early as the beginning of our century, P. Gardner related these electrum coins to the period of the Ionian revolt. These coins, as well as silver examples, were minted from 499 B.C. onwards in many districts of western Asia Minor and on the nearby islands (see Bengtson 1960:45; Gardner 1908:107-138; Tozzi 1978:81-92).

Herodotus' account, which is our main source for the Ionian revolt, clearly demands a critical reading because of his antipathetic attitude towards the insurgents.[1] To Herodotus, the territory of Asia Minor, just like the rest of Asia, belonged to the Persian king. The Ionians, therefore, had to live in peace with the Achaemenid king without revolting against his legitimate power. From this point it is possible to conclude that the native town of Herodotus, Halicarnassus, did not join the revolt. Whatever the case, Herodotus, being a subject of the Persian king, regarded the revolt as mad, as a 'whim' and as a sign of the stubbornness of the Ionians (Burn 1970:197; Lur'e 1947:66-68). It is not surprising, therefore, that Herodotus relates the reasons for the revolt to certain unsavoury intentions of its instigators (according to Herodotus, they were intriguers and adventurers), and in particular to Aristagoras' fear of reprisals from the side of the Persians after his unsuccessful campaign against Naxos. Herodotus also sought another motive for the revolt in

---

[1] See the monograph by P. Tozzi (1978), which deals with this revolt. It contains a thorough analysis of literary, epigraphic, archaeological and numismatic sources which refer to the various events and their chronology (pp. 22-99). The book also contains plans and maps of military operations (pp. 100-230) and an extensive bibliography (pp. 231-236). See also Tozzi 1975; 1976-1977; 1977. Cf. Balcer 1984:227-282.

Histiaeus' wish to return to Miletus. He had become extremely bored at Susa and hoped that Darius would send him back to Asia Minor to crush the rebels. It is possible that Aristagoras and Histiaeus were really adventurers and had no purposeful programme of actions against Persian domination. If this were the case, then the question arises as to why the call for revolt found such widespread support among the Greeks. It is clear that there must have been some very serious reasons.

First of all, the annual tribute of 400 talents of silver, which the Greeks of Asia Minor had to pay together with the Carians, Lycians and certain other and smaller population groups, caused dissatisfaction with the Persian rulers, the more so because only a small part of this sum was returned to Ionia. This hindered the development of money-commodity relations. By itself, however, this would not have been the main reason for the revolt, for approximately the same sum had been paid by the Greeks since the time of Croesus and it was not regarded as a heavy burden. Probably, the Greeks in general were not content with the system of local autonomy. When, more than forty years before the outbreak of the Ionian revolt, the Persians had conquered Asia Minor, the dominant form of government in the Greek cities had been that of tyranny. In those days tyrants were popular leaders who received widespread support from the farmers, craftsmen and traders in their struggle against the old ranks of the aristocracy. When autonomy was granted to a certain subject people, Persian administration, as a rule, remained indifferent towards the internal political structure of the population. In Asia Minor, therefore, the Persians did not alter the traditional political order, and they showed support for the tyrants who, gradually, changed into loyal servants of the Persian king. Herodotus (IV 137) writes that each of the Greek tyrants could only rule their towns because of the support they received from the Persian authorities. The Persian government, however, only supported the tyrants out of tradition. Thus the widespread view that the Persians were in all cases on the side of the tyrants and remained adverse to democracy, is incorrect (cf. Graf 1985:86).

After one or two generations (apparently starting by the time of the Persian conquest of Asia Minor), however, tyranny had fulfilled its function of democratic dictatorship and had become an unpopular force which was against the spirit of the time, notably as it had changed into an impediment to social development (see Burn 1970:195; Lur'e 1940:188; Tozzi 1978:121; Walser 1984:16-19). By the end of the sixth century B.C., social life on mainland Greece had developed without significant outside pressure, and as a result tyrannies either grew into oligarchies, or were, as in Athens, replaced by democracies. In Ionia the craftsmen and merchants also strove to take power and were discontent with tyranny. It appeared to the Ionians, however, that it was impossible to discard the tyrants without first liberating themselves from Persian domination.

It should finally be noted that many Greeks suffered under the yoke of the Persians and hoped for their freedom. It is fully possible, therefore, that this point, as already suggested by H. Bengtson, was the main reason for the Ionian revolt (Bengtson 1960:43).

Scholars have published much about the economic motives behind the revolt. As far as conclusions can be drawn from the historical sources, craftsmen, sailors and traders played an active role in the revolt, rather than the population of the countryside which in the main remained on the fence. It is not possible, therefore, to exclude the idea that the city dwellers, whose prosperity depended on the market system, had become oppressed by various mercantile problems. According to S. Ja. Lur'e, leading groups within the trade and producers' classes in Asia Minor had become involved in trade with the Black Sea area and Thrace, where they could export their products and whence they could import cheap grain. When by the end of the sixth century the Persians conquered the Hellespont, and trade through these straits came under their control, the trade with Black Sea grain fell into the hands, according to Lur'e, of the Phoenicians. This, in his words, was the 'crash of the time' for the Ionian traders, and therefore they started the call for revolt (Lur'e 1940:186). It is, however, difficult to agree with these suggestions. In the first place, Persian officials did not impede the trade of the towns of Asia Minor with the Black Sea littoral. On the contrary, after the Persian conquest of the Hellespont this trade was completely safe. In the second place, the Phoenicians had never been interested, either in grain from the Black Sea area, or in the timber from Thrace, because they could obtain the pertinent products for a lower price from lands adjacent to Phoenicia (i.e. Egypt, Babylonia and Lebanon). The Phoenicians had become strong competitors of the Ionian merchants in their trade with the lands of the Near East, but Persian domination is not reflected in a trade war with the Ionians for the markets of the northern littoral of the Black Sea. The competition from the side of other Greeks, however, was certainly not less. For example, after the fall of Egypt to the Persians the Greek colony of Naucratis, in Egypt, became a rival to the merchants of Asia Minor. To an even greater degree this point can be applied to the Athenians. Archaeological finds in northern Syria testify to the fact that by the end of the sixth century B.C. Athenian ceramics had to a large extent replaced the pottery products of producers from Asia Minor. It is possible that the economic decline in Ionia was started by unsuccessful competition with the Athenian merchants.

This development may have caused the discontent of the traders and craftsmen of Ionia (see Sealey 1976:177).

Whatever was the case, the revolt spread to other districts, and soon had a huge territory in its grip, stretching from the Hellespont in the north to Caria in the south. In 499 B.C. the leader of the rebels, Aristagoras, sailed to mainland Greece to ask for assistance.

Aristagoras first went to Sparta, which was at that time the strongest military city-state of the Greeks. He addressed the Spartan king Cleomenes and asked that the Spartans should liberate the Greeks of Asia Minor from the Persian yoke. He tried to convince the Spartan king that the Persians were only armed with bows and short swords and would therefore be easily defeated as the Greeks were superior to the Persian soldiers, both in weaponry and in tactics. Aristagoras also displayed a map on a bronze plate. This map was made, according to certain scholars, by the Milesian scholar Anaximander on the basis of earlier Babylonian maps. On this map, which the Spartans would long remember because they had never seen such a thing before, the whole world was depicted, such as it was known in those days to the Greeks of Asia Minor. Aristagoras pointed out on the map where particular peoples lived that were subject to the Persians, and how rich they were in gold, silver and livestock. He called upon the Spartans to conquer these riches, instead of waging war upon their poor neighbours from whom there was nothing to gain. Cleomenes promised an answer within three days. When at the appointed time Aristagoras appeared again, Cleomenes refused assistance, on the grounds that it would take three months to travel from the Ionian Sea to Susa, the capital of the Persian king. He furthermore ordered Aristagoras to leave Sparta before the sunset of the same day. Of course, the Spartans had realized that they were not in a position to undertake a successful campaign to the hub of the Achaemenid empire. In addition, they had bitter experiences from previous alliances against the Persians, first with Lydia, and thereafter with Egypt. Sparta also had to prepare for war on the Peloponnesos itself, with its traditional enemy, Argos. Finally, Sparta had the long tradition of not sending, as far as possible, any large bodies of troops beyond the borders of Greece.

Aristagoras left for Athens, which after Sparta was the most powerful Greek city-state. In Athens there lived many groups of people, especially the noble and influential family of the Alcmeonids which occupied many important state functions, who agitated against a conflict with the Persians. They did so because their own prosperity was based on trade with Asia Minor. In 507 B.C., not long before the Ionian revolt, the Athenians, expecting an invasion by a strong force of Spartans and their allies, had sent messengers to the Lydian satrap Artaphrenes in order to conclude a treaty with Persia and to ask for military assistance. Artaphrenes[2] agreed to this alliance which was directed against Sparta. His agreement, however, included the demand that the Athenians would present 'earth and water', which meant that they had to recognize the suzerainty of the Achaemenid king. According to Herodotus (V 73), this condition was accepted by the Athenian ambassadors and the treaty was concluded. The arrival of Aristagoras in Athens was therefore greeted with hostility by many inhabitants of the city.

Nevertheless, Aristagoras came at a fairly favourable moment, as the relationship between Athens and the Persians had become tense due to the following event: The tyrant Hippias, deprived of his power in Athens and exiled from the city, had by 505 B.C. turned towards the Persian satrap at Sardis and had urged him to subject Athens to Darius. Hearing about this, the Athenians sent their ambassadors to Sardis in order to prevent Hippias' plans coming to fruition. Artaphrenes, however, demanded from the ambassadors that the Athenians took Hippias back. They refused the ultimatum and commenced preparations for war with the Persians. The ambassadors who had concluded the treaty with the Persians in 507 B.C. were accused of having exceeded their mandates. Cleisthenes, the leader of Athenian political life, was severely criticized because of the treaty; the pro-Persian Alcmeonids and their adherents were ousted from power. When in 507 B.C. the Athenians had sought a temporary alliance with Persia in order to protect their land against Sparta it would appear that the leaders of Athens did not realize that the Persians by this treaty would regard them as their voluntary vassals for all times (see Orlin 1976:264).

Appearing at the popular assembly of the Athenians, Aristagoras tried to convince his audience that the Persians used no shields or spears and were therefore easy to defeat. Consequently it would not be difficult to conquer the wealth of Asia. Aristagoras also referred to the fact that Miletus was an Athenian colony and therefore was entitled to help from the Athenians when in need.

After a long speech Aristagoras succeeded in obtaining a promise of assistance from the Athenians. In his report on this event, Herodotus (V 97) adds that it is easier to deceive a large group of people, than one man,

---

[2] According to Herodotus (V 105), before 507 B.C. Artaphrenes and the Persians had no idea whatsoever who the Athenians were, and where they lived. This piece of information, however, does not seem to reflect historical truth. According to L. Orlin, Athenian presence in the Hellespont and its influence on the cities along the Ionian coast started at least by 600 B.C. (Orlin 1976:264, n. 28; for an extensive account of the Perso-Greek relations in the early period, see Sealey 1976:170-230).

as the Spartan king Cleomenes was not convinced by Aristagoras' words, while the Athenian assembly promised help to the rebels. This promise, according to the 'Father of History', became a source of undescribable misery, both for the Greeks and for the Persians and all their subjects. Referring to the Athenian decision, Herodotus (I 4) also writes that the Greeks attacked the Persian dominions in Asia before the Persians attacked Greece.

In reality, however, Aristagoras did not have a great deal of success in Athens, because the influential part of the population, headed by the Alcmeonids, decisively argued against any assistance to the rebels, on the grounds that it could lead to an open war with the Persians. In the end, Athens only sent twenty ships in support of the rebels. This was an open challenge to Persia, although it could not influence the outcome of the revolt. The Eretrians on the island of Euboea, who had long since established close trade links with Miletus, also replied positively to the request by the rebels, but they could only send five triremes.

Having returned to Miletus, Aristagoras sent a messenger to the tribe of the Paeonians, who twenty years before on the orders of the Persian general Megabyzus had been deported from the valley of the Strymon (in Thrace) to Phrygia in Asia Minor. The messenger presented the Paeonians with a proposition from Aristagoras: if they wanted to regain their freedom and return to their home land, then the rebellious Ionians could be of assistance. With the help of the Greeks the majority of the Paeonians returned to Thrace. This, however, could hardly help the rebels. It only aggravated Darius' anger, a fact which had been anticipated by the acute Aristagoras.

When the Athenian and Eretrian ships arrived at Miletus, Aristagoras sent a fleet and troops to Sardis. The rebel army crossed Mount Tmolis and occupied Sardis, while Artaphrenes, the Persian satrap, and his garrison remained in possession of the acropolis. The Greeks did not succeed in occupying the Persian stronghold. During the pillaging of the town, fire broke out, burning down almost all the houses, whose roofs were thatched. In addition, the sanctuary of the Lydian goddess Cybele was destroyed. This destruction set the Lydians against the rebels. They thus joined the Persians in Sardis, and together they assembled on the market place and commenced battle with the Ionians. The latter fled back to their ships, having lost all hope of support from the Lydians.

On hearing the news of the initial defeat at Sardis, the Persian leaders in Asia Minor assembled their forces and marched towards Lydia. At the same time the Ionians withdrew to Ephesus, where, in the summer of 498 B.C., they were decisively beaten by the Persians. The remnants of the rebel army fled in chaos to their different towns. When the rebels started to lose ground, persophil groups in Athens gained the upper hand, and after the election of 496 B.C. the party of the Alcmeonids regained its former power. Immediately afterwards the Athenians recalled their ships, leaving the Ionians to their fate and ignoring a further appeal for help by Aristagoras. The Eretrians followed the example of the Athenians. The Ionians, however, who had no hope for a pardon from the side of Darius, continued the war.

Hecataeus of Miletus, who at first had tried unsuccessfully to keep his fellow citizens from rebellion, now pointed out that as the Ionians were not capable of defeating the Persians on land, it was necessary to build a huge fleet and to gain supremacy at sea. The Ionian rebels, however, did not have the money to build new ships. Hecataeus, therefore, called for the Milesians to use the treasures of the temple of Apollo at Branchidae, near Miletus, which had been deposited there by Croesus. This would also mean that, in case of Persian successes, these goods and riches would not fall into the hands of the enemy. The superstitious rebels, however, did not heed the advice of Hecataeus.

The Ionians sent their fleet to the Hellespont. They conquered the city of Byzantium and other towns. As a result the Thracian satrapy was cut off from the other Persian provinces. A large part of Caria and Lycia came over to the side of the rebels. Not long afterwards the revolt also spread to Cyprus. The people of the island consisted of Greeks and Phoenicians, and a struggle had been going on between them for a long time. Particularly bitter was the rivalry between Salamis, the main Greek settlement on the island, and the Phoenician city of Kition. The Greeks, headed by their tyrants, revolted, while the Phoenicians remained loyal to the Persian king. When Salamis defected to the Ionian side, its king Gorgus fled to the Persians.

Thus, the revolt extended from the districts around the Hellespont to the island of Cyprus. The unrest on Cyprus was of particular danger to the Persians because it made a considerable fleet available to the rebels, plus the rich copper mines of the island. In addition, by occupying Cyprus, the rebels could stop Phoenician ships from entering the Aegean Sea.

The rebellious Cyprians besieged the town of Amathus, which had remained loyal to the Persians. The Persian army, commanded by Artybius, advanced by sea towards Cyprus, in cooperation with the Phoenician fleet. Thereupon the Ionians came to the assistance of the Greek Cyprians. The rulers of the Greek Cyprian towns selected Onesilus as the commander of their united forces. He was a younger brother of the Gorgus who had fled to the Persians. In the ensuing sea battle the Ionians defeated the Phoenicians, while on land Artybius and

Onesilus fought man to man. The specially trained horse of Artybius hit the shield of Onesilus with his hoof, but just at that moment the shield-bearer of Onesilus cut off the hoofs of the horse with his scimitar. Artybius fell and was killed. However, during the course of the battle, part of the Cyprian army fled from the scene, and the victory went to the Persians. Onesilus and many of his adherents were killed. The Persians reinstated Gorgus at Salamis. In the years 497-496 B.C. they reconquered the rest of Cyprus.

We are acquainted with certain details concerning the siege by the Persians of the Cyprian towns. Thus, at the time of the siege of the town of Idalion, near modern Nicosia, 'the Medes and the Kitians' (namely, the Persians and the people from the Phoenician town of Kition, on the same island) had been opposed for a long time by the people from Idalion, who were headed by their king Stasicyprus. According to the information on a bronze tablet, written in the syllabic, Cyprian script, a family of healers, to be precise "Onasilus, the son of Onasicyprus, and his brothers", was solemnly promised a reward for having treated wounded people free of charge during the long siege.[3] Between 1950 and 1953, during the course of archaeological excavations at the town of Paphos, a ramp was discovered along which the Persians must have made an attack on the besieged city. Part of the ramp consisted of statues which the Persians had apparently taken from a nearby cemetery. In the ramp were found hundreds of arrowheads. These belonged to arrows which the besieged had shot from the town walls towards the workers constructing the fortifications (for literature, see Burn 1970:203ff.).

After having been defeated in the war on land, the Ionians left Cyprus and the Persians started to subdue one after the other the towns of Asia Minor. Towards the end of 496 B.C., the Persians fought a bitter battle with the revolting Carians along the banks of the River Marsyas. In this battle, 2,000 Persians were killed, and many more Carians. During the battle the Ionians came to the assistance of the Carians, but the Persians were victorious. The remaining Carians continued their resistance, defeating many Persian troops by laying ambushes.[4]

---

[3] GD, No. 60; ICS:235. Many scholars, beginning with J. Beloch, relate the information on this tablet to the time of the Ionian revolt. Some scholars, however, suggest that the tablet refers to events which took place between 478 and 470 B.C., when Idalion was occupied and annexed by the kingdom of Kition with its pro-Persian, Phoenician population. Other historians hold the opinion that the text refers to the expedition by Cimon in 449 B.C. According to P. Tozzi, the *terminus ante quem* for the siege of the town of Idalion, mentioned by the bronze tablet, is 470 B.C. (see Tozzi 1978:93ff. The same study also contains references to relevant literature).

[4] In 1954 a Greek inscription was published (it dates to a period slightly earlier than 478 B.C.) which indicates that in the 80's of the fifth century B.C. there were many

The Lydian satrap Artaphrenes and the general Otanes united their forces and started a planned campaign against the rebels. The depressed Aristagoras, the instigator of the revolt, handed his authority over to one of the citizens of Miletus. Together with those who had no will or strength to continue the fight, Aristagoras fled to the district of Myrcinus in Thrace. Soon afterwards he died.

While the revolt was still in full swing, Darius summoned Histiaeus and asked him about Aristagoras' actions, wondering whether there had been any intrigue from his side. Histiaeus tried to convince Darius that he was innocent and he added that there would have been no unrest if he had been in Ionia. In addition, Histiaeus promised that, if the king would send him to Miletus, he would soon put an end to the revolt and turn Aristagoras over to Darius. Darius believed the words of Histiaeus and sent him to Asia Minor, ordering him to return to Susa after the subjugation of Ionia.

Histiaeus arrived at Sardis in 496 B.C. There the satrap Artaphrenes, alluding to his role in the preparations of the revolt, told him: "You made the shoe, and Aristagoras put it on." In fear of punishment by Artaphrenes, Histiaeus fled from Sardis, initially conspiring with certain of his companions (according to Herodotus these were Persians) to start a revolt in Lydia. When Histiaeus arrived on an island along the coast of Asia Minor, he was met without enthusiasm. The inhabitants of the island interrogated him, asking why he had urged Aristagoras to revolt and involve them in such hardships. Histiaeus answered that Darius had planned to deport the Ionians to Phoenicia and this had forced him to plan a revolt. According to Herodotus (VI 3), this was a lie concocted in order to justify himself. Subsequently when Histiaeus attempted to get into contact with his fellow conspirators in Sardis, his messenger betrayed them and they were executed by Artaphrenes. Shortly after this Histiaeus went to Miletus. The citizens of the city, however, who had set up democratic structures of administration, were not inclined to receive back their former tyrant. Subsequently Histiaeus sailed to the island of Lesbos. He persuaded the people of the island to equip eight triremes and to send these together with him to Byzantium, a town along the Hellespont. There they commenced to seize any ships whose sailors refused to join the revolt. In effect, they took to piracy.

Carians living at Athens. Apparently they were participants in the Ionian revolt who had escaped Persian revenge. H. Bengtson suggests that among them were also some leaders of the revolt, such as Heraclides, the former tyrant of the Carian town of Mylasa, and the famous explorer Scylax of Caryanda (Bengtson 1955:301f.; in the same study references are made to pertinent literature; see also Drews 1973:34f.).

In one of the battles, near the town of Malene in the north of Asia Minor, the Ionians fled, and Histiaeus was captured by the Persians. At the moment that the Persian soldiers were about to kill him as a common prisoner, he cried out in Persian, being overcome by cowardice, that he was Histiaeus. Subsequently they brought him to Sardis. The Persian generals Harpagos and Artaphrenes, fearing that Darius would pardon him and that Histiaeus would again become an influential person, crucified him and sent his decapitated head to the Persian king at Susa. The latter showed great dissatisfaction with the fact that Histiaeus had not been brought to him alive. Remembering the past deeds of Histiaeus, Darius ordered a funeral for his head.[5]

During the spring of 494 B.C. the Persians started to lay siege to the city of Miletus, which was the main centre of the revolt. A large army, collected from all of Asia Minor, was concentrated along the walls of the town. A fleet anchored nearby. The ships were manned by sailors from Phoenicia, Egypt, Cilicia and Cyprus. Friendly Ionian towns decided to assist Miletus in protecting it from the sea. Together with the Milesian ships they mustered a fleet of 353 vessels, a large part of which came from the islands of Samos, Chios and Lesbos. According to Herodotus, the Persian fleet numbered 600 ships, but A. R. Burn regards this figure, not without reason, as being far too high and perhaps symbolic, because the same number of ships, according to Herodotus, participated in Darius' Scythian campaign and also at the disembarkation of his army in the plain of Marathon (Burn 1970:210).

The Persian commanders decided not to join in combat. They ordered the former tyrants of the cities of Asia Minor, who had fled to the Persians during the revolt, to address their countrymen with a call to come over to the other side on the promise that their goods and temples would be safe. If they continued their resistance, the Persians threatened that they would enslave them; their land would be given to other people and their daughters would be taken to distant Bactria. This message was passed on by the tyrants to the Ionians. The Ionians, however, refused to follow the call.

Dionysius, leader of the Phocaeans and also the commander of the whole Greek fleet, thoroughly prepared for the coming battle by forcing the seamen to do continuous military exercises. Herodotus, whose account of the Ionian revolt is not always objective and who is sometimes even malicious towards the rebels, writes that the Ionians were not used to heavy labour and that they soon became irritated by the fatiguing

---

[5] In addition to literary references to Histiaeus, there is also his dedication text from the temple of Didyma (see Tozzi 1978:92).

exercises. They stopped, still according to Herodotus, to follow the orders of Dionysius, on the basis that he had only brought with him three ships. In reality, the position of the rebels was very difficult, because in the middle of the summer they had to transport every mouthful of water and every crust of bread in boats from a distance to their main camp on the small island of Lade, near Miletus (see Burn 1970:210). Discipline in the Greek fleet was low, and eventually the case of the Ionian rebels became hopeless.

The decisive sea battle took place near Lade in 494 B.C. When the Phoenician ships attacked the Ionian fleet, 49 of the 60 Samian ships left the scene and returned to their island. They did this on the instigation of the exiled tyrant of the island, called Aeaces, who resided in the Persian camp. Soon after this desertion, which took place at the very beginning of the battle, many other ships disappeared. These desertions decided the outcome of the fight. Only the men from Chios, which had sent one hundred vessels, and the sailors from several smaller islands refused to give in to the enemy. Nevertheless they were heavily defeated, and subsequently the remaining ships from Chios fled to their island.

Having defeated the Ionian fleet, the Persians were able to besiege Miletus from all sides. In the autumn of 494 B.C. they brought siege engines to the walls of the city, and thereafter took it by storm.

The Persians almost totally destroyed Miletus. They killed a large part of the male population, and the survivors, together with many of the women and children, were led in chains to Susa. Darius settled them near Ampe, not far from the mouth of the Tigris in the Persian Gulf. Herodotus (VI 22) reports that after the crushing of the revolt the Persians occupied the territory of Miletus and began to settle there themselves. At the same time, they settled Carians in the Milesian countryside. Herodotus also says that none of the original population was left in Miletus. In fact, archaeological excavations have shown that massive destruction took place at Miletus in the year 494 B.C. (Mellink 1974:114f.; Tozzi 1978:77-79, with extensive bibliography). The story, however, about the complete destruction of the town is certainly exaggerated, and from the work of Herodotus himself we learn that Miletus continued to exist. Fifteen years after the punishment of the rebels, at the time of the battle at Plataea, a Milesian contingent was incorporated into the Persian army. We may note in passing that it is known from the *Hellenica* by Xenophon (I 1.31) that Miletus still existed in the fourth century B.C. The city, however, never regained its former glory. The town's harbour district was left in ruins and the western quarters were deserted (see Burn 1970:214ff.).

It is known that the Persians robbed and burnt down the temple of Apollo at Branchidae (Didyma), near Miletus. This event is reported, not only by written sources, but also by archaeological data (for references, see Tozzi 1978:205). Herodotus' account (VI 19, 32) about the removal by the Persians of the treasures of this sanctuary, were confirmed at the time of the excavations by French archaeologists at Susa in 1911. There they found a massive, bronze statue with an inscription in Ionian characters reporting on its dedication to the temple of Apollo. Many other objects were found at Susa, which had originally been removed from this temple (Haussoullier 1905:156). There was also a statue of Apollo, which Seleucus I returned to the Milesians in 294 B.C.[6]

During excavations at the site of Karaburun, in the ancient land of Lycia, a tomb was found dating to the beginning of the fifth century B.C., with a mural painting. In this painting the owner of the tomb, a Lycian prince subject to the Persians, is depicted as a victor over the Greeks. His warriors are armed with Greek shields and the Persian akinakes. Apparently, he participated in the crushing of the Ionian revolt (Mellink 1972:263ff.).

In the spring of 493 B.C. the Phoenician fleet also conquered the islands of Chios and Lesbos, ravaging the land, and in addition they occupied several towns along the Hellespont. Thus, the link between the rest of the Persian empire and the Thracian satrapy was re-established. The Persians punished the rebels severely, catching them with fish nets, burning their temples, turning the boys into eunuchs, and sending the attractive girls to the royal court (cf. Meuli 1954:63ff.).

Six years after its start, the revolt had been finally crushed, and everywhere the tyrants were reinstated into their former positions. The Ionians, led by their cowardly leader Aristagoras, were, in fact, deserted by the other Greeks and left to their fate. They eventually had to lose, because of their own limited resources. The Ionians saw the weak points of the Persians, but ignored the warnings of Hecataeus, who said that the Persian king, in order to crush the revolt, had at his disposal limitless resources and reserves in manpower. In addition, from the very beginning the Ionians did not fully agree among themselves. The Greek population in the countryside, being dependent on farming, was afraid of wide-scale destructions of their property and refrained from active

---

[6] Pausanias (I 16.3) reports that this statue was removed on the orders of Xerxes, and transported to Ecbatana. According to Strabo (XIV 1.5; XVII 1.43), the temple at Didyma was burnt down by Xerxes, and its inventory was handed over to the Persians by the priests of the sanctuary. They then fled to Iran, because they were afraid of being accused of sacrilege. The temple was subsequently rebuilt by the Milesians, but the dimensions of the building were so large that no roof could be provided.

participation in the revolt. Many Greek families had been linked for decades to the Persian ruling class, and decisively acted against the revolt. It is therefore not surprising that not all of the Greek cities participated in the insurrection. Apparently even such a large city as Ephesus remained neutral. Finally, there was no consensus in the general staff of the rebels; the rivalry between the various towns was too great. Although the revolt covered a huge territory from Ionia to the Hellespont and Cyprus, the leaders were unable to coordinate effectively the military activities on such a large scale.

After crushing the revolt, the Persian administration showed great political suppleness and in many cases readiness to refrain from taking revenge upon the Greek population. The Lydian satrap Artaphrenes summoned the tyrants of the cities of Asia Minor and ordered them to conclude agreements among themselves, and not to wage war on each other, but rather to let a court of arbitration judge over their points of disagreement. However, while previously the Ionians held many privileges in comparison to the other subject nations, retained from as long ago as the reign of Cyrus II, they were now included in the common system of satrapal rule. As a reward for his crushing of the Ionian revolt, the Lydian satrap Artaphrenes also received authority over Ionia and Caria. The border lines between the various towns were determined anew; the land was measured out, and in accordance with these measurements the taxes were levied. Herodotus reports with praise on the reforms by Artaphrenes, regarding these measures as beneficial to the Greek population. The taxes he regarded as sufficiently moderate. According to Diodorus (X 25, 4), Artaphrenes recognized the traditional laws of the Ionian cities.

After the crushing of the revolt, however, Ionia lost its former importance and its international trade decreased. Over a period of time its economy went into decline. From then on the leading role in the Greek world was to be taken over by the city-states of the mainland, in particular by Athens and Sparta.

CHAPTER EIGHTEEN

THE BEGINNING OF THE PERSIAN-GREEK WARS

Having re-established his authority in Asia Minor, Darius started preparations for a military campaign against mainland Greece. He realized that Persian domination in Asia Minor, in Thrace and on the islands of the Aegean Sea, would be in danger as long as the Greeks on the Balkan peninsula retained their independence. At that time Greece consisted of a multitude of city-states with various political systems. These small states lived in a permanent state of hostility and war with each other. It therefore seemed that the subjugation of Greece would not cause too many problems for the Persians, who had at their disposal a large, well-equipped army and the best fleet of its time.

When the Athenians and rebellious Ionians burnt down Sardis, Darius, if Herodotus (V 105) can be believed, asked who the Athenians were. When he had received the answer, Darius ordered one of his servants to repeat before every dinner the words: "Lord, remember the Athenians."

It is true that the Athenians did everything to avert a war with the Persians. When the playwright Phrynichus presented in 493 B.C. his tragedy 'The Fall of Miletus', the whole audience broke into tears of pity for those who were killed, and out of shame for the fact that the Ionians had been left on their own. The authorities, however, fined Phrynichus one thousand drachmas because of his commemoration of recent, unsuccessful Athenian foreign policy. Many leading politicians of Athens, and especially the Alcmeonids and followers of the deposed tyrants of the Pisistratids, and also the popular masses led by them, were against a confrontation with the Persians, or were of the opinion that it was necessary to do all that was possible to prevent a war. As a result, they agitated against the use by their opponents of the theatre for political propaganda.

The adherents of a more active policy, however, did not remain idle. When, by the end of the sixth century B.C., Darius started to control the sea lanes leading to the Black Sea, the Athenian merchants could apparently still trade with the coastal regions of the Black Sea. During the Ionian revolt, however, and after its crushing, the sea straits were blocked. This was a heavy blow against the vital interests of a significant number of Athenian craftsmen, namely those who produced items for the export and those who were dependent on the importation of grain. Such a situation could lead to an economic crisis. At the same time the Athenians were also deprived of the possibility of importing timber needed for their shipyards from Thrace and Macedonia, because these lands had been conquered by the Persians. There was therefore in Athens no lack of an anti-Persian feeling among part of the population, and it was these people who only waited for suitable leaders.

During the spring of 493 B.C., there arrived in Athens the former tyrant of the Thracian Chersonesus, called Miltiades. He had fled when his town was occupied by the Persians. It was evident to all that Miltiades was an adherent of the war faction, and he was therefore immediately sued by his opponents, namely the Alcmeonids, who accused him of having established a tyranny at the Chersonesus. The court, however, justified Miltiades, and he thereupon started to unite his adherents from the party of landowners. In the same year of 493 B.C., Themistocles was chosen as one of the archontes (the highest officials of Athens). He was the first radical democrat of Athens. He was supported by the craftsmen and merchants. He commenced the building of navy ships for the expected war with the Persians. All this testified to the fact that soon after the fine was imposed upon Phrynichus, public opinion changed radically, and the determined opponents to a pro-Persian orientation acquired the upper hand. The persophil groups lost their power although they still maintained considerable influence on Athenian politics.

Darius, a brilliant strategist as he was, realized the difficulties of the impending war, and commenced extensive preparations. In particular, the Persian rulers took an important and intelligent step, which testified to their wide perception and political tolerance. In 492 B.C. the Persian general Mardonius ordered a change from tyranny to democracy for the majority of Greek cities in Asia Minor. He did so in order to prevent dissatisfaction among the Greeks who were subject to the Persians, and to assure the Persian king of their loyalty. This fact also indicates that in the end the Ionian revolt did achieve some of its objectives, and shows that the Persians were not particularly troubled by the inner political structures of their satrapies in Asia Minor, and were ready to support the popular political groups which did not agitate against Persian suzerainty. However, the information provided by Herodotus (VI 43) about the establishment of democratic rule in the Ionian towns does not relate to all the Ionian districts of the Achaemenid empire, because on some islands tyrannical rule was not changed (see Burn 1970:222). For instance, according to Herodotus (VIII 132; IX 90) there was still a tyrant on the island of Chios, by name Strattis, in 480 B.C.; while after the battle at Salamis a tyrant called Theomestor was installed on the island of Samos, as a reward for his loyalty to the Persians. According to Thucydides (VI 59, 3), the sons and grandsons of Hippoklos succeeded him as tyrants of the town of Lampsacus on the Hellespont.

In the same year of 492 B.C., the Persian army and fleet started their campaign. The Persian forces were commanded by Mardonius, who was married to a daughter of Darius called Artozostre. Having arrived in Cilicia, Mardonius sailed with his fleet to the Hellespont. The land army then also marched to this area. Thereupon the Persians crossed over the Hellespont and marched to Macedonia and Thrace, which together with the northern littoral of the Aegean Sea had been conquered twenty years previously. Persian authority had, however, not proven to be stable in these regions. At the time of the Ionian revolt it had been necessary to withdraw the garrison troops to Asia Minor and since then the provinces had been lost to the Persians. Mardonius advanced along the Thracian coast, re-establishing Persian authority and at the same time depriving Greece from the possibility of obtaining timber from the northern regions of the Balkan peninsula.

However, near Cape Athos, on the Chalcidice peninsula, the Persian fleet was destroyed by a violent storm, and about 20,000 people were drowned, while approximately 300 ships were wrecked. In addition, there was a night attack on the Persian camp by the Thracian tribe of the Brygoi. Many Persians were killed and even Mardonius was wounded. Thereafter the army and fleet of the Persians had to withdraw to Asia Minor. Preparations for the military campaign against Greece had to be started all over again. It should be noted in passing, that H. Bengtson and S. Ja. Lur'e, contrary to E. Meyer and other historians, have suggested that the campaign by Mardonius was not directed against Greece, but rather had the objective of restoring Persian authority north of the Aegean Sea (Bengtson 1965:47; Lur'e 1940:195). Against this hypothesis it can be stated that following this aborted campaign Mardonius was relieved from the command of the army and the fleet.

In the same year of 492 B.C., Persian ambassadors were sent to the still independent islands and cities of the mainland, with the demand for 'earth and water'. The acceptance of this demand would signify the people's readiness to acknowledge the suzerainty of the Persian king. At the same time messengers were sent to the Greek cities of Asia Minor with the summons to start building war ships and cargo vessels, to be used in the coming war. The majority of the islands, and many of the mainland cities (including Thebes, Argos and Aegina) reacted positively to the call from the king's ambassadors; only Sparta and Athens refused to recognize the authority of Darius, and even killed his ambassadors (the Athenians dropped them down a precipice; the Spartans into a pit). H. Bengtson regarded this piece of information from Herodotus as being contrary to historical probabilities, because previously the Athenians had helped the rebellious Ionians, and were consequently in a state of war with the Persians. Therefore, according to Bengtson, Darius would certainly not have sent his ambassadors to Athens (Bengtson 1965:47). It is, however, difficult to agree with these arguments, because, in the first place, the Athenians had left the Ionians to their own fate, and, in the second place, Darius had many adherents in Athens.

The Persians thus prepared for a new military campaign. It was officially declared that the objective of the war was the punishment of the Athenians and Eretrians for helping the Greeks of Asia Minor during the Ionian revolt. The real reason, however, was different: Darius considered that the conquest of Attica and its capital Athens would lead to the subjugation of all of Greece. In addition, Darius was instigated towards the conquest of Athens by the tyrants of the Pisistratids, who had been exiled from Athens and subsequently fled to the Persians. They hoped to be reinstated into their former position.

In 492 B.C., as indicated above, Darius relieved Mardonius from his command, blaming him for the unsuccessful results of the first campaign against Greece. The new commander of the army was Artaphrenes, the son of the Lydian satrap with the same name, and also the nephew of Darius. The Mede Datis was appointed as the commander of the fleet (for this official, see Lewis 1980). According to Herodotus the fleet counted 600 ships; the greatest part of this fleet, however, consisted of cargo vessels for the transport of infantry and cavalry. Both generals received the orders to defeat the Athenians and Eretrians and to bring them to Darius.

During the summer of 490 B.C., the Persian fleet, including the freighters for the transport of the horses, was concentrated along the Cilician coast. The cavalry and infantry also assembled in Cilicia. By experience from the previous disaster, the commanders of the Persian army decided to transport their soldiers by ship across the Aegean Sea in order to prevent the fleet from being subjected to the same dangers as before near the ever treacherous Athos cape, and also to bypass the coastal regions of Thrace, which had proved to be extremely difficult to control effectively.

The Persians disembarked on Naxos, which was still independent. They conquered the island and pillaged it. The majority of the people of the island fled to the mountains. Thereupon the Persian army sailed to the town of Eretria on Euboea. At that time Eretria suffered from the strong antagonism between two political parties. The aristocrats wanted to defend their town, while the democrats were inclined to surrender. The Eretrians offered resistance against the Persians for six days. On the seventh day, the democrats surrendered their city in the hope that the Persians would give them the power over Eretria. The Persians, however, burnt and destroyed the city and its temples, and led away its people into captivity. They were deported to Susa and thereupon by orders of Darius settled in the village of Arderikka in the Elamite district of Cissia (see Grosso 1958:350ff.).

Thus, one of the objectives of the campaign was achieved, and the Persian generals could hope for similar successes as regards Athens. The excessive cruelty of the Persians at Eretria, however, strengthened the resoluteness of the Athenians. Some days after the destruction of Eretria, the Persian army with the assistance of experienced Greek guides sailed in their ships to Attica and disembarked on the plain of Marathon, 40 kilometres from Athens. The plain has a length of nine kilometres and is about three kilometres wide. The area was selected for the disembarkation because it offered the Persian cavalry room for manoeuvre. In addition, at one time the landowners of this plain and beyond had been of support to the tyrant Hippias, who was now urging the Persians to march against his native town, Athens. Datis was of the opinion that either the Athenian army would come to Marathon and he would subsequently smash it, or the Athenians would not come out, in which case the Persians would be able to move up towards Athens itself. This was at a time when the Persians still controlled the seas and could easily cut off Athens from the sea, thus threatening its supply of grain.

The Persian army cannot have included more than 15,000 men, and it would have been difficult to accommodate many horses on the ships. There may also have been Babylonians in the Persian army, as is perhaps attested by the find on the battlefield of Marathon of a Babylonian cylinder seal (see Pallis 1954:29). The statement by Cornelius Nepos, to the effect that 100,000 Persian soldiers disembarked on the shores of Marathon, is a concoction from a much later period, meant as a tribute to the Athenian soldiers.

CHAPTER NINETEEN

THE BATTLE OF MARATHON

The Athenians were in a difficult position and they had no reason to hope for assistance from outside. The neighbouring district of Boeotia had turned against them and openly welcomed the advent of the Persians. In Athens itself the strife continued between the aristocrats and the democratic party. Some of the Athenians were prepared to help the Persians and without publicly acclaiming so, hoped for their victory. Hippias, who had been the last tyrant of Athens and twenty years previously was deprived of his power and exiled from Athens, had been appointed by the Persians as governor of the town of Sigeum, on the Hellespont. Now, at an advanced age, he returned with the Persian army to Attica where his secret adherents awaited him. In particular, there was the noble family of the Alcmeonids, who had been deprived of their power by their political opponent Miltiades, and who at the time of the Persian attack united itself with the adherents of Hippias. Hippias hoped to return to power with their help. Many people were opposed to the risky war with the Persians, fearing that with a defeat they would lose their riches and influence. Some were tempted to surrender the city to the Persians and to take all possible advantage from this voluntary submission. Many Athenians accused the Alcmeonids of siding with the enemy and with Hippias. It is true that Herodotus strongly refutes this point, but, in the first place, he does not deny that the Persians had some sympathisers inside Athens, and, in the second place, he strives hard to refute the accusation that the Alcmeonids had been siding with the Persians. Herodotus' motives may lie in the fact that he himself belonged to the literary circle around Pericles, the great Athenian statesman, who belonged to the family of the Alcmeonids and who was admired by Herodotus. As we have seen previously, Cleisthenes, who also belonged to the family of the Alcmeonids, had in 507 B.C. given 'earth and water' to the Persians, and he was still a very influential persophil in Athens. It should be noted that during the Persian-Greek wars, the Alcmeonids became aware of the resolution of the people to fight against Persian domination, and consequently they adopted a new policy. As a result, Athens was to gain several prominent democratic leaders from among the family of the Alcmeonids.

When the Persian army disembarked at Marathon, there was considerable disagreement in the Athenian assembly concerning the tactics for the impending battle with the Persians. Miltiades, the leader of the conservative farmers, who was one of ten Athenian strategoi (the highest military commanders), feared betrayal from the side of the pro-Persian faction and therefore insisted on an immediate advance upon the Persians. The leader of the radical democrats, Themistocles, fervently supported this suggestion, and after long deliberation it was accepted by the assembly. According to information given by the second century A.D. writer Pausanias (I 32.4), the Athenians also included into their army slaves who were promised their liberty after the battle.

The Athenian army consisted of about 10,000 men who marched to the plain of Marathon. There were also approximately 1,000 men from the allied Bocotian town of Plataea, located at the border of Attica. At the same time the famous runner Pheidippides was sent to Sparta. He arrived there on the second day and he presented to the Spartans the Athenian request for help. The Spartans promised assistance, but they did not hasten to send out their soldiers as there was an old belief that it was impossible to start a campaign before a full moon. The Athenians did not expect help from the other Greeks, because at best the Greeks were indifferent towards the fate of Athens, which had the impudence to wage war against 'the Great King'. They thought that the outcome of the battle was inevitable. The famous poet Theognis of Megara, who before the disembarkation of the Persians at Marathon had called for resistance against 'the Medes', had become frightened when confronted with the real danger. He proved to be only capable of asking Apollo for help. The main sanctuary of Apollo, however, which was the temple of Delphi, was on the side of the Persians and in fact tried to paralyse the resistance of the Greeks (for the literature, see Olmstead 1948:160). At the same time, the Athenians had outspoken enemies among the Greeks themselves. Thus, the neighbouring island of Aegina, which for long had been a rival of Athens, was prepared to ally itself with the Persians. Aegina was only kept from doing so by the resistance of its protector, Sparta. Sparta was afraid that the Persians, after conquering Attica, would advance towards the Peloponnesos and set up a naval blockade of the peninsula.

Many historical and military studies have been dedicated to the reconstruction of the battle of Marathon. The traditional account of the course of events, such as presented by most historians, is as follows: The Athenian strategoi still disagreed about the tactics for the battle. Many were opposed to immediate action. Miltiades and his adherents, however, finally managed to persuade the Athenians to attack and defeat the Persians.

In reality, the course of events must have been different. At Marathon both parties waited for several days, without joining in battle. It should be noted that the Persian army was encamped in the open plain where it was possible for them to deploy their cavalry. The Athenians, who were without cavalry, had assembled in a narrow part of the plain and were not intent on leaving this place, as it offered no advantages to the Persian horsemen. In the meantime, the situation of the Persian army had deteriorated, and the Persian commander Datis, awaiting in vain some sign from his friends in Athens, was forced to take a decision as to the necessary course of action. He apparently knew about the Spartan decision to march towards Attica after the next full moon, and wanted to decide the war before their arrival. At the same time he was unable to move his army towards the defile where the Athenians were entrenched. Datis attentively followed events at Athens, whence he expected the signal (a shield lifted up above the city walls) which would indicate that the city had come under the control of the adherents of the dethroned tyrant, Hippias. In Athens the supporters of the Persians were ready to act, but they could not decide on whether to take the risk or not. Thus, in their turn, they waited for the Persian army to defeat the Athenians.

At the time that the Spartans were about to arrive in Attica to join forces with the Athenians, Datis realized that he could not wait any longer. He decided to send part of his army by boat to Athens in order to occupy the city. To do so he had to split up his forces. This was a risky decision, which he had not dared to take thus far. A part of the army, including the cavalry, were embarked. Apparently this happened at night by the light of the moon. The success of the operation depended on the factor of surprise. Miltiades, however, guessed the plans of Datis. Or, which is also possible, he was accurately informed about the Persian plans by the Ionians in the Persian army. They may have told Miltiades that the cavalry had already been embarked while only lightly armed infantry was left in the plain.[1] Thus Miltiades had no longer any reason to fear his Persian opponents.

The battle commenced on the morning of the 12th of August, 490 B.C. (for the chronology, see Burn 1970:257). The Athenians quickly lined up, left their defensive position in the narrows and in a quick march descended down the defile to the enemy, firmly resolved to fight a decisive battle. The front line of the Athenians was as wide as that of the Persians, although in the centre the Athenian ranks were not as deep.

---

[1] In the Byzantine lexicon called the Sudas it is said, under the rubric 'the horsemen away', that, when Datis started to withdraw from Marathon in order to sail to Attica, the Ionians climbed into the trees and sent signals to the Athenians, informing them about the withdrawal of the cavalry. Miltiades, being informed about the Persian withdrawal, started the attack and gained a victory (see, however, also Sealey 1976:190f., where doubts are expressed as to the accuracy of the information provided by the Sudas).

The disposition of both armies was in accordance with the traditions of both sides: the Persians positioned the best troops in the centre, while the Greeks usually attempted at all cost to fight a victory on the flanks and subsequently to turn upon the centre of the enemy ranks.

The soldiers of the Achaemenid army fought bravely. In the centre the Athenian ranks were driven back and pursued by the Persians and Sakas. On the flanks, however, the Persian ranks were insufficiently deep and the soldiers were defeated by the Athenians and Plataeans, who subsequently turned inward towards the Persians in the centre. Thereupon the Persians started to withdraw, suffering heavy losses. As a result of the Athenian tactics, the best part of the Persian army, being placed in the centre, suffered heavily when it found itself surrounded by hostile troops. Many soldiers fled into the muddy lake of Marathon and were butchered without mercy (cf. Burn 1970:246-250; Lur'e 1940:196ff.). On the battlefield remained 6,400 men of the Achaemenid army, and in total 192 Athenians. The Plataeans also suffered some losses, but the exact number is unknown.

The remaining part of the Persian army fled on board the ships and sailed towards Athens. The Athenians captured seven Persian vessels and then hastened home, where they arrived before the Persians. Thereafter nothing remained for the Persians but to return to Asia Minor.

When full moon had come, Sparta sent 2,000 soldiers to the assistance of the Athenians. This force, however, arrived when the battle had already been decided. The Spartans looked with interest at the corpses of the fallen Persians, as most of them had never seen Persians before. Shortly afterwards the Spartans returned home.

The victory at Marathon was the first success of the Greeks in the wars with the Persians who had previously seemed invincible. Essentially, the battle was won by the Athenians. The poet Simonides, a contemporary of the battle, called them the leaders in the war for the freedom of the Hellenes.

The defeat of the Persians was caused by a combination of factors. Firstly, although their army to a certain degree surpassed in number that of the Athenians, only part of the Persian troops could take part in the battle, while the cavalry could not join in at all and had to remain idle. Secondly, the Persians were campaigning in an unknown country and had been forced to make a long journey to arrive at Marathon. Thirdly, the heavily armed Greek foot soldiers, the hoplites, were protected by iron armour, and as a result the lightly armed Persian elite troops could not breach their ranks. Fourthly, and of considerable significance, is the fact that the Athenian army was commanded by the talented general Miltiades, who was well acquainted with Persian military tactics. He was knowledgeable about the Persians because at the time of the Scythian campaign he had served in Darius' army. Finally, it is important to remember that the Athenians were fighting for their own land, for their freedom, and for the maintenance of their democratic political structure which was still in its infancy. The Athenians knew that if they were defeated they would be enslaved and sent away from their homeland. The Athenians were therefore left with the choice between fighting or dying.

The Athenians were very proud of their victory at Marathon. According to Pausanias (I 15.3), scenes of the battle at Marathon occupied an honorary position among the paintings in the public buildings at Athens. These paintings depicted the advancing Athenians and Plataeans, while the fleeing Persians were pushing each other out of the way. Some of the Persians were depicted seeking refuge on board the Phoenician ships. In addition, a Persian helmet has been preserved which was dedicated to one of the temples as a trophy of the Marathon battle. The inscription on it says: "To Zeus from the Athenians, who took this from the Medes."

The victory at Marathon, however, had more significance for the morale of the Greeks than any real military importance. Only a small part of the Persian army was defeated and Darius could justifiably say that he had lost a battle, but not the war. There were also some grounds for him to say that he had achieved a victory on the Greek mainland, as many cities had given him the 'earth and water'. He, therefore, stated in one of his inscriptions, that his empire included "the Ionians, who live along the sea, and those beyond the sea" (DSe, 27-29).

In Athens the attitude towards the battle at Marathon was different. They thought that the war was over. The acute Themistocles, however, held a very different opinion, namely that Marathon was only an episode and the beginning of a long and serious war. Because of the succeeding crisis within the Achaemenid empire, however, the Greeks were fortunate to win a respite of ten years.

CHAPTER TWENTY

REVOLTS IN EGYPT AND BABYLONIA

Darius never abandoned plans for a new campaign against Greece. After the battle at Marathon, he was convinced that it was impossible to conquer Greece with only a small army. Preparations for the next campaign demanded much more time. Darius sent his messengers to the different parts of his empire with the call to muster military contingents; to collect ships, and to gather provisions and military equipment. Preparations for the war continued for three years. In the fourth year (486 B.C.), however, a revolt broke out in Egypt which caused a break in these preparations. Some of the reasons behind the insurrection included the heavy taxes and the deportation of thousands of craftsmen to Iran for the construction of the royal palaces at Susa and Persepolis. It would also seem likely that knowledge of the Persian defeat at Marathon contributed to the commencement of the revolt.

A lively account of the beginning of the revolt is contained in a letter of an Egyptian official called Khnumemakhet to the Persian satrap Pherendates. The letter was sent from the island of Elephantine on October 5, 486 B.C. The letter reports that the Egyptian official Osorwer had ordered Khnumemakhet to take with him Artabanus, who was the Persian commander of the Jewish garrison on Elephantine, and to sail to Nubia in order to fetch grain by ship. The imported grain was unloaded on the order of Artabanus. In the meantime the insurgents had become so impudent that they showed themselves by daylight, while at night they could attack and carry off the grain. The sender of the letter therefore asked the satrap of Egypt whether he would order Artabanus to guard the ship and to unload only as much grain as could be transported in a small boat to the town of Syene (modern Aswan) at Elephantine (see Spiegelberg 1928:604ff.). Thus, at the beginning of October the unrest had extended to Elephantine and quickly spread over the south of Upper Egypt. At the end of the month the unrest had developed into open rebellion.

In October 486 B.C., Darius died at the age of 64.[1] He had ruled for 36 years. He did not have the time to re-establish his authority in Egypt.

---

[1] According to Ctesias (fragment 19; König 1972:9), Darius died at the age of 72. This is contradicted by Herodotus (I 209), who reports that in around 530 B.C. Darius was about 20 years old.

Before his death he had ordered the construction of his tomb, which is located five kilometres to the northwest of Persepolis, in the cliffs now bearing the name of Naqsh-i Rustam, 'Depiction of Rustam' (a medieval legend attributes the monument in the rock to this legendary hero). In the Elamite texts from the Persepolis fortifications a place is referred to with the name of Nupishtash (from Old Persian *nipišta*, 'written'), which I. Gershevitch and W. Hinz, quite independently of each other, have identified with Naqsh-i Rustam as its most ancient appellation. Both scholars base their hypothesis on the mention by the 12th century author Ibn al-Balxī of a mountain called Kuh-i Nibišt ('Inscribed Mountain') near the town of Istakhr, which is located near ancient Persepolis. According to the Persepolis texts, there were royal so-called paradises (enclosed parks) near Nupishtash. Apparently, the appellation of Nupishtash (in Elamite rendering) was given to this place because of inscriptions of Darius in the rock-face (if not because of an even earlier Elamite relief). The earliest reference in the documents to the site of Nupishtash dates from 497 B.C. It is known that work on the construction of the tomb in the rock-face continued for many years, as in 490 B.C. an additional work force of stone masons was sent to the place (see PTT, 9; Gershevitch 1969:177-179; Hinz 1970:425ff.).

Many centuries prior to Darius, an Elamite king had ordered his work force to carve out a relief with his depiction in the rock-face of Naqsh-i Rustam. It was at the site of this older Elamite relief that, at a height of approximately twenty metres, the tomb of Darius was constructed. According to ancient Iranian traditions it was carved out in the rock. In the tomb chamber three solid sarcophagi are placed in deep niches. In one of these sarcophagi Darius' body was laid. The other two were reserved for other members of his family. Outside the tomb a portico was carved out with four columns. Above the portico rises a relief which depicts Darius surrounded by his courtiers. They are all located on top of a dais which is lifted up by representatives from thirty peoples within the Empire. Great attention was paid to the anthropological and ethnographical characteristics of these delegates. The depictions are accompanied by inscriptions which indicate the identity of each of the thirty representatives. In his left hand Darius holds a bow, while his right hand is raised towards a depiction of Ahura Mazda, who floats above the whole monument. To the right of Darius stands an altar for the sacred fire.

To the left of Darius there are depictions of three of his most important bodyguards. One of them, according to the accompanying inscription, was called "Gaubaruva, the Patischorian, spear bearer of King Darius." He holds a long spear, which appears to represent the weapon belonging to Darius himself. In addition, Gaubaruva is armed with a bow and quiver. The second bodyguard is called Aspathines. He is equipped with a war axe and a quiver. His depiction is accompanied by the following text: "Aspathines, the quiver bearer of King Darius" (Aspathines is also depicted in reliefs in the Throne Hall and in the Treasury of Persepolis, but without inscriptions). The third official carries Darius' mace (see Borger 1972:388ff.; Hinz 1969:53ff.; Schmidt 1953-1970, Vol. I, pp. 133ff.; 165ff.; Vol III). According to Ctesias (frag. 15), Hystaspes, Darius' father, died at the age of seventy when he fell during a visit to the construction works of his son's tomb. Taking this detail as a starting point, W. Hinz has suggested that the tomb was completed in approximately 510 B.C., the year when Hystaspes died (Hinz 1970:425f.). As we have seen above, however, work parties of stone cutters were still sent to the site in 490 B.C.

Near the tomb of Darius there are three more tombs of Achaemenid kings, but none of them carry any inscriptions. In all probability, they belong to Xerxes; Artaxerxes I and Darius II. Their tombs are referred to in the work of Diodorus (VI 17, 71).

Even before Darius' death, continuous quarrels and harem intrigues had arisen over the question of who would succeed Darius to the throne. Before he became king, Darius had three sons by a daughter of Gobryas. The eldest of these was called Artobazanes. Following Darius' accession to the Persian throne, he had four more sons by Atossa, the daughter of Cyrus II. Problems concerning who should succeed Darius arose because Persia did not have strict succession laws. The choice of the successor was left to the monarch. In the end Darius chose Xerxes[2], his eldest son by Atossa. He based his decision on the fact that Xerxes was born while his father was king. In addition, he was a grandson of Cyrus II. Thus runs the fully reliable account by Herodotus. Plutarch (*Mor.* 488 D) wrote that the eldest son of Darius was called Ariamenes, but that Ariamenes left the throne to Xerxes, because Persian laws demanded that the throne should be given to the eldest of those princes who were born after their father became king. This acquiescence by Ariamenes was praised by Plutarch as an example of "brotherly love unpolluted by anything." According to Herodotus, the quarrels about who should succeed Darius took place a year before his death. According to Plutarch, the problems were only solved after the king died.

F. W. König, and following him some other scholars, have expressed the opinion that Darius abdicated the throne when he was fifty-two years old and that during the last eleven years of his life he remained a private

---

[2] In Old Persian *Xšayāršā*, 'ruling over heroes', although Herodotus (VI 98) tells that the name of Xerxes meant 'warrior' (cf. Schmeija 1975).

person, while the throne was occupied by his son Xerxes. Not so very long ago W. Nagel argued in favour of this hypothesis, saying that Persian kings were wont to abdicate at the age of fifty-two. Nagel adds to this point the condition that, if the monarch was fifty-two and the successor to the throne had not yet reached the age of twenty-six, the king could continue to rule until the crown prince had attained the required age. E. Herzfeld, F. H. Weissbach and J. Junge have suggested that Xerxes was co-regent with Darius. They based themselves on an inscription which was discovered at the foundation of one of the palaces at Persepolis (XPf) (Herzfeld 1932a:4-7; *idem* 1932b:117-125; *idem* 1938:38; Junge 1940:24, n. 4; König 1938a:95; Nagel 1975:356ff.; Weissbach 1933:318-321; cf. also the criticism towards this conclusion by H. H. Schaeder 1935:503f.). Such an hypothesis, however, is contradicted by the historical data. In the above mentioned inscription of Xerxes it is said: "When my father Darius left the throne, I became king by the favour of Ahuramazda." The phrase 'left the throne' is taken by the above mentioned scholars to mean that Darius withdrew from the affairs of the state and transferred his power to Xerxes. The Akkadian version of the same text, however, contains the following phrase 'he went to his fate', which means that Darius died, after which Xerxes became king. According to Herodotus (VII 3), as already said, Darius appointed Xerxes as his successor one year before his death. This does not mean that Xerxes became his co-regent.

In the same inscription Xerxes says: "My father was Darius. The father of Darius was Vishtaspa. The father of Vishtaspa was Arshama. Both Vishtaspa and Arshama were still alive when Ahuramazda had the wish to make Darius king ... king in this world ... Darius had other sons, but it was the wish of Ahuramazda that Darius appointed me as the greatest after himself." Here, apparently, we hear the echoes of the power struggle with which Xerxes had been confronted.

In certain reliefs from Persepolis, Xerxes is depicted as the successor of his father Darius. He stands behind Darius who is sitting on the throne. These reliefs are not normally accompanied by a text, but one sculptured portrait at the entrance to the palace depicts Xerxes in courtly costume next to Darius. This relief is accompanied by the inscription: "Xerxes, the son of Darius, the Achaemenid."

When Xerxes ascended the throne in November 486 B.C., he was about 36 years old and many a difficult task awaited him. For example, while the campaign against the Greeks had long been planned by his father, Xerxes obviously needed time to consolidate his authority and to carry through certain changes in the higher echelons of his government, a process which is common in the case of a change of power. It should be noted that Xerxes started with the presentation of the same moralistic-ethical principles which had earlier been proclaimed by Darius in one of his inscriptions at Naqs-i Rustam (DNb). Xerxes ordered the addition of an analogous text in his name. The inscription was found near Persepolis and is essentially a copy of the Darius text (see Hinz 1969:45ff.). Xerxes, who literally repeats the credo of Darius, tells that he was intelligent and active, a friend of the truth and an enemy of lawlessness, a king who protected the weak from oppression by the strong while protecting the strong from injustice by the weak. He was able to control his emotions, and he did not make hasty decisions. He punished or rewarded everyone in accordance with their deeds and merits. In the inscription Xerxes also talks about his excellent physical qualities as a warrior. It should be conceded that this part of his apology is not contrary to the information provided by Herodotus. It says that Xerxes, when he became king, was a tall, dignified and good-looking man in the prime of life.

In January of the year 484 B.C., Xerxes managed to crush the Egyptian revolt. This date can be deduced from information contained in inscriptions by a Persian official. These texts derive from Coptos and date from the years 486 and 484 B.C. Some scholars suggest that Xerxes commanded the punitive expedition himself (Böhl 1962:112), but the sources lend no support for this hypothesis. Under Xerxes, Egypt suffered a merciless chastisement for its revolt. The property of many temples was confiscated. Xerxes' treatment of Egypt was completely opposite to that by his predecessors. Darius and Cambyses tried to convince the Egyptians that they were continuing the ancient traditions of the pharaohs. In addition, they adopted the relevant titles. They offered sacrifices to the local Egyptian gods and in all possible manners stressed their respect for the ancient culture and its customs and they called themselves kings of Egypt. It was Xerxes who demonstratively treated the country as a conquered province. Contrary to his predecessors, Xerxes never went to Egypt (in this point he was later followed by Artaxerxes I) and he did not adopt the title of King of Egypt. In the Egyptian texts he is called 'The Great King', and in an Aramaic inscription from Memphis he is called 'king of kings' (Cooke 1903, No. 71). There are no buildings in Egypt whose construction can be related to the name of Xerxes. It is true that work continued in the Wadi Hammamat stone quarries, and six inscriptions have been preserved here, which are dated to the reign of Xerxes (Gauthier 1907-1917:8). The stone, however, which was quarried there was not used for buildings, but rather for sarcophagi. Starting from the reign of Xerxes, until the rule of Darius II, Egyptian officials occupied the lowest positions in the state apparatus. Many decades later, the priests of the temple of Buto called Xerxes "that wicked man", because of his confiscation of temple land (Kienitz 1953:68f.; Struve 1928:203).[3] Still before the death of Darius, a magnificent sarcophagus of granite had been made for the burial of the sacred bull; but the epitaph of the grave has been scratched in a hasty and careless manner (Olmstead 1948:235). Apparently the burial took place at the time of the crushing of the revolt and the priests were not in the position to carry out the customary, elaborate rites.

Xerxes appointed his brother Achaemenes as governor of Egypt, instead of the satrap Pherendates, who was apparently killed during the revolt.

After crushing the revolt, Xerxes started to prepare plans for a campaign against Greece. During the month of Du'ūzu, however, in the second year of Xerxes' reign (June-July 484 B.C.), another insurrection broke out, this time in Babylonia (Böhl 1962:110ff.; Cameron 1941:314ff.; San Nicolò 1934:335; Ungnad 1907:464ff.; *idem* 1960:73ff.). The motives for the revolt, just like in Egypt, included the burden of taxation, the deportation of people for construction work in Iran, and the huge expenses incurred in the upkeep of Persian garrisons and the satrapal court. The rebels were led by a certain Bel-shimanni. According to the relevant documents which are dated to his reign, the insurgents managed to occupy Babylon as well as the cities of Borsippa and Dilbat.

The news about the revolt in Babylon reached Xerxes at his summer residence in Ecbatana. It turned out, however, that the revolt was easily suppressed (possibly after only two weeks, as indicated by some Babylonian documents which date to the reign of Bel-shimanni). The initiators of the revolt were punished, but Xerxes refrained from a harsh retaliation. He knew Babylon well, as he had lived, starting from 498 B.C., at the royal palace of Babylon. The palace was especially built for him, and it is likely that he did not wish to destroy the city he loved. During the summer of the year 482 B.C., however, the Babylonians revolted again, this time under the leadership of Shamash-eriba.[4] The rebels initially achieved a number of important successes, including the occupation of Babylon, Borsippa, Dilbat and other cities. They could do so because

---

[3] According to E. Bresciani, however, the reference to 'the wicked one' on the so-called Satrap Stela of Ptolemaeus I, which was inscribed in 312 B.C. and testifies to the confiscation of land of the temple of Buto, refers to Artaxerxes III, rather than Xerxes (Bresciani 1958:167). Whatever the case, Xerxes is mentioned in the text as the conqueror of Egypt.

[4] M. San-Nicolò suggested that the revolt by Shamash-eriba followed almost immediately after the crushing of the previous insurrection by Bel-shimanni. F. M. Th. Böhl, however, has shown that a period of two years elapsed between both events (Böhl 1968:150; *idem* 1962:110ff.; San Nicolò 1934:337).

most of the Persian soldiers stationed in Babylonia had been directed towards Asia Minor in order to participate in the intended military campaign against the Greeks. This second revolt was particularly dangerous because Xerxes had already decided to start a war against the Greeks. This revolt in the rear could therefore not be tolerated.

The task of crushing the second Babylonian revolt was put into the hands of Megabyzus (in Old Persian: *Bagabukhša*), the son-in-law of Xerxes, and grandson of the Megabyzus who had participated in the murder of Gaumata. The siege of Babylon continued for several months, and apparently came to a conclusion in March, 481 B.C.[5], with a severe chastisement. The city ramparts and other fortifications were demolished. It is possible that many private houses were also destroyed, although, according to archaeological data, the majority of the houses were left unscathed. The course of the Euphrates was also changed and the river, at least for some time, was allowed to separate the residential districts of the city from its sanctuaries. A number of priests were executed. The main temple of the land, the Esagila (the sanctuary of the supreme Babylonian god, Marduk) and the ziggurat of Etemenanki were severely damaged and many objects from the treasury of this temple, deposited there by the Assyrian and Babylonian kings, were transferred to Persepolis. It is worth noting that in the ruins of the Persepolis Treasury royal seals were found with the depictions of the Babylonian gods Adad and Marduk. On the seal of Adad there is a text which says: "Property of the god Marduk. The seal of god Adad from the temple of Esagila" (Schmidt 1953-1970, Vol. I, pp. 174, 179; Vol. II, pp. 56ff., 64, 67). It is also recorded that the golden statue of Marduk, which weighed twenty talents (about 600 kilos), was brought to Persepolis and appears to have been melted down.[6] Thus, Xerxes dealt the most significant blow to the old city, because after the removal of Marduk's statue, in Babylonian

---

[5] Apparently, before the New Year festival, which was celebrated in March, as Shamash-eriba was not crowned and so his name is not mentioned in the Babylonian kings' lists.

[6] For this ravaging and plundering, see Aelianus, *Var.* XIII 3; Arrian, *Anabasis Alexandri* III 16.4; VII 17.2; Ctesias, *Persica* XII 9; Diod. II 9.9; XVII 112; Herodotus I 183; Plinius, *Hist. Nat.* VI 120; Plutarch, *Mor.* 173 C; Strabo XVI 1.5. Arrian, however, dates the Babylonian destructions to a time subsequent to Xerxes' campaign against Greece. According to Strabo, the tomb of Cyrus was also subjected to destruction. This structure, Strabo writes, consisted of a quadrangular pyramid, built of burnt brick. In this case, however, the Babylonian Tower (Etemenanki) is meant. Aelianus writes that Xerxes opened the tomb of Bel (one of Marduk's names), and was later punished for this crime. Several Babylonian documents from the years 483-482 B.C. are dated to the reigns of Akshimarshi and Shikushti, who are sometimes regarded as the rebellious kings (see Ungnad 1907:464). G. G. Cameron, however, has shown that we are here dealing with incorrect Babylonian renderings of the name of Xerxes (Cameron 1941).

eyes, nobody would be able to call himself the legitimate king of the city. It must be realized that it was necessary for the incumbent to receive the crown out of the hands of Marduk at Esagila at the time of the New Year festival. In this manner the previous Assyrian, Babylonian and Persian rulers, including Xerxes himself, had become the legitimate rulers of the country. From that moment on, there was no statue of Marduk in Babylon, and the New Year festival ceased to be celebrated. Thus Xerxes liquidated the Babylonian kingdom, which formally from the time of Cyrus onwards had been regarded as a separate entity within the Achaemenid empire, although linked by a personal union with the Persian kings. Babylonia was reduced to the status of a common satrapy and its capital lost forever its political significance (one and a half century later, Alexander of Macedonia planned to make Babylon his capital, but after his death these plans were dropped).[7] At the same time certain important changes were made in the organization of the satrapy. During the reign of Cyrus the whole territory of Babylonia and the districts west of the Euphrates, covering almost all the land of the former neo-Babylonian empire, were united into one satrapy. Further to this, although under Darius the satrapy had been split up into two, both parts were still governed from Babylon, a detail which is clear because the governor of the areas west of the Euphrates owed responsibility to the governor in Babylon. According to certain instructions given by Xerxes, Babylonia was incorporated into the new satrapy of Assyria, while the lands west of the Euphrates ('Across-the-River') became an independent province which soon occupied a leading position amidst the western satrapies. Following this alteration, the traditional title of the Achaemenid kings, namely 'king of Babylon, king of the lands', officially carried by Cyrus and his successors in Babylon, lost its significance. At the very beginning of his reign, Xerxes still carried the title, but in his first year he augmented the title into 'king of Persia and Media, king of Babylon and king of the lands' (VS, Vol. IV, 194). Beginning from 481 B.C., the scribes of Babylonian legal and economic documents began to refer to Xerxes with his Iranian title 'king of the lands', although this change in the titles was gradual. Sometimes, even many years later, he was still called 'king of Babylon, king of the lands' (see for references Stolper 1985:9, n. 25). In Iran, Xerxes maintained the original Iranian title, 'king of the lands, king of kings', and it is interesting to note that

---

[7] Arrian (*Anab. Alex.* VII 17.2) writes that Xerxes destroyed the temple of Bel (the Esagila), but Alexander of Macedonia decided to restore the building. He ordered the removal of the rubble of the fallen walls. This piece of information is corroborated by several Babylonian documents, according to which in 331 B.C. a beginning was made with the preparation of the building site (see for references, McEwan 1981:193).

his successor Artaxerxes I, in the Aramaic-Lydian bilingual text from Sardis, called himself 'king of kings' (Torrey 1917-1918:185).

After the suppression of the revolt, Babylon lost its position as a sacred city and as an important economic centre. This last point in particular is indicated by the sharp decline in the quantity of texts relating to economic matters. In addition, after the second year of Xerxes' reign, there are no documents known which come from Sippar, thus it is possible that J. Oelsner was correct in suggesting that the city of Sippar was also destroyed (Oelsner 1971:145). After the eclipse of Babylon, Nippur became the most important city of Mesopotamia. Oppenheim has even suggested that Nippur was the economic capital of the newly created satrapy called The Land of Akkad (see Oppenheim 1985:579). If Plutarch (*Mor.* 173 C) can be believed, the Babylonians were forbidden, after the crushing of their revolt, to carry weapons. The *Historiae* of Herodotus, however, indicates that the Babylonians participated in the war with Greece. Diodorus (II 9.9) wrote that after the revolt only a small part of Babylon was still inhabited, while the greatest part was made into arable land. Throughout the whole country, the lands which belonged to those who took part in the revolt were confiscated and handed over to the Persian nobility. Herodotus' account (I 196) concerning the destruction of Babylon probably relates to the period immediately after the quelling of the revolt under Xerxes. It is to be noted, however, that in later times Babylon managed to recover a certain degree of its former significance as the economic centre of the land. Herodotus, who visited Babylon some twenty or thirty years afterwards, describes Babylon as a city with a hundred gates. Much of his account, however, is taken from oral stories, rather than from personal observation. Thus, he refers to a tower with eight floors, but by his time the Etemenanki lay in ruins, although the walls still stood upright. In any case, Herodotus cannot have seen the sanctuary of Marduk at the top of the tower. In addition, as can be deduced from archaeological data, by the time of Herodotus' visit Babylon no longer had any city walls, so, although Herodotus frequently refers to these walls, he could only have seen their foundations (Meuleau 1965:338).

Despite the destruction which was carried out during and after the suppressing of the second Babylonian revolt, the city still retained its status as a royal residence, next to Susa and Ecbatana. Fragments have been found at Babylon of several building inscriptions of Darius II and Artaxerxes II (Wetzel & Schmidt & Mallwitz 1957:48ff.). It is also known that the Persian kings laid out gardens with pavilions at Babylon, while in 345 B.C. Artaxerxes III ordered the building of an Apadana in the city. In addition, Darius II lived for a long time in Babylon before the commencement of his reign. As regards Babylonia as a whole, it is evident from the *Anabasis* of Xenophon that around 400 B.C. it was once again a rich and prosperous country.

CHAPTER TWENTY-ONE

XERXES' WAR WITH GREECE

Mardonius, the son of Gobryas and son-in-law of Darius, who was commander of the Persian army at the time of its campaign in Thrace and who was relieved from his command because of the lack of success of his leadership, was subsequently rehabilitated when his successor Datis lost the battle at Marathon. Mardonius urged Xerxes to set off once more against Greece. At the same time there arrived from Thessaly, a Greek district south of Macedonia, messengers who invited the Persians to campaign against the Greeks of the mainland and who promised their full support for such an undertaking. A similar request was also put forward by exiles from Athens. Herodotus (VII 8-11) tells that Xerxes summoned a council of noble Persians in order to answer the request for military action. In this council Mardonius pronounced himself decidedly in favour of such a campaign. Artabanus, however, a son of Hystaspes and an uncle of Xerxes, described the difficulties of a war against the Greeks and declared that he did not favour such an undertaking. If Herodotus can be believed, the admonitions by Artabanus were met with approval by the Persian noblemen who had assembled in the council.

Xerxes, however, strove to achieve world supremacy and he realized that as long as the Greeks of the mainland remained independent, Persian power in Asia Minor and in the northern lands of the Balkan peninsula remained at risk. Thus, in 483 B.C., Xerxes ordered to start all the necessary preparations for the war. The official objective of the campaign was the subjugation of Athens and Sparta, which had refused to offer 'earth and water'. In reality, Xerxes wanted to conquer all of Greece.

In the same year of 483 B.C., it was decided to dig a canal in the eastern part of the Chalcidice peninsula, through the promontory of the mountain of Athos. This project was ordered in order to protect the fleet from another storm, similar to that which raged in 492 B.C. Traces of the canal have been brought to light during recent archaeological work (see Bengtson 1965:51). These activities, extensively described by Herodotus (VII 22-24), were carried out for two years under the command of the Persians Bubares and Artachaees. Different segments of the canal were allocated to the working parties from various nations (including local Greeks). The labourers were forced to work without stopping, urged on by the whip of their supervisors. The width of the canal was sufficient to allow two triremes to pass through the canal simultaneously.

To transport the army across the Hellespont, two pontoon bridges were constructed at Abydos, with a length of seven stadia (c. 1360 metres). The Phoenicians and Egyptians made cables from flax and papyrus for the bridges. Later classical writers and orators (Isocrates and others) ridiculed all these preparatory activities as another indication of the stupidity and megalomania of Xerxes. The digging of the canal, however, was less dangerous and cheaper than drawing the ships overland, while the bridges would have saved the Persians from having to load a huge army with a large number of horses, camels and mules onto ferries across the Hellespont, followed by their subsequent unloading (see Burn 1970:318-320).

At the same time supply dumps were established at previously indicated points, and hence transport ships carried grain from Asia. Many of these depots were located at specially selected points along the Thracian and Macedonian littoral. The provisions brought there by the Persians were augmented by local produce.

There were also diplomatic preparations for the war. In essence, the Persian allies against the Greeks were the Carthaginians. They had for long been the main mercantile rivals of the Greeks and long since waged war with them for the control of certain districts of Sicily and southern Italy. Now Persian diplomats started to set the Carthaginians against the Greeks of Sicily in order to keep the latter from extending assistance to their fellow Greeks on the mainland. If Diodorus (XI 1.20) and other classical authors can be believed, Xerxes concluded a treaty with Carthage. Both parties promised to advance upon the Greeks in the spring of 480 B.C. While Xerxes moved overland against Greece, the Carthaginians were to send their war ships and a large army to Sicily (see Bengtson 1965:52-54f.; Elayi 1981:21f.; Meyer 1939, Vol. III, pp. 356ff.).

In the meantime Themistocles continued trying to persuade the Athenians to prepare for resistance against the Persians. He pointed out the necessity of a strong fleet, as the Persians had one which consisted of Phoenician, Ionian and Egyptian vessels. Athens therefore used, above all things, the ten year lapse in the war with Persia to build a war fleet. The profits from the Laurion silver mines in Attica, which previously had been divided among the Athenian citizens, were now directed towards the construction of new ships. Two hundred triremes were built which formed the basis for the future strength of Athens as a maritime power.

The attitude of many Greek states towards the impending war had changed during the ten years after the battle of Marathon. They were now prepared to confront the common enemy with a united resistance. On the invitation of Sparta, a congress was organized of thirty Greek states. The meeting took place on the Isthmus of Corinth. These thirty states had either decided to oppose the Persians, or they were still unsure as to whether they should fight or capitulate. A leading role at the congress was played by Sparta and Athens, and the nucleus of the future alliance lay among the states of the Peloponnesos. As a result of this meeting, all wars between the various Greek states were halted. In addition, the congress decided that the Greek cities which voluntarily submitted to the Persians, without having been forced to do so in the face of the most pressing circumstances, would be punished and a tithe of their possessions would be given to the gods. This did not refer to a confiscation of a tenth part of the possessions of possible allies of the Persians, but a complete destruction of these cities and a subsequent presentation to the gods of a tenth part of the booty.

Many Greek states ignored the invitation to send their representatives to the congress and decided not to fight against the Persians. The Greeks were certainly not united in the war, and the call by Sparta and Athens to put up a united front gained only limited success (cf. Gillis 1979). The new patriotic slogans, referring to the fact that all Greeks had a common language and religion and that they were related to each other and were therefore obliged to fight together against the enemy, were not accepted by the majority of the population and did not become popular. The idea that the Greeks constituted one people had not yet taken root, and only a few Greeks regarded the allies of the Persians as traitors and turncoats. The Greeks looked upon themselves as citizens of different states. At that time no Greek taught his children patriotic love for Greece. Several centuries later, Plutarch wrote that at the commencement of the fifth century B.C., as well as much later, the Greeks regarded themselves as one people. In his opinion, when the Persians invaded Greece, the Hellenes were united in their common hatred against the barbarian enemy. As suggested by S. Ja. Lur'e, however, even Aeschylus, who personally participated in the war with Persia, did not call for a unification of all Greeks against the Persians. To the contrary, he suggested that all of Asia, including its Greek inhabitants, should belong to the Achaemenid empire (Lur'e 1947:83).

According to Herodotus (VII 138), the majority of the Greek states did not want to wage war against the Persians. Some even openly sided with them. There were many reasons for this apparent fatalism. The most important of these was the widespread conviction that resistance was useless and ill-advised. The agricultural districts of Thessaly, Boeotia and Locris, which were headed by tribal aristocracies, were unhesitating in preparing to join the side of the Persians. Thucydides (III 62.3) astutely remarks that at Thebes, the capital of Boeotia, power lay in the hands of a few and the latter called for the Persians in order to strengthen their position even further and to keep the masses under control. Other states, such as Achaea to the north, did not want to be involved in a war just for the sake of Athens and other Greek cities which wanted to resist the Persians. Similarly, the people from Argos, who shortly before had been defeated in a war with Sparta and who had lost thousands of men, did not burn from desire to fight against the Persians under command of the Spartan kings. Certain people even suggested that the Argives had invited the Persians to Greece, in order to frustrate their main enemy, Sparta. It should be added that the Delphian priests gave the Argives the clear advice to remain neutral if they wished to remain unscathed, and the people from Argos were pleased to follow this advice. The priesthood of Delphi, which played an important role in the political life of Greece, was convinced that the Persians were invincible and therefore, not wishing to risk their wealth, maintained a pro-Persian orientation and urged the Greeks more towards a capitulation than towards resistance (cf. Elayi 1978). The priests of Delphi were also aware that the Persians had treated the sanctuaries of Apollo with respect and that in particular the Persian general Datis had dedicated costly gifts to the temple of Apollo on Delos.

Thus, the energetic diplomatic activities of the Greek patriots, directed towards a unification of all Greeks against the Persians, did not meet with a great deal of success.

Greek ambassadors were also sent to Gelon, the tyrant of the city of Gela on Sicily, who had organized a powerful state on the island. The messengers warned Gelon that, if he would not help the Greeks of the mainland, the Persians would conquer all the lands with a Greek population, one after the other, including Sicily. According to Herodotus, Gelon received the ambassadors very insolently and reminded them of the fact that the Greeks of the mainland had not helped him when he waged war on the Carthaginians. Nevertheless, if Herodotus is correct, Gelon promised to send 200 war ships for the war against the Persians, together with 20,000 hoplites, 2,000 cavalry, 2,000 archers, 2,000 slingers and 2,000 lightly armed horsemen. He also promised to provide the Greek army with food and equipment. The promise, however, was made on the condition that he would be the overall commander of the army. When the Spartan ambassadors categorically stated that the Spartan kings would lead the Greek army, Gelon demanded for himself at least the leadership of the fleet. This the Spartans were willing to accept, but the Athenians, having decided to command the fleet, told Gelon that they had come with a call for assistance, not to ask for his leadership. Thus the consultations, according to Herodotus, were concluded without result, and Gelon decided to await the outcome of the war. If Xerxes won, Gelon would then indicate his willingness to offer 'earth and water'.

It should be admitted that E. Meyer was correct in regarding Herodotus' account of the discussions between Gelon and the Greek messengers as absurd, because at the time of Xerxes' campaign the people of Syracuse were involved in a war against Carthage (Meyer 1939, Vol. III, p. 356). This is evident, even from the work of Herodotus (VII 165-167) himself, who refers to Carthaginian and Sicilian sources stating that the Carthaginian army, together with their allies, attacked Sicily. This would make it very unlikely that the mainland Greeks would have asked Gelon for assistance against the Persians.

Greek ambassadors were also sent to Corcyra, an island in the Adriatic Sea, to the west of the Balkan peninsula. The people of Corcyra, who possessed a large fleet, promised assistance, assuring the messengers that they would not allow Hellas to be enslaved. But during the course of the war their behaviour was ambivalent. They equipped sixty ships and sent them to the Peloponnesos. However, they did not sail any further, but awaited the outcome of the war. Thus whatever happened, they would have the right answer. If Xerxes won, they planned to tell him that they sympathized with the Persians, and that they had not extended any assistance to the Greeks. If the Greeks were victorious, the Corcyraeans were prepared to say that it had been impossible for them to arrive at the battle scene in time, because of adverse winds.

The people of Crete, who also received requests for help, sent their ambassadors to Delphi in order to ask the oracle what they should do. The oracle, being pro-Persian, gave them, as they had done in similar circumstances, an ominous prophecy and called for the Cretans to refrain from assisting the Greeks. As a result, the Cretans decided to remain neutral. Thus, the number of Greek states that had decided, at the hour of greatest need for Greece, to fight for their freedom was limited, and they remained without outside allies.

After a long and detailed preparation, Xerxes commenced the campaign at the head of a, for that time, huge army. All the satrapies from Egypt to India had sent military levies; some dispatched infantry, others cavalry (in particular, the camel riders from Arabia, and charioteers from India). Others sent war ships and cargo vessels. Herodotus presents an extensive list of this multinational army which consisted of soldiers from 46 different nations. He also describes their costumes and weaponry and introduces the names of their commanders. As was suggested by various historians, this part of Herodotus' *Historiae* is based on official Persian written sources. Twenty-nine Persian generals took part in the campaign, including eight brothers of Xerxes. For example, the Bactrians and Sakas were led by Hystaspes or Vishtaspa, a brother of Xerxes; the Utians and Mukoi were commanded by Arsamenes, another son of Darius. In addition, Masistes was present. He was a son of Darius and Atossa and thus a full brother of Xerxes. Another general was Megabyzus, who shortly before had crushed the Babylonian revolt. There was also Mardonius, the son of Gobryas, and Smerdomenes, the son of Otanes. The Persian fleet was made up of vessels from the Egyptians, the Phoenicians, the Cyprians, the Carians and the Greeks of Asia Minor. The people from these nations did not have to join in the land army. The fleet was commanded by the satrap of Egypt, Achaemenes, another brother of Xerxes. In the general staff of the whole army, less important functions were given to Medes, Babylonians, and representatives from other subject nations. The nucleus of the army consisted of Iranians, namely Persians, Medes, Bactrians and Sakas. Although the ships were manned by Phoenicians, Cyprians and sailors from other naval peoples, there was on every ship a certain number of Persian and Saka soldiers, who had to prevent a mutiny or defection by the sailors to the other side.

According to Herodotus (VII 184), at the time of Xerxes' campaign to Greece his army included 1,700,000 foot soldiers; 80,000 horsemen; 20,000 camel riders and charioteers; the crew for 1,207 war ships, and auxiliary troops, in the aggregate 5,283,220 men. According to Ctesias (XIII 27)[1] and Ephorus, the army of Xerxes counted 800,000 men; Diodorus (II 3.7) tells that there were more than 800,000 men. According to other classical authors, there were 700,000 soldiers. All contemporary scholars state without any doubt that these numbers are absurd and exaggerated and that in those times it would have been impossible to feed such an enormous army. In addition, according to military specialists, such a large army would have stretched over thousands of kilometres. H. Delbrück and following him many other contemporary scholars of military history have suggested that Xerxes' army may not have counted more than between 50,000 and 75,000 men, and such an army, according to the standards of those times, must have seemed to the Greeks a huge host. According to E. Meyer and the majority of other scholars, the maximum number of people in the Persian land army at the time of the Greek campaign cannot have been higher than 100,000. Evidently, when presenting the numbers, Herodotus followed an oral tradition which was gradually being absorbed into Greek literature and which was designed to show that a tiny, freedom-loving people was

---

[1] J. M. Bigwood correctly remarked that Ctesias' references to the number of soldiers in various armies, are, in all cases, without any foundation (Bigwood 1976:10ff.).

attacked by the huge army of a despotic king (Bengtson 1965:54f.; Meyer 1939, Vol. III, pp. 240ff., 374ff.). As an example, reference may be made to an inscription at the pass of Thermopylae. The text reads: "At this place 4,000 Peloponnesians fought hand to hand against 300,000 men" (see Burn 1970:322). According to A. R. Burn, Herodotus, in the opinion that Xerxes' army counted approximately 2,100,000 men, doubled this number because he believed that the number of cooks, grooms and women, who followed the army, cannot have been less than the number of active soldiers, and he thus came to the number of 5,283,220 people. According to Herodotus, there were 10,000 men in the contingent of the Immortals, while each other contingent included 60,000 men. As suggested by Burn, the Persian army, similar to the Immortals, was organized according to the decimal system, and, consequently, every contingent counted 10,000 soldiers. Starting from this point, he came to the conclusion that Xerxes' army counted 200,000 men, but that it must have been impossible to lead this whole army to Greece, or even to concentrate it at one point because of problems in providing food and other necessities. Indeed, during his campaign Xerxes established garrisons and thus had to spread his army. According to Burn, the rear of the army was protected by soldiers from the subject nations, while the Iranians together with their king advanced upon Greece (Burn 1970:326-332; cf. Cook 1983:101-112).

According to Aeschylus, who was a contemporary and participant in the Persian-Greek wars, the Persian fleet counted 1,207 vessels, of which 207 were fast going ships. According to Herodotus, the Persian fleet of 1,207 vessels was later augmented by 120 ships from Greek colonies in Thrace and neighbouring districts. Herodotus extensively relates which district provided ships and how many. He must, therefore, have had access to a contemporary source. He did not start from the simple wish to adapt the numbers which were known to him, to those provided by Aeschylus. As suggested by Burn, the numbers of vessels in Herodotus' *Historiae* originate in the information provided by Greek reconnaissance. Nevertheless, the numbers are exaggerated. According to Burn, in quantity of war ships the Persians were not superior to the Greeks. This point is also attested to by the tactics of the Persian commanders, who felt insecure when a clash with the Greek ships was imminent. Greek reconnaissance, apparently, was aware of how many ships and how many soldiers each Persian satrapy could provide, but these numbers carried a more theoretical character. In particular, 674 old ships were used to build the pontoon bridges across the Hellespont (see Burn 1970:330-332). E. Meyer was of the opinion that before the decisive battles the Persian fleet outnumbered the Greek forces, but after losses during the voyage the Persian fleet equalled that of the Greeks, and at the battle of Salamis the Persian fleet was not stronger than that of their adversary. At Salamis, there were between 300 and 400 Greek triremes, while the Persian fleet counted between 400 and 500 vessels (Meyer 1939, Vol. III, pp. 374ff.).

In relation to the attempt to determine the size of Xerxes' army, much weight can be given to a piece of information provided by Thucydides (VI 33.5). The Greek historian states that the large armies of the Greeks and 'the barbarians', when undertaking long campaigns, usually had no success because the local people and their neighbours, united in their fear of the attackers, were always larger in number than the invaders. This remark, such as it has been transmitted by the great historian when he alludes to Xerxes' campaign, truly reflects the real state of affairs on the side of the Persians at the time of their campaign against Greece.

The assembling point for the land army was located in Cappadocia. Hence, in the autumn of 481 B.C., the Persian army crossed the River Halys (the modern Qizil Irmaq). At the city of Celaenae in Phrygia, according to Herodotus (VII 27-29), a rich Lydian by name of Pythius welcomed Xerxes and his army in a grand style. This pleased Xerxes so much that he turned towards Pythius and said: "Since I left Persia, I have not met anyone who wished to entertain my army." From Phrygia Xerxes and his forces advanced upon the capital of Lydia, Sardis, and from there, in 481 B.C., he sent ambassadors to Greece with the demand for 'earth and water'. He did not send, however, anyone to Athens or Sparta, as these cities had previously killed the ambassadors of Darius. In 481 B.C. there also arrived certain Greek spies at Sardis, who wanted to collect information about the Persian fleet, but they were soon apprehended and sentenced to death. When Xerxes heard about these sentences he ordered that the spies should be set free, and, after showing them the whole Persian army, he allowed them to return home unscathed. According to Herodotus, Xerxes did so in the hope that the Greeks, after being informed about the size of his army, would decide to lay down their weapons.

But misfortune awaited Xerxes at the very start of his campaign. A storm destroyed both bridges across the Hellespont. According to Herodotus (VII 35), when Xerxes was informed about this calamity, he was enraged and commanded that the waters should be whipped, and in order to tame the Hellespont he ordered chains to be thrown into the water. In addition, the supervisors of the construction work of the bridges were beheaded. Two new pontoon bridges were built; one of 360 and the other of 314 vessels. Thick cables were stretched in layers over the boats, and planks were laid on top. The planks were covered with

compacted earth, and on both sides of the bridge a railing was constructed, so that the horses and other animals would not become frightened by the view of the sea.

In the spring of 480 B.C. the bridges were completed and the Persian
army left Sardis and was ordered to march to Abydos. Here a throne was
constructed on top of one of the hills. The throne was made of white marble, and from this seat Xerxes was able to review his army. Subsequently, the army crossed the Hellespont. The cavalry and infantry used one
bridge, while the army followers and the beasts of burden used the other.
According to Herodotus (VII 56), the crossing continued for seven days
without a pause, and the rivers in the area did not contain enough water
for the troops and animals. The army then went to the city of Doriscus
along the Thracian coast. Here Xerxes arranged his army into fighting
ranks, dividing his forces into national contingents. At the same time the
ships were hauled onto the nearby beaches and repaired. While on the
march, the army incorporated new contingents from Thrace and
Macedonia. The army was largely fed by the districts it passed through,
a burden which put considerable pressure upon the local populations.

From Doriscus the army marched westward in three parallel lines.
One third of the army, commanded by Mardonius and Masistes, the
brother of Xerxes, advanced along the coast and escorted the fleet. The
second line was commanded by Tritantaechmes and Gergis. This part of
the army marched deep inland; the third line was commanded by
Xerxes, together with Megabyzus and Smerdomenes. This line marched
between the two others. During the march the Thracian peoples
presented guides, who, in reality, appear to have been hostages. When
the army came to the city of Acanthus, Xerxes gave its inhabitants Median clothes as a reward for their enthusiasm in digging the canal near
the mountain of Athos. Near the city of Therma, in the north of Greece,
the fleet and land army, which operated in close cooperation, came
together. Xerxes visited the landmarks of the region, he listened to local
legends and enjoyed the Thessalian mountains. In the meantime the ambassadors returned who had been sent out to demand 'earth and water'.
The Thessalians, Achaeans, Thebans, and the inhabitants of other
districts and many other cities had declared their willingness to
acknowledge the supreme authority of Xerxes.

It should be noted that the capitulation of the Thessalians could to a
certain degree be regarded as enforced. When the Persian army marched
from Asia to Europe, the Thessalian representatives at the Congress on
the Isthmus of Corinth had stated that they would protect Greece from
the Persians, if a common Greek stand was made to hold the passes of
the Olympus which led into Thessaly. If the other Greeks turned down

this demand, the Thessalians threatened to join the side of the Persians. Subsequently, the Greeks sent 10,000 hoplites to Thessaly, mainly soldiers from Sparta and Athens. This force was strengthened by the Thessalian cavalry. Afterwards there arrived in the Greek camp messengers from Alexander, the king of Macedonia, who had previously stated that he was prepared to welcome the Persian army, because Macedonia already formed part of the Achaemenid empire. On behalf of Alexander the ambassadors tried to convince the Greeks to leave the Olympus Pass so that the Persians would not annihilate the complete Greek forces. In giving this counsel, Alexander assured the Greeks that he did so out of sympathy with the Hellenes. In reality he was trying to prevent the Persian army from staying long in Macedonia, thereby consuming all local supplies of food (see Burn 1970:344). But independent of Alexander's advice, the Greek hoplites were insufficient in number to defend the passes of the Olympus. The Greeks feared that the Persians would bypass them via other mountain routes and surround them. In addition, the local people of Thessaly were, to a certain degree, inclined in a friendly manner towards the Persians as they were headed by the pro-Persian family of the Aleuadae. It was, therefore, difficult for the Greeks to hold this rich land. All these points convinced the Greek generals that they should leave the northern part of Greece to the enemy, although at that time the Persians were still engaged in crossing from Abydos to Europe. Under these circumstances, the Thessalians, who long since had been looked upon with mistrust by the Greek patriots, went over to the side of the Persians and during the course of the whole war assisted them with considerable energy.

CHAPTER TWENTY-TWO

PERSIAN VICTORY AT THERMOPYLAE

Leaving northern Greece undefended against the Persians, the Greeks assembled again for a council at the Isthmus of Corinth. They decided to resist the advancing Persians at the narrow defile of Thermopylae. Through this gorge lay the route to Boeotia and Attica, while to the east of Thermopylae stretched the sea. It was an easy position to defend as there was no room for the Persians to unfold the flanks of their army and to deploy fully their cavalry.

The Spartan authorities, however, either regarded the defence of central Greece as a hopeless case or did not want to risk their forces so far away from their homeland. They urged the other delegates to evacuate the whole of central Greece, without offering any resistance to the Persians, and to defend the Isthmus of Corinth. When this suggestion was turned down by the majority of the Greeks, Sparta sent only a small force of three hundred hoplites to Thermopylae, commanded by their king Leonidas. The latter only took with him those soldiers who had sons, so that no family of Spartans would die out. As is apparent from this point, the Spartan authorities hoped to preserve in safety the main forces of their army, and they thus purposefully sacrificed the life of their king and of three hundred men in order to prevent discontent among the other Greeks, especially the Athenians, for without the Athenian fleet it would have been impossible to conduct the war with any hope of success.

The total number of Greek soldiers that arrived for the defence of Thermopylae amounted to 6,500. The nucleus of this force consisted of 4,000 men from the Peloponnesos. Four hundred Thebans who also joined in the united defence, were suspect of planning to defect to the Persian side. When the Greeks arrived at Thermopylae, they restored a wall in the gorge which had been constructed many years previously. At the same time the Greek fleet sailed to the narrow sea lane of Cape Artemisium, which divides the northern point of the island of Euboea from Thessaly. The fleet was to be used to prevent the Persians from attacking the Greek land forces at Thermopylae in the rear. The Greek fleet thus acted in close cooperation with the land army. The further course of events, however, showed that the commanders of the Greek fleet were irresolute, while the army that held Thermopylae was too small in number to protect the access to central Greece.

In the meantime the Persian army advanced into Thessaly. According to Herodotus (VII 197), Xerxes showed the greatest respect towards the sanctuaries of the land and did not allow his troops to commit any act of sacrilege. Expecting a successful Persian advance into central Greece, the Greek states that had refused to give 'earth and water' regretted their decision, while those who had showed their willingness to do so, and thus had recognized Xerxes' suzerainty, rejoiced in their apparent foresight. At the most dangerous hour, when Greece was threatened by bondage to a foreign power, the number of those willing to defend their freedom was very small. The majority of the Greeks were only concerned in trying to survive these difficult times.

The Persian fleet left Therma in the direction of the shore of Thermopylae. During the voyage the Persians managed to capture two reconnaissance ships of the Greeks. The Persians enslaved the sailors. One of the crew, although heavily wounded, had shown extraordinary braveness. This evoked the admiration of the Persians and they treated his wounds by applying myrrh and bandaging the injuries with fine linen. The crew of a third ship hastily abandoned their ship and fled to Athens. Subsequently the Greek fleet left Cape Artemisium, which meant that Persian ships could approach the coast of Thermopylae without meeting any opposition. They assembled in the waters off Chalcis on Euboea, southeast of Thermopylae. Shortly afterwards, however, a heavy storm sprang up which lasted for three days. The storm wrecked hundreds of Persian ships and killed many people. On being informed of this, the Greeks returned to Artemisium and captured fifteen ships which had been separated from the main fleet. Following these events the Persian vessels left for Aphetae, a port of Magnesia.

When the Persian land forces approached Thermopylae, the majority of the Greeks who guarded the gorge wanted to leave their position and withdraw towards the Peloponnesos in order to dig themselves in at the Isthmus of Corinth. The Phocians and Locrians, however, turned against this suggestion, as such a withdrawal would mean that their lands would be turned over to the enemy. Leonidas, therefore, who commanded the united Greek forces, decided to hold the mountain pass and he sent messengers to the allied Greek cities to ask for assistance.

According to Herodotus, Xerxes waited four days, in the hope that the Greeks would withdraw from the passes. After these four days he sent in his troops for a frontal attack. At first he sent Medes and Cissians, with orders to defeat the Greeks and to lead them to him. For the whole day the troops of Xerxes attacked the Greek positions. The places of the fallen were taken over by replacements, but the attack remained without success and eventually the Persians were forced to withdraw after suffering heavy losses. Xerxes sent in his Immortals, headed by their general Hydarnes. These troops could not spread out their ranks in the small gorge, and found themselves in the same hopeless position as their predecessors. In addition, their lances were shorter than those of the Greeks. As a result the attack was thrown back. While the Persians were thus making frontal attacks for three consecutive days, a certain commoner called Ephialtes, probably in the hope of receiving a large reward, told the Persian leaders about a little known path which led around the mountain and that night he guided the enemy troops to the top of the pass. Later in history many Greek writers have asserted that if Ephialtes had not been there the Persians would never have taken Thermopylae and subsequently the city of Athens. However, the whole account by Herodotus about the battle at Thermopylae, describing Xerxes as a stupid despot, and Herodotus' reflection upon the point that the Persians had many people, but few men, is evidently far from the truth. The legend about the betrayal by Ephialtes, known to everyone from the school benches, also demands a critical consideration. For four days Xerxes remained inactive before Thermopylae. Of course, he did so not because he hoped for a withdrawal of the Greeks, but because he waited for the arrival of his main forces. It should also be noted that even on the first day after its arrival at Thermopylae, Persian cavalry must have started to reconnoitre the district and they, accustomed to the mountains, may have discovered without the help of a traitor the path which led around the top of the mountain. A. R. Burn, having studied the topography of Thermopylae, remarked that there are at least two paths, and one of them could easily have been spotted by the Persians from a distance. In addition, there were also other circuitous routes. Because of these paths Xerxes did not need to send his troops into a senseless frontal attack against the Greeks (see Burn 1970:407-413). Without a great deal of effort the Persians could also find good guides, who could have shown them a circuitous route around the gorge of Thermopylae. Herodotus was aware of various versions about such guides; amongst the Greek traitors, he mentions in particular a certain Onetes from the island of Euboea and some others. As was said above, Greece consisted of dozens of autonomous states and many of these had gone over to the side of the Persians and acted as their allies. Depending upon the point of view, those who acted as guides could be seen as traitors or allies. But, if their psychology is studied, it should be admitted that they did not violate any law; they did not have a common motherland, and certain Greek states even invited the Persians to Greece. Many Greeks were even convinced that Zeus had arrived in person in their country, personified by Xerxes (cf. Dovatur 1957:118). According to Herodotus (VII 115), the Thracians still regarded the road which was followed by Xerxes, decades after Xerxes' campaign, as sacred.

When the Persians via the circuitous path had surrounded the Greeks and started their attack, the position of the Greeks became hopeless. The Greek troops were distributed unequally; only 1,000 soldiers held the top of the mountain, while the remaining Greeks were positioned in the adjoining narrows. The mountain top was taken without much opposition, and thereupon the majority of the defenders returned to their towns as there was nothing which would stop the Persian advance into central Greece. Herodotus relates that Leonidas ordered the allied troops to withdraw. He remained, however, with his Spartan soldiers, because Spartan law did not permit him to withdraw. Only the Thespians remained voluntarily with the Spartans. Leonidas did not dismiss the Thebans, whose pro-Persian feelings were well known, because they could act as his hostages. In total there remained about a thousand soldiers with the Spartan king. The motives behind Leonidas' decision were the topic of numerous discussions, even amongst the classical writers, and this polemic has been continued by contemporary writers. A. R. Burn has correctly remarked that if all the Greeks had withdrawn, the Persian cavalry would have pursued and routed them. It is likely, therefore, that Leonidas remained with his men in order to cover the withdrawal of the others, so that they could safely regroup and continue the war against the common enemy (Burn 1970:419). Later in history, many legends sprang up around the figure of Leonidas. These tales were officially diffused by the Spartan leaders. The Athenian playwright Aristophanes, in his comedy 'Lysistrata', regarded the battle at Thermopylae as the most famous page in the military history of Sparta. In fact, the soldiers giving their life for the freedom of their motherland, deserved eternal fame, independent of the point that their heroism was based on a definite policy of Sparta, which put the fate of a significant part of central Greece into the hands of so few men.

Apparently, the Persians at first shot arrows at the defenders of Thermopylae. On the battlefield a large collection of arrowheads has been found which are mainly three-edged in shape, and which are characteristic for the Scythian, Persian and Median troops (Burn 1970:420). When the attack on the position of Leonidas started, the Persians, according to Herodotus, urged troops from their subject lands to the front, under the threat of whips. At the time of the battle, the Thebans defected to the side of the Persians. Nevertheless the majority of them, on the command of Xerxes, were branded with the 'royal mark', which meant that they were enslaved. In close combat the spears of most of the Spartans were broken, and the Spartans started to fight with their swords, and even with their bare hands. All of them bravely resisted to the very end, and all were killed. The Persians also suffered heavy losses. Xerxes lost two of his brothers in addition to many noble Persians. In spite of the fact that the Persians behaved in general with respect towards a brave adversary, it occurred that when the body of the Spartan king was found, Xerxes ordered it to be decapitated (subsequently, the remains of Leonidas, according to Pausanias, were transported to Sparta, and buried).

After the battle, Xerxes was convinced of the truth of the words once spoken to him by the former king of Sparta, Demaratus, who had fled to the Persians. Demaratus had said that the Spartans were not afraid of the enemy, whatever the outcome of the battle would be, and they would fight until victory or until they perished. It is characteristic of this attitude that two of the Spartans, who before the battle were sent by Leonidas to the allied cities with a request for assistance, were subsequently met at Sparta with contempt. On the battlefield, on top of a hill, there still stands a memorial to Leonidas, with some verses by the famous poet Simonides: "O stranger, tell the Spartans that here we lie, obedient to their orders" (see Lur'e 1940:202).

By the beginning of August, 480 B.C., while at Thermopylae the Greeks still continued their resistance, several sea battles took place between the Greeks and their enemy. The former Spartan king Demaratus advised Xerxes to occupy, with 300 ships, the island of Cythera, along the south coast of Laconia, and thereupon to attack Sparta. Thus, it was argued, the Persians would prevent the Spartans from helping the remaining Greeks. Achaemenes, however, the brother of Xerxes and commander of the Persian fleet, was opposed to an independent action by the fleet, and preferred close collaboration between the fleet and land forces. The latter advice was followed by Xerxes, although, apparently, Demaratus' opinion about a campaign against Sparta was correct.

The united Greek fleet was anchored near Cape Artemisium, not far from Thermopylae. In total the fleet counted 271 vessels, of which 127 were provided by the Athenians; 40 by the Corinthians, and the remaining by other Greek city-states. The fleet, just like the army, was under the command of Spartan leaders, as the allies did not want Athenian commanders. The reason for this was that Corinth had long been a mercantile competitor of Athens and rivalry continued to that time. In addition, Aegina, which had a significant number of ships at her disposal, was known as the most bitter enemy of Athens, and an open war between the two had been going on to the very beginning of Xerxes' campaign. At the same time Corinth and Aegina were loyal allies of Sparta. The Athenians categorically demanded for themselves the command of the fleet, because almost half of the vessels were Athenian. The leading Athenian politician, Themistocles, however, managed to stop the quarrels for the sake of the common cause. Finally the Spartan Eurybiades was appointed as commander of the united Greek fleet. Many captains of Greek vessels had decided not to participate in the fight and were prepared to flee to the Peloponnesos. If Herodotus can be believed (VIII 4-5), the Euboeans, who had not yet succeeded in bringing their families and goods from the island to a safe place, bribed Themistocles with thirty talents of silver, in order to persuade the remaining generals not to withdraw. From this sum, Themistocles, as if it was his own, passed five talents on to Eurybiades, and three to the Corinthian admiral Adeimantos, who had planned to sail away from Artemisium. The remaining sum Themistocles kept for himself. As a result of this, according to Herodotus, the Greeks remained at their anchorage near Cape Artemisium and joined in the battle. This whole story is repeated by Plutarch. Many modern historians have accepted this account as true, in the supposition that Themistocles, even at the moment of greatest danger for his motherland, would not forget to fill his pockets with gold. E. Meyer, however, has correctly remarked that this piece of information is not reliable, and that it originated in political slander from the side of the aristocrats directed towards the leader of the radical democratic party (Meyer 1939, Vol. III, pp. 396f.).

The Persians, in an attempt to cut off the retreat of the Greeks, sent 200 ships around the island of Euboea. The Persian vessels were lighter than Greek ships and they came close to achieving their objective. Soon, however, a storm rose up, and many Persian ships were wrecked. The battle which took place soon afterwards remained inconclusive, but Greek hopes, namely that the ships of the Greeks from Asia Minor would change sides, were not justified. The latter, to the contrary, fought vigorously in the hope of receiving a reward from the Persian king. The next morning fifty-three more triremes came from Attica, and the Greek fleet attacked some ships from Cilicia, and sunk them. Subsequently a second battle took place near Artemisium. The fleets on both sides were approximately equal in strength, as the Persians could not deploy all of their maritime strength. On the Persian side the Egyptians distinguished themselves to a high degree. Indeed they managed to capture five Greek vessels, together with their crew. Both sides suffered heavy losses; half of the Athenian ships were damaged, and the battle, which continued for three days, was indecisive. Nevertheless, it proved to a certain degree to be a victory for the Greeks, because they were now convinced that they could resist the enemy. Later, the famous ancient Greek poet Pindar said that at Artemisium the Athenians laid the foundation for their subsequent victory.

After the battle of Artemisium, the Greeks heard about the fall of Thermopylae. The news of the defeat reached the admirals of the fleet at sunset on the same day that the Persians had destroyed Leonidas and his forces. Thereupon the Greek fleet left Artemisium and withdrew towards Attica. Before the withdrawal, however, Themistocles went in a fast ship to fresh water springs and anchorages, and ordered inscriptions to be carved into nearby stones with a call to the Ionians and Carians, incorporated into the Persian army, to come over to the side of the Greeks. In these inscriptions it was said that the war originated in the impartial help which the Athenians had given to the Ionians at the time of their revolt against the Persians. The objective of Themistocles is clear: the Ionians would either defect and join the Greek forces, or they would not do so, but in that case the Persians would start to doubt their loyalty. From his side, however, Xerxes also decided to use subterfuge. He ordered the burial of the Persian soldiers who had fallen at Thermopylae, except for only a few, and to cover the graves with leaves. Thereupon the battlefield was shown to the Ionians. About 4,000 Greeks were lying there. Many of them were Helots, serving in the army train. The Persians told the Ionians that they had chastised the Greeks with great ease. This deceit, however, was not completely successful, because the Ionians discovered the graves which had been covered with leaves.

After the fall of Thermopylae and the withdrawal of the Greek fleet into coastal waters, all of central Greece as far as the Corinthian Isthmus lay open to the Persians. They occupied Doris; Phocis; Locris and the other areas of central Greece, and destroyed various cities and towns that offered resistance. The sanctuary of Delphi, well known for its pro-Persian attitude, remained neutral towards all military actions and suffered no damage at all. The people of Boeotia came to the side of the Persians. Finally, the Achaemenid army was able to advance without opposition towards Attica and Athens.

CHAPTER TWENTY-THREE

THE BATTLE OF SALAMIS

Athens was now in immediate danger. The inhabitants of the city, however, remained steadfast in their decision to fight, although it had
become evident that they could not count on assistance from their allies,
who had hastened to dig themselves in on the Corinthian Isthmus. In
Athens a law was passed which allowed political exiles to return to their
motherland and participate in the war. Amongst those who returned was
the former leader of the landholders, Aristides, who had been ostracized
in 482 B.C. The war for the freedom of the motherland brought temporary reunification between the democratic party and their opponents,
the aristocrats.

Just before the fall of Thermopylae, Athenian messengers were sent to
Delphi in order to ask the oracle which tactics they should adopt for the
war. The answer was ominous, because the oracle predicted that the
Athenians would suffer a heavy defeat. For the second time the
messengers turned towards the oracle begging Apollo for a more
favourable prophecy. Receiving a new prediction, the messengers
recorded it and transmitted the message to the popular assembly at
Athens. It was still necessary, however, to explain the prophecy which
was given to them, because it was very obscurely worded, so that should
the Athenians lose, it would be possible to blame them for not correctly
interpreting the words of the god. The prophecy stated that the Athenians should hide themselves behind wooden walls. Many disputes arose
as to the interpretation of these words. Specialists in predictions called for
an evacuation on ships, after which they would sail to Italy to find a new
home. Themistocles, chosen as strategos with unlimited powers, argued
that the oracle when talking about wooden walls was referring to the war
ships, and that the Athenians should continue the war by fighting the
Persians at sea. This opinion was accepted by the majority of the
assembly. It was impossible to protect Athens against the huge army of
the Persians. It was therefore decided the leave the city. All able bodied
men would take up arms and embark on the ships, while the women,
children and the aged would be evacuated, together with their possessions, to the islands of Salamis and Aegina, and to Troezen. The latter
city was located in Argolis in the northeast of the Peloponnesos, and had
long since been friendly to the Athenians. Many Athenians opposed this
decision, as they did not want to leave the temples of the gods and the

graves of their ancestors. The aged people cried and begged not to leave their city, but the younger people were unrelenting and the evacuation was organized and carried out under command of the Areopagus (the highest executive of the state).

It cannot be excluded, however, that the dramatic description of the evacuation, as presented by Herodotus, is incorrect. In 1960, an inscription was published which was found on the territory of ancient Troezen. The text contains a decree of the Athenian assembly, published in 480 B.C. This decree refers to the evacuation of Athens at the instigation of Themistocles. If this text can be believed, the decision to leave Athens was not taken after the death of Leonidas and the defeat of his troops at Thermopylae, but long prior to it and before the retreat of the Greek fleet from Artemisium. If this is correct, then the battle at Salamis was only one aspect of the strategic plan which long before had been premeditated by Themistocles and which had been approved by the Athenian assembly. The objective of the defensive actions at Thermopylae and Artemisium was therefore to slow down the advance of the enemy, in order to prepare for the premeditated and decisive battles. If this is correct then the activities of Sparta were without reproach and based on agreements with the Athenian generals. The experience of military history, however, testifies against the possibility of such acuteness, not only of one leader, but of a whole people. Themistocles, of course, may have foreseen the coming events, but it is unlikely that he would have been able to convince the assembly of the necessities of an evacuation, long before the moment when danger was most imminent. In any case, on the basis of a number of peculiarities in the inscription which contradict the situation in the eighties of the fifth century B.C., but which reflect the policy of the Athenian assembly in the fourth century B.C., and on the basis of certain other points which we cannot discuss here, it would appear that the inscription from Troezen is a fake, made in Athens during the fourth century B.C. in order to glorify the city and Themistocles. It is therefore difficult to trust this text completely (for a survey of the various opinions, see Gluskina 1963:35ff.).

Whatever really happened, the Persians occupied Attica and destroyed and burnt down the city of Athens, which had been deserted by its inhabitants. Only a few citizens had entrenched themselves on the Acropolis. They were, in the main, the keepers of temple goods who were convinced that the prophecy of the Delphi oracle as regards the necessity to hide behind wooden walls related to the gates of the Acropolis. The Persians started to shoot fire arrows from the opposite hill, but they could not take the fortress. After having discovered an undefended place on the rock, the Persians managed to climb to the Acropolis. Some of the defenders, when they saw a contingent of the enemy forces above them, jumped from the wall and died. The others tried to hide in the temples. The attackers, however, killed them all. Then they burnt the Acropolis. Thereupon Xerxes ordered the removal of the bronze statues of the tyrannicides Harmodius and Aristogeiton. These statues were transported to Susa. Much later Alexander of Macedonia returned them to Athens.

Having conquered the capital of Attica, Xerxes sent messengers to Susa in order to proclaim his victory. Three months had passed since the Persian army crossed over into Europe.

The Greeks, who were unwilling to risk their army, kept to their tactics of warfare at sea. According to the wishes of the Athenians, the combined Greek fleet was anchored in the narrow gulf between the island of Salamis and the coast of Attica. This fleet was comprised of almost 380 vessels, of which 147 were provided by the Athenians. These 147 ships had been newly built with due observance of all demands of maritime warfare. Eurybiades, the commander of the fleet, summoned a war council and asked all of the leaders to point out, if they so wished, the best place to fight a battle. The subsequent course of events is described by Herodotus as follows. The majority of the war leaders were of the opinion that the best course of action would be a withdrawal to the Isthmus of Corinth. They feared that in case of a possible defeat at Salamis the Greeks would find themselves completely cut off on the island and that they would perish. If they could not defend the Corinthian Isthmus, then they could disperse and return to their own towns. While the discussions continued, the news arrived about the Persian cruelties towards the defenders of the Athenian Acropolis. At that moment, several of the war leaders, without even waiting for the outcome of the council, sailed to the Peloponnesos. The remaining captains also decided to sail to the Corinthian Isthmus and there to join battle with the enemy. This plan coincided with the tactics of the Spartans, who for long had wanted to leave northern and central Greece to their fate, and to concentrate all the Greek forces for the defence of the Peloponnesos. The Athenians, however, resisted these plans with vigour. Without their fleet the allies would not be able to continue the war at sea. Also, in the case of a withdrawal of the fleet from Salamis, the Athenian women and children would fall into the hands of the Persians. Therefore, while preparations for the withdrawal were under way, Themistocles turned to Eurybiades with the request to recall the council, while pointing out that, when the fleet would leave Salamis, it would scatter. Eurybiades agreed to the proposal. Themistocles then used all his rhetorical skills and his great personal influence and asked those who were present to join in battle against the

Persians near Salamis, in the narrow strait where the Persian fleet would lack the space to spread out and manoeuvre. Themistocles argued that they should not surrender Salamis, Megara and Aegina to the enemy without a fight, and subsequently lead the Persians towards the Pelopon-nesos, as a battle on open sea near the Corinthian Isthmus would be too disadvantageous to the Greeks because they had fewer ships than the enemy. According to Herodotus, the Greeks held the Persians in con-siderable awe, and it fell hard on Themistocles to convince the remaining leaders to decide for action. He again spoke out and tried to show that in the war against the Persians the fleet had been the main defence of the Greeks. Thereupon he threatened that, if the Greeks decided to leave Salamis, the Athenians would pick up their families and sail to the Italian town of Siris. According to an ancient oracle, they were destined to settle there. In such an event, the other Greeks would find themselves without the military support of a strong fleet. In fear of the realization of such a threat, Eurybiades decided to join in battle against the Persians at Salamis.

In the meantime the Persian advance continued. The Persian forces were strengthened by militia from Malis; Doris; Locris; Boeotia and other Greek districts. The Persian fleet arrived at Athens, and Xerxes summoned a war council which included the ships' captains and the leaders of the various contingents. The council was headed by the king of the Phoenician city of Sidon; following him there was the king of Tyre. Xerxes asked Mardonius to question every representative in turn whether they should join battle with the Greeks in the Gulf of Salamis, or not. All of them were in favour of a battle, except Artemisia, the queen of the city of Halicarnassus in Asia Minor. She argued that all of Greece was already at the mercy of the Great King and the Persian army should therefore refrain from any overhasty and dangerous action. She argued in favour of an advance upon the Peloponnesos in a combined operation of the land forces and the navy. Xerxes, however, decided to heed the advice of the majority of the captains. He said that he would follow the course of the battle himself, thus encouraging his warriors. Thereupon the Persian fleet drew up in battle array near Salamis.

The night fell before the day of the decisive battle. The Greek camp, according to Herodotus, was still in the grips of the previous discussions and completely overcome by fear of their mighty adversary. As on pre-vious occasions, the majority did not want to fight at Salamis, and most of the captains wanted to escape to the Peloponnesos, where at the same time defensive structures were being built without any effort being spared.

The route to the Peloponnesos was blocked in order to prevent an attack by the Persians, and straight across the Isthmus tens of thousands of

Spartans, Arcadians, Corinthians, and people from other districts were engaged night and day in the construction of a wall, made from stone, brick and timber. Many Peloponnesian towns, however, sympathized with the Persians, and therefore sent no people to help in the construction of these fortifications. Helots and other groups of dependents, of course, awaited the advent of the Persians as if they were their liberators. The combined Greek land army was commanded by Cleombrotus, a brother of the dead Spartan king Leonidas. To the majority of the Greek soldiers, the wall across the Corinthian Isthmus seemed to be the only hope, and the decision to order the fleet to join in battle against the Persians near Salamis seemed suicidal. Therefore a new war council was summoned.

In this council all of the war leaders, except the representatives from Athens, Aegina and Megara, whose land was immediately threatened by the Persians, showed themselves in favour of an immediate withdrawal to the Peloponnesos. At that moment Themistocles sent in secret his loyal slave, who was a Persian by extraction, to the camp of Xerxes. He told the Persians the following: Themistocles was on the side of the Persians and wished them to win. He also said that there was no unity among the Greeks and they were planning to withdraw. If the Persians attacked the Greek fleet, they would gain a victory.[1]

Xerxes decided to annihilate the enemy fleet in one stroke and thereby end the war with a Persian victory. The Persians disembarked some troops on the island of Psyttaleia, in order to prevent the Greeks from fleeing. Thereupon, under the cover of darkness, they surrounded the Greek fleet without being noticed. According to Herodotus, the disputes within the Greek camp were coming to an end when the famous Athenian politician Aristides suddenly came in and informed Themistocles that the Greek fleet had been surrounded by the Persians. At the request of Themistocles, Aristides entered the council and told those present that the discussions were no longer of any use and that the Greeks were left with only one choice, namely a sea battle. The majority of the leaders did not believe Aristides' information, but shortly afterwards a captain of one of the Ionian ships who had defected from the Persian fleet came to the council, and told the military chiefs that the Greek fleet had actually been surrounded. The dawn had already risen, when Themistocles addressed the soldiers, who were now, against their will, forced to fight. The Greek ships lifted anchor and set out for battle.

---

[1] According to S. Ja. Lur'e, this story about the sending of a messenger to Xerxes was a later fake, concocted in order to glorify Themistocles (Lur'e 1940:203). However, Aeschylus, who was a participant in the battle of Salamis, also said through the mouth of a Persian courier that a Greek came to Xerxes from the Athenian camp and told him that the Greeks were going to escape to save their lives. See also Plutarch, *Themist.* 12.

Many modern historians, not without foundation, have expressed doubts as to the version of events related by Herodotus. An army that was ready to flee and whose leaders could not agree about the course of action to be taken, is unlikely to set out to join battle and subsequently gain a decisive victory. Apparently, the battle tactics of Salamis had long before been discussed and adopted by the leaders of the combined Greek forces. The initiator of this plan must in fact have been Themistocles, who, according to Thucydides (I 138), was quickly able to detect the best way out of even the most difficult situation. Herodotus writes that the most stubborn advocate of a withdrawal was the Corinthian admiral Adeimantos. In this piece of information, scholars have correctly detected some slander, the reason for which was the uncordial relationship between Corinth on the one hand, and on the other Athens, where Herodotus wrote the greatest part of his work. From Plutarch's essay *De Malignitate Herodoti* (39) it is known that in certain texts the name of Corinth was mentioned in the third place after Sparta and Athens. These texts were engraved on goods which were captured after the battle of Salamis, and which were dedicated to the gods. Plutarch also refers to another text, which has been preserved to the modern time and which relates that the Athenians permitted the Corinthians to bury their men who had fallen in the battle of Salamis, in the neighbourhood of Athens. It is clear that Herodotus in an attempt to please the Athenians shows some subjectivity in his report on the battle of Salamis (Burn 1970:436; Lur'e 1947:73; Meyer 1899, Vol. II, pp. 204ff.; *idem* 1939, Vol. III, p. 387).

The battle took place in the Gulf of Salamis on September 28th, 480 B.C. These waters are only 5 kilometres long and 1.5 kilometres wide. The battle started at sunrise and continued to the evening. The Greeks were the first to attack. Xerxes followed the course of events, sitting at the foot of a mountain, and dictating to his scribes the names of commanders who distinguished themselves. A poetic description of the battle is contained in Aeschylus' 'The Persians'. According to this playwright, 399 Greek vessels participated in the battle (Herodotus gives the round figure of 400). On the Persian side there were approximately 650 ships, but only about half of them could actually take part in the fight. Not long before the battle, during a storm, the Persian fleet had suffered heavy losses and many vessels were wrecked upon the rocky coast.

The Phoenicians were fighting on the left flank, opposite the Athenians; the Ionians were opposite to the Peloponnesians. The sailors of the Persian fleet fought stubbornly and bravely. The majority of the Ionians, contrary to the summons by Themistocles, remained loyal to Xerxes and stoically fought for him. If Herodotus (VIII 10) can be believed, they were even pleased when some Greek soldiers were killed. The Ionians captured several Greek ships, and as a reward for this act the Persians later appointed the Ionian Theomestor as tyrant of Samos; Phylacus, another Ionian captain, was listed among the royal benefactors. In spite of the courage of their soldiers, the Persians suffered a heavy defeat. The greater part of their fleet was destroyed in a piecemeal fashion by the Greeks. The Persian fleet was impeded in its manoeuvring by the narrowness of the waters between the island of Salamis and the mainland; their ships could not spread out in battle array, and they had to fight individually. In the chaos they often bumped into each other. In addition, the strength of the Persians was diminished because some of their vessels had to cut off the escape route of the Greeks. As regards the Greek ships, they were relatively small and could therefore be more easily manoeuvred. Finally, in this battle the Greeks were left with the choice between dying or gaining a victory, and the recognition of this fact presented them with all the necessary decisiveness. The patriotic feelings of the Greek warriors finds clear reflection in the following verse from Aeschylus' 'The Persians':

> ".... Forward, sons of Hellas, Save the motherland, save your wives, your children, the shrines of your ancestral gods, and the graves of your fathers; fight now, for everything"

In his biography of Aristides, Plutarch (9) tells that three nephews of Xerxes and many other noble Persians were taken captive on the island of Psyttaleia and sacrificed by the Greeks to their god Dionysus. The fate of the Persian contingent at Psyttaleia is described by Aeschylus (*Persae*, 426-427) through the mouth of a Persian messenger: "never in one day have so many persons lost their lives."

A large part of the Persian fleet was destroyed during the battle. Once again the Greeks showed their superiority in military tactics over the Persian commanders. After the battle at Salamis the Greeks decided to reward the bravest of the commanders with a laurel wreath. Every commander, however, regarded himself as the one most worthy of the reward. As the second best, nevertheless, they all regarded Themistocles: a sure sign of the fact that he had been the brain behind the victory. This victory came to the Greeks as a complete surprise. At the same time, however, they clearly overestimated its significance in expecting that the Persian empire was from that moment onwards doomed to fall. Aeschylus, who looked upon the Persians without enmity and who saw them as victims of the thoughtlessness of Xerxes, wrote that Persian authority would crumble; the Asian subjects would no longer submit to their king and they would stop paying tribute. The people would talk about freedom for all and attempt to break loose from the bondages of slavery. These expectations of the Greeks, however, did not come true. The battle at Salamis did not exercise significant influence on the fate of the subjects of the Persian king, except for the Greeks of Asia Minor (cf. Dovatur 1957:121f.).

The defeat at Salamis was the first major set-back for the Persian fleet. Supremacy at sea now remained with the Greeks, and the Persians could no longer provision their huge army by ship. A large part of Xerxes' army, therefore, had to return to Asia. In leaving a major land force in Greece, however, it is clear that Xerxes still hoped to win the war.

The undamaged Persian ships fled to Phalerum, where the land forces were encamped. Xerxes feared that the Greeks would sail to the Hellespont and destroy the bridges, thus threatening him and his army in the rear. He therefore decided to return to Asia Minor. In order to hide his intentions, however, he started to take demonstrative measures to make the Greeks believe that he was preparing for another sea battle. Mardonius, the initiator of the Greek campaign, and whom the Persians now regarded as the cause for all their misery, urged Xerxes that military activities should be continued and that they should advance upon the Peloponnesos. According to him, the Persians had lost the sea battle because of the cowardice of the Phoenicians, Egyptians, Cyprians and Cilicians, but the fate of the war on the Peloponnesos would depend on the brave Persian infantry. Xerxes, however, was no longer prepared to risk all of his army and he sent his ships to the Hellespont in order to protect the bridges, but at the request of Mardonius he decided to leave part of the forces behind, in order to conquer the rest of Greece.

Mardonius and his army had to spend the winter in Thessaly to continue the war in the succeeding year, namely in 479 B.C. Mardonius was allowed to hand pick his own troops, and he chose contingents from the Immortals and cavalry and infantry forces from the Persians, Medes, Sakas, Bactrians and Indians. According to Herodotus, Mardonius' army counted approximately 300,000 men, but modern scholars regard this figure as grossly exaggerated and suggest that only between 40,000 and 50,000 men were left in Greece.

As long as the main Persian forces remained in Attica, the Greeks knew nothing about the intentions of Xerxes to leave for Asia Minor. On being informed, however, that the Persian vessels had left for the Hellespont to protect the bridges, they realized that Xerxes was planning to withdraw. Thereupon the Greeks met in council to decide the further course of action. Themistocles advised the pursuit of the Persian ships and the destruction of the bridges, whereupon the Persian land army would be left in Greece without support and at the mercy of the Greeks.

Apparently, such a plan could have been carried out. The Peloponnesians, however, were of the opinion that this would defy fate. The Spartan admiral Eurybiades said that if the Persian route of retreat was cut off, the enemy, pushed to the extreme, would be brought to despair and that they would subsequently destroy the Greek cities. The majority of the Greek leaders decided to leave the Persians an escape route and thereupon to bring military operations into enemy territory. According to Herodotus (VIII 109), Themistocles did not insist on the execution of his plan, but worked out a way to turn the situation to his own advantage. He sent his slave in secret to the camp of the Persians. He ordered him to tell Xerxes that Themistocles, wishing to render the king a favour, had dissuaded the Greeks from destroying the bridges. Herodotus relates that Themistocles attempted to provide himself of a place of refuge in Persia, in case he was later exiled from Athens. Many historians, however, regard this account by Herodotus as unreliable and logically unlikely, because following the battle at Salamis, Xerxes would hardly heed the information provided by a messenger from Themistocles. It is possible that the story was concocted much later by enemies of Themistocles from the aristocratic camp (see Burn 1970:469).

Xerxes started the retreat of his army to central Greece, and hence to Thrace. After 45 days he crossed over to Asia. The troops subsisted on plunder, and when there was nothing to plunder, they ate grass and the bark of trees. Some of the troops died at Abydos from eating too much and too quickly after a long period of fasting. The remaining troops advanced together with Xerxes to Sardis. There the king permitted the Egyptian troops to return home. The Phoenician sailors were also allowed to go. According to Diodorus (XI 19.4), they went home almost in state of rebellion, because Xerxes had executed the Phoenician captains, whom he had accused of cowardice during the battle of Salamis.

At the same time the Persian garrisons on the Cyclades were evacuated. The 300 undamaged Persian ships had sailed to the island of Samos, while the Greek fleet of 110 vessels regrouped itself along the coast of Aegina.

In the meantime, during the spring of 480 B.C. the western Greeks of Italy and Sicily gained a victory over the allies of the Persians, the Carthaginians. The troops of Carthage had disembarked at the settlement of Panormus on the island of Sicily. The Syracusan tyrant Gelon, contrary to the mainland Greeks, was superior in cavalry forces and with the help of these horse troops he defeated the enemy near the town of Himera, east of Panormus.

CHAPTER TWENTY-FOUR

THE DEFEAT OF MARDONIUS

After the retreat of Mardonius' army to Thessaly, the Athenians returned to their own city and started to rebuild the houses which had been
destroyed by the Persians. For the time being, however, the women and
children were left at the place where they had been evacuated. In the
spring of 479 B.C., the Athenians chose Aristides and Xantippus as their
new strategoi. Both of these men had returned from exile to their
homeland at the beginning of the war. In the meantime a revolt had
broken out in the rear of the Persian army, namely in Chalcidice, in
Macedonia. The Persian general Artabazus, who had accompanied
Xerxes in his retreat, prevented a spread of the insurrection and laid
siege to the town of Potidaea. After three months of unsuccessfully attempting to conquer the town, Artabazus decided to lift the siege and to
join forces with Mardonius in Thessaly.

Mardonius tried to conclude a separate treaty with the Athenians in
order to secure for himself the domination over the remaining Greeks
with the help of the strong Athenian fleet. The Persians sent Alexander,
their subject king of Macedonia, to Athens to discuss a peace treaty.
Mardonius promised to grant Athens autonomy (apparently, local self-
government, such as was granted to the Phoenician cities); to repay all
damages caused by the war, and to rebuild in Athens the temples and
houses that had been destroyed. From his side, Alexander, linked by
rules of hospitality with the Athenians, called for the latter to conclude
a treaty with Mardonius, saying that the Greeks could never defeat the
huge army of the Persians. The Spartans were informed about this mission of Alexander, and fearing that the Athenians would accept the offer
by the Persians, sent ambassadors to Athens. On behalf of Sparta, the
ambassadors asked the Athenians not to abandon the common cause of
the Hellenes. In the words of the ambassadors, the Athenians had been
praised of old as the liberators of the Greeks, and they could therefore
not take part in the enslavement of Greece. The ambassadors also suggested that the Spartans would feed the families of the Athenians to the
end of the war, because the Athenians had had to miss two harvests. The
Athenians ordered Alexander to tell Mardonius that they would continue
the war with the enemy who had burnt down their sanctuaries. They
promised the Spartans that they would try not to be a burden on them
because of their families, but they requested the Spartans to send an

army with all speed to Attica, before another invasion by the Persians could take place.

The rulers of Thessaly, where Mardonius resided in expectation of Alexander's return, showed the Persians all possible support, and they urged them to invade Attica once again, as the Thessalian nobility looked upon the democratic party of Athens with hostile feelings. Having received the Athenian refusal of the peace which he had offered, Mardonius directed his army towards Attica. When the Persians, on the way to Athens, entered the region of Boeotia, the Thebans invited Mardonius to set up camp in their territory, and thereupon to send costly gifts to influential leaders among the Greeks, and thus to create disorder in the Greek city-states. After doing so he could deal with them one by one. Some decades later, the Persians would adopt this tactic of bribery as the main basis of their policy towards the Greeks, but in 479 B.C. the Persians under Mardonius were still convinced of their own military strength, and Mardonius issued the orders to re-occupy Athens. The Spartans, who again feared a great battle with the Persians, refrained, as before, to send troops for the defence of the city, and the Athenians once again had to evacuate their city and retreat to Salamis. The fall of Athens was announced to Xerxes, at that time residing in Sardis, by a series of signal fires on the islands of the Aegean Sea.

Having entered the empty city, Mardonius again turned to the Athenians with an offer for peace. One of the Athenian citizens was bold enough to say that it was not a matter of course to refuse at once the Persian offer, but that it was necessary to pass the Persian offer on to the Athenian assembly for public discussion. The man was stoned to death on the spot. Thereupon the Athenians went to his house and also killed his wife and children. The Athenians sent messengers to Sparta, to reproach the Spartans for not assisting them, thus forcing them once again to leave their city. The messengers added, that, if the Spartans would not send troops to fight the Persians, the Athenians would look after their own interests. By that time the construction of a defensive wall across the Isthmus of Corinth had been completed, and the Spartans, feeling themselves comparatively secure, did not hurry to answer the Athenian request. Not wishing to put their troops at risk, the Spartans expressed the idea of sending the fleet to the coast of Thrace and Ionia. This suggestion, however, had little effect, especially as the strength of the fleet depended on Athenian ships. The Spartan ephors told the Athenian messengers, who insisted on immediate assistance, that an answer would be given on the following day. The messengers, however, had to spend a total of nine days in Sparta, while the ephors delayed in making a decision. Out of fear that the Athenians would go over to the side of the Persians, the Spartans finally decided to send a force of 5,000 heavily armed soldiers to the assistance of the Athenians. They did not, however, communicate this decision to the messengers. On the tenth day the Athenian ambassadors appeared again before the ephors, and they said what they saw, namely that the Athenians were without allies, and the Spartans would regret it. Subsequently the ephors informed the messengers that a Spartan army was already on the way to Attica. The Spartans also sent a further 5,000 lightly armed *perioikoi*, dependents of the Spartans, to follow the hoplites. In total, the Peloponnesos sent 17,000 soldiers to the assistance of the Athenians. Argos, the old enemy of Sparta, where Persian gold had been distributed in large amounts, was unable to withstand the advance of the Peloponnesian warriors, and the Argives sent their fastest messenger to Athens in order to warn Mardonius of the impending danger and to inform him of the size of the Greek army which advanced upon Attica.

Mardonius had not yet given up hope of concluding a peace treaty with the Athenians and so he refrained from destroying the city for a second time. Being informed, however, about the Spartan advance, the Persians burnt down the whole city and levelled it to the ground. Because the terrain of Attica was unsuitable for cavalry manoeuvres, the Persian army moved towards friendly Thebes. There they were joined by local levies from Greek districts in Thessaly and Boeotia. The united Greek forces assembled in Boeotia, near the town of Erythrai. The Greek army counted in the aggregate approximately 50,000 soldiers, coming from the various Greek states. Included in this number were about 30,000 hoplites. The Persian army, including the contingents from their allies, came to approximately the same number.

A bloody battle started when the wounded horse of the Persian commander Masistius threw off his rider. Thereupon a large group of Athenians fell upon the Persian nobleman. Masistius was a man of extraordinary strength and he defended himself desperately, and the Athenians only managed to kill him with the greatest of difficulties. Following his death a long battle ensued over his body. When the Persians finally managed to take the body away, other Greek troops came to the assistance of the Athenians, forcing the Persians to withdraw, leaving the body of their commander behind. Thereupon the Greeks hoisted the body of Masistius on a wagon and showed it to their own troops.

In the main, however, the battle was indecisive. The Greeks then decided to move to the town of Plataea in Boeotia, where there were many springs of water, and to draw up in battle array. Not long afterwards the Persian army also advanced on Plataea.

The right wing of the Greek army was formed by 10,000 Lacedaimonians, half of whom were Spartans. Behind them stood 35,000 lightly armed helots, who were representatives of the dependent people of Lacedaimonia. Next to the Spartans the ranks were formed by 1,500 hoplites from Tegea. Further along the line stood 5,000 Athenians commanded by Aristides, together with soldiers from other districts. All the Greeks, apart from the helots, were hoplites, and they totalled, without the helots, 38,700 men. In addition, there were also 34,500 lightly armed troops in the Greek army. If Herodotus can be believed (IX 29-30), the Greek army at Plataea counted 110,000 men. The opinions, however, of contemporary scholars as regards these figures differ. M. Rostovtzeff suggested that the united Greek army totalled 100,000 heavy-armed and light-armed soldiers (Rostovtzeff 1963:133). E. Meyer brought forward the idea that Sparta could not muster more than 5,000 soldiers, of whom less than half were originally Spartan citizens. The total number of Greek troops at Plataea did not exceed, according to Meyer, 30,000 men (Meyer 1939, Vol. III, p. 407). H. Bengtson adopts this figure as convincing. According to him, the Persians were superior in number to the Greeks; their forces were between 40,000 and 50,000 men in total (Bengtson 1965:62). Herodotus related that Mardonius' army counted 300,000 men. According to Diodorus and Ctesias, the Persian army included 200,000 or 120,000 men (Ctesias makes the mistake of suggesting that the battle of Plataea preceded the sea battle at Salamis). According to A. R. Burn, the solution to the problem of the size of Mardonius' army and of that of his Greek allies is presented by the size of the almost square field of about 900 acres, on which the army was positioned. This size was twelve to fourteen times as big as the Roman military camp that housed a complete legion. These calculations permit the suggestion that the Persian army counted around 60,000 or 70,000 soldiers and that the cavalry was not larger than 10,000 men. Burn is inclined to hypothesize that the combined Greek forces were somewhat larger than the Persian troops (Burn 1970:511).

While the Greeks prepared for the decisive battle, a conspiracy arose in the Athenian camp, directed towards a reconciliation with the Persians. Many aristocrats, who during the war had lost their wealth and influence, were prepared to go over to the side of Mardonius. On being informed about the conspiracy, Aristides, the commander of the Athenian forces, refrained from punishing the plotters, who belonged to the same social group and political party as himself. He gave certain of the ring leaders the opportunity to escape, and thereupon turned towards the whole Athenian contingent with a call for unity in the face of the Persian threat.

Mardonius drew up his Persian soldiers opposite the Lacedaimonians, while the Medes were placed against the Corinthians. The Greek allies of the Persians were positioned opposite the Athenians, Plataeans and Megarians. These allies included the Boeotians, Locrians, Thessalians, Phocians, and the Macedonians.

For ten days both sides refrained from an active engagement. They waited, neither side wishing to be the first to start the battle. On both sides soothsayers, at the instigation of the generals, had predicted that the party which started the battle, would perish. The Greek army, especially the Spartans, were stoic in their defence and showed great trust in their heavy armour. It was clear to Mardonius that he could only win the battle if it was fought in open terrain where his cavalry had space to manoeuvre. The Greeks had no cavalry at all. Gradually the position of the Persians became more difficult as the Greek army was continuously augmented by troops from both near and far-away towns. The Persians, who were dependent on local resources and who lacked any transport over sea, had to look for provisions, while the Greeks received these from the Peloponnesos and other districts. The Greeks were encamped along the mountain slopes where the Persians could not deploy their cavalry. As any further procrastination by the Persians would be dangerous to them, Mardonius decided to call for a war council.

In this council the noble Persian Artabazus suggested that they should not fight at Plataea, but withdraw to Thebes, where there were sufficient provisions for the army and fodder for the horses. According to Artabazus, the Persians, while at Thebes, should send money to the most influential Greeks, and thus create tension among the enemy. From Artabazus' suggestion it is evident that the Persian commanders realized the difficulty of their position and foresaw a defeat. Mardonius, however, ignored Artabazus' advice and decided to join in battle on the following day.

That night, King Alexander of Macedonia came in secret from the Persian camp to the Greeks. He wanted to cover himself in case of a Persian defeat. He told the Greeks that the Persians would attack in the morning, because they only had provisions left for three days. Thus, the Greeks had the opportunity to prepare against the attack by the enemy. The Spartan commander Pausanias, in charge of the allied Greek army, suggested that the Athenians should take the place of the Spartans opposite the Persians, saying that the Athenians were already acquainted with the military tactics of the Persians. The Athenians, without hesitation, thereupon swapped places with the Lacedaimonians. At sunrise, however, the Persians noticed the changes in the Greek camp and informed Mardonius about this development. The latter regrouped his ranks, and again placed the Persians opposite the Lacedaimonians. Subsequently, the Lacedaimonians returned to their previous place. When Mardonius heard about this, he sent a messenger to Pausanias and accused the Spartans of cowardice and suggested that the Spartans and Persians should decide the outcome of the battle with an equal number of men, and thus determine who would be victorious. The message, however, was not replied to, because the Lacedaimonians remained unconvinced and in fear of the Persians.

Since there had been no answer from Pausanias, Mardonius ordered his cavalry bowmen to shoot at the Greeks. Thereupon the Persians succeeded in driving the Greeks from the fresh water springs, and also from a supply route for provisions from the Peloponnesos. When night fell, the Greeks under cover of darkness withdrew to the town of Plataea, where the decisive battle was about to be fought (479 B.C.). Under the false idea that the Greeks were fleeing, the Persians started in pursuit. This was a grave mistake by Mardonius, for he urged his troops to go uphill to the Greek positions, who anyhow preferred to fight in the hills rather than in the open plain, out of fear of the Persian cavalry. Soon the Persians clashed with the Spartans and a man-to-man fighting ensued. The other Greeks did not yet know that the decisive battle had commenced, and did not join in. When the Persians fell upon the front ranks of the Lacedaimonians, Pausanias offered to the gods in order to find out whether he should join the battle or not. The sacrifices took a considerable amount of time. Meanwhile the stoic Spartan hoplites were dying without any real resistance, because Pausanias had not given the order to attack due to the poor results of the offerings. In reality, Pausanias wished to draw the Persians far enough uphill deep into the Spartan ranks, so that they would not be able to withdraw under cover of their cavalry (see Burn 1970:538). Mardonius, at the head of a thousand selected men, started to push back the Lacedaimonians, and killed many of them. Soon afterwards, however, he died together with his bodyguards, and the Spartans started to gain the upper hand. As it is stated by Herodotus (IX 62-63), the Persians were not inferior to the Lacedaimonians in bravery and physical strength; they advanced courageously towards the long thrusting spears of the hoplites and broke them with their bare hands. The Persians, however, lacked heavy armour, and in the art of warfare they were inferior to the Greeks. The Persians were provided with a first class cavalry, but because of the accentuated terrain the horsemen could not take part in the battle. The Persian army was also split up into various contingents which acted without much coordination. The remaining forces withdrew under command of Artabazus, and after a desperate struggle with the Lacedaimonians, who fought bloodthirstily and took no prisoners, the Persians were defeated. The foreign contingents within the Persian army had already fled from the battlefield before the commencement of the fight. Commenting upon this, Herodotus (IX 68) relates that all the strength of the 'barbarians' was held by the Persians. Only the Boeotian cavalry fought bravely, covering the retreat. Next to the Persian horse troops, the Saka cavalry distinguished itself by its bravery.

In his biography of Aristides, Plutarch (19) writes that 1,360 Lacedaimonians died in the battle at Plataea. Apparently, this figure only covers the fallen hoplites and excludes the light-armed troops that died; they were citizens without full rights.

The Lacedaimonians captured the body of Mardonius and showed it to all the Greek troops. A certain Greek from Asia Minor, however, subsequently stole the corpse and gave it a burial. Much later he was given costly presents by Mardonius' son. According to Herodotus (IX 82), Xerxes, when he left Greece, presented Mardonius with his rich household utensils, including golden vessels, beds and tables, and also multi-coloured carpets (in fact, they belonged to Mardonius himself, but the Greeks thought that only a king could possess such wealth). Having captured Mardonius' tent, Pausanias ordered the Persian servants to prepare the same meal as they used to make for their former master. When the meal was served on golden tables, around which multi-coloured carpets were laid, Pausanias ordered his own servants to prepare the normal meal of the Lacedaimonians. Subsequently, he invited the Greek commanders and pointed out to them the difference between Persian and Spartan food, and he talked about the folly of Mardonius, who, being used to such riches, came to Greece to rob the Hellenes of their poor crumbs.

After the withdrawal from Plataea, the Persian army entrenched itself within a previously prepared wooden fortification. The Athenians, however, well acquainted with siege tactics, managed to scale the walls and to push the Persians back, and finally to annihilate their forces. Only one contingent, headed by Artabazus, managed to escape in time and to reach Byzantium, having lost many people because of starvation, and in clashes with Thracians. From there the remnants of the Persian army crossed by ship to Asia Minor.

In the meantime the Greek army began to take revenge upon the Greek states which had allied themselves with Persia. The Greeks besieged Thebes and demanded the surrender of the leaders of the pro-Persian party. The latter stated that they had not been alone in joining the Persian side, but that they had done so with the support of the whole city. Nevertheless, they were prepared to go voluntarily to the Greek camp, to prevent the destruction of Theban land. These leaders of the oligarchic party hoped to save themselves with money. Pausanias, however, ordered that they should be sent to Corinth and there be executed as traitors of Greek freedom. Only one of the Theban leaders managed to escape. Thereupon the Thebans handed his children to the Greeks. Pausanias, however, sent them back, with the meaningful words that the children were not guilty of the misdeeds of their father. The execution of the Theban oligarchs, however, was almost the only act of vengeance upon the Persian allies. The oath by the Greek patriots to destroy all the Greek towns that voluntarily joined the Persians and to give a tenth of their wealth to the gods, was not fulfilled. It would have been very difficult to go through the mountainous districts of central and northern Greece with a sword and torch in hand. In addition, soon after the repulsion of the Persian troops, the rivalry between Sparta and Athens came to the forefront. They were the two states which had carried the brunt of the war.

CHAPTER TWENTY-FIVE

THE BATTLE OF MYCALE AND THE SIGNIFICANCE
OF THE PERSIAN-GREEK WARS

After the battle at Plataea, the Greek fleet under the command of the Spartan king Leotychides anchored at Delos. Without the knowledge of Theomestor, who had been appointed by the Persians as tyrant of Samos, the Samian citizens sent messengers to Delos to call for the Greeks to attack the Persian garrison on Samos. They promised that the Greeks of Asia Minor would revolt against Xerxes. The Greek fleet thereupon sailed from Delos to Samos. The Persians, however, did not join in battle, because the Greeks possessed a superior number of ships. The Phoenician ships had long been sent home, and the greater part of the Persian fleet consisted of vessels of the Asian Greeks, which each had thirty Persians aboard to prevent mutiny.

The Persians sailed to Mycale, a cape and mountain in Ionia, between Ephesus and Miletus, where about 60,000 soldiers had assembled under the command of Tigranes. The ships were hauled ashore for repair, and around the ships a rampart was thrown up.

On Samos the Greek commanders started the draw up plans for further military action. The Peloponnesians, who had a strong land force, but lacked a significant war navy, were of the opinion that it would be impossible to gain a foothold in Asia Minor. They therefore suggested that they should liberate the Greeks living in that area and transport them to the western mainland. The Athenians, however, answered that the Ionians were their colonists and that they would look after the Ionian settlements, and therefore on no condition would they leave the land to its fate. After long discussions the decision was finally taken to go to Mycale.

Having arrived at Mycale, the Greeks faced the Persian forces which had drawn up in battle array. Thereupon the Greeks turned to the Greeks from Asia Minor who formed part of the Persian army, and called for them to join the side of the Greeks. This call had the following objective: if the Ionians would not want to deceive the Persians, the latter would nevertheless start to mistrust them. In fact, the Persians disarmed the troops from Samos, while the Milesians were sent away from the battlefield, with orders to protect the passes to the top of the mountain of Mycale.

Subsequently the Greeks disembarked and advanced upon the Persians. The battle was fought in August, 479 B.C. According to a Greek tradition, the battle took place on the very same day that the battle at

Plataea was fought. Modern historians, however, regard this point as untrustworthy.

The Persians stoically awaited the Greek attack. They protected themselves from the hostile spears by a barrier formed with their shields. Very soon, however, their commander Tigranes was killed, followed shortly afterwards by the fleet commander Mardontes. The Persian troops, which had become split up in different groups, fought bitterly, but they were completely defeated. During the battle the Greeks from Asia Minor defected from the Persian side and joined the mainland Greeks. When the remnants of the Persian army commenced to withdraw and flee to the heights of Mycale, the soldiers from Miletus fell on them and killed many. The victory at Mycale signalled a revolt of the Ionian cities in Asia Minor against Persian domination. The islands of Chios, Lesbos and Samos joined the Greek cause, and many Persian garrisons perished. The Greeks, however, showed themselves unable to bring all of Ionia under their control; they had to limit themselves to the liberation of the islands in the Aegean Sea. It meant, however, that the Greeks could now freely traverse and patrol these waters.

Survivors of the Persian army managed to reach Sardis, where a brother of Xerxes, Masistes, accused their surviving general Artayntes of cowardice. The Greek troops, meanwhile, set sail for the Hellespont in order to secure the supply of grain from the Black Sea littoral. Thereupon the Peloponnesians, who felt that the war had ended, returned home. The Athenians, however, laid siege to the town of Sestos, a heavily fortified city in the Chersonesus. The siege continued for a long time, and the Persians, being completely cut off from their own troops and allies, were forced to eat leather. With the assistance of the Greeks in the Chersonesus, the Athenians finally managed to reduce the town in the spring of 478 B.C. They executed the Persian satrap Artayctes and then they returned home. It should be remarked that with the fall of Sestos, Herodotus concludes his *Historiae*.

The Greeks and Persians remained in a state of war with each other until 449 B.C., when both parties concluded a peace treaty. The brilliant Greek victories at Salamis, Plataea and Mycale forced the Persians to accept that they were not capable of conquering Greece.[1] After Mycale, military confrontations occurred on islands in the Aegean Sea and on the territory of Asia Minor. It is therefore, at this point, appropriate to discuss the significance of the Persian-Greek wars.

---

[1] Thucydides (I 23.1) wrote that the outcome of the war was based on the sea battles at Artemisium and Salamis, and the land battle at Plataea. He did not include the battle at Mycale within this group. As regards the Persian-Greek wars, he only discussed two years, namely 480 and 479 B.C.

The famous historian Arnold Toynbee has suggested that it would have been better for the Greeks if they had accepted Persian domination without offering any resistance. This, according to Toynbee, would have prevented the Greek states from the interminable, internecine wars which characterize Greece in the period which lasted 450 years between Darius I and Emperor Augustus. On the other hand, it has been stated in many works on ancient history that the Greeks during the wars with the Persians fought for the survival of their culture and for the protection of their religion. It is impossible to agree with Toynbee and with those who were of the opinion that the Persians posed a threat to Greek culture. S. Ja. Lur'e, H. Bengtson and many other outstanding specialists in the study of Greek history have correctly stated that the Persian-Greek wars formed one of the most important pages in the development of human society, but the Persians did not strive to annihilate the Greeks, or to destroy their culture and temples. They only wanted to conquer Greece. In this intention the large Greek sanctuaries, especially that of Delphi, were of great and loyal support to the Persians. E. Meyer remarked that the intellectual culture, science and philosophy of the Greeks could have showed further development under Persian domination. In this context Meyer points at classical scholars such as Anaximander, Hecataeus and Heraclitus, who devoted themselves freely to their studies, although they were subjects of the Great King. As regards international trade, of such great importance to the Greeks, the Asian Greeks being under protection of the Persians managed to become great competitors of the Phoenicians. The real danger to the Greeks lay elsewhere. The Persians knew very well that the large Greek sanctuaries were influential counsellors of the people and of the states, and even strove to become the political leaders of the whole country. It is therefore not surprising that the Persians supported the Greek priests by dedicating costly gifts to the temples. In their turn the priests advised the Greeks to refrain from opposing the Persian military advance. The Persians, some isolated cases excepted, did not destroy Greek temples. To the contrary, they were prepared to worship the Greek gods together with the Greeks themselves. If the Persians had succeeded in conquering Greece, this would have led to a dominant position in the country of the priesthood, such as occurred with direct support of the Achaemenid administration in Egypt and Judah. In such a case the theological system of thinking would have enchained the intellectual freedom and development of the Greek polis and its political system, which was incompatible with the Oriental despotism of the Persian king. If the priests had ruled Greece, the country would have acquired a religious bias (see Bengtson 1965:68; Meyer 1939, Vol. III, pp. 444-446). It is, therefore, possible to say truthfully that the Greek victories created the possibility of an unimpeded development of a secular culture, which, free from the chains of a theological system, could reach an unprecedented height.

From our schooldays onwards, we are used to read that at the time of Xerxes' campaign, the small people of Hellas united in order to withstand the numberless and well-equipped Persian army, thereby showing the excellence of democracy above monarchy. In reality, however, at the decisive battles the forces on both sides were almost equally distributed; the Greeks had a better armament than the Persians; they also were superior to the Persians in fighting methods and military tactics. In addition, the Greeks fought in their own country, while the Persians had to deal with the greatest difficulties to provision their army. Contrary to general opinion, the Greeks were not united at all in the war against the Persians, and many districts of the country joined the invaders. This, however, does not diminish the significance of the great heroism of those Greeks (especially the Athenians and Spartans), who did not wince at the sight of the power and resources of the huge Empire; who, at the cost of many thousands of lives, gained a victory in a decisive struggle and thus kept their freedom and political organization, to which modern civilization owes so much.

The great victories of the Greeks were chanted by many Hellenic poets. Apart from Aeschylus' tragedy 'The Persians', the Persian-Greek wars were also celebrated by the poet Simonides in his work 'The Sea Fight with Xerxes'. Depictions of the heroic past also became popular in figurative art. Greek artists produced paintings which depicted episodes from the war, and showed them in public places or dedicated them to temples. The Persian attack was forever imprinted onto the consciousness of the Greek people and in Greece the question could often be heard: "How old were you when the Mede (namely, Xerxes) came?" (see Dovatur 1957:18). Pausanias (III 11.3) wrote that in the central square of Sparta a building was erected, the roof of which was supported by pillars with a depiction of the vanquished Persians, including Mardonius, and the queen of Halicarnassus, Artemisia. According to his testimony (IX 2.5), the graves of those who had fallen in the war with 'the Medes' could still be seen in the second century A.D. along the road leading to Plataea. The fallen Lacedaimonians and Athenians were buried in separate graves; the others were interred in mass burials.

An essential question arises: What was the influence of the Persian-Greek wars on the Persians? According to a classical writer from the first century A.D., Dio Chrysostomos, the Persians wrote in relation to these wars that "Xerxes, having undertaken an expedition against the Greeks, defeated the Lacedaimonians at Thermopylae and destroyed the city of

Athens. All who could not escape were enslaved. After having imposed tribute on the Greeks, Xerxes returned to Asia'' (see Lur'e 1947:88). There is no doubt that the Persians (in any case, in their official tradition), did not regard themselves as being defeated, because the previously proclaimed objectives had been accomplished: Athens was taken twice; the Eretrians were taken away in captivity. The real objective of the war was of course different: under the pretext of a punitive expedition against Athens, the Persians wanted to occupy all of Greece. On Persian seals with depictions of the war with the Greeks, who are armed with shields and spears, the Hellenes are usually depicted as having collapsed to the ground, or fallen onto their knees (see Lur'e 1947:88). As noted previously, Aeschylus and the other Greeks exaggerated the significance of their victories when they expressed the hope that Xerxes' empire would fall apart. To the Achaemenid empire, with its huge extent and enormous resources, the defeat in Greece had the character of a minor set-back along the periphery of its realm.

CHAPTER TWENTY-SIX

WARS IN THE AEGEAN SEA AND IN ASIA MINOR, 478-469 B.C.

After the withdrawal of the Persians from Greece, the war entered a new phase. The majority of the Greeks were captured by a burst of patriotic unity in the war against the common enemy. The acute Themistocles, however, had a different view on the situation. He was led by cool political foresight. Thucydides (I 138.3) wrote that Themistocles was "the best judge of a situation, and best of all foresaw the events of the distant future." Having a sixth sense for politics, the Athenian leader always took the right decision at the right time. He was of the opinion that the Athenians had no interest in a complete defeat of Persia, because, as he saw it, the greatest political and military danger to their state was Sparta, and not distant Persia. Therefore, immediately after the victory at Salamis, which for the greater part was achieved under his leadership, Themistocles was prepared to adopt a farsighted policy of rapprochement and peace with Persia. He attempted to establish friendly relations with the Persian king in order to prepare Athens for a war with Sparta. Amidst the Greek states, which together had opposed the common enemy, there emerged a latent disagreement. In the autumn of 479 B.C. the Athenians, on the initiative of Themistocles and supported by Aristides, the leader of the aristocratic party, started to strengthen their city and to build ramparts in order to make Athens independent of Sparta. The neighbours of Athens, including their old enemies the Corinthians, fearing an increase of the military might of Athens, started to incite Sparta against Athens. The Spartans were also of the opinion that the fortifications of Athens would threaten their dominant position in Greece, so they demanded a halt to the building of the walls around Athens. To justify their ultimatum, the Spartan leaders brought forward the argument that the Persians could again occupy Athens and then use the city fortifications in the war against the Greeks. The Spartan attempt, however, to make use of the difficult situation of Athens after the war and to dictate its will upon the city was bound to fail. Themistocles told his fellow citizens that he personally would go to Sparta for consultations. The people of Athens, however, should continue night and day with the erection of the city walls. Having arrived at Sparta, Themistocles started to gain time by delaying a meeting with the Spartan leaders. When he finally had to answer the ephors, he told them that the Athenians were not engaged in building city fortifications at all. He also said that this could be easily checked by sending their observers to the city. When the latter arrived at Athens, they were detained and held as hostages, so that Themistocles could safely return home. Thus, the Spartans were confronted with a *fait accompli*.

After the victories of 480 and 479, the Athenians increased their number of navy and merchant vessels and gained a superiority at sea which nobody could now contest. The founder of Athenian sea power was Themistocles, who was the most influential political leader in Athens. The democratic party gained new successes in home politics. Power in the state lay in the hands of the popular assembly, which was made up of all the Athenian citizens. Everywhere in the Greek world the Athenians started to lend their support to democratic parties. This policy clashed with Sparta, which was an oligarchic republic led by two kings, the power of whom was limited by a council of elders.

In addition, there was disagreement between Athens and Sparta about the tactics for the further war with Persia. Sparta did not wish to be involved in a protracted war in Asia Minor, because it was an agricultural land with limited resources and without a fleet with which a maritime war could be fought. Sparta was also not interested in trade markets. To the Athenians, however, war in Asia Minor was inevitable in order to secure their trade, and they also felt it necessary to repel the Persian garrisons from the Thracian littoral, and especially from the coasts of the Hellespont, so that the import of grain from the Black Sea could be taken up again. The Athenians also strove to extend their influence over the cities of Asia Minor, which were still under the domination of Persia. The Athenians were therefore the initiators of an aggressive policy towards Persia. Sparta, however, did not want to relinquish its leading role in the war against Persia, and so, in the spring of 478 B.C., it appointed its king Pausanias, the victor at Plataea, as commander of a combined Greek fleet. Pausanias headed twenty ships from the Peloponnesos; thirty vessels from Athens and a number of ships from the islands of Lesbos, Chios and Samos. With this fleet he set sail to Cyprus and captured the greater part of the island. In the summer of the same year the fleet went to Byzantium and also captured it.

Soon afterwards, however, Pausanias entered into secret contacts with Persia and started to correspond with Xerxes. He promised the king his acquiescence in the imposition of Persian hegemony over Greece. Pausanias, however, had far reaching plans to establish his own power over all of Greece. In Sparta itself he intended to abolish the oligarchy and to free the helots from bondage. He asked assistance from the Persians, and wanted to marry a daughter of the king in order to strengthen his relationship with Xerxes. Pausanias secretly released some relatives of the king, who were captured during the siege of Byzantium. He later told the Greeks that they had fled.

Having received Pausanias' letter, Xerxes appointed Artabazus, a son of Pharnaces, who had previously fought in Greece in the army of Mardonius, as satrap of Phrygia with his residence at Dascyleium. He was ordered to give gold and silver to the Spartan commander and to conduct secret negotiations with him, with all necessary caution. Via Artabazus Xerxes sent a letter to Pausanias, which was signed with the royal seal. This letter is quoted in the work of Thucydides (I 129.2). In style it is strongly reminiscent of the Achaemenid inscriptions and it appears to be an original source. Apparently it is a copy of a Greek translation of the Persian original (compare Olmstead 1933:156ff.). In this letter Xerxes informs Pausanias that after the release of the Persian prisoners, Pausanias "was in our house for ever assured of our favour. Do not stop day or night to do what was promised to me."

Thus, while one year before, after the battle at Plataea, Pausanias had laughed about the luxury of the Persians and had praised the Spartan simplicity and plainness, he now, at the time of the withdrawal from Byzantium, went dressed in Persian costume; he was accompanied by Persian and Egyptian spear bearers, and his servants prepared for him Persian dishes. The arrogant behaviour of Pausanias and his open adoption of the Persian style of life aroused resentment in the Greek army and in the Greek towns which had been liberated from the foreign yoke. The Spartan leaders, therefore, recalled their general. He, however, did not return to his native city, but remained as a private person living in the Hellespontine region to continue his negotiations with the Persians. The ephors again sent a messenger to Pausanias, demanding his immediate return. He decided to present himself to the court of ephors, as there was no direct evidence against him. In Sparta, Pausanias continued his negotiations with the Persians. One of his loyal men, who had been ordered to convey a letter to Artabazus, feared for his fate, as one of Pausanias' previous messengers had not returned from the Persians. On reading the letter, the messenger realized that it contained the request to kill him after he had delivered the letter. Having convinced himself of his suspicions, the messenger handed the letter over to the ephors. Finally, some eight years after his victory at Plataea, and as a result of the above related evidence, Pausanias was forced to flee the city to one of the nearby temples, where he died of starvation.

Instead of Pausanias, another Spartan general was appointed, but the Greek allies refused to recognize him. Thereupon Sparta recalled its forces from the united Greek army, as a result of which the Greek states which wanted to continue the war against Persia started to orientate themselves towards Athens.

Meanwhile, in 478 B.C., representatives from Athens, Samos, Chios, Lesbos and other Aegean islands met on the island of Delos and agreed upon an alliance for the war against Persia. They also set up a common treasury to finance the war. Those of the Ionians and inhabitants of the islands who used to belong to the Persian empire and who had participated in Xerxes' campaign against mainland Greece, were to contribute the same sum to the treasury as they used to pay to the Persian authorities as tribute. Above all the Delian League attempted to secure its domination on both sides of the Aegean Sea and to liberate Thrace and the Hellespont from the Persian garrisons. In those districts, however, the Greeks met with stubborn Persian resistance. In 476-475 B.C., the Greeks, under the command of the Athenian general Cimon, laid siege to the Persian fortress of Eion, which was located at the mouth of the River Strymon. When provisions dwindled to nothing and further resistance seemed hopeless, the commander of the fortress, Boges, to whom Cimon had promised a safe conduct to Asia Minor, refused the offer. He killed his children, wives, concubines and servants; he threw all his gold and silver and other precious objects into the river, and thereupon threw himself on a funeral pile.

In these years important political changes took place in Athens. The enemies of Themistocles had united their forces in an attempt to remove him from the political scene. In the backrooms of the aristocratic party thousands of ostraca were prepared bearing the name of Themistocles. Subsequently they put the question to the Athenian assembly whether Themistocles should be exiled. The opponents of Themistocles used all means, above all slander, in order to convince the Athenian citizens that his influence and wealth had become a danger to their state. After a counting of the sherds (some of which have been preserved to the present day), Themistocles, the leading politician of Athens, was subjected to an ostracism and was forced to go into exile. He fled Athens not long after Pausanias had been forced to leave Sparta. Themistocles went to Argos. When the Spartans heard about Pausanias' secret relations with the Persians, they also accused Themistocles of high treason. At the request of the Lacedaimonians, the Athenians ordered Themistocles to return to the city and they sent officials to arrest him and lead him back to stand trial. Themistocles, however, knew better than to give himself up to his political enemies, independent from the question whether he was guilty or not. He therefore fled to Corcyra and hence to Epirus. Finally, he reached the territory of the Persians. The Athenian court sentenced him in his absence to death and confiscated all his property.

The leading figure in Athens now became Cimon, the leader of the aristocratic party. He was the son of Miltiades, the victor of Marathon. During the time of Cimon good relationships were established between Athens and Sparta, as the Athenian aristocrats had always sympathized with the Lacedaimonians.

While Athens was engaged in internal matters, the Persians re-established their control over Cyprus. Thereupon the Persian fleet sailed westward. The fleet of two hundred vessels was commanded by Tithraustes, while the land forces were headed by Pherendates. Overall command lay with Ariomandes, a son of Gobryas. The fleet anchored at the mouth of the River Eurymedon, in the south of Asia Minor. There they awaited the arrival of a further eighty Phoenician ships from Cyprus. Cimon, who commanded the fleet of the Delian League, with two hundred triremes, joined in battle with the Persians, in 466 B.C., before the Persian fleet had been strengthened by the Phoenician vessels. The Greeks gained a decisive victory. Thereupon the Greeks fell upon the Persian infantry which showed stubborn resistance. After a bloody battle, the Greeks were victorious once again, but at a heavy price. Finally the Greeks attacked the Phoenician ships. The Phoenician captains had not heard about the Persian defeat, and their forces were completely destroyed.

After the battle at the Eurymedon many Greek cities along the southern coast of Asia Minor joined the Delian League. Cimon even managed to bring the Carian and Lycian towns into the League. The Aegean Sea had now become a Greek sea, where the Persians had lost their strongholds. Their only important sea bases now lay in Palestine, Syria, Phoenicia and Egypt. Gradually the Greeks also succeeded in expelling the Persian garrisons from Thrace and the Hellespont, except for the town and fortress of Doriscus along the Thracian littoral. This settlement had been founded by Darius I in 512 B.C. The governor of Doriscus, Mascames, repelled all Greek attempts to reduce his fortress. When Herodotus wrote his *Historiae* during the second half of the fifth century B.C., Doriscus was still subject to the Persians.

CHAPTER TWENTY-SEVEN

PALACE REVOLUTION IN PERSIA

Persia continued its active foreign policy, in spite of the defeats in Greece and in the Aegean basin. In particular, the Saka people of the Dahae were subjugated. This people lived east of the Caspian Sea. They are first mentioned in a list of subject peoples which was drawn up during the reign of Xerxes. The latter also extended his conquests in the far east, occupying the land of Akaufaka (from Iranian *kaufa*, 'mountain'. The word corresponds to Greek *Oreitai*, 'mountaineers'), located in the modern borderlands of Afghanistan and Pakistan (see Junge 1944:376; Schaeder 1942:131).

During Xerxes' reign the main danger for the survival of the Persian empire became apparent, namely satrapal revolts. Thus, around 478 B.C., Xerxes' full brother Masistes fled from Susa to his satrapy of Bactria in order to start a revolt. Loyal soldiers, however, stopped Masistes on his way to Bactria and killed him together with those of his sons who accompanied him. Herodotus (IX 108-113) relates the bloody history of his death. Apparently, Xerxes fell in love with the wife of Masistes, without arousing similar feelings in her. Thereupon he arranged a marriage between his son Darius and a daughter of Masistes, hoping that this would give him the possibility of coming closer to Masistes' wife. Subsequently, however, he fell in love with the daughter of Masistes, Darius' wife. She agreed to sleep with him. This became known to Xerxes' wife Amestris. During a festive dinner which was organized once a year, namely on the king's birthday, it was permitted to ask the king a favour, so Amestris asked the king for Masistes' wife, whom she regarded as the cause of all her troubles. Once in the power of Amestris, Masistes' wife was treated in a most cruel manner. Afterwards Xerxes summoned Masistes and told him that he would give him his daughter in marriage, to replace his mutilated wife. Masistes, however, preferred to flee to Bactria (see Sancisi-Weerdenburg 1980:51-83).

During the reign of Xerxes intensive building programmes were carried out at Persepolis; Susa; Van (Armenia); near the mountain of Elvend, near Ecbatana; and at other places. To strengthen the central authority of the state, the king also ordered religious reforms, which have become known to us via his so-called Daeva inscription.

The figure of Xerxes is described in Aeschylus' 'The Persians'. The action of the play takes place in Susa. It also contains a list of Xerxes' troops and the names of his generals. The play describes the battle of Salamis, after which the playwright makes Xerxes responsible for the misery caused to both Persians and Greeks. According to the play, Xerxes' mother, Atossa, had a dream which predicted a defeat for the Persians. She tells the Persian elders about her dream. At that moment a messenger arrives with the information about the Persian defeat at Salamis. Thereupon the ghost of Darius appears, predicting further misery for the Persians. The elders relate the dangers which could ruin the Empire. In the play the free Hellenes are opposed to the Persians, who are all, except for the king, portrayed as slaves. At the end of the play Xerxes appears on the scene, lamenting his defeat.

In the works of other Greek authors, Xerxes is depicted as being surrounded by stupid eunuchs. Plato (*Leg.* 695 D) wrote that Xerxes was excessively spoilt in his youth, and that starting with him, the Persian kings were great in name only, but not in reality. Contemporary historians often regard Xerxes, in accordance with Greek writers, as a man of weak character and a toy in the hands of his eunuchs (see, e.g., Mayrhofer 1970:161). The official Persian sources, however, depict Xerxes as a wise statesman and a tried warrior. Apparently, both the Greek and Persian sources are tendentious and subjective, but they nevertheless supplement each other.

To characterize the person of Xerxes, the following account by Herodotus (VII 134-136) carries some significance. After the murder by the Lacedaimonians of the Persian messengers who had been sent by Darius I to request 'earth and water', the Spartan priests stopped seeing favourable omens. Thereupon the Spartans sent two volunteers to Xerxes in Susa, in order to expiate the crime of the Spartans by their deaths. When they arrived in Susa and told the king about the objective of their mission, Xerxes told them that he did not want to imitate people who do not respect the customs of international relations. He thereupon sent both Spartans back home, unharmed, relieving the Lacedaimonians from the guilt of the messengers' death. Elsewhere in Herodotus' *Historiae* (VII 31), he is depicted as an admirer of beauty, when he became fascinated by the sight of a beautiful plane tree which he found in Lydia.

According to Ctesias, Xerxes was at the end of his life under the influence of the commander of the palace guard, Artabanus. This man originated from Hyrcania. Another important figure at Xerxes' court at that time was a eunuch, called Aspamitres (he was referred to as Mithridates by Diodorus). The position of Xerxes at that time was apparently not very stable. In any case, it is known from documents from Persepolis, that in 467 B.C., i.e. two years prior to Xerxes' death, there was a famine in Persia. The royal storehouses were empty, and the prices for grain had risen to a level seven times as high as before. To pacify the discontent in Persia, Xerxes, in the course of one year, discharged about one hundred state officials, starting with those who were placed at the highest positions (see Hinz 1976-1979, Vol. II, p. 24).

In August, 465 B.C., Artabanus and Aspamitres, apparently on the instigation of Artaxerxes, the younger son of Xerxes, killed the king in his bedchamber. At that time Xerxes probably was in Persepolis, being 55 years old. He was buried at Naqsh-i Rustam in a previously constructed tomb. Information about the date of this plot was given by Babylonian scribes in an astronomical text (LBAT, 1419). The Babylonians, undoubtedly, regarded the murder as a punishment by their god Marduk, whose temple had been destroyed by Xerxes (see Wiseman 1974). In a later Egyptian text it is stated that Xerxes was killed together with his eldest son in his palace and that his death was a punishment by the gods for the confiscation of land of the temple of Buto in Egypt (Kienitz 1953:69; Struve 1928:204ff.). According to Aelianus (*Var.* XIII 3), Xerxes was killed in his sleep by his own son (it is not clear whether he meant Darius or Artaxerxes). If credence can be given to Diodorus (XI 69.4), after the murder had been committed the conspirators told Artaxerxes that the murder had been carried out by his elder brother Darius. They then advised him to kill his brother. Darius was led to his brother and stabbed to death, in spite of the assurance by the doomed man that he was not guilty of anything. Together with Darius his children were also killed. The third son of Xerxes, Hystaspes (Vishtaspa), resided at that time in Bactria as the satrap of the province, and for the time being remained outside of the struggles.

When Artaxerxes became king, the real power came into the hands of Artabanus. The chronographers even reckoned him as a king who ruled for seven months. If that is correct, Artaxerxes was only formally the king. Artabanus also planned to kill Artaxerxes and to occupy the throne himself. With this objective in mind he tried to draw the noble Persian Megabyzus, the son of Zopyrus, into a conspiracy. Megabyzus was married to a daughter of Xerxes, but at that time was at odds with her. Megabyzus, however, warned Artaxerxes about the danger threatening him. Thus Artaxerxes was able to defend himself and punish Artabanus, as well as Aspamitres, together with their sons, relatives and adherents. Artaxerxes I (in Old Persian, *Artaxšaça*, 'having a kingdom of justice') was nicknamed 'Long arm' (*Makrokheir*) by the Greeks, because his right arm was longer than the left.

During the year 464 B.C. Artaxerxes was occupied with the reorganization of the administrative system. He appointed his loyalists as satraps. His brother Vishtaspa, however, who was the satrap of Bactria, planned to win the throne with the help of the Bactrian nobility and with this intent in mind he rose in revolt. He was, however, defeated in two battles and killed. Fearing a palace revolution, Artaxerxes ordered the deaths of all his remaining brothers. From this point onwards the court intrigues gained increasing importance for the further development of the Persian empire.

Themistocles fled to Persia soon after Artaxerxes' accession to the throne. There are several versions about his arrival in Persia. The most credible seems to be the one which is presented by Thucydides (I 135-138). When the Athenians sent their men to Argos to arrest Themistocles, he, evidently being informed about this threat, fled to Ionia. Here he came into contact with a Persian. Travelling deep into the mainland, together with the Persian, he sent from there a letter to Arta- xerxes. Themistocles wrote that he had caused the house of the king more misery than anyone else among the Greeks, as long as it had been necessary to protect his Greek motherland against the Persian army. He also, however, had done Xerxes much good, in assisting Xerxes in his escape from Greece. And now, Themistocles continued, "I arrive in the land of the king, being accused by my own men of sympathy for the Per- sians." The letter also contained a promise to render Artaxerxes great services. Finally Themistocles wrote that he wanted to spend a year in the domains of the king, in order to master the Persian language, and subsequently to appear in the presence of the king. According to Thucydides, Artaxerxes agreed to these proposals.

Plutarch states that Themistocles fled to Asia Minor and hence in a closed wagon he was conducted to the Persian court in the guise of a Greek girl who was being brought to the harem of a noble Persian. There, with the help of a Greek concubine of the above mentioned Ar- tabanus (or, according to Ctesias, Artapanos), the commander of the royal guard (the *hazārapatish*, or in Greek, *chiliarch*), who had access to the king, he requested an audience with the king. In doing so, Themistocles hid his real name and said that he planned to inform the king of impor- tant matters. The courtier, well aware of the Greek dislike of executing the proskynesis (a humiliating bowing to the ground), answered that if he did not want to bow before the king, he would not be able to see him and would have to present his information via a third party. Themistocles, however, expressed his wish to perform the proskynesis. He thereupon received permission to see the king. During the audience, he mentioned his name. He said that the Greeks regarded him as their enemy because of the favours he had rendered to the Persians. Themistocles continued by saying that the Greeks wanted to arrest him, and he therefore asked the king to save his life and to grant him asylum. Artaxerxes was very pleased with the fact that the famous Greek politician asked him for asylum and ordered him to return on the following morning. When Themistocles appeared for the second time before the king, the courtiers, who knew his name and deeds all too well, openly showed their hostile feelings and threatened him with severe punishment. Artaxerxes, however, with much greater foresight than his officials, showed magnanimity to the Greek and ordered that Themistocles should receive the two hundred talents which had been promised to the man who would bring Themistocles to court, because the Greek had come of his own accord. When Artaxerxes commenced to ask about the situation in Greece, Themistocles replied by saying that the human speech was like a patterned carpet, for when the carpet is rolled up, the patterns are deformed. In this manner Themistocles made it clear that he did not want to converse with the help of an interpreter, thus taking the chance of being misunderstood. Thereupon, according to Plutarch, for a year Themistocles studied the Persian language so that he could talk to the Persians without an interpreter. Cornelius Nepos wrote that Themistocles studied the Persian language and literature so diligently and thoroughly, that when he appeared again before the king he knew more than those who were born in Persia. Thucydides, however, who did not like exaggerations, said that Themistocles mastered the Persian language and the customs of the country ''as much as possible.'' Thucydides added that Themistocles gained considerable influence over the king, indeed more than any other Greek had achieved. According to Plutarch, Themistocles' status at the Persian court was considerably different from that of any of the other foreigners. He went hunting together with the king and he was invited by Artaxerxes' mother to her company. In addition, Themistocles received such gifts from Artaxerxes which were usually given only to noble Persians. If Diodorus (XI 57.5) can be believed, the king married Themistocles to a noble Persian woman. Because Artaxerxes carried through many changes in the Persian administration, court officials started to hate Themistocles, as they thought that all the alterations were made at his instigation.

Later, Themistocles received certain towns as a gift from the king, so that he could live from the taxes paid by these settlements. According to Thucydides (I 138.5), Themistocles received Magnesia-ad-Meandrum (in Asia Minor) 'for grain'. This town paid him an annual tribute of fifty talents. The town of Lampsacus, rich with vineyards, was given 'for wine'. Also included in the gift was the town of Myus, 'for spices'. It is clear from the work of Thucydides that Themistocles became the ruler of Magnesia, although still owing allegiance to the Great King. Athenaeus (XII 533 D) wrote that Themistocles received at Magnesia the position of archont stephanephoros. Coins have been preserved, minted by Themistocles, with a depiction of an eagle and the deity Apollo. The information that Lampsacus was given to Themistocles is supported by an inscription from the third century B.C. from the same town, according to which there was an annual festival in honour of Themistocles, and his ancestors were given honorary rights (for references, see Lur'e 1941:370, n. 168).

Themistocles died around 462 B.C. There are several versions about his death. According to Thucydides (I 138.4), he died of an illness. Thucydides, however, also presented a widespread story according to which Themistocles swallowed poison because he did not want to participate in a war against the Greeks, although he had promised to assist the king in this matter. Thucydides saw with his own eyes a memorial to Themistocles on the main square of Magnesia. In his biography of Themistocles, Plutarch (32) wrote that at Magnesia there was a beautiful tomb for Themistocles.

CHAPTER TWENTY-EIGHT

THE REVOLT OF INARUS IN EGYPT

In 460 B.C., a new revolt broke out in Egypt, as a result of which the country was drawn into the Persian-Greek conflict. Reliable information about this event is contained in the work of Thucydides (I 104, 109-110); certain details can also be found in the *Persica* of Ctesias (XIV-XV), although it remains impossible to verify his statements. In addition, Diodorus (XI 71, 74-75, 77; XII 3) also refers to the Egyptian revolt, as does, to a lesser extent, Herodotus (III 12, 15; VII 7). According to Diodorus (I 44.3; XI 71.3), the motives for the revolt were the heavy burden of taxation; severe mismanagement, and the contempt shown by the Persian officials towards the local sanctuaries.

The insurgency started in the western Delta and was led by the Libyan Inarus, son of a certain Psammetichus (possibly a descendant of the old royal dynasty from the city of Sais). The initiative for the revolt was apparently taken by Libyans. The rebels drove the Persian tax collectors out of the region and established their control in the Delta. Subsequently the revolt spread into the Nile valley. Not long afterwards, another rebel leader joined Inarus. This was Amyrtaeus from Sais. Memphis, however, the capital of the Egyptian satrapy, together with Upper Egypt, remained under the control of the Persians. From those areas documents have been preserved which are dated to the fifth and tenth years of the reign of Artaxerxes I (Bresciani 1984:362).

Achaemenes, the satrap of Egypt and a brother of Xerxes (Ctesias incorrectly refers to Achaemenides, the brother of Artaxerxes; see König 1972:13), assembled a considerable army and marched against the rebels. In 460 B.C. a decisive battle was fought at Papremis. According to Ctesias, 400,000 soldiers fought on the Persian side (this figure is undoubtedly a fantastic exaggeration). The Persians also had a fleet of eighty vessels, of which twenty were captured by the Egyptians, together with their crew. Another thirty ships were sunk. Herodotus (III 12) visited the battlefield of Papremis about twenty years after the event, and he wrote that the place was still covered with the skulls of the fallen soldiers. The Persian army was completely defeated, and Achaemenes was killed. The Egyptians sent his body to Artaxerxes in order to ridicule the Great King, who was the nephew of Achaemenes.

Having achieved a number of victories over the Persians, Inarus turned to the Greeks for assistance. The latter, at the end of the sixth century having had the experience of losing their markets along the Black Sea where they collected their grain, willingly agreed to help the Egyptians. The Athenians hoped to end the Persian hegemony in Egypt and to establish unhampered trade relations with this country and to meet most of Athens' needs for grain. In 459 B.C. the Athenians sent a fleet of two hundred vessels to assist the Egyptians. The fleet also included ships from the allied Greek states. At first the fleet sailed to Cyprus, which still form- ed part of the Persian empire. The Greeks then plundered the island. Thereupon the ships sailed to Egypt. Going up the Nile, they annihilated the Persian fleet. Subsequently the Greek vessels advanced on Memphis, where the Persian forces were centred. They succeeded in taking the city and the Persian garrison was forced to withdraw to the citadel called 'The White Fort'. The garrison was augmented by the Persian and Median population in Egypt, and also by those Egyptians who remained loyal to the Persian king and did not believe in the success of the revolt.

The siege of the citadel continued for almost a year and the Athenians suffered heavy losses. In the meantime the Peloponnesian states, headed by Sparta, advanced on Athens. At first the Persians and Peloponnesians acted independently and the Athenians fought both wars with success. Soon, however, the situation changed.

According to Thucydides (I 109-110), in 458 B.C. there arrived at Sparta the Persian ambassador Megabazus with a large sum of money. He urged the Lacedaimonians to carry out a direct attack on Attica, so that the Athenians would be forced to recall the Athenian fleet from Egypt. The Spartan leaders accepted the Persian gold and gave their con- sent to a campaign against Athens. In 457 B.C. the Spartans united with the Thebans and in a battle near Tanagra in Boeotia they heavily defeated their adversaries. Soon, however, the Athenians beat the Thebans. The Spartans felt themselves insecure, as shortly before they had suffered a heavy earthquake and there were insurrections by the local helot population. The money, therefore, which had been presented by Megabazus, was directed to other objectives and not to the war. Megabazus was forced to return home without having fully accomplished what he wanted to do and with only a fraction of the gold which he had taken with him to Sparta.

In the meantime the rebels in Egypt were still unable to take the White Fort, although they continued the siege. In 456 B.C. Artaxerxes sent to Egypt his satrap in Syria, Megabyzus, who had participated in the war against Greece in 480 B.C. He was also a grandson of the Megabyzus who had been one of the conspirators against Gaumata. This satrap had a strong army and a Phoenician fleet at his disposal, which he used to defeat the Athenians and Egyptians and to retake Memphis. Inarus, together with his remaining adherents and the Athenians fled to the island of Prosopitis in the western Delta. There they were surrounded by the Persians. The besieged were able to withstand the Persians for another year and a half. In 454 B.C. the Persians sent their ships inland along one of the branches of the Nile. They then beached the ships and drained this branch, while the water level of the Nile was at its lowest, by allowing the water to flow in another direction. The Persians then constructed a dam which united the island with the mainland. As a result of these actions the Persians were able to take the island. The majority of Egyptians and Athenians were killed, although Inarus together with some of his remaining followers and some Athenians, were taken captive by Megabyzus. He had given them his assurance that all captives would be kept alive. An extensive account of the last phase of the revolt is given by Ctesias. His data, however, are not reliable, and his figures of the number of soldiers are completely imaginary (see Bigwood 1976:20ff.). Ctesias wrote that Megabyzus led 200,000 men against Inarus, together with 300 ships. Both sides, however, suffered heavy losses in a number of great battles. Inarus himself was wounded in the waist by Megabyzus. Throwing all forces into the battle, the Persians were finally victorious, and Inarus had to flee to Byblos. According to Ctesias, this was the most heavily fortified city in Egypt, but other sources do not mention the existence in Egypt of such a city (see Bigwood 1976:23). The Persians reconquered all of Egypt, except for the inaccessible fortress of Byblos. Megabyzus sent messengers to the besieged with the offer that they should surrender on the condition that no harm would come to them. They surrendered and Megabyzus himself went to Artaxerxes and received from him the promise that the captives would be pardoned. In any case, Megabyzus did all what was possible to keep his word.

Only a few Athenians managed to escape from the island of Prosopitis. After a journey westward they reached Cyrene and hence they went back to Athens. In the meantime fifty vessels with Athenian and allied soldiers had sailed to Egypt in order to relieve the forces which had been previously sent and whose ultimate fate was still unknown to Athens. These vessels anchored in one of the eastern branches of the Nile, not suspecting the presence of the enemy so nearby. The Persians made a surprise attack by sailing, together with the Phoenician fleet, from the sea upstream to the Greek vessels. Most of the Greek ships were sunk, although some of them did escape. This was a heavy blow to Athens, which was left almost defenceless. As a result, the Athenians, against whom the Spartans had also moved with the assistance of Persian gold, were forced to leave the Egyptians to their fate.

Thus, in 454 B.C., after a revolt which had lasted for six years, Egypt once again became a Persian satrapy, and only in the western Delta did Amyrtaeus, one of the leaders of the revolt, manage to consolidate his position. In the large expanses of marshlands he was elusive and they were unable to catch him.

There was now among the Persians all justification to be content with the successes which they had achieved in Egypt, and indeed the land along the River Nile remained quiet almost to the end of the fifth century B.C. A chalcedony cylinder seal, which was found in the northern littoral of the Black Sea and which contains a cuneiform inscription, depicts Artaxerxes I with a high, golden crown on his head; a bow and quiver behind his back, and a spear in his hand. He leads three captives whose hands are fastened behind their backs. The captives are bound to each other with a rope. Because one of the men has an Egyptian crown on his head, it would seem as if the seal depicts the victory of Artaxerxes over Inarus (the seal is now housed in the Pushkin Museum of Fine Arts, Moscow, and was published by V. K. Šileiko (Šileiko 1925:17ff.; see also Hinz 1976-1979, Vol. II, p. 31; cf. Schmitt 1981:37). Impressions of comparable seals have been found at Persepolis (see Schmidt 1953-1970, Vol. II, p. 10). Another seal kept in the Hermitage Museum, Leningrad, depicts the triumph over the insurgent Egyptians. According to W. Hinz, the seal belonged to Megabyzus, who suppressed the Egyptian revolt (see Hinz 1976-1979, Vol. II, p. 31).

Cyprus was also brought back under Persian control, and the Phoenician fleet became the dominant force throughout all of the Mediterranean, and for some time the Phoenician vessels even appeared in the Aegean Sea, where they plundered the islands.

In 454 B.C. Megabyzus returned to Syria and Arsames was appointed as the new satrap of Egypt. He was, apparently, a grandson of Darius I. According to the information provided by Greek sources, the new governor held his post until at least 423 B.C. (see AD:10ff.). In the Aramaic papyri from Elephantine, Arsames is recorded as Egypt's satrap between 428 and 408 B.C. (see AP, 17, 21 etc.). Babylonian documents which date to the years between 423 and 403 B.C., also refer to prince Arsames (see Stolper 1985:64ff.). Even letters have been preserved from the same Arsames, which are addressed to the stewards of his domains in Egypt. As is evident from one of these letters, at the time of writing its author resided in Babylon (AD, XI; cf. also *ibid.*:10-12). The letters are not dated, but there is no doubt who was their author. It is the very same Arsames who in the Elephantine papyri is referred to as the governor of Egypt. Ch. Clermont-Ganneau has suggested the identification of the Arsames of the Elephantine papyri with the Arsames who is referred to by Greek sources as satrap of Egypt in 454 B.C. (see AD:10-12). In that case he kept his position for half a century, from 454 to 403 B.C. G. R. Driver was inclined to suggest that the Arsames who sent the letters from Babylon was the son of the identically named Arsames, the governor of Egypt, who at the time of Xerxes' campaign against Greece commanded one of the contingents of the Persian army (AD:92ff.). It is unlikely, however, that father and son would carry the same name. It would seem more likely that the Arsames of the Greek sources and the *Aršama* of the Aramaic and Babylonian documents were one and the same person. This hypothesis becomes more plausible when it is realized that, according to W. B. Henning, reference is made in one of the fragments of Arsames' letters to a certain *'nrw*, who may be the well-known leader of the rebellious Egyptians. It is true that in that case the conclusion should be drawn that Arsames was the governor of Egypt for more than fifty years, and lived to an age of at least 75 or 80. This cannot be excluded, as the Achaemenids were famous for their longevity. Herodotus (III 22) wrote that the oldest Persians lived to an age of 80.

According to Driver, the letters from Arsames' archive date to the period between 411 and 408 B.C., when Arsames was absent from Egypt, but residing in Susa and Babylon (cf., e.g., AP, 27, which testifies to the fact that Arsames had gone to the king). W. B. Henning, however, together with I. M. Diakonoff and J. Harmatta, dated the archive of Arsames to the period after Inarus' revolt (see Diakonoff 1959:84f., n. 62; Harmatta 1963:201). The Semitologist I. N. Vinnikov presented the same hypothesis in his lectures at Leningrad University. Harmatta correctly remarked that in Egypt between 411 and 408 there was no significant revolt against Persian rule, while the archive illustrates a situation which must be dated after a major insurrection which involved both Upper and Lower Egypt. Driver related the unrest commented upon in Arsames' letters to the destruction in 410 B.C. of the Jewish temple of Yahweh at Elephantine, which took place at the instigation of Egyptian priests (see below). This, however, was an episode which had no effect on the districts beyond Elephantine.

As remarked by certain scholars, the following reference in one of the letters (AD, 5) may also be used to support a mid-fifth century date for the archive. When Egypt revolted, thirteen Cilician *garda* (labourers in the household of the king and of high officials), who belonged to Arsames and who were housed in barracks[1], did not manage to flee to the citadel

---

[1] M. N. Bogoljubov, basing himself on the etymology of the Iranian word with which the profession of these *garda* is indicated, suggested that they were cattle drivers (personal communication).

and were captured by the insurgents. This piece of information may be related to a remark by Diodorus (XI 74), to the effect that after the battle at Papremis the Persians fled to the fortified part of Memphis, called the White Fort. It cannot be excluded that in Arsames' letter and in Diodorus' work reference is made to the same citadel. This point, however, is not totally acceptable, because in the pertinent letter the fortress mentioned may be identical with that of Elephantine or indeed any other fortified site in Egypt (Cazelles 1955:98f.).

After Darius I the Persian kings were basically uninterested in the internal affairs of Egypt. Only a few inscriptions in the stone quarries of the Wadi Hammamat have been found which date to the reign of Artaxerxes I (see Posener 1936:125-128). On the other hand, however, a relatively large number of stoneware vessels have been found which carry the name of Artaxerxes I, written in Egyptian hieroglyphs, together with the common trilingual cuneiform texts. These vessels were made in Egypt for use in the royal household.

CHAPTER TWENTY-NINE

THE PROVINCE 'ACROSS-THE-RIVER'
DURING THE SECOND HALF OF THE FIFTH CENTURY B.C.

Soon after crushing the revolt in Egypt (around 450 B.C.), one of the noble Persians, Megabyzus, satrap in the province 'Across-the-River' (*Abar-Nahara*), rose in rebellion against the king. According to Greek writers, whose sources go back to unreliable information provided by Ctesias, the reason for the revolt was the fact that Artaxerxes I had not heeded the promise made by Megabyzus that Inarus and the other captive Egyptians and Greeks would be pardoned. Five years after their arrest, Amestris, the mother of the king, succeeded in her wish of having them executed in order to avenge the death in Egypt of Achaemenes (according to Ctesias, Achaemenes was her son. This is apparently incorrect, because Achaemenes was the brother of Xerxes). Inarus was impaled while the Greeks were decapitated. According to Thucydides, however, Inarus had already been executed in 454 B.C.

Megabyzus twice defeated the forces of the king. Subsequently (possibly in 449 B.C., when an Athenian fleet headed by Cimon attacked Cyprus), he was reconciled with Artaxerxes and he concluded a favourable peace. He kept his position as satrap. Some time later, in 445 B.C., his son Zopyrus defected from the Great King. He fled to Athens where he was well received. Soon afterwards, after having taken service in the Athenian forces, he perished.

It would appear that the tomb inscription of the Sidonian king Eshmunazar dates to the time when Megabyzus was governor of the province 'Across-the-River' (see Galling 1937:46). In this text it is said: "Whoever may find this sarcophagus, do not open it and do not disturb me, for I have no gold, silver or precious stones with me. I am all alone here in this sarcophagus."

Palestine, which lies next to Syria and which formed part of the province of Megabyzus, was at the time of Artaxerxes I one of the quietest areas. The district of Ashdod successfully repelled recurring attacks by nomadic tribes (see Galling 1937:46).

In the district of Judah, forming part of Palestine, events took place which would prove to be of great importance for the future. Even before the Babylonian captivity, serious conflicts had broken out over religious matters. Some of the religious leaders of the people stated that the Jews should worship only one God, Yahweh (the monotheistic group), while others, supported by the greatest part of the common people, worshipped in addition to Yahweh other deities as well, such as Astarte. Because the conviction that Yahweh was the only god was particularly dominant among the prominent Jews who were for the greater part exiled to Babylonia, it resulted in the dominance in Judah of that group which regarded Yahweh as the highest among a number of gods (cf. M. Smith 1965:356ff.). A similar belief was also widespread among the Jews of Elephantine in Egypt (cf. below).

During the Babylonian captivity, a considerable part of the Jewish exiles began to worship, along with Yahweh, other gods as well. When under Cyrus II the Babylonian Jews, still predominantly monotheistic, were given permission to return to Jerusalem, which, according to Deuteronomy, was the only place to worship Yahweh, only a minor part of the Jewish exiles were prepared to return to their old motherland. The representatives of the priestly families, however, wanted to return in order to regain their former position and enjoy the income from the temple service. The plans of the repatriates to reinstate the monotheistic cult met with strong opposition from the local Jewish population who had never left their land, and also from the people of the neighbouring districts. The attempts, therefore, of the adherents of the monotheistic party to force their point of view upon the population remained unsuccessful. It is for this reason that between 515 and 458 B.C. in the temple of Jerusalem, other gods were worshipped together with Yahweh.

It appears as if the monotheistic party and its opponents were used to accusing each other before their Persian overlords. In addition, ,the district officers of the neighbouring lands complained about the activities of the monotheistic party, accusing their representatives of planning a revolt against the Great King. As a result the king, in 458 B.C.[1], sent the Jewish scholar Ezra, his counsellor on Jewish affairs and official in the royal chancellery, from Susa to Jerusalem. The king provided him with the necessary funds and provisions for the journey and gave him the authorization to carry out a codification of the laws, apparently along the same lines as had previously been carried out under Darius I for the laws of Egypt.

Ezra arrived in Jerusalem with his assistants and with costly presents for the priests in order to gain their support. He also presented a codicil,

---

[1] I adhere to the traditional date for the activities of Ezra and Nehemiah (cf. Stern 1984:73). Certain scholars have presented the view that Ezra was not sent to Jerusalem during the reign of Artaxerxes I, rather than in 398 B.C. during the reign of Artaxerxes II. H. Kreissig dates the activities of Nehemiah to 445 B.C., and those of Ezra to 430 B.C. (for a discussion of the problem, and pertinent literature, see Albright 1950:52, Boyce 1982:190; Kapelrud 1949:63; Kreissig 1973:16ff.).

known as the Pentateuch ('The Law of Moses', or the Torah), which was edited during the Babylonian captivity and which would form part of the Old Testament. During his journey through Mesopotamia, Ezra had also persuaded many of the Mesopotamian Jews to follow him to Jerusalem. The rich among them refused to go, but they did provide financial assistance to those who decided to go back to Judah.[2]

From that time onwards a new period started in the history of Judah. This phase resulted in the seclusion and isolation of the Jerusalem community (cf. Galling 1964:60). As remarked by E. Meyer, Judaism is a product of the Achaemenid empire. Although its ideas originated in Palestine, they could not have been realized without the assistance of the economic strength of the Babylonian diaspora, whose representatives succeeded in assuring themselves of the support of the Persian kings. With their assistance the laws of the Pentateuch were established, not only in Judah, but also amongst the Jews of the diaspora (Meyer 1912:96).

In 455 B.C. Ezra declared the Pentateuch compulsive for all members of the Jewish community, both in Judah itself, and beyond its borders. Basically this was a scroll containing myths, legends and cultic laws, but in which civil and criminal law was hardly discussed. Ezra's attempts, however, to have his laws recognized met with strenuous opposition, not only from the masses, but also from a part of the nobility. In particular, the inhabitants of Jerusalem were irritated by Ezra's unyielding demand that mixed marriages with the Samaritans, who worshipped Yahweh and other deities, should be dissolved. The people of Judah also continued to worship other gods along with Yahweh, and Ezra was unable to change this situation. The adherents of Ezra were reluctant to permit the Samaritans to take part in the temple service, in order not to share with them the profits related to the status of the citizens of the town of Jerusalem. Ezra's attempts to surround Jerusalem with a defensive wall were also doomed to fail. When he ordered the people of the town to rebuild the walls, the governors of the neighbouring districts complained to Artaxerxes I, saying that they ate "the salt from the royal table" and that is was therefore hard for them to witness how harm was being done to the king, by Jerusalem preparing for a revolt and stopping paying tribute. As a result of these complaints the work on the construction of the walls was halted (Ezra IV 13-15). The further fate of Ezra is unknown. It is possible that he was recalled to Susa. Judah now became

---

[2] According to estimates by I. P. Veinberg, around the middle of the fifth century B.C. there lived in the area of Jerusalem about 42,000 people, or about 20% of the whole population of Judah. By the end of that century the number of people who constituted the temple community of Jerusalem had swollen to 150,000, which equalled about 70% of the total population of the province (Veinberg 1974).

ruled by a Persian satrap, and communal matters were directed by the high priests.

In 445 B.C. there arrived in Jerusalem another Jewish official from the court at Susa. He bore the name of Nehemiah, and was the royal counsellor in Jewish affairs and cup bearer of the king. Usually scholars think that the office of royal cup bearer was occupied by eunuchs, but such an opinion has recently been rejected by M. Heltzer (1988:127). Nehemiah succeeded in obtaining from the king permission to go to Judah as the new governor and to enforce the Laws of the Pentateuch. The king also presented his cup bearer with letters to the governors of Syria and Palestine, ordering them to give Nehemiah unhampered conduct through their territories. In addition, Artaxerxes ordered the guardian of the royal forests in Syria, Asaph, to provide building timber for the Jerusalem temple and for the construction of the city walls.

Nehemiah, just like Ezra, was a staunch supporter of monotheism, and was therefore welcomed with a considerable degree of hostility, not only by the people of the neighbouring districts of Judah, but also by a large part of the Jewish population. Jerusalem was suffering from inroads by the surrounding people of the Ammonites, Arabs and Edomites. Thus, the task awaiting Nehemiah was difficult; Ezra had proved incapable of coping with these difficulties. With the same fanaticism as Ezra, he differed from the latter by his acuteness and feeling for politics.

In the function of Persian governor, Nehemiah was in command of the garrison. To use the garrison against his own people, however, was full of risks and for Nehemiah's objectives quite useless. In order to win the masses to his ideas, he first decided to end the bitter social-political strife within the Jewish community. To do so, he proclaimed a number of social reforms; he decreed the annulment of debts and loans against interest and he returned pawned goods to the debtors. In addition, he exempted the people from taxes for the maintenance of the satrapal court. On October 30, 445 B.C., Nehemiah declared that the laws which had been collected and codified previously by Ezra, should be enforced. Subsequently, Nehemiah returned for some reason to the royal court; he was possibly recalled after complaints by the Jewish nobility and priesthood who were discontent with his social reforms. In 432 B.C., however, he again returned to Jerusalem and recommenced his religious reforms. First of all he banned Tobiah from the temple. The latter was the district's officer of the land of the Ammonites, on the other side of the River Jordan. He had a room for himself on the terrain of the Jerusalem temple, which he had received from the High Priest himself. The eviction of Tobiah led to the first direct confrontation between Nehemiah and the priesthood led by the High Priest. Nehemiah, however, instead of increasing tension, took an unexpected step: he strengthened the position of the priestly class of the Levites by presenting them with the use of a tithe on agricultural profits and exempting them from taxes. He thus drew the Levites into his camp, who adopted the position of a privileged class. Thereupon Nehemiah achieved the enforcement of the law on religious cleanliness and the maintenance of the Sabbath. Subsequently, with the support of the Persian garrison, the Levites and the common folk who had been freed from debts, Nehemiah finally turned towards the most difficult and unpopular task: the annulment of the mixed marriages. Forcing his opponents to silence by beating and the pulling out of their hair, he expelled the grandson of the High Priest, who was married to the daughter of Sanballat, the governor of Samaria, from Jerusalem. He also evicted other people who had not agreed to be separated from their foreign wives. All of them worshipped, along with Yahweh, other deities. Although Sanballat carried a Babylonian name (Sinuballit, '(the god) Sin kept (me) alive)', he had given his sons theophoric names compounded with the name of Yahweh.

It then became possible to make a renewed start with the construction of the fortifications around Jerusalem. Sanballat, however, and the governors of other neighbouring districts, angrily opposed these activities and they accused Nehemiah of planning a revolt against the Persian king. These officials and their men went to Jerusalem and tried to force the people of the city to stop their work. The Jews, however, selected from among themselves some military groups to defend the labourers, and soon Jerusalem was transformed into a well-protected city (Neh. II 19; IV 7-21). Thus, with the support of the Persian king and acting on his behalf, Nehemiah succeeded in consolidating Judaism as the dominating ideology in Judah (cf. Meyer 1896:243). Gradually the Laws of the Pentateuch were also brought to the Jews of the diaspora. This is particularly attested by an Aramaic papyrus which contains an interesting piece of information about a decree of Darius II. This decree was proclaimed in 419 B.C. (AP, 21). Via his satrap in Egypt, Arsames, the king ordered the Jews who lived at Elephantine to celebrate the festival of the Passover from the 15th to the 21st of the month of Nisan, as had become common in Judah (see Kraeling 1953:94; Meyer 1912:91ff.). The decree was apparently issued, not only to the Jews of Elephantine, but also to all the Jews living within the borders of the Persian empire.

Having accomplished his mission, Nehemiah returned to the royal court at Susa. The fortifications of Jerusalem, however, composed a threat of Jewish secession from Persia, so the Persian government appointed the trusted Bagoas as the successor of Nehemiah. He is also referred to by Josephus Flavius (*Ant. Jud.* XI 7.1), and in the Aramaic papyri from Elephantine, where he is called Bagohi. It is difficult to say something definite about the ethnic origin of this man. His name is Iranian, but in the sixth century B.C., not to mention during later periods, certain Jews started to carry Iranian names. In addition, all three of the known governors of Judah before Bagoas, from the end of the sixth to the second half of the fifth century B.C., were Jews (Sheshbazzar; Zerubbabel; Nehemiah).

CHAPTER THIRTY

THE PEACE OF CALLIAS

When the Athenian fleet which had been sent out to assist the Egyptians, was defeated, the Athenians, if at all possible, did not want to fight a war on two fronts against the Spartans and the Persians. Although the Persians still urged the Spartans to attack Athens, the Lacedaimonians, however, preferred to occupy themselves with internal affairs. According to Thucydides (I 112.1-4), three years after the Persian victory over Inarus, the Peloponnesians and Athenians concluded a peace treaty which was to last for five years. Now the pro-Spartan, Athenian politician Cimon started to concentrate all the Athenian forces upon the war with the Persians, while at the same time trying to avoid a conflict with Sparta.

In 449 B.C., a fleet of two hundred vessels from Athens and other members of the Delian League, headed by Cimon, set sail for Cyprus. Part of the island, disrupted by internal warfare, was soon conquered by the Athenians, who had declared themselves as the liberators of the Greeks. The greater part of the population of the island, however, showed little enthusiasm for the advent of the uninvited guests. Only Salamis and certain other cities with a Greek population joined the army of Cimon (it is possible that they were even pressed to do so).

Cimon sent sixty ships to Egypt to assist Amyrtaeus, who still continued in his opposition to the Persians in the marshes of the Delta. Cimon hoped that with the help of the Athenian flotilla Amyrtaeus would be able to stir another general revolt in Egypt. With the remaining ships Cimon advanced on the city of Kition, which was the main Phoenician settlement on Cyprus.

During the siege of Kition Cimon died of an illness. In the meantime the Syrian satrap Megabyzus collected his forces in Cilicia in order to attack the Athenian ships. The Persian army included a large fleet. The Greeks, who were short of provisions, lifted the siege of Kition and sailed back to Salamis, where a battle ensued with the Persian fleet. In a great battle the Athenians gained a complete victory over the Phoenician, Cilician and Cyprian ships, and captured one hundred hostile vessels.[1] At the same time the Athenians were also victorious on land (Thucydides, I 112; Plut., *Cim.* 18).

---

[1] This victory is extensively reported by Diodorus (XI 62), who, however, incorrectly relates the information to the battle at the Eurymedon.

These were the two last battles of the Persian-Greek Wars. The Athenians, together with their allies, had grounds to regard themselves as the victors. Following decades of exhaustive warfare, however, both parties realized that they were not capable of achieving the results they wanted by military means. They knew that the time had come to initiate peace negotiations. Thus, there came an end to a long period of bloody warfare between Persia and the Greek states, in which both opponents had gained victories and suffered defeats. Apparently, the Persian nobility held the opinion that Persian policy towards Greece needed alteration. In any case, according to Diodorus (XII 4.4), Megabyzus and the satrap of Dascyleium, Artabazus, informed Athens that Artaxerxes wished to conclude a peace treaty. Following the death of Cimon, power in Athens had come in the hands of the peace party headed by Pericles. The Athenians had lost interest in the war with the Persians and expressed their hope for peace. When, in the Athenian popular assembly, the question was discussed as to what must be done next, the active adherents of the war party, together with the majority of the army, were on Cyprus and could therefore not participate in the discussions.

Pericles devoted himself to concluding peace with Persia in order to break with Sparta and to prepare for war with the Lacedaimonians. In addition, the Athenians experienced many problems with their allies. The Delian League, which in the middle of the fifth century B.C. counted approximately two hundred members, was primarily formed as a coalition of independent Greek states to continue the war with Persia. However, although at the very beginning of the League Athens had only occupied a leading position as *primus inter pares*, she had gradually started to dominate her allies. The Athenians also started to dominate the Greeks of Asia Minor and to interfere in their affairs, under the pretext that the latter had submitted to the Persians. Many Greeks were simply forced to join the alliance. Thus, a large fleet headed by Pericles sailed to the coastal regions of the Black Sea and incorporated many towns into the Delian League. In 454 B.C. the Athenians removed the treasury of the League from Delos to Attica and started to use the economic resources of the allies for their own internal needs. In this manner, the Delian League turned into an Athenian Sea Empire, and the former allies became the subjects of Athens. During the course of time the Greek cities of Asia Minor and the islands of the Aegean started to suffer more from the Greek liberators than from the Persian oppressors. From bitter experience during decades of war, the Greeks who had been submitted to Persian hegemony knew very well that the slogans about their liberation were empty demagogic tricks and that the deeds of the politicians and generals of Athens were not directed by ideals of liberating their

fellow Greeks from the Persian yoke, but exclusively by the egotistical objectives of their state (cf. Starr 1975-1977, part I, p. 74). For instance,
when the islands of Naxos, Lesbos, Chios and certain others made an attempt to leave the Delian League, the Athenians defeated them and
destroyed their houses. The town of Byzantium, which had revolted
against Athens, was razed to the ground by their opponents. The people
of the majority of the Greek cities of Asia Minor, therefore, preferred to
be under Persian domination and to pay a moderate tribute which would
guarantee them a peaceful life and unhampered trade. The Greeks of
Asia Minor thus gradually started to break their strong links with the
states of the Greek mainland, which had shown that they were always
ready to betray the interests of their fellow Greeks. Many Greek towns
in Asia Minor were loyal to the Persian king, and on arrival of Athenian
vessels put up a resistance. Following the death of Cimon the Athenians
conquered Samos and installed there a democracy. Many islanders fled
the island to the mainland of Asia Minor, where they concluded an
alliance with the governor of Sardis, Pissouthnes, son of Hystaspes.
Subsequently the combined Persian and Samian forces attacked the
island and expelled the Athenians.

All of these events and the fact that the war with Persia was without
perspective, forced the Athenians to seek peace with the Great King. In
449 B.C., therefore, the decision was made to withdraw the fleet from
Cyprus and Egypt and to send an embassy to Susa to negotiate a peace
treaty. The embassy was headed by the most experienced Athenian
diplomat, Callias. The Greek states which were allied to Athens also sent
their ambassadors. The Athenians, having previously successfully expelled the Persians from the Aegean Sea, hoped to gain important concessions from Artaxerxes I.

Within the same year, 449 B.C., a peace was concluded between Persia on the one hand and the members of the Delian League on the other.
This peace, which received the name of Callias, became, even in antiquity, the subject of lively discussions.

Callias was prepared to leave the Mediterranean to the Persians; to
evacuate Cyprus, and to give a promise to refrain from meddling in
Egyptian affairs. In return, he wished the recognition of an Athenian
sphere of influence in Asia Minor, and an annulment of Persian claims
on those Greek cities of Asia Minor which were in fact already under the
control of the Athenians. The Persians, however, could not agree to an
official limitation of their influence and an abdication of their rights on
the Greeks of Asia Minor, because this would affect the sovereignty of
the king. Persia, however, also wanted peace, because at that time Amyrtaeus was still continuing his opposition to Persian authority in Egypt.

Besides, the Athenians were ready to return Cyprus, and many Greek cities of Asia Minor had not paid any tribute for a long time and there was no hope that they would pay it in future. Both sides had to make concessions, and the following compromise was reached.

The Greek cities of Asia Minor remained nominally under the domination of the Great King, but in certain cases the right to levy tribute was granted to the Athenians. The amount of tribute would remain the same as it was under the Persians. In addition, Athens was granted the right to govern these cities. Contrary to the information provided by Plutarch (*Cim.* 13), however, the Persians never relinquished their supreme sovereignty over the Greek cities. As is evident from the work of Herodotus (VI 42) and Thucydides (VIII 5.6), these territories in Asia Minor were regarded to be originally Persian, and thus Demosthenes, referring to the Peace of Callias, says nothing about the independence of the Greeks of Asia Minor.

Under the conditions of the treaty, the Persian army was not allowed to station troops within the distance of one day's march on horseback from the coast of the Aegean Sea.[2] In addition, the ships of the Persian navy were not allowed to patrol between west of Phaselis to the south and the Kyaneai to the north, which meant that they could not sail in the waters between the exit of the Bosphorus into the Black Sea to the north, and the Mediterranean to the south. Thus, the coastal regions of the Aegean Sea and the Propontis actually fell to Athens. It is true, nothing was said about it in the treaty, but all concerned realized that Athens would not permit the Greek cities she already controlled to become independent of Athens, although according to the treaty, Greek cities could voluntarily join the Achaemenid empire, and Athens would not oppose such a move. Certain districts along the coast, which previously had not formed part of the Delian League (Smyrna; Gergis in the Troad; a number of cities in the Propontis, etc.), were left under Persian rule, as before. In this manner, the Peace of Callias divided the sphere of influence of both parties (see Lur'e 1947:83; Meyer 1939, Vol. IV, p. 617).

During the third century B.C. the text of the treaty was included in the 'Collection of Decrees', drawn up by Craterus, which has been transmitted to us in the biography of Cimon (chapter 13), written by Plutarch (see also Diodorus XII 4.4ff.). Based on the rendering by Craterus, the text of the treaty was written, not in Attic characters, but in Ionian, which only came in use in 401 B.C. This point led the ancient

---

[2] This information is provided by Plutarch (*Cim.* 13), who, however, incorrectly connects this condition with the battle at the Eurymedon. According to Diodorus (XII 4.4), the Persians could not approach the sea to a distance of a three day's ride on horseback.

historian Theopompus to regard the Peace of Callias as a concoction by
the Athenians (see FGrH, II B, I, No. 115, frag. 154), and many modern
historians share this conclusion. They also base themselves on the fact
that Thucydides does not refer to the treaty, and the earliest reference to
it is made by Isocrates in a speech which was delivered in 380 B.C., i.e.
some seventy years after the conclusion of the Peace (for the text of the
treaty, see H. Bengtson, who is inclined to believe that it is original)
(Bengtson 1962: No. 152).

As remarked by E. Meyer, S. Ja. Lur'e and A. R. Burn, doubts about
the Peace of Callias of 449 B.C. miss sufficient grounds. Let us dwell on
this point in more detail. The fact that Thucydides in the short introduction to his work remained silent about the treaty, does not prove that there
never had been such an agreement, because he omitted many events
which are known to have occurred. Much more important, as pointed out
by Burn, is a particular piece of information provided by Thucydides
(VIII 56), namely that in 412 B.C. Darius II expressed the wish, via his
satrap in Asia Minor, Tissaphernes, that Athens in the course of negotiations would recognize the Persian right to send ships to the Aegean Sea.
This fact points at a revision of a previous treaty (see Burn 1970:563). At
the same place in his work, Thucydides (VIII 56) wrote that in 411 B.C.
the Athenians, who were in a very difficult position because of their wars
with Sparta, did not object to the Persian occupation of Ionia. When,
however, the Athenian politician Alcibiades, who had fled to the Persians,
demanded that the Athenians should allow the Persian fleet to sail through
the Aegean Sea whenever the Persians wanted and with as many ships as
they desired, the Athenians were indignant. Consequently, the Peace of
Callias must have included an article which forbade the Persians to sail
the Aegean Sea. A certain reflection of the Peace of Callias can also be
detected in the point that in 405 B.C. the Persian satrap Cyrus the
Younger gave the Spartan commander Lysander the administration of
certain of the Greek cities of Asia Minor and the right to levy taxes (see
Diodorus XIII 104.4; cf. Xenophon, *Hell.* II 1.12).

Callias' journey to Susa is also referred to by Herodotus (VII 151),
although, it should be admitted, without an indication of its goal. The
reason for this apparently lies in the point that Herodotus often strove
to hide events which were unfavourable to the Athenians, and in Athens
the Peace of Callias was not regarded as a great success. The people of
the city were dissatisfied with the conditions of the treaty, and they were
of the opinion that the treaty had put them to shame. They accused
Callias of having been bribed by the Great King. Demosthenes (XIX
273) wrote that the Athenians almost condemned Callias to death
because of the conditions of the treaty to which he had consented. In 447

B.C., when Callias laid down one of his functions, legal proceedings were started against him, and he was requested to pay a fine of fifty talents, the same sum which he, according to some Athenians, had received from the Great King during his sojourn in Susa. At the same time several friends of Pericles, who was the son-in-law of Callias, were officially accused of pro-Persian sympathies (Lur'e 1947:71).

According to E. Meyer, the Peace of Callias was an oral agreement. A formal, solemn conclusion of the treaty never took place, and there was therefore no textual copy of the treaty at Athens. This is evident from Plutarch's biography of Cimon (chapter 13), where with reference to Callisthenes it is said that the Persians had not formally accepted the treaty, but observed its conditions, thus preventing a clash with the Greek naval ships in the Aegean Sea.

With regard to the version of the treaty which was included by Craterus in his survey of the decisions of the Athenian assembly, it can be hypothesized, with Burn, that this was one of the reconstructions from the fourth century B.C. of the conditions of the Peace, which by that time was regarded as a symbol of the golden age (see Burn 1970:563). After sixty years, the Peace of Callias had become an object of pride to the Athenians. This, however, was only in retrospect, as the treaty which the Athenians concluded much later with Artaxerxes II was much more unfavourable to the Athenians. According to the conditions of the new treaty the Athenians ceded all of Asia Minor to the Persians. It is at this time that Athenian orators started to laude the Peace of Callias. For instance, Isocrates (*Paneg.* 120) said that the Athenians had prevented the Persian king from using the Aegean Sea and had set limits to his power. It is exactly at this time that one of the reconstructed texts of the treaty was presented, as a propagandistic document which was considered to be a forgery by Theopompus (Burn 1970:563; see for an extensive bibliography: Bengtson 1960:206).

After the conclusion of the Peace of Callias, the Athenians strove to heal their wounds and to restore the heavy damage, both in human life and in economic affairs, which the long wars had inflicted upon them. Now a period started which lasted for almost two decades in which the forces of both sides were almost of equal strength, and in which possibilities were opened up for unhampered trade and economic growth. The peace also strengthened the position of the Phoenicians, especially on Cyprus. For instance, Idalion, which previously had been in the hands of the Greeks, fell to the Phoenician king of the city of Kition. At Salamis, on Cyprus, where previously kings of Greek extraction had reigned, now Phoenician officials occupied leading positions.

CHAPTER THIRTY-ONE

A REVISION OF PERSIAN POLICIES

The continuing revolts by subject peoples, together with military defeats and satrapal revolts with the assistance of Greek mercenaries, forced Artaxerxes I and his successors to change their policy towards Greece in a drastic manner. Well acquainted with Greek affairs, the Persian politicians realized that while Greece was divided she could not constitute a threat to the Persian empire. The Persians therefore began to adopt the regular policy of bribery and bringing Greek politicians and orators into discredit, thus following the creed of 'divide and rule'. The influx of Persian gold effectively brought about the division of Greece. The Persians commenced to set one state up against the other in order to occupy them fully with internal matters and so not to give them time to turn their attention to the Persians.

Above all Greece was divided according to political principles: the states with an oligarchic government were drawn towards Sparta, while those with democratic institutions drifted into the arms of Athens. The political controversies between Sparta and Athens did not diminish. Two allies of Sparta, the states of Corinth and Megara, were trade rivals of Athens and they anxiously followed the strengthening of Athens' position, and urged Sparta to declare war on Athens. Finally, in 431 B.C., the Peloponnesian war broke out, to the great satisfaction of the Persians. This war was fought between the Peloponnesian union headed by Sparta, and the maritime Athenian empire. The war would prove to be one of the most devastating events for ancient Greece and it was to be the cause of incalculable misery for the Hellenes. It continued until 404 B.C. During the course of this war the political situation in Athens would change a number of times. Both sides appealed to the Persians for assistance, and so Persia at one moment helped Sparta, and then Athens. Persia was only interested in the weakening of both parties.

When the war broke out, contention arose between the democratic and oligarchic parties in various Hellenic states, and the representatives of these groups turned to Athens and Sparta respectively, inviting them to send forces to defeat their rivals.

At the commencement of the war Athens suffered a heavy loss, because in 430 B.C. the city witnessed the outbreak of an epidemic of the plague (see Alekseev 1966:134). According to Thucydides (II 48), the epidemic started in Ethiopia, and hence spread over Egypt, Libya and the greater part of the Persian empire, eventually reaching Athens.

At that moment, however, the Spartans were not in a position to inflict a decisive defeat upon the Athenian army and fleet, because in order to continue the war they needed money. As Persia could provide them with the necessary funds, the Spartans started to accept Persian gold without remorse, promising in return to bring the Greeks of Asia Minor back under Persian rule. The execution of this agreement, however, was delayed. Persia feared the excessive strength of Sparta, while the satraps in Asia Minor acted separately, and each of them was led by his own political objectives. From their side, the Spartans also delayed the negotiations with the ambassadors of the Great King, as they had decided that they should not immediately betray the interests of the Greeks of Asia Minor. Nevertheless the Spartans asked the Persians to send a Phoenician fleet to assist the navy of the Peloponnesian alliance and also to pay the wages of the sailors on board the Peloponnesian vessels. The activities of the Spartan leaders, however, were inconsistent. Thucydides (IV 50) remarked that at the mouth of the River Strymon in Thrace the Athenians captured Artaphernes, who had been sent by Artaxerxes I to Sparta. In his baggage the Athenians found a letter in 'Assyrian' (i.e., Aramaic) characters, in which it was said that the king did not know what the Lacedaimonians wanted, because all of their ambassadors contradicted each other.

While the war continued in Greece, the long reign of Artaxerxes, which had been poor in glorious moments, came to an end.

CHAPTER THIRTY-TWO

THE REIGN OF DARIUS II

Artaxerxes I died between December, 424 B.C., and February, 423 B.C. (see Stolper 1983:225ff.). On the same day that he died, his wife Damaspia also passed away. Both of them were buried at Naqsh-i Rustam. The news of their death gradually spread over the Empire. In the Nippur region of Babylonia, for example, the scribes continued for some time to date the documents to the reign of Artaxerxes after he had died.

Xerxes II, a son of Artaxerxes, became king. He was the only legitimate successor, but he only managed to occupy the throne for 45 days, before he was murdered in his bedroom by several members of the court nobility. Early in the year 423 B.C., royal power was passed on to another son of Artaxerxes, by one of his concubines. He was called Sekyndianos (according to other sources, he was called Sogdianos). He, however, lacked any serious support. From among the influential people at court he was only supported by the eunuch Pharnacyas, and the king's cousin Menostanes, the son of the Babylonian satrap Artarios. According to Ctesias, Menostanes became commander-in-chief of Sogdianos' army.[1] Sekyndianos tried to persuade his half-brother Ochus (in Old Persian, *Vahuka*), who was the satrap in Hyrcania, to come to Susa and ascend the throne. Ochus, however, suspected, not without reason, that he was not being invited to Susa to adopt kingship, but to be buried. He therefore did not hurry in going to the capital. Ochus was not in his Hyrcanian residence, but probably in Babylonia. At least by February, 423 B.C., he was in Babylon and declared his claim to the throne (see Stolper 1983:224f.). In the meantime, according to Ctesias (XVIII 78-79; König 1972:19, paragraph 47), Arbarius, the commander of the cavalry, together with Arxanes (Arsames), satrap in Egypt, and the powerful eunuch Artoxares, who was a Paphlagonian in origin, came over to the side of Ochus. Sekyndianos, after having reigned for six and a half months, abdicated in the hope that he would receive

---

[1] The same Menostanes is referred to in several documents of the Murashu archive from Nippur, in which he is called Manushtanu, the 'royal prince', son of Artareme. As seen from the texts, he held a prominent fiscal and administrative position in the Nippur region. Yet Menostanes was not able to deliver any serious support to Sogdianos since all of Babylonia stood firmly on the side of his adversary Ochus (see Stolper 1983:232ff.).

clemency from the new king. This hope proved to be in vain, as he was subsequently executed.[2]

In February 423 B.C., as said before, the Hyrcanian satrap Ochus, the son of Artaxerxes I and a Babylonian concubine (on this basis he was given the Greek nickname *Nothos*, 'bastard'), had proclaimed himself as the king of Persia, adopting the throne name of Darius II.[3] After defeating Sekyndianos, he ordered the execution of all those who, together with Sekyndianos, had participated in the murder of Xerxes II. Subsequently, a brother of Ochus, called Arsites, instigated a revolt, apparently in Syria, in order to occupy the throne himself. The suppression of this insurgence occupied much time. Against him the king sent Artasyras who initially suffered two defeats, but he was victorious in the third battle after having bribed the Greek mercenaries in the rebel camp. Having too much trust in the clemency of his brother, Arsites gave himself up and was later executed (see Lewis 1977:79).

At the same time in Greece the Peloponnesian war continued with defeats and successes on both sides. The course of events was followed with great attention by the Persian diplomats Pharnabazus and Tissaphernes, who in alliance with Sparta commanded the military activities against Athens and who strove to return control over the Greek cities in Asia Minor to the Great King. Pharnabazus was the son of Artabazus, the Persian general who together with Mardonius was left by Xerxes with orders to subjugate Greece. In 413 B.C. Pharnabazus was appointed to the position his father had formerly occupied, namely as satrap of Hellespontine Phrygia and all the northwestern regions of Asia Minor, with Dascyleium as capital.

Around 413 B.C. the satrap of Lydia, Pissouthnes, rose against Darius II. He based his strength on Greek mercenaries under the Athenian general Lycon.[4] Tissaphernes was commissioned to crush the revolt. He was the son of the noble Persian Hydarnes, who had participated in

---

[2] According to Diodorus (XII 71.1), Sekyndianos ruled for seven months. The same historian wrote that Xerxes II ruled for two months.

[3] In the Babylonian sources Sekyndianos is not mentioned at all. The latest text which was dated to the reign of Artaxerxes I, was written on February 26th, 423 B.C., although at that time Artaxerxes was no longer among the living. It can be suggested that some scribes took a very careful position, not knowing what would be the outcome of the struggle for the Persian throne. In the meantime they continued to date their documents to the reign of the already deceased king. The earliest reliable reference in a Babylonian document to the reign of Darius II is dated to February 13th, 423 B.C. Three documents, however, have been preserved which are dated to "the 41st year of Artaxerxes (I), the accession year (of Darius II)." The earliest of these contracts was drawn up on August 16, 423 B.C. (see Lewis 1977:72, n. 145; Parker & Dubberstein 1956:18).

[4] This revolt is sometimes dated to the summer of 422 or 421 B.C. (Lewis 1977:80ff.; the same passage also presents relevant literature).

Xerxes' campaign against Greece in 480 B.C. as commander of the 'Immortals'. Tissaphernes was a great state official and gifted diplomat, although not always particular about his means. In spite of the fact that his brother Teriteuchmes had started a conspiracy against the royal family, and consequently had been executed together with the majority of his relatives, Tissaphernes managed to retain his influence (cf., however, Burn 1985:342f., n. 5, and p. 349, n. 1, in which it is suggested that Hydarnes, the father of Teriteuchmes, and Hydarnes, the father of Tissaphernes, were different persons). Having received orders to suppress Pissouthnes' revolt, Tissaphernes bribed the Greek mercenaries of the rebel, and in a treacherous manner captured him. Darius ordered to throw him into a furnace. As a reward Tissaphernes received the Lydian satrapy, Caria and the Ionian cities. In his turn, he presented the Athenian general Lycon, who had betrayed Pissouthnes, with large estates.

Taking advantage of the Athenian difficulties, Darius II ordered Tissaphernes to collect and send to him the tribute from the Greek cities of Asia Minor. In order to execute this order, it was necessary to divert Athenian attention away from these areas. In addition and at the same time, there was a revolt in Caria which was led by an illegitimate son of Pissouthnes, called Amorges. The Carian revolt was supported by the Athenians. Darius ordered Tissaphernes to bring Amorges to Susa, either dead or alive. All these points forced Tissaphernes to seek Spartan support. He therefore sent an ambassador to Sparta with propositions for an alliance. At the same time there arrived at Sparta two Greeks who were employed by Pharnabazus and who on his behalf asked the Spartans to send warships to the Hellespont. Pharnabazus, imitating Tissaphernes, attempted to conclude an alliance with Sparta in order to obtain tribute from the Greek cities in his satrapy.

The two ambassadors, however, first of all attempted to expand their own power and therefore acted independently of each other, each wanting to show the Great King that it was his own endeavour which made Sparta an ally of Persia. Inevitably, during the negotiations at Sparta, the messengers of Tissaphernes and Pharnabazus incessantly quarrelled among themselves. Eventually the Spartans decided to accept the conditions which were proposed by Tissaphernes. While the negotiations continued, the city of Miletus revolted against Tissaphernes and came over to the side of Sparta. Thereupon Tissaphernes decided to hasten the conclusion of the talks. The contents of the treaty, which was concluded in 412 B.C. and which was not very favourable to the Spartans, were extensively reported by Thucydides (VIII 18). According to the conditions of the treaty, all the land and cities which the Persians ruled and used to rule, came to the Great King. The Persian king and the Lacedaimonians would combine forces in order to prevent the Athenians from levying any tribute in these areas, and they should end the war against Athens only on the basis of a mutual decision. If one of the pertinent towns or districts revolted against the king, the Spartans should regard them as rebels and thus as their enemies. In the same way the Great King would regard those who revolted against the Lacedaimonians as his enemies. In addition, the Persians took upon themselves the obligation of assisting the Spartans with money.[5]

Having become allies, Tissaphernes and the Spartans took the city of Iasus in Caria. There the Spartans captured the rebel Amorges and handed him over to Tissaphernes in order to be brought before Darius. In addition, they handed over to the Persians all the inhabitants of the city, both free and slaves, and received one stater for each person. During these events, the Lycians also gave Tissaphernes their energetic support. They were commanded by their king, who was a subject of the Persians and a long-time enemy of the Athenians. On a certain Lycian stela from Xanthos reference is made to the war against Amorges, and the exploits of the Lycian prince Kheriga, the son of Harpagos. It is true, the name of this king in the inscription is damaged, but it has been reliably reconstructed on the basis of certain legends on coins, issued by the same person (see Childs 1981:62-64; Lewis 1977:83; Shahbazi, *Enc. Ir.*, s.v. 'Amorges'). Relatively recently, another stela was found at Xanthos, which refers to the same events. This text tells about a victory of the Lycian general Kheriga over a certain rebel called Tlos. It also refers to a defeat suffered by Ionians and Amorges. On the stela Tissaphernes is depicted as a famous hero, who defeated the Athenians (information provided by M. Mellink). There are also coins which were issued by Kheriga in 410 B.C.

After the victory over Amorges, Tissaphernes went to Miletus and there, in agreement with the treaty, he paid all the sailors of the Peloponnesian vessels one drachma per day for every man. He proclaimed, however, that from that moment onwards he would only pay half of that amount, namely three obols. He promised that, if the king sent money for provisions, the payment would be raised to one drachma.

The Peloponnesians were dissatisfied with the conditions of their alliance with the Persian king. They regarded the treaty as being unfavourable to them, so they started new negotiations. According to Thucydides (VIII 37), the second treaty ran as follows: The Lacedaimo-

---

[5] For the text of the treaty, see H. Bengtson 1962, Nos. 200-202. As regards the authenticity of this and two other treaties between Persia and Sparta, see A. T. Olmstead 1933:157.

nians and their allies concluded a treaty of friendship and cooperation
with the king, with the sons of the king and with Tissaphernes, with the
following conditions. The Lacedaimonians or their allies would not wage
war upon, or inflict any damage upon any territory or city which belongs
to the king, or which belonged to his father and ancestors. The
Lacedaimonians and their allies would not levy tribute from these towns.
The King Darius (II) and his subjects would not wage war against the
Lacedaimonians and their allies, nor inflict any damage upon them. If
the Lacedaimonians or their allies had any claim against the king, or if
the king had any claim against the Lacedaimonians or their allies, then
everything that they decided in full agreement, would be regarded as
binding. The king and the Lacedaimonians should cooperate in the war
against the Athenians and their allies, and if a peace treaty was concluded, then they should also act together. The king was obliged to pay the
expenses for the upkeep of all troops which were stationed in his land at
his request. If a certain town, forming part of the treaty, attacked royal
land, then the remaining towns had to act and help the king, as much
as was in their power. And if one of the inhabitants of royal land, or of
land subject to him, attacked the land of the Lacedaimonians or of their
allies, then the king had to act and assist the Lacedaimonians or their
allies as much as possible.

Soon afterwards, however, Lacedaimonian ambassadors again had a
meeting with Tissaphernes. The Spartans were of the opinion that both
of the previous treaties had been incorrect in their wording, because
under the conditions of the treaties the king could claim all the land
which one time had been conquered by the Persians, including in particular the islands of the Aegean Sea, Thessaly, and even all of Hellas as
far as Boeotia. The Lacedaimonian ambassadors therefore wanted to
conclude a new treaty. Tissaphernes was indignant and he left the discussions unfinished. The Spartans, however, were not in any position to
maintain their fleet without Persian money.

In the meantime the political intrigue was joined by the distinguished
Athenian general and politician, Alcibiades, a nephew of Pericles. At the
time of the Athenian campaign against Sicily in 413 B.C., which was unsuccessful, Alcibiades had been accused of sacrilege and had fled to Sparta. He started to assist the latter in the war against Athens and even
presented the Spartan leaders with the military plans of the Athenians.
In addition, Alcibiades incited almost all the Greek towns of Asia Minor
to revolt against Athens. At Sparta, however, many were discontent with
his power, and, if Plutarch (*Alcibiades* 24) can be believed, conspired to
kill him. When Alcibiades heard about this plot in 412 B.C., he fled the
city and went to Asia Minor and Tissaphernes. He soon acquired a high

position at the court of the satrap. The intelligence and dexterity of his new counsellor and eminent partner fascinated Tissaphernes. Alcibiades feared further strengthening of the Lacedaimonians and wanted to take revenge upon them. He therefore strove to hamper the negotiations between Sparta and Tissaphernes. Alcibiades advised the latter not to hurry in ending the war, but to wait for the outcome of the conflict between Athens and Sparta, so that the Hellenes would exhaust themselves. Alcibiades also persuaded Tissaphernes not to pay the Peloponnesians regularly, and only to pay three obols for every man, instead of the Attic drachma. He argued his proposition by saying that too much money would make the sailors weak. All this was clearly realized by Tissaphernes who did not need a teacher in politics; without the advice of Alcibiades and long before the latter's arrival, Tissaphernes had formulated the same policy. Alcibiades, however, had only given this advice in order to win Tissaphernes' trust. In reality he had other objectives. The Athenians, who were now totally on the defensive and who endured many hardships, repented the fact that they had ever condemned Alcibiades. Very carefully, Alcibiades therefore started to move Tissaphernes towards an alliance with Athens. He did so by telling the Persian satrap that the Lacedaimonians strove for superiority on land, and when the opportunity arose they would try to liberate the Greek cities of Asia Minor from Persian domination. The Athenians on the other hand, according to Alcibiades, only wanted hegemony at sea and therefore did not constitute the same danger to the Persians as the Lacedaimonians. Tissaphernes agreed that it would be unwise to give the Spartans the opportunity to become too strong. He decided to give them only a small sum of money, and to oppose their interests in secret. As regards an alliance with Athens, Tissaphernes gave the impression that he was prepared to discuss the subject. It would seem likely that under favourable circumstances he was not adverse to such an alliance. Alcibiades, however, overestimated his influence on the Persian satrap.

In the meantime Alcibiades was in contact with his adherents of the oligarchic party in Athens. His supporters in Athens openly started to move towards the establishment of an oligarchy, saying that otherwise the Persians would not agree to form an alliance with Athens, and thus the state would be manoeuvred into a very critical situation. Alcibiades also secretly sent his messenger to the Athenian leaders on the island of Samos, promising to acquire for them the sympathy of Tissaphernes, provided 'the best people' would take the matter of saving the motherland into their hands. Alcibiades, however, only sought for the possibility of returning to Athens and was not an adherent of any political party. Amidst the adherents of an oligarchy who formed part of the Athenian garrison on Samos, a conspiracy was formed with the objective of overthrowing the Athenian democracy. According to Thucydides (VIII 48), the soldiers in the army were gradually drawn into the conspiracy "in the hopeful expectation of royal salary", in the opinion that Darius had no confidence in the democrats of Athens and would be interested in the establishment of an oligarchy in the city. Thus, among the civilian population of Athens, and the army on the island of Samos, there were many people who were prepared to change the political system in Athens, in order to gain the favour of the Great King or his satrap Tissaphernes.

The adherents of Alcibiades sent a trusted messenger called Peisander from Samos to Athens. He was dispatched to prepare the coup, to liquidate the democracy and to establish an oligarchy. Soon afterwards an embassy was sent from Athens, headed by Peisander, to negotiate a peace treaty with Tissaphernes. The embassy arrived at the city of Magnesia in Asia Minor, but Tissaphernes was not really interested and ordered Alcibiades to conduct the negotiations on his behalf. According to Thucydides (VIII 56), this was all done to cheat the Athenians. The Athenians were prepared to give up all of Ionia and the adjoining islands. Alcibiades, however, also wished permission for the Persian ships to sail along the Athenian possessions. The Athenian ambassadors could not agree to this point and were forced to return to their city.

Tissaphernes now became afraid that the Athenians would defeat the Peloponnesians in a sea battle, and that in their search for food the latter would start to plunder his domains. He therefore suggested that the Lacedaimonians should conclude another treaty, promising them no further hostilities and regular payment for the sailors. The treaty was concluded in 410 B.C., in the valley of the Meander river. It contained the following conditions: the Great King would exercise his authority in Asia Minor as he pleased. The Lacedaimonians and their allies would not step on the king's land with hostile intentions. In return, Tissaphernes was obliged to pay wages to the sailors of the Peloponnesians, until the arrival of the royal vessels, namely those from Phoenicia. When these arrived, the Peloponnesians, if they so wished, could keep their fleet. If they preferred to receive support from Tissaphernes for the upkeep of their fleet, he had to give it to them, but after the end of the war the Lacedaimonians and their allies were obliged to return to Tissaphernes all the money which they had received. When the royal ships arrived, they would wage war on Athens in cooperation with the Peloponnesian vessels.

When the treaty was concluded, Tissaphernes created the impression that he would take measures to call for the Phoenician ships. At the same time, however, he kept the Lacedaimonians from a decisive battle, fearing for a too rapid end to the war. In addition, true to his policy,

Tissaphernes continued to pay the sailors of the Peloponnesian fleet very irregularly and not as much as he should have done under the conditions of the treaty.

Consequently the Lacedaimonians decided to assist Pharnabazus, instead of Tissaphernes. Pharnabazus also promised to support the Peloponnesian fleet. Thereupon the Spartans sent forty vessels to Byzantium, which the Persian satrap could use as he pleased. For two years Pharnabazus supported the Peloponnesian fleet. Nevertheless, his endeavour to return the Greek towns north of the Hellespont to Persian domination had no significant success.

In the meantime the people of Miletus attacked the fortress of Tissaphernes, which was located within the city, and forced the Persian garrison to withdraw. Disturbed by the destruction of his fortress at Miletus and by the Spartan decision to join the side of Pharnabazus, Tissaphernes sent a close adviser to Sparta to conduct negotiations. The ambassador was a Carian called Gaulites. He spoke, apart from his own language, fluent Greek. Gaulites accused the Milesians of destroying Tissaphernes' castle. He did so in the hope of inducing the Spartans to take action against them. The Milesians, however, had also sent messengers to Sparta with complaints about the activities of Tissaphernes.

While Tissaphernes tried to reorganize his relations with Sparta, the position of Athens was gradually improving. In October, 411 B.C., Alcibiades and the ships which he had at his disposal joined the side of the Athenians during a sea battle between the Athenians and Peloponnesians, near the town of Abydos. As a result the Peloponnesians were defeated. The soldiers of Pharnabazus assisted as much as possible in rescuing the damaged Peloponnesian vessels. Pharnabazus himself came to the shores on his horse. Alcibiades was of the opinion that he had done Tissaphernes a favour. The latter, however, feared the anger of his king because he had hampered the cause of the Lacedaimonians. Tissaphernes arrested Alcibiades, who had come to him with gifts of hospitality, and imprisoned him in Sardis, in the hope that the Spartans would not blame their defeat on him.

Very soon afterwards, however, Alcibiades managed to escape his guards. He obtained a horse and fled during the night to the town of Clazomenae. There he slandered Tissaphernes by saying that he had set him free. Thereupon he went to the camp of the Athenians where he was well received and given back his citizen's rights. In the course of the ensuing years the Athenians, led by Alcibiades, gained a number of significant victories, including one over the cavalry of Pharnabazus. At that time the position of the Persians became extremely weak because the Medes had undertaken a revolt against Darius II and the king was forced to concentrate all his forces in Media to suppress the revolt. The Athenians also managed to conquer the town of Sestos on the Chersonesus from the Persians, and they used the place as an observation post for the Hellespont. In 409 B.C., the Athenian fleet headed by Alcibiades gained a great victory over the Peloponnesian fleet in the harbour of Cyzicus. The ships of Pharnabazus were also involved and the Persian satrap himself was forced to flee. The Athenians conquered Cyzicus and, controlling the Hellespont, started a successful attack on the Peloponnesian and Persian forces. Subsequently Alcibiades surrounded Chalcedon, which had previously annulled its treaty with Athens and had welcomed a Spartan garrison. Efforts to prevent the fall of Chalcedon proved unsuccessful, and in 408 B.C. Pharnabazus concluded at Cyzicus the following agreement: He was obliged to pay the Athenians a certain sum of money, while the latter would no longer plunder and threaten Pharnabazus' domains. In addition, Chalcedon was to remain under the control of the Athenians. Alcibiades also besieged Byzantium, which had broken off its alliance with Athens. The town ran out of provisions and, in spite of the presence of a Spartan garrison, was given up by its population to the Athenians.

Unfortunately for Athens, however, a change was taking place in Persian policies. Darius II decided to stop his former balanced policy as regards Athens and Sparta and to extend his full support to the Lacedaimonians. Tissaphernes, having successfully played off for a long time both adversaries, was now recalled from his duties as satrap of Lydia and a number of other districts. He was left with merely the satrapy of Caria.

In 408 B.C., Parysatis, the wife and half-sister of Darius II, who had considerable influence at court, succeeded in obtaining the appointment of her favourite son Cyrus the Younger as satrap of certain provinces of Asia Minor, namely Lydia, Phrygia, and Cappadocia. According to Xenophon (*Hell.* I 4.3), Cyrus was given the authority over all the lands along the sea. In order to secure his position, he carried a letter with the royal seal. In addition, the new governor was appointed as supreme commander of all Persian forces in Asia Minor. These had been assembled for military inspection in the valley of Castolus, in Lydia. According to information which is provided by Xenophon, Cyrus, in the function of commander, carried the title of *karanos*, which he translated as 'commander' (apparently, the word was derived from Old Persian *kāra*, 'army'; Bivar 1961:123, n. 5). He was an energetic ruler and an acute general. In his relations with other states he acted in almost complete independence, and classical writers tended to call him 'king'. Having arrived in Asia Minor, he defeated the rebellious Mysians and Pisidians, who lived between Lydia and Cilicia. He also appointed his own governor to rule these peoples.

In the same year of 408 B.C., Athenian messengers, in the company of guides provided by Pharnabazus, went to the Great King for negotiations. On the way they met Spartan messengers who were just returning from the royal court and who told the Athenians that they had already come to a favourable agreement with the king. On being informed about this point and also knowing that the new governor in Asia Minor had been ordered to extend his full cooperation to the Spartans, the Athenians requested their guides either to take them to their king or to allow them to return to Athens. Cyrus, however, ordered Pharnabazus not to permit the ambassadors to return home, so that the Athenians would be kept in the dark as regards the true state of affairs. Pharnabazus was dissatisfied with this order and held the opinion that the Persians should not set the Athenians against them. Nevertheless, and against his own volition, he kept the Athenian ambassadors under arrest for three years before sending them to a sea port in Mysia. From there they reached Athenian troops.

In 407 B.C., almost simultaneously with Cyrus the Younger's appointment as governor of Asia Minor, the command of the Peloponnesian military forces came into the hands of an experienced Spartan general, called Lysander. Cyrus started to conduct a pro-Spartan policy, and he supported the Peloponnesians energetically, although he did not break definitively with Athens. This development created the opportunity for a friendship between the two leaders and they met for negotiations at Sardis. During the discussions, Lysander accused Tissaphernes of the fact that he, although under orders of the king to support Sparta against Athens, had allowed the Peloponnesian fleet to be almost completely destroyed. Cyrus was pleased to hear these accusations against a man whom he, with justification, regarded as his enemy. Cyrus promised to pay the sailors of the Peloponnesian fleet four obols per day, instead of the three obols which were paid previously. He also presented Lysander with 10,000 darics. Cyrus added that in support of Sparta he was prepared to spend all his personal property and even to disassemble his throne of gold and silver if more funds were needed. According to certain Greek orators, Darius presented Sparta, via his satraps, with a sum of more than 5,000 talents for the war against Athens (Andoc., *De pace* 29; Isocr., *De pace* 97). With this money it was possible for the Spartans to pay the crews of a hundred vessels an amount of four obols a day per man, for a period of five years. When Lysander started to pay his crews the daily salary of four obols, the Athenian vessels gradually had to withdraw because the sailors tended to defect to the other side due to the higher pay. The position of the Athenian fleet, commanded by Alcibiades, which had been invincible until that time, became desperate.

After the dismissal of Tissaphernes from his post as satrap of Lydia, the Greek cities of Asia Minor remained in his power. Soon, however, they were all, apart from Miletus, occupied by Lysander and following the installation in these towns of an oligarchy, handed over to Cyrus. Thereupon Lysander started to plunder the possessions of Pharnabazus. The latter complained to the Spartan leaders about these activities, reminding them of his former assistance in their war against Athens. As a result Lysander was relieved from his post. Receiving the orders to return to Sparta, Lysander, who at that time was residing in the Hellespont, asked Pharnabazus to write to Sparta a letter in which he would give his assurances that he had not been damaged in any way by the activities of the Spartan leader. Pharnabazus was pleased to agree, but, before impressing his seal, he deftly changed the letter which had been agreed upon with Lysander, by another one, which had been written before, and this he handed to the Spartan. In Sparta, Lysander handed the letter, without suspecting anything wrong, to the ephors. He was convinced that these, after reading the letter, would soon restore him in his former function. When the ephors, however, showed him the contents of the letter, he realized that Pharnabazus had deceived him.

In 407 B.C., Alcibiades, after a military defeat, was in his absence sentenced in Athens and he was forced to flee to Pharnabazus in Phrygia in the hope of obtaining his assistance to go, just like Themistocles before him, to the royal court. Pharnabazus received him well, but soon the military and political situation changed. The Persian and Peloponnesian fleet repelled the Athenian vessels from the coasts of Asia Minor and from many of the islands of the Aegean Sea and attempted to deprive Athens from the chance of obtaining provisions from the northern Black Sea area. The Athenians sent a fleet to protect the passage through the Hellespont. In 406 B.C. the Athenian fleet gained a victory over the Peloponnesians at the battle of the Arginusae, near Lesbos. The Athenians, however, lost many men as a result of a storm. During the battle the newly appointed Spartan admiral Callicratidas was also killed. These events enabled Lysander to return to Asia Minor. Although he was not appointed as admiral, the actual command of the Peloponnesian ships came into his hands. In the winter of 405 B.C. Lysander unexpectedly attacked the Athenian fleet, which was anchored at the mouth of the River Aegospotami in the Hellespont. He was able to capture 170 of the 180 Athenian ships. The 3,000 Athenians who were captured, were then executed. This was a heavy blow to Athens. Soon afterwards Lysander and the Peloponnesian army appeared before the walls of Athens, an event which created the most dangerous threat to the city. In 404 B.C. Athens was forced to accept the peace conditions which were dictated by Sparta. Lysander installed in Athens the Government of the Thirty Tyrants. At the request of these men, who feared that Alcibiades would restore democracy, Lysander sent a letter to Pharnabazus with the demand that he should kill his Athenian guest. Pharnabazus gave this order to his brother Bagaeus and uncle Sisamitres, and in the autumn of 404 B.C. Alcibiades ended his eventful life in a Phrygian village.

Thus, in 404 B.C. the Persians in alliance with Sparta had won back their former hegemony along the coastal lands of Asia Minor.

CHAPTER THIRTY-THREE

THE REVOLT OF AMYRTAEUS IN EGYPT

The Peloponnesian war gave the Persians the opportunity to deal with their own, internal problems. The Achaemenid leaders, however, could not use this interlude to its full advantage. Characteristic for the reign of Darius II is the further weakening of central authority, combined with court intrigues and conspiracies in which Queen Parysatis played an important role. The influence of the court nobility was also increasing. In addition, from the end of the fifth century B.C. onwards the satraps of Asia Minor were continuously at war with each other, in particular for the possession of the rich city of Miletus, while the Achaemenid kings remained aloof and maintained a policy of non-interference. Several governors also rebelled against the central authority, and, with the support of Greek mercenaries, tried to gain complete independence. Furthermore, the subject peoples themselves occasionally revolted. These insurgencies were caused by the fact that the government of the later Achaemenids brought severe impoverishment upon the population of the subject lands. The rulers no longer tried to find support for their government in the conquered lands, but tried to overcome all problems by military means and bribery with gold. Between 410 and 408 B.C. there were serious revolts in Asia Minor and Media, which were only crushed with great difficulty.

At the same time unrest broke out again in Egypt. This led, in particular, to the destruction of the temple of the Jewish garrison at Elephantine. For more than 150 years the relations between the Jews and the local population in that area had been peaceful and even friendly; mixed marriages were concluded, and business relationships were maintained. Contrary to the many Greek mercenaries, who had been hated by the local population at the time of the later Saite government, the Jews had many customs in common with the Egyptians (for instance, circumcision, and in certain nomes a prohibition against the eating of pork, etc.). By the end of the fifth century B.C., however, the Egyptians started to behave hostilely towards the Jews of Elephantine. The reasons for this change of mood are difficult to ascertain. It is difficult to agree with F. K. Kienitz, who suggested that the temple of the Jews at Elephantine had been destroyed due to religious intolerance by the Egyptians (Kienitz 1953:75). It may be significant that in those chaotic times the Egyptians revolted several times against Persian rule, while the Jews, together with other military colonists who found themselves in a strange country and in the military service of the foreign rulers, had to step forward in loyal support of the Persians. All that is known to us with any degree of certainty, is that in the month of July, 410 B.C., the priests of the Egyptian god of Khnum incited the Egyptians at Elephantine to destroy the temple of the god Yahu (Yahweh). In doing so they were not stopped by the Persian governor, who was called Vidranga. Possibly he was not even in the position to stop them. Vidranga, if the colonists can be believed, was bribed by the Egyptian priests, both with money and with various precious objects. He was even accused of having sent his son Nefayan, the commander of the garrison at Syene, together with a group of soldiers, to help the Egyptians in the destruction of the temple. The sanctuary was destroyed and the cult objects were plundered or burnt. In the report from the Jewish military colonists, sent to various officials, it is stated: "In the fourteenth year of the King Darius, after our lord Arsames had gone to the king, the priests of the temple of Khnum enacted this evil deed at the fortress of Elephantine, with the approval of Vidranga, who was the commander here. They gave him silver and goods ... They destroyed the temple" (AP, 27; cf. Bogoljubov 1969:69ff.; Porten & Yardeni 1986:62; Struve 1938).

The complaint of the Elephantine Jews was first passed on to the High Priest and other religious functionaries at the Temple of Jerusalem, and subsequently to Arsames, satrap of Egypt, who at the time of the pogrom resided outside of Egypt. The report was also sent to Bagohi, the governor of Judah. In their letters to these officials, the Jews of Elephantine asked for an inquiry into the affair and for assistance in the rebuilding of the temple. In particular, the fact is emphasized that when the Egyptians rebelled against Cambyses, the colonists remained loyal to the Persian king and did not leave their fortress. Cambyses had therefore not inflicted any damage upon the temple of Yahweh while he did destroy some Egyptian sanctuaries.

The priests of Jerusalem, however, did not reply to the complaint. At that time the dogmatic cult of Yahweh, intolerant towards the worship of other gods, had become well entrenched in Jerusalem. The religion of the Elephantine Jews, who next to Yahweh also worshipped other deities, was regarded by the Jerusalem priests as a heresy. In addition, according to the point of view of Deuteronomy, the temple of Yahweh could only be located at Jerusalem. The priesthood at Jerusalem therefore refrained from assisting the colonists in Egypt.

The afflicted Jews of Elephantine, however, found full sympathy with the sons of Sanballat, the governor of Samaria, who followed a very similar cult of Yahweh as that practised at Elephantine. The sons of San-

ballat made considerable efforts to ask Arsames for a decision concerning
the rebuilding of the temple to its former state and according to its former
plan (possibly, at state expenses). Bagohi, to whom two identical complaints were addressed (AP, 30, 31; Porten & Yardeni 1986:71-75), also
promised to direct the case to Arsames. In the meantime, both the Egyptians and the Jews tried to bribe the Persian officials.

The reply of Arsames, if it was presented in written form, has not been
preserved. It is only known that after his return to Egypt Arsames removed Vidranga and his son from their duties and confiscated their goods.
It is also known from one of the letters that all the treasures which had
been acquired by Vidranga were lost, and the people who had caused
damage to the temple were killed. In two Aramaic papyri, however,
which are dated to the end of the fifth century B.C. and to 399 B.C. respectively, a certain Vidranga is mentioned, who (in any case in the first
of these documents) is referred to as a commander of a garrison (AP, 38;
Kraeling 1953, no. 13; cf. also *idem*:283). If this is the same man as the
governor of Elephantine during the year 410 B.C., then Vidranga was
not executed, but merely removed from office. In all probability, the Persian government also took a positive decision about the rebuilding of the
temple. It is possible that the reconstructions could not be carried out
because of a revolt which broke out in Egypt under the command of
Amyrtaeus II from Sais. He was apparently a grandson of the same
Amyrtaeus who some fifty years before had resisted the Persian forces in
the western Delta. The initiative of the revolt, as before, came from the
Libyans who lived in the Delta.

It is difficult to give an accurate date for Amyrtaeus II's revolt. E.
Meyer and following him many other scholars have suggested that even
by 404 B.C. all of Egypt was in the hands of the rebels (Bickerman
1934:77ff.; Meyer 1912:90; *idem* 1939, Vol. V, p. 180). Later, however,
other Aramaic papyri have become available which indicate that the
Elephantine garrison remained loyal to the Persian king until at least
December 401 B.C. As remarked by Kraeling, it is evident from the
Anabasis of Xenophon that by 401 B.C. Amyrtaeus was still engaged in
establishing his control over Egypt, because in the spring of that year the
Spartan general Clearchus offered Tissaphernes a contingent of Greek
mercenaries to retain Egypt for the Persians. In 402-401 B.C. the Persians still controlled Elephantine, and in all probability, also most of the
rest of Upper Egypt. A number of papyri from this period are dated to
the third and fourth years of the reign of Artaxerxes II (Kraeling 1953,
nos. 9-13; cf. also *ibid.*:111ff.). Apparently, Amyrtaeus started his insurgency in 405 B.C., and during the first years of the revolt his control
remained limited to Lower Egypt. By 400 B.C., the rebels also

dominated Upper Egypt, including Elephantine. On the basis of one specific Aramaic papyrus, the Jewish colonists entered the service of the new pharaoh (AP, 35). Subsequently they were apparently assimilated with the local population.

In the meantime the rebels gained one victory after the other, and soon the whole country was in their hands. The commander of the Persian forces in Syria, Abrocomas, gathered a large army in order to suppress the insurrection. At that time, however, Cyrus the Younger started a revolt against his brother, Artaxerxes II, in the centre of the Achaemenid empire. The army of Abrocomas was ordered to assist the king, and Amyrtaeus, making use of this opportunity, even transferred his military operations as far north as Syria. Thus, at the beginning of the reign of Artaxerxes II, the so-called first period of Persian domination in Egypt came to an end. According to Manetho, Darius II was the last pharaoh of the 27th dynasty, while Amyrtaeus became the first, and the last, ruler of the 28th dynasty. The Egyptian revolt was not suppressed by the Persians until sixty years later, i.e. in 342 B.C., and not long before the fall of the Achaemenid empire. The loss of Egypt was a heavy blow to the Persians, because it deprived them of the main granary of the Empire.

CHAPTER THIRTY-FOUR

THE REVOLT OF CYRUS THE YOUNGER

Cyrus the Younger had hoped to ascend the Persian throne with the help of his mother Parysatis, who held a strong influence on Darius II. The king's eldest son Arsaces (according to Deinon he was called Oarses), however, had already been appointed as successor, and Darius did not wish to change his decision. According to Plutarch (*Art.* 2), Cyrus based his claims to the throne on the fact that he had been born when Darius II was king, while Arsaces was born when he was still a private person. According to Plutarch, Cyrus was about eighteen years old when his father died. This piece of information, however, seems unlikely, because four years previously he had been appointed as governor of Asia Minor.

At the beginning of the year 404 B.C., after being told about his father's disease, Cyrus went to Babylon where the royal court was currently residing (according to another version, the Persian king was in Media). In March, 404 B.C., Darius died and Arsaces became the new king after attending the ancient ceremonies at the old Persian capital of Pasargadae. He adopted the throne name of Artaxerxes (II). Because of his exceptional memory, the Greeks called him *Mnemon*, 'the mindful one'.

Tissaphernes, the satrap of Caria, whose daughter was married to Arsaces, attended the coronation and told the new king that Cyrus was conspiring against him. This accusation was supported by a magus who was Cyrus' tutor when still a child. If Xenophon (*Anabasis* I 1.3) can be believed, Cyrus did not plot against his brother at this time. Tissaphernes, according to Xenophon, was merely slandering him. Artaxerxes ordered the arrest of his brother in order to have him executed, The widowed Queen Parysatis, however, after much supplication, managed to achieve the release of her favourite son, who in 403 B.C. was sent back to Asia Minor unharmed.

Cyrus realized that the Achaemenid empire was slowly falling into decline, and he attempted to revive its former might and fame. It is difficult to say which objectives, apart from conquering the Persian throne, the young man had set himself, and among which social classes he hoped to find support. It is possible that he hoped to diminish the influence of the Persian nobility and to create a centralized government, comparable to those which were established in the Hellenistic period. Thus, in some manner he may have anticipated the social and political programme of the successors of Alexander of Macedonia (cf. Plutarch 1941:28; I. M. Diakonoff 1956:29).

In any case, the figure of Cyrus made an ineffaceable impression on his Greek friends. Xenophon in his *Anabasis* (I 9.1) wrote that according to people close to Cyrus, "he was the most talented and worthy of all the Persians after Cyrus the Elder (Cyrus II) to occupy the throne." According to the same writer, he was a very modest and inquisitive man, a brave hunter, a dexterous and courageous warrior, he respected the elders and generously rewarded his friends, and above all he remained loyal to once concluded treaties and alliances. Whole towns and many private people therefore trusted his word. If he concluded a treaty with his enemies, they could never doubt its durability. Cyrus commanded experienced troops, intelligent assistants and loyal friends. Many noble Persians from the entourage of his brother and of Tissaphernes came to join him. According to Plutarch (*Art.* 6), Cyrus was a man with brilliant talents and in the science of the magians he was better qualified than his brother.

Cyrus was acquainted with Greek culture and could express himself in Greek without the assistance of an interpreter. Nevertheless, he remained a typical Oriental despot. For instance, according to Xenophon (*Hell.* II 1.8), during the time that he was governor of Asia Minor, he ordered the execution of Autoboesaces and Mitraeus, grandsons of Xerxes, because they had not taken their hands out of their sleeves in his presence[1], although it was only for the Persian king who was to be met in that manner. He also reduced the people of the town of Kedreiai in Caria into slavery, because they had been allied to Athens.

Returning to Asia Minor, the young prince started to gather a large army to try to conquer the Persian throne. With this objective in mind he hired in secret a large force of Greek mercenaries. Some of the soldiers, and via them the Persian king himself, were told that military preparations were being made for a war with Tissaphernes. Artaxerxes II, who was engaged in plans to bring order to the chaos that he had inherited, believed these assurances by Cyrus, because internal strives between the satraps for the extension of their domains had become normal in the eyes of the Persian government. In addition, Cyrus continued to send the king the tribute of the lands of Asia Minor which were under his satrapal rule.

In the meantime the Spartans, who in 404 B.C. had gained a victory over Athens in the Peloponnesian war and now played a leading role in Greece, were not willing to heed their promise to give the Greek cities of Asia Minor back to Persian control after their successful conclusion of the

---

[1] *Kora*, according to Xenophon, was the Persian word to indicate the very long sleeves which impeded the arms to move freely.

war with Athens. The Spartans did so because they realized such a step would have repercussions in the public opinion of the Hellenes. Soon afterwards, therefore, the relations between Sparta and Persia started to become tense.

However, in 402 B.C. Cyrus the Younger sent his ambassadors to Sparta with the request that they should provide him with some of their troops. This request was honoured; in addition, the Spartan general Clearchus was ordered to obey Cyrus in all matters and to assist him in the selection of mercenaries. Sparta, which foresaw the rebellion by Cyrus, also concluded a treaty with Egypt, where the insurrection of Amyrtaeus was gathering momentum.

There was no shortage of mercenaries in Greece, as the Peloponnesian war had ended and many professional soldiers were prepared to serve whosoever seemed fit to them. The Spartan Clearchus received from Cyrus 10,000 darics, and on the Thracian Chersonesus he started to gather an army. The Thessalian Aristippus, connected with Cyrus by links of hospitality, collected 4,000 mercenaries in his motherland. Cyrus also ordered the Boeotian Proxenus to come to him with an army, under the guise of an expedition against the Pisidians, who were wont to make inroads into the lands of Asia Minor (about the raids by the Pisidians and other mountain peoples, see Briant 1976). Finally, Sophaenetus from Arcadia and Socrates from Achaea, also connected with Cyrus by links of hospitality, were ordered to present themselves with the greatest possible number of soldiers, this time under the pretext of a war against Tissaphernes. Thereupon Cyrus also recalled his warriors who were besieging from land and sea the city of Miletus, which at that moment was in the hands of Tissaphernes, and he ordered an inspection of all his troops, both the Persians and Greeks, at Sardis. Some of the mercenaries were to join Cyrus' army along the way. At Sardis there were assembled 9,600 Greek hoplites; 2,100 peltasts (light-armed foot soldiers); 200 Cretan bowmen, plus a large Persian force. In addition, Cyrus commanded cavalry troops and a fleet and he had drawn to his side some of the closest advisers of Artaxerxes II. In the early spring of 401 B.C. Cyrus marched off from Sardis, telling everybody that he was planning to bring the Pisidians under his control.

After being informed about the strength of the army which was clearly too large simply for the subjugation of the Pisidians, Tissaphernes hastened to the king to inform him about the situation. Subsequently a quarrel broke out in the royal harem between Parysatis and Artaxerxes' wife Stateira. The latter accused her mother-in-law of secretly supporting her younger son Cyrus. In the meantime, Artaxerxes hectically prepared for war and collected all his forces.

At the same time Cyrus marched towards Phrygia and there, at the town of Colossae, another 1,500 mercenaries joined his forces. Thereupon Cyrus directed his army to the rich Phrygian town of Celaenae, where he possessed a palace and a large park for the hunting of wild animals. Hence came even more mercenary troops, and here Cyrus again reviewed the Greek forces. Cyrus' army now included 11,000 hoplites and 2,100 peltasts. Cyrus then had some financial problems, as the mercenaries had not been paid for more than three months, and they were beginning to complain. At the town of Caustroupedion, however, he was joined by Epyaxa, the wife of the Cilician king Syennesis. She, being in love with Cyrus, presented him with the necessary funds, thus allowing Cyrus to pay four months of wages to his mercenaries.

Thereupon, advancing through the territory of Cappadocia, Cyrus marched to Cilicia, along a precipitous and almost impossible route which had been left undefended by the Persian king's forces. He then went to Tarsus, the capital of Cilicia, where the palace of Syennesis was located. The king of Cilicia, however, together with the majority of his people, had left the city and fled into the mountains. This allowed the Hellenes to plunder the city and palace. Via a courier Cyrus summoned Syennesis to present himself, but the latter refused to come. Epyaxa, who received from Cyrus the assurance that her husband would not be hurt, finally persuaded her husband to accept the invitation. Syennesis' position was difficult, because he feared punishment from the side of Arta-xerxes if the rebellion was suppressed. Syennesis therefore attempted to give Artaxerxes the impression that he was hostile towards the leaders of the revolt, while at the same time he had refrained from opposing Cyrus' advance through the inaccessible Cilician mountain passes, hoping for a reward in case Cyrus won. According to Diodorus (XIV 20), Syennesis conducted a double policy, sending one of his sons with a military contingent to Artaxerxes, in order to inform him about the intentions of Cyrus, while he sent another son to Cyrus, also with a group of soldiers. Whatever the case, the meeting between Syennesis and Cyrus was conducted in a friendly atmosphere. The Cilician king gave Cyrus money for the payment of his mercenaries, and Cyrus promised not to plunder his land any further. In addition, Cyrus presented Syennesis with presents which the Persian king usually gave to his closest followers: a horse with golden reins; a golden torque; a bracelet, an akinakes, and Persian clothes.

The Greeks started to suspect that Cyrus was planning to lead them against the king, and fearing for their fate refused to continue. Their commander Clearchus, of course, knew far in advance the real objective of the campaign. Cyrus, however, convinced the mercenaries that he was leading them against the Phoenician governor Abrocomas who hated him, and who was residing along the banks of the Euphrates. The Greeks did not fully believe Cyrus, but nevertheless decided to follow him in return for a rise in their pay. Cyrus promised to pay them one and a half times as much as before, namely instead of one daric a month, the mercenaries were to receive one and a half darics (for the wages of Cyrus' soldiers, see Marinovic 1958:70ff.).

When Cyrus and his army arrived at the large port of Issus in Cilicia, he was joined by 35 Peloponnesian ships and 25 from Ephesus, commanded by the Egyptian admiral Tamos, one of Cyrus' friends. In addition, another 400 Greek hoplites joined the army. These troops had defected from Abrocomas. There were also several hundreds of Greek mercenaries who joined Cyrus. The Spartan admiral Samios sailed along the Cilician coast at the head of his fleet, to stop any activity from the side of Syennesis, if indeed the Cilician king still had any hostile intentions.

The rebel army thereupon reached the Syrian gates between Cilicia and the highlands of Syria. The pass was blocked by two walls. The first was protected by Cilician guards, while the second wall should have been guarded by a Persian garrison. The passage through the gates was narrow and had steep uprising walls which went down to the sea. Above the walls rose the towers. This gate was regarded as impregnable, and with this point in mind Cyrus ordered his fleet to land troops on the other side of the walls, in case he and his army were stopped at the gates. Abrocomas, however, whose duty it was to guard the gates, heard about Cyrus' advance, and cowardly decided not to put up any resistance, and to lead his troops to the Persian king.

There were many discontented mercenaries who feared that they were marching upon the king, and two of the Greek commanders secretly fled by sea. Cyrus, after having summoned the remaining Greek commanders, told them that he could have captured the fugitives or arrest their families, which were living in the town of Tralles in Caria, but that he had decided not to do so. Instead he allowed their families to go wherever they liked in return for the former services of the Greek commanders. These words made a deep impression upon the Greeks, and subsequently they followed him deep into Mesopotamia.

In Syria, along the banks of the River Dardanus, Cyrus ordered the destruction of the parks and palaces which belonged to the satrap of the province 'Across-the-River', called Belesys.[2] When they finally arrived

---

[2] Belesys is also mentioned in Babylonian documents, with the name of Belshunu, the governor of Across-the-River (EKBK, 25, etc.; see Stolper 1987:389ff.).

at the town of Thapsacus in Syria, Cyrus summoned the Greek commanders and told them that he was leading them against the king in Babylon. He ordered them to tell this to the soldiers and to persuade them to follow him. The mercenaries took the opportunity to ask for another pay rise. Cyrus promised to pay each of them five silver minas per month and to continue the payment until the soldiers' return in Ionia.

While passing through Syria, the soldiers could collect wine and grain for their provisions. Soon afterwards, however, when the army passed through an open stretch of land along the left bank of the Euphrates, they had to eat their beasts of burden, as there was nothing else left to consume. While passing through a marshy area some of the carts got stuck and Cyrus thought that the soldiers were too slow in extracting the vehicles. In his anger, he ordered the surrounding Persian noblemen to occupy themselves with the matter. Taking off their purple coats, clothed in their luxurious chitons, with torques around their neck and other jewellery on their arms, they threw themselves in the mud and extricated the carts.

When Cyrus had passed through Syria, he began to speed up, correctly thinking that the more time he spent marching, the more time Artaxerxes would have in collecting an army. Eventually, when the army arrived in more fertile areas, it turned out that the grass had been burnt by the troops of Artaxerxes. The noble Persian Orontas, who had considerable experience in military matters, suggested to Cyrus that he, with a thousand horsemen, should hunt and kill the fire raisers. Cyrus agreed, but thereupon Orontas wrote a letter to Artaxerxes, informing him that he would come over to his side with his cavalry contingent. The letter was sent via a man whom Orontas regarded as trustworthy. The man, however, informed Cyrus about Orontas' intentions. Subsequently, Cyrus arrested the traitor. He summoned seven noble Persians plus Clearchus to his tent, and ordered the Greek hoplites to surround the place.

Cyrus told the assembled leaders that he wished to treat Orontas according to divine and human laws. Reminding the commanders that much earlier Orontas had betrayed him three times, but that he had forgiven him and had offered his right hand, Cyrus asked the accused, whether he, Cyrus, had done him any injustice. Orontas answered in the negative. Thereupon Cyrus asked Orontas whether once again he could become his friend. Orontas answered that Cyrus would never again trust him as a friend. Those present sentenced Orontas to death, and as a sign of their judgement they touched his belt. Thereupon they took Orontas to the tent of one of Cyrus' closest followers, his staff bearer Artapates. No one ever saw Orontas again.

When Cyrus arrived in Babylonia he drew up his forces in battle order as he expected contact with the king's army to be quickly established. On the following morning there arrived in the camp some defectors from the army of Artaxerxes. Shortly afterwards Cyrus summoned the Greek generals for counsel. If Xenophon (*Anab.* I 7.3) can be believed, Cyrus told them that the Greeks were stronger than 'the barbarians' and he urged them to be worthy of the freedom which was their fortune. According to Cyrus, the king's army was merely a huge body, and if the Greeks could withstand them from the very start of the battle, then victory would be theirs. Reminding them of the fact that the Persian empire was huge, saying that it stretched from the lands where it was too hot to live, to those areas in the far north where habitation was impossible because of the cold, he promised the Greeks that when they would win the battle, he would give his Greek friends the rule of complete districts, and, in addition, would remunerate every Greek soldier with a golden laurel wreath.

According to Xenophon (*Anab.* I 7.10-11), the army of Cyrus, at the beginning of the battle, consisted of 12,900 Greek mercenaries, 100,000 Persians and soldiers from other peoples, together with 20 scythe chariots. These chariots killed any man or beast which came in their way while they were moving. Artaxerxes' army, 'according to rumours', consisted of 1,200,000 men (the figure is undoubtedly exaggerated); 200 scythe chariots and 6,000 horsemen, commanded by the Persian Artagerses. According to Diodorus (XIV 19-21), Cyrus' army counted 70,000 Persians (including 30,000 horsemen) and 13,000 Greeks; Artaxerxes' army included 400,000 men. The same figure for the king's army is also presented by Plutarch in his biography of Artaxerxes (ch. 7) on the basis of information provided by Ctesias. E. Meyer has correctly suggested that these numbers were considerably exaggerated, as it would have been impossible for so many men to travel through the Syrian desert in one group. According to Meyer, there were not very many more Persians than Hellenes in Cyrus' army, while Artaxerxes' army may not have exceeded 40,000 men. Thus, the forces on both sides were roughly equal (Meyer 1939, Vol. V, p. 185).

The king's army was commanded by Abrocomas, Tissaphernes, Gobryas[3] and Arbaces. Abrocomas, however, was at the time travelling with his forces from Phoenicia to Babylonia, and he arrived too late at the battlefield.

---

[3] In texts from the Murashu archive, which date to a period between 421 and 417 B.C., reference is made to 'the governor of Akkad' (i.e. Babylonia), called Gubaru (BE X, 101 etc.). It would appear that this is the same man who is referred to by Xenophon with the name of Gobryas (see Röllig 1971:672; Schwenzner 1922-23:247).

Artaxerxes' army withdrew, leaving the crossing over the Euphrates and some of its tributaries open to the rebels. Cyrus concluded that the king feared a battle and had fled. The rebels therefore advanced at all ease, some even without carrying their weapons, because they thought they had won without a fight. Soon, however, the noble Persian Pategyas, one of Cyrus' closest followers, arrived on a horse which had foam at its mouth, and cried out in Persian and Greek that Artaxerxes and his army were closing in. Panic broke out in Cyrus' camp, because the soldiers thought that they could not prepare for the battle in time. Cyrus, however, descended from his vehicle, put on his armour, and mounted his horse. He took his spear and ordered his troops to arm themselves and to draw up the ranks.

The battle was fought on September 3, 401 B.C., 90 kilometres to the north of Babylon, near the village of Cunaxa. The Greeks were placed on the right wing of Cyrus' army, together with approximately a thousand Paphlagonian horsemen. They were commanded by Clearchus. The main assistant of Cyrus, Ariaeus, was placed on the left wing, together with part of the Persian forces. Cyrus took up his place in the centre. He was surrounded by 600 horsemen, clad in armour and armed with Greek swords. Cyrus, however, did not wear a helmet, thus showing his contempt of danger. The king's forces advanced with measured steps in absolute silence. They were drawn up according to their ethnic origin. On the left wing were the horsemen and troops in white armour, who were commanded by Tissaphernes; next to them there were the light-armed troops and the Egyptian hoplites with long wooden shields. At a significant distance in front of these troops there were the scythe chariots.

With the help of an interpreter, thus to prevent any misunderstanding, Cyrus instructed Clearchus to lead the Greek mercenaries to the centre of the enemy, where the king would be. Clearchus, however, fearing being surrounded by the greater number of the enemy, eventually did not obey the order and answered that he would take care that all would be well, and he also asked Cyrus not to take any risks. Thus, Clearchus, who was well experienced in military tactics, did not fulfil his main strategic duty, namely to defeat the centre of the enemy ranks. He remained at the right wing and confronted the troops of Tissaphernes.

When the Greek mercenaries attacked, the left wing of the royal army was pushed back. The dreaded chariots proved to be of no avail to Artaxerxes as the Greeks simply let them pass. When it was seen that the Greeks pushed back and pursued the fleeing soldiers of the king, those surrounding Cyrus bowed to the earth and greeted him as their new ruler.

Artaxerxes, who was in the centre of his army, outside of the main battle area, started to withdraw his forces in a half-circle formation. Fearing that the king would attack and destroy the Greek soldiers from the back, Cyrus and his 600 horsemen plunged forwards into the centre of the king's army. He forced a group of horsemen who protected the king to withdraw and then killed with his own hands their commander, Artagerses. During the fight, however, the bodyguards of Cyrus became dispersed and Cyrus was left almost without support. When he spotted the king, Cyrus exclaimed: ''I see him'', and again he plunged forwards, to wound his brother in the chest, straight through the cuirass. At that moment, however, Cyrus received a heavy blow with a lance on his head and he was killed together with eight of his closest followers from among the Persian nobility. When Artapates, the prince's staff bearer, saw Cyrus' body, he dismounted from his horse and, dropping himself on Cyrus' body, committed suicide, thus showing his sympathy for his deceased friend. The closest followers of the king, ''according to a Persian custom'', decapitated the body of Cyrus and Artaxerxes held it by the hairs, showing it to all to convince them that Cyrus was dead. According to Ctesias, not less than 20,000 soldiers of Artaxerxes were left behind on the battle field, although the king was told that only 9,000 had died (see: Plutarch, *Art.* 13).

After Cyrus' death, his Persian troops which were commanded by Ariaeus fled from the scene of battle, while the Greek mercenaries continued the fight, not knowing that the prince had died. They came to regard their tactical success as an overall victory. On being informed of Cyrus' death, the following day, the Greek commanders offered to take Ariaeus to the Persian throne. He answered, however, that many Persians were higher in status than he was, and that they would never recognize him as their new king. He suggested that the Greeks should withdraw together with him to Ionia. The Greek commanders and Ariaeus promised not to betray each other. They killed a bull, a wild boar and a sheep under a shield, whereupon they put their swords and the points of their lances in the blood, as a symbol of their pledge.

On the day after the battle, messengers arrived in the Greek camp, who were sent by the king and Tissaphernes. In their midst was a Greek who was in the service of Tissaphernes. They proposed that the mercenaries should lay down their weapons and ask the king for clemency. The mercenaries replied that they were the victors, rather than the king, and so refused to disarm themselves. Some days later, other messengers arrived, this time bringing the proposition of an alliance. Tissaphernes promised the mercenaries, because he lived in Asia Minor himself, to lead them back to their homeland. An agreement was made, to the extent that on their march the Greeks would not plunder the land, but should buy their provisions; the Persians were obliged, under the conditions of the treaty, to lead the Greeks back to Ionia, so that hence they could return to Greece. As a sign of the treaty the two parties swore solemn oaths and shook each other's right hand.

After this, Ariaeus and his followers were visited by their brothers and other relatives. They convinced them that the king would show mercy when they would come over to his side. As a result of these talks, the followers of Ariaeus began to behave in a more unfriendly manner towards the Hellenes.

Having reached the city of Opis in Babylonia, the mercenaries saw an army which came from Ecbatana and Susa to assist the king. Being experienced in military matters, Clearchus ordered his men to advance forward, two by two, and to halt from time to time. This gave the Persians the impression that they were dealing with a large army.

When the Greeks arrived at some villages in Babylonia which belonged to Parysatis, the mother of the Persian king, Tissaphernes permitted them to plunder, only forbidding them to take away the slaves.

Having been hindered by hostile actions from the side of Tissaphernes, Clearchus again spoke to him and suggested that the Greek mercenaries should be used to suppress the Pisidians and Mysians, who caused considerable damage to the Persians by their raids, or for the suppression of the Egyptian revolt. The deceitful Tissaphernes tried to pacify Clearchus and invited him for dinner and in passing remarked that only one could carry the upright tiara, but that supported by the Greek mercenaries, everyone could dream about it. Tissaphernes asked Clearchus and his commanders to come to him for consultations, and to remove all misunderstandings. When the Greek leaders arrived in Tissaphernes' camp, the officers were treacherously killed, while those in high command were arrested (later they were taken to the king and decapitated). Only one of the officers, seriously wounded in the abdomen, managed to reach the Greek camp and, holding his intestines with his hands, informed the mercenaries about what had happened. At approximately the same time the Persian army under Ariaeus went over to the king's side. Thus the Greeks found themselves far from their homeland, in a strange country, surrounded by the enemy, without allies and provisions and even without a command of their own. They did not panic, however, but chose new leaders and at the cost of heavy losses (of the 13,000 men only 8,600 survived the campaign) they reached the city of Trapezus on the Black Sea in March 400 B.C. The march from Mesopotamia to Trapezus, which lasted for fifteen months, took them straight through the regions of Assyria and Armenia (for their marching route, see

Barnett 1963). Further to the west, in Asia Minor, the mercenaries were eventually added to a Spartan army which under the command of Thibron fought against Pharnabazus and Tissaphernes.

The campaign of the Greek mercenaries was at first glance an ephemeral event, soon to be forgotten by the Persians. In reality, however, it had been of great significance for future events. With their own eyes the Greeks had seen the fantastic riches of the subject peoples of the king, and at the same time they had noticed the weakness of the state and the strength of their own forces which offered the possibility of defeating the Persians on their own territory. Xenophon (*Anab.* I 5.9) acutely observed that "the empire of the king is strong in the expanse of its territory and the multitude of its peoples, but its weakness lies in the long distances of its communication routes and the dispersal of its forces in case of a sudden attack from the outside." Having returned to Greece, a poor country which was going through a deep crisis, and where the masses of impoverished people did not know how to feed themselves, the mercenaries told their compatriots about the richness in provisions, herds of cattle, gold and silver of the Achaemenid empire, and how easily they could extricate themselves from their miserable situation by occupying the lands of the Persians. Historians therefore correctly regard the journey by Cyrus' mercenaries as a significant precedent for the military campaigns of Alexander of Macedonia.

After his victory, Artaxerxes refrained from conducting a harsh policy towards Cyrus' followers, who were protected in all possible manners by Parysatis; only later did he remove, one by one, the old friends of Cyrus. As a first move in this course of action Artaxerxes only punished the Mede Arbaces, who during the battle had defected to Cyrus, but after his death returned to the king. Artaxerxes did not accuse Arbaces of defection, but of cowardice. Artaxerxes ordered him to go, for one whole day, through a busy square, putting on his neck a naked whore. For his double policy, Artaxerxes removed Syennesis from the throne of Cilicia. The land was turned into a regular satrapy (see Diodorus XIV 20).

Artaxerxes remunerated those men who had distinguished themselves in the crushing of the revolt and who had saved his life. These rewards, however, turned into a bloody tragedy for those who received them. Artaxerxes ascribed to himself the killing of Cyrus. A Carian, who had given Cyrus the lethal wound, was acclaimed by the king as the first messenger of Cyrus' death. The simple-minded Carian started to say that he received the reward for having killed Cyrus. Being informed about this, Artaxerxes ordered his decapitation. Parysatis, however, remarked that such an easy death would not be proper, and, after having asked that the Carian would be handed over to her, ordered the executioner to torture him for ten days, and subsequently to tear out his eyes and to fill his throat with molten copper. The noble Persian Mithridates, who had afflicted Cyrus with the first wound, was rewarded by Artaxerxes for having found Cyrus' horse blanket. Mithridates remained silent about the insult, and complained to nobody. Soon, however, Mithridates was tricked. One day he appeared at a court dinner dressed in a valuable garment and with costly jewellery, which had been given to him by the king. During the occasion he had too much to drink. A clever eunuch congratulated Mithridates with the high honours shown to him by the king for only finding Cyrus' horse blanket. The drunken Mithridates then loudly proclaimed that his spear had wounded Cyrus in the temple. These words were immediately passed on to Artaxerxes, who ordered that the braggart should be severely tortured. They put him in a trough and placed a second trough on top, so that only his head and hands stuck outside while the rest of his body remained inside. Thereupon they put the troughs into the sun, which blinded the eyes of the man. Subsequently Mithridates was fed, and when he refused to take more food, they forcibly put the food into his mouth. After feeding him, they put a mixture of milk and honey into his mouth and covered his face with it. Flies landed on the head of the unfortunate man, and worms appeared in his bodily waste inside the trough. Gradually Mithridates' body was eaten while he was still alive. Death came slowly to Mithridates, and seventeen days were past before he died.

Now only two enemies remained for Parysatis to deal with: Tissaphernes and the eunuch Masabates, who had cut off the head and hands of Cyrus. Tissaphernes remained in the king's favour, however, and Masabates' behaviour was beyond reproach. Delaying revenge on the influential Tissaphernes, Parysatis played dice with the unsuspecting Artaxerxes, with one of their eunuchs as the stake, and when she won, she received Masabates from the king. For his death, she chose to have him skinned alive.

CHAPTER THIRTY-FIVE

THE PEACE OF ANTALCIDAS

After the crushing of Cyrus' revolt, the Spartans expected a military reaction from the side of the Persians as a consequence of their assistance to Cyrus. Besides, the Greek cities of Asia Minor, which had previously been governed by Cyrus and subsequently gained their independence, asked Sparta for assistance. Tissaphernes, who in addition to Caria had received command over all the lands which were formerly controlled by Cyrus, and who now also fulfilled the function of commander-in-chief of all Persian forces in Asia Minor, was at the height of his power. He attempted to subject the various Greek cities along the coast in order to collect their taxes. This wish was completely in accordance with the treaties with Sparta, concluded in the years 412-410 B.C. Sparta, however, after its victory over Athens, had become the leading power of Greece, and would not openly leave the Greek towns of Asia Minor to their fate. It should also be noted that by the end of the fifth century B.C., the Greeks of Asia Minor gradually started to feel a common bond, and in favourable circumstances would have been prepared to fight for their liberation from Persian domination (Seager & Tuplin 1980:141ff.).

In 400 B.C., Sparta sent five thousand soldiers to Ephesus in Asia Minor, under the command of Thibron. The relatively small force was, however, not capable of an active policy, and only strove to defend the Greek towns of Aeolis against the Persians. From their side, the Persian administrators, after the crushing of Cyrus' rebellion, moved closer towards the democratic regimes, and started to remove the aristocratic rule from some of the Greek towns of Asia Minor. At about the same time the influential groups of the urban population strove towards independence from the Persians, while the Greek farmers in the countryside apparently preferred Persian rule to that by the Spartans or Athenians (see Lewis 1977:115ff.).

Cyprus also quickly became involved in the hostilities between Sparta and the Persians. Around 425 B.C., Baalmilk II, king of Kition and Idalion, conquered the city of Salamis with the help of a Phoenician fleet, and he killed the local Greek tyrant. The son of the tyrant, Evagoras, managed to escape from the island. He returned in 411 and successfully attacked the palace during the night. As a result he was able to reestablish his family's authority in the city. In the following year, Evagoras sent grain to the Athenians, who at that time were at war with

Persia, and in return he was granted Athenian citizen rights. When in 405 B.C. the Athenian fleet was defeated by the Spartans at Aegospotami, the Athenian admiral Conon, together with the ships that were saved, fled to Evagoras. With the help of the Athenians Evagoras started to expand his authority, subduing neighbouring Greek and Phoenician towns. Because of this development Evagoras' relationship with the Persian administration became tense. He could, however, only carry out his plans as a subject of the Great king. On the advice of Conon, Evagoras turned towards the Persian king. In this he was helped by certain Greeks who resided at the royal court, including the king's personal physician, Ctesias. He asked the king to recognize his conquests on Cyprus. Simultaneously Evagoras sent tribute and gifts to the Persian court. In addition, he asked Artaxerxes to equip, in secret, a fleet on Cyprus and to appoint Conon as its commander. Artaxerxes decided to grant both of Evagoras' requests, and he appointed Conon as the commander of a Persian fleet. At the beginning of 397 B.C. the satrap Pharnabazus arrived on Cyprus, bringing five hundred talents of silver for the equipment of the fleet. In the meantime the building of the fleet was hidden from the Lacedaimonians, who in 398 B.C. had sent ambassadors to the Great King in order to conclude a peace treaty. Tissaphernes and Pharnabazus gave the impression that they were prepared to negotiate with Sparta. The king's officials, however, dragged their feet over the consultations.

In 397 B.C. open war broke out between Sparta and Persia. The Spartan king Agesilaus arrived in Asia Minor to command the Lacedaimonian forces in the area. The Spartan army was forced to conduct a somewhat defensive war due to their limited numbers. Nevertheless, Tissaphernes was left without any advantages and so, in the spring of 396 B.C., he agreed with his adversaries to a cease-fire of three months. At the same time he promised to suggest to the king that autonomy should be granted to the Greek cities of Asia Minor. Tissaphernes, however, did not intend to grant independence to the Greeks. Instead he asked the king to send a large army for a renewal of the war. Simultaneously he asked for assistance from Pharnabazus. He could do so in his capacity of supreme commander of the Persian forces in Asia Minor. The Persian leaders, however, disliked each other. Pharnabazus insisted that it was necessary to conduct an open war with the Greeks. Tissaphernes decided against this, mainly because he was not used to such a course of action. Thereupon Pharnabazus went to the king with a complaint about the inactivity of Tissaphernes. Artaxerxes, however, did not take this complaint seriously, although he provided Pharnabazus with money for the building and equipment of a large fleet.

In the year 396 B.C. Tissaphernes had collected together a large army and he renewed the war. At the same time Agesilaus, whose army by then counted about 20,000 men, sent Lysander with a large force to the Hellespont. The latter managed to win the influential Persian Spithridates for the Spartan cause. Previously Spithridates had been an official of Pharnabazus. He arrived in the Spartan camp together with two hundred horsemen and certain treasures that had been under his protection. He betrayed his own leaders because his daughter was kept in Pharnabazus' harem as a concubine, after having been promised a marriage. Pharnabazus still held great hopes of marrying one of the king's daughters.

Agesilaus unexpectedly invaded Hellespontine Phrygia and destroyed many towns, after having given the impression of planning that he intended to invade Caria, where Tissaphernes' residence was located and where the latter was concentrating his forces. In the spring of 395 B.C., while Tissaphernes' main forces were still in Caria, Agesilaus attacked and defeated a Persian corps of cavalry near Sardis. These unexpected raids caused considerable damage to the Persians. In particular, the paradise and the estate of Tissaphernes in Lydia were destroyed. Some days later Persian cavalry arrived in the region and killed many Greeks who were engaged in plundering. This was, however, only a minor success for the Persians. For the rest, their position in Asia Minor was weak. Yet, the Persians adhered little significance to their difficulties in Asia Minor, and they regarded these problems as forming part of the many border fights which harassed the Empire.

On the advice of Conon, the Persians subsequently tried to gain a victory at sea. The Athenian admiral managed to clear some islands along the Ionian coast from Spartan garrisons. But Conon only succeeded in equipping forty ships, because the main part of the money, destined by the king for the equipment of the fleet, had fallen into the hands of Persian officials. At the beginning of 396 B.C. Conon sailed towards the southern borders of Caria. Having managed to increase his fleet to twice its former size, he attacked Rhodes and forced the Lacedaimonians to leave the island. Thereupon Conon succeeded in confiscating a large transport of grain, which had been sent by the Egyptian pharaoh to Sparta. At Rhodes, Conon's fleet was joined by eighty Phoenician and Cilician vessels. He did not receive, however, more money to continue the war, and his request for more funds, directed to Tissaphernes, remained unanswered. If Cornelius Nepos can be believed (*Con.* 2-3), Conon personally went to the king to complain about Tissaphernes, and Parysatis was pleased to hear these accusations against the main enemy of the late Cyrus, her younger son. Conon, however, could not personally see the king, as he did not want to make a proskynesis (for which the Athenians could prosecute him), and he expressed his complaints about Tissaphernes to the king via the chiliarch Tithraustes. Having received more money and the mandate to continue the war at sea, Conon returned at the beginning of 394 B.C. to his fleet.

Parysatis now moved towards the fulfilment of her dearest wish, namely the punishment of Tissaphernes, and in all possible manners attempted to incite the king against him. Artaxerxes finally decided that Tissaphernes had played a double game and that he had the ultimate purpose of handing over to Sparta Persian interests in Asia Minor. In 395 B.C. he ordered the death of his leading commander and diplomat, a man with a wide horizon and a match for his Greek opponents. The execution was entrusted to Tithraustes. The king handed him two letters. One of these was addressed to Tissaphernes. In it the king wrote that he left it to Tissaphernes' insight how to wage the war with Sparta. The other letter was addressed to Ariaeus, the former friend of Cyrus the Younger. This letter contained an order to assist in the execution of Tissaphernes. At that time Ariaeus resided in Colossae, in Phrygia. Having received the king's letter, he invited Tissaphernes for a discussion of some urgent matters. Tissaphernes arrived with thirty Greek bodyguards, leaving his army at Sardis. Inside Ariaeus' palace, he started to undress before having a bath. When Tissaphernes had laid down his akinakes, Ariaeus and his men overpowered him, put him inside a closed vehicle and sent him off to Tithraustes, who was at Celaenae in Phrygia. There Tithraustes decapitated Tissaphernes and sent the head to the king, who, in his turn, passed it on to Parysatis. Silver coins are still extant which bear the portrait of Tissaphernes, wearing the Persian tiara. On certain of these coins there is the symbol of Athens, namely the owl, and a Greek legend saying 'king'. These coins were probably minted by Tissaphernes to pay his Greek mercenaries (for references about the relatively recent find of these coins, see Schwabacher 1957:28; for Tissaphernes, see Walser 1984:84ff.; Westlake 1981).

As a reward for his actions, Ariaeus received the satrapy of Caria, while Tithraustes occupied Tissaphernes' place. When Conon told Tithraustes that funds were lacking for a continuation of the war, the latter gave Conon two hundred talents of silver from the property of Tissaphernes. Contrary to his predecessor, however, Tithraustes was not particularly competent in warfare and diplomacy, and nobody expected much of him in that direction. He made it known to Agesilaus that he would recognize the political autonomy of the Greek cities of Asia Minor, as long as they continued to pay tribute to the king, including arrears for the previous years. In addition, Tithraustes added that Agesilaus and his troops could now return to the mainland, because the culprit for the misery inflicted upon Greeks and Persians alike, had been executed. In his reply Agesilaus stated that only the Spartan authorities could decide how to answer these proposals. Thereupon Tithraustes gave Agesilaus thirty silver talents for 'travel expenses' and asked him, while waiting for an answer from Sparta, to go to the domains of Pharnabazus and to plunder them. Agesilaus agreed to maintain a cease-fire for six months and accepted the offered funds.

In the autumn of 395 B.C., Agesilaus left Tissaphernes' former lands and started to pillage the domains of Pharnabazus. Otys, the prince of Paphlagonia, who had defected from the Persian king, joined forces with the Lacedaimonians. The Spartan forces were also strengthened by the fugitive Persian Spithridates. Ariaeus, who was trying to gain independence, was also prepared to join the coalition. It was decided that the war with Persia should be continued with united forces. During the winter months Agesilaus remained in Dascyleium, the capital of Pharnabazus' satrapy, where he destroyed the paradise and estate.

Soon afterwards, Agesilaus met Pharnabazus, at the latter's request, for negotiations. The adversaries shook hands and, according to etiquette, Pharnabazus, the elder of the two, was the first to speak. Reminding Agesilaus that in the past he had assisted Sparta, Pharnabazus complained about the plundering by the Lacedaimonian forces of his palace, and also about the destruction of his beautiful parks, full of trees and wild animals. Agesilaus answered that he was at war with the Persian king, and that his actions were a result of this war, but that he felt no personal feelings of hostility towards Pharnabazus. In addition, he suggested that Pharnabazus should join the Spartan alliance. Pharnabazus answered that he would conclude a treaty with Sparta, if the Great King did not appoint him as the supreme commander of the Persian forces in Asia Minor. If this position fell to him, he would support the cause of Artaxerxes. The professional mercenary Agesilaus fully understood the intentions of his opponent and agreed with his sly decision. In addition, he, from his side, promised not to plunder, at least if not pressed by urgent needs, the lands of Pharnabazus. After this Agesilaus and Pharnabazus' son concluded a treaty of hospitality, which would prove to be of the greatest help to the Persian young man, when he was later forced to flee to the Peloponnesos. Although the Lacedaimonians withdrew from the domains of Pharnabazus, the latter nevertheless, on the advice of Conon, started to send money for the bribery of Greek political leaders in order to ensure that they would set up their city states against Sparta.

Soon a rift became apparent between the Lacedaimonians and Spithridates and his followers, who, although allies of Sparta, were left out from the distribution of the war booty. With his forces Spithridates marched to Sardis for negotiations with Ariaeus concerning a change over to the side of the king.

While Sparta was conducting an offensive war against Persia, the bloodthirsty and vindictive Parysatis was continuously engaged in palace intrigues. Her name (Old Persian *Parušyātiš*) literally means '(having) much blessing', but in reality she caused only misfortune and misery. Stateira, the wife of the king, and Parysatis were not friends, and each of them was seeking the opportunity to get rid of her opponent. They had to meet regularly, because the king was used to eating with his mother and wife, whereby the first was seated higher than the king, and the other lower. It is true that Artaxerxes tried to change these old established customs, and he also invited his younger brothers for dinner. Stateira also infringed upon the etiquette of the court by showing herself to the people in an open vehicle and permitting the spectators to come closer and to greet her. Parysatis used these activities of her daughter-in-law to bring her into discredit, because according to ancient customs the queen should not show herself to the people. Parysatis, however, who at that time was an old woman, allowed a much more serious breach of court etiquette. For instance, a certain Orontes was accused of having slept with her, and on the orders of the king he was sentenced to death.

Stateira and Parysatis, when they had to dine together, ate from the same dish and from the same plates, because they both feared poisoning. With the help of one of her slave girls, however, Parysatis showed extreme ingenuity. She cut open a bird which was to be eaten at dinner with a knife which on one side was covered in poison. Parysatis ate some of the bird while the poisoned portion was handed to Stateira. The Queen soon died in extreme pain. In Persia there was a law against poisoners, according to which the head of the accused was laid upon a flat stone. Thereupon the head was pressed with another stone until the skull burst open. The king's mother, however, did not fear such punishment. Artaxerxes ordered her to be exiled to Babylon and added that as long as she lived he would never go there.

After some time, however, Parysatis not only managed to return to Persia, but also regained her former influence over the king. In the meantime Artaxerxes had fallen in love with his own daughter Atossa, and Parysatis persuaded him to marry her. Such a marriage was forbidden by law, but Parysatis said that the king was Persian law himself, and its sole judge, whether it was good or not. On the basis of the work by Heraclides of Cyme, Plutarch said that Artaxerxes also married his second daughter, Amestris.

The king's courtiers, being involved in various intrigues, paid little attention to developments in Asia Minor, even though the Persians suffered one defeat after the other. This incited Tithraustes to take the well tried-out road of diplomatic bribery. He sent Timocrates of Rhodes to Greece and provided him with gold to bribe important politicians so that these should press their fellow citizens to wage war on Sparta. With the help of Persian gold, the cities of Corinth, Athens, Argos and Thebes concluded an alliance to fight against Sparta. Thus, in 395 B.C., the so-called Corinthian War broke out, and Sparta had to fight a simultaneous war on two fronts, against Persia and against a coalition of Greek city-states. Egypt refrained from assisting Sparta, in spite of the help that it had received from the Lacedaimonians in the past. Apparently, the Egyptian pharaoh was under pressure by Evagoras from Cyprus, the ally of Athens. On August 10, 394 B.C., the combined Persian Greek fleet, consisting of ninety vessels from Cyprus, Rhodes and Athens, and commanded by Conon and Pharnabazus, defeated near Knidos the Spartans who were commanded by Peisander. Of the 85 Spartan triremes, 45 were sunk, and 40 ships, together with 500 men, were captured. Peisander died in the battle. Sparta would need a further ten years to recover from this defeat. All the islands west of the coast of Asia Minor defected from the Spartan side, and certain Greek towns, such as Ephesus, Mytilene, etc., voluntarily joined the Persian camp. Thus, the Persians achieved great successes and even started to organize raids upon the coastal regions of the Greek mainland.

In 394 B.C., the Spartan king Agesilaus was forced to return to Sparta. As a reason for his return he said that "30,000 Persian bowmen[1] have driven me out of Asia Minor." According to Plutarch, the sum of 30,000 darics was distributed on behalf of Artaxerxes II among Athenian and Theban politicians, to form a coalition against Sparta. In July, 394 B.C., Sparta succeeded in defeating the coalition near Corinth, and again in August near Coronea. At the same time the Lacedaimonian army, under the command of Thibron, raided the royal domains in Asia Minor.

Around 392 B.C., important administrative changes took place in Asia Minor. The dominant position of the Lydian satrap was weakened. Struthas was appointed as satrap of Ionia, and Autophradates was made satrap of Lydia. Simultaneously Caria fell into the hands of a local leader called Hecatomnus. In 391 B.C., the Persians led by Struphas defeated the Spartan army of Thibron, and the latter was killed in the battle.

In 390 B.C., Evagoras, the king of Salamis on Cyprus, who up to then had acknowledged his allegiance to Artaxerxes II and had actively par-

---

[1] A shooting bowman is depicted on one side of the Persian darics.

ticipated in the talks between the Athenians and the Persians, started to act in a more independent manner and to bring more towns under his rule. The people from Soli, Kition and Amathus, however, who were predominantly of Phoenician descent, did not submit to him and sent messengers to the Great King with a request for help. Artaxerxes ordered the Lydian satrap Autophradates and the Carian leader Hecatomnus to equip a fleet and land army, in order to attack Evagoras. The latter, in his turn, turned for help to the Athenians, and they sent their general Chabrias to Cyprus, at the head of a fleet and an army. In 389 B.C. a military alliance was concluded between Evagoras, Athens and Achoris, who was the pharaoh of Egypt, which was directed against Persia. Then, to demonstrate his independence from Persia, Evagoras started to issue golden coins with the legend 'king Evagoras'. With the help of Chabrias' troops he managed to subdue almost all of Cyprus. Soon afterwards Hecatomnus, who commanded the Persian fleet against Cyprus, started secret negotiations and assisted Evagoras with funds. Around 388 B.C., Artaxerxes recalled Struthas and appointed Tiribazus as satrap of Lydia and Ionia. Tiribazus was his old, trusted counsellor and the former satrap of Armenia. Pharnabazus was also recalled to Susa under the pretext of his marriage to a daughter of the king, and in his place the king appointed Ariobarzanes as the new satrap of Phrygia. In 387 B.C. Tiribazus imprisoned Conon, on the accusation that he was not interested in the re-establishment of Persian control over the Greek cities of Asia Minor; instead he wished to use Artaxerxes' fleet for the strengthening of Athens' power. Conon, however, succeeded in escaping to Evagoras on Cyprus, where soon afterwards he died of an illness.

The military activities continued, but once again Persian gold proved stronger than Greek weapons. Sparta was defeated by the Persian fleet, which subsequently became master of the Aegean Sea and carried out destructive raids on the Peloponnesos. Thereupon the Lacedaimonians decided to enter into negotiations with Artaxerxes. Sparta was also driven to seek peace by the threat that Athens would again emerge as a major state. From their side, the Persians hoped to obtain a free hand to contain the aspirations of Evagoras and to bring Egypt back into the folds of the Empire. Tiribazus therefore secretly supported the Spartans with money, with the objective that they would withdraw from the war. In addition, Persia demanded that the Corinthian League would stop its military actions against Sparta. The Athenians, however, did not want peace, because they feared to lose their domination of certain islands in the Aegean Sea. The Thebans also feared peace negotiations, because they were afraid to lose their grip on Boeotia.

In 387 B.C., there arrived, at the satrapal court of Tiribazus at Sardis,

a Spartan delegation headed by Antalcidas, with the objective of concluding a peace treaty (on this and other Greek embassies to Persia, see
Hofstetter 1972:94ff.). Hence also diplomats from other Greek states, including Athens, appeared. Showing the king's seal, Tiribazus listed the
conditions demanded by Artaxerxes. The Athenians, dreaming of a
return of their authority over the coastal regions of Asia Minor, rejected
the proposals, and thus the negotiations dragged on. The Athenians,
however, could not prevent the conclusion of a coalition between Sparta
and Persia, while at the same time important Athenian politicians filled
their pockets with Persian gold.

In 386 B.C., at Susa, the so-called King's Peace, or the Peace of Antalcidas was concluded and ratified by Persia and all Greek states. Essentially, this was not a peace treaty concluded by two equal powers, but a
decree which was dictated to the Greeks by the Persian king Artaxerxes
(for the text of the treaty, see Von Scala 1898:114; cf. Wilcken 1942). According to this treaty, which was a humiliation to the Greeks, and ex-
cerpts of which are contained in the 'Greek History' by Xenophon
(*Hellenica* V 1.31), the Persians won back their domination over the
eastern coast of the Aegean and re-instated their control over the long lost
cities of Asia Minor, which were now made fully subject to the Persian
king. Cyprus also had to return to Persian domination. The king granted
independence to the remaining Greek towns and districts, bar the islands
of Lemnos, Imbros and Skyros, which remained in Athenian hands. All
Greek states were obliged to heed the conditions of this Peace, and any
infringement by one of them would bring war, not only from the side of
the Persians, but also from all the other Greeks. The Peace of Antalcidas
also forbade any coalition between the Greek states. The only exception
was made for Sparta and its allies, who were subservient to the Persians
and, giving the cities of Asia Minor to the Persians, had attempted to win
hegemony in Greece at this high price. It is not surprising, therefore, that
Artaxerxes favoured Antalcidas above all Greek ambassadors. During a
festive dinner, the king took off his head wreath, submerged it in perfume, and handed it to Antalcidas. Later on, the dissatisfied Athenians
executed their greedy ambassador Timagoras, who had accepted the
king's gold, silver, a luxurious couch and even eighty cows with herds-
men on the pretext that he had developed some illness and therefore
needed a continuous supply of fresh milk. The carriers, who had
transported Timagoras to the coast, were paid four talents of silver from
the royal treasury. In addition, another Athenian accused Timagoras of
the fact that, at the time of their stay in Susa, he did not want to be in
the same tent as him, and often in his speeches supported the Theban
case. Only the Theban ambassador Pelopidas declined the costly presents

from the king, apart from those which were symbols of a good relationship. At the Theban's request, Artaxerxes declared that the Thebans had been old allies of the king, because at the time of Xerxes' campaign against Greece the Thebans had sided with the Persians.

Thus, with the help of his gold Artaxerxes II succeeded in defeating the Greeks, something which since the time of Darius I and Xerxes had proved to be impossible to achieve with weapons. Still in 411 B.C., the Athenian playwright Aristophanes (*Lysistr.* 1133-1134) had pointed out that the Greeks had one common enemy, namely Persia. And after the suppression of Cyrus the Younger's revolt this idea was also upheld by Xenophon. Persian diplomacy, however, managed to divide the Greeks and to defeat them without a fight.

The Greek states, however, were dissatisfied with the policy of Sparta, which submissively heeded the conditions of the Peace. Soon a democratic revolution took place at Thebes, the oligarchic rulers were deposed, and the Spartan garrison which was stationed at Thebes was forced to capitulate. In defiance of the conditions of the Peace, certain Boeotian towns united around Thebes, which after 378 B.C. became the most powerful political force in Greece. This coalition, directed against Sparta, was also supported by Athens. In the same year, the Athenians founded the Second Athenian Sea Empire. Sparta suffered defeats from both of these coalitions and lost its hegemony in Greece. The Persian king acted as intermediary in this internal Greek war and in 366 B.C. sent an embassy in order to persuade the warring parties to conclude an all-embracing peace treaty. Thus ended the Boeotian War, which had lasted for five years.

Taking advantage of the peace with the Greeks, Artaxerxes II made an attempt to subdue the tribes of the Cadusians in the Median satrapy, along the Caspian Sea. The punitive expedition, however, proved unsuccessful, and the king lost many men and almost all of his horses. In fact, he was lucky to escape with his life. The Persians were unable to defeat the Cadusians who had long ago been submitted by Cyrus II, but who had rebelled in the middle of the fifth century B.C. During the reign of Artaxerxes II, the Cardouchoi, the Tibareni and other peoples also succeeded in gaining their independence.

CHAPTER THIRTY-SIX

WAR WITH EGYPT AND THE GREAT REVOLT
OF THE SATRAPS

At the end of the fifth century B.C., the Egyptians had successfully revolted against Persian domination of their country. The Peace of Antalcidas provided the Persians with the possibility of making an attempt to bring the country back under their control. In 400 B.C., Tamos, an Egyptian from Memphis, who at the time of Cyrus the Younger had been deputy governor of Ionia (some classical writers wrote that he was the hyparch of the region), remained loyal to his friend after Cyrus' death. He fled together with his sons (apart from Glos, who later became one of the generals of the Persian king), the fleet and treasury to Amyrtaeus in Egypt, to ask him for protection against the wrath of Tissaphernes.[1] Amyrtaeus, however, ordered the execution of all the refugees and he confiscated their possessions. In the following year he was dethroned himself (he possibly died in the coup). An Aramaic letter, dated October 1, 399 B.C., contains important political news about the change of power (Kraeling 1953, no. 13; see also Porten & Yardeni 1986:46). According to Manetho, Amyrtaeus was the only king of the 28th dynasty and ruled for six years, from 404 till 399 B.C. The Demotic Chronicle reports the following about Amyrtaeus: "The first pharaoh that emerged subsequent to the foreign Medians, was Amyrtaeus ... His son did not succeed him" (DC; cf. Meyer 1915:297ff.). The Egyptian throne was then occupied by the founder of the 29th dynasty, Nepherites I, from the town of Mendes in the central Delta (for Egyptian sources about this king, see Gauthier 1907-1917:161ff.). In 395 B.C. he sent many ships in support of the Spartan fleet which was assembling at Rhodes, but these vessels fell into the hands of the Athenians who were currently at war with Sparta. During the reign of Nepherites there apparently came an end to the Jewish military colony at Elephantine.

In 393 B.C., Nepherites was succeeded by his son Achoris. He reigned until the year 382 B.C. and followed an active policy in the Mediterranean area. Notably, he entered into anti-Persian alliances with the Athenians, Evagoras of Cyprus, the city of Barka in Libya, and also with the rebellious tribes of the Pisidians in Asia Minor and the Arabs in

---

[1] Diodorus (XIV 35.3) reported that Tamos fled to Psammetichus. This is an obvious mistake, for at that time Amyrtaeus was pharaoh.

Palestine. Meanwhile he started to transform Egypt into a maritime power and he strengthened his army with Greek mercenaries. Many monuments have been preserved which date back to his reign. They testify to economic growth and large-scale building activities. Egypt, however, proved unable to reach the economic level which it had attained during the reign of Amasis before the conquest of the country by the Persians. Although Egypt had witnessed considerable economic growth during the reign of Darius I, the country sunk into decline during the later Achaemenids because of the continuous drain of silver, in the form of tribute, to Persia. This silver was used as money in Egypt. The continuing wars and insurgencies also negatively influenced the land's economy.

The Persians decided to deal a simultaneous blow to Egypt and to its ally, Cyprus. Tiribazus advanced with a fleet against Evagoras, while Pharnabazus, Abrocomas and Tithraustes, around 385-383 B.C., campaigned against Achoris. The attempt to reconquer Egypt was doomed to failure. In the end it was Achoris who started to expand his territory by supporting rebellions against the Great King in Phoenicia and Cilicia. He even extended his control over Tyre and with the assistance of a fleet of ninety triremes established his authority over the eastern half of the Mediterranean. Thereupon the Persians assembled their main forces against Evagoras, who had become the ruler of almost all of Cyprus and possessed a strong fleet and land army. Apart from generous help from Egypt, Evagoras also received financial assistance from Hecatomnus, who was planning to turn his province of Caria into an independent state.

By 382 B.C. Tiribazus had completed his preparations for a war against Cyprus. He had collected a strong land force in Cilicia, commanded by Orontes, a son-in-law of the Great King. The nucleus of the army consisted of Greek mercenaries. In addition, Tiribazus had a fleet of three hundred Ionian vessels at his disposal. Evagoras' army consisted of Cyprians and Greek mercenaries, and he received grain, money and sixty ships from Achoris. In the aggregate he had two hundred triremes. The mercenaries who served in the Persian army expressed their discontent with the non-payment of the wages, but Glos, the commander of the fleet and the son of the Egyptian Tamos, and at that time the son-in-law of Tiribazus, managed to restore order. In 381 B.C. a sea battle took place near the Cyprian city of Kition. Although at the beginning the initiative was taken by Evagoras' vessels, the Persians were victorious because of the quantitative superiority of their fleet. Evagoras decided to withdraw to Salamis and to reinforce the town. Thereupon he personally set off to Egypt in order to ask Achoris for help. The latter, however, could only grant a limited sum of money. Meanwhile Tiribazus received from the king reinforcements for his army. Evagoras finally had to turn to Tiribazus with the proposition that he would pay tribute to the king and relinquish his conquests. Tiribazus was prepared to accept this offer, on the condition that he would openly submit to the king as a slave to his master. Evagoras, however, was only prepared to submit to Arta-xerxes as king towards another king, and thus the war continued, although the outcome seemed inevitable.

Soon afterwards several important events took place. Orontes com-plained to the king that Tiribazus was conducting a sitting war and was planning for secession. Artaxerxes ordered the arrest of Tiribazus and his move to Susa. This significantly weakened the Persian position. Glos, whose father-in-law was removed from office and arrested, now con-spired against his king and concluded a secret treaty with Egypt and Sparta. Evagoras turned for help to the Spartans and started to provide Glos with information which would compromise Orontes in the eyes of the king. In 380 B.C., under the threat of this blackmail, Orontes con-cluded a treaty with Evagoras, according to which the latter was obliged to pay tribute to the king, but not as the king's slave, but rather as a sub-ject monarch. When Artaxerxes judged that the war, which had cost 15,000 talents, had not reached the desired results, Orontes fell into disfavour and Tiribazus was released from arrest. Soon afterwards Evagoras died, but not before giving his power to one of his sons. Glos, who had concluded an alliance with Achoris, was eventually killed, thus averting his planned rebellion.

Achoris' son Psammuthis failed to retain the throne. Nepherites II, the next pharaoh, only ruled for some months until he was deposed by Nec-tanebo I from Sebennytus in the Delta. He ruled from 380 to 363 B.C. and was the founder of the 30th dynasty. During that period all political initiative in Egypt derived from the Delta region, a fact which can partly be explained by its opportunities for contacts with the other lands around the Mediterranean.

The Athenian admiral Chabrias had already been allied to Pharaoh Achoris, and he was now found willing to assist Nectanebo. In 379 B.C., however, when relations between Athens and Persia were improving, Chabrias was recalled from Egypt on the demand of Persia. Thereafter the Athenians sent their general Iphicrates with an army to participate in the Persian campaign against Egypt. In 373 B.C. a considerable Per-sian army[2], supported by a fleet under the command of Pharnabazus,

---

[2] According to Diodorus (IV 29.4), this army consisted of 200,000 soldiers, exclusive of 20,000 Greek mercenaries, and 300 ships.

advanced against Egypt. In the meantime Nectanebo had fortified all the outlets of the River Nile and at Pelusium he blocked the entrance to the country by digging canals and erecting earthen ramparts. It proved impossible for the Persians to advance via this route. Pharnabazus' fleet, however, circumvented the fortifications and disembarked men at one of the Nile outlets. When this Persian army entered Egypt, the soldiers started to loot the land and its temples, and caused a massive bloodbath among the local population. Other captives were enslaved.

The Persians and mercenaries advanced upon Memphis. Iphicrates advised Pharnabazus to march as fast as possible to the city, in order to prevent a build-up of its defences. Pharnabazus, however, did not trust Iphicrates and ignored his counsel. While the Persian commanders were assembling all their forces, the Egyptians succeeded in strengthening the town of Mendes in the Delta. Meanwhile the Nile started its annual rise, and the Persian army was forced to withdraw from Egypt with heavy losses. During the following years, Persian plans to reconquer Egypt were doomed to failure because of instable conditions in the western part of the Empire, revolts by subject peoples, insurrections by satraps in Asia Minor, and finally because of Greek assistance to the Egyptians.

Under Nectanebo Egypt went through a period of significant economic growth, and from this period many objects of art have been preserved. These pieces testify to a return to ancient traditions from before the time of Persian domination.

In 362 B.C. Nectanebo was succeeded by his son Tachos. In the same year he concluded an alliance with Ariobarzanes, a son of Mithridates, who in 387 B.C. had replaced Pharnabazus as satrap of Phrygia and later defected from the Persian king. The new pharaoh set himself the objective of invading and occupying Syria and Palestine, which had proved to be rebellious against Artaxerxes II. To achieve his ambitious goals, Tachos equipped a large fleet and a strong army and started to look for possible allies. Any enemy of Persia was essentially an ally of Egypt[3], and the pharaoh turned to Athens and Sparta with a demand for mercenaries. In 361 B.C., there arrived in Egypt, together with hoplites who were attracted by Egyptian money, the aged, but still indefatigable Spartan general Agesilaus, who by then was more than eighty years old. In the same year the Athenian admiral Chabrias arrived, together with his mercenaries.

Agesilaus and Chabrias, however, quarrelled incessantly among each other for the post of commander, and Tachos, wishing to pacify them,

---

[3] Aristoteles (*Rhetor.* II 20.3-4) wrote that the Greeks should assist the Egyptians and other enemies of the Persians, because if the latter won, they would attack Greece.

took the command himself, appointing the Spartan king as leader of the mercenaries and Chabrias as commander of the fleet. In all Tachos commanded 80,000 Egyptian soldiers, 10,000 Athenian mercenaries and 1,000 Spartan hoplites. The fleet consisted of 120 triremes. Another 50 vessels were sent by the rebellious satraps of Asia Minor, together with 500 talents of silver.

Soon, however, Tachos was confronted with a shortage of money which was needed to pay his mercenaries. These refused to serve against payment in kind. Because the sums involved a considerable amount of money, Tachos decreed, in 361 B.C., on the advice of Chabrias, certain important economic reforms.

According to Pseudo-Aristoteles (*Oec.* II 25-27; cf. Polyaenus III 5-7), Tachos told the Egyptian priests that because of the excessive costs of the war some temples had to be closed and a large number of the priests and temple servants had to be dispersed. Under this threat, the priests presented the state with loans, taken from the gold and silver of the temples. Then the pharaoh said that he could only present one tenth of the traditional gifts of the state to the temples, and that the remaining provisions would be given after the victory. In addition, everything in the country, including the building of new houses, was taxed. It was also decreed that one tenth of the harvest, of the profits made by craftsmen and of all purchasing and selling transactions, should be paid to the state. The population of Egypt was forced to lend all their precious metals to the state. The Egyptians hoped to receive a high percentage on these enforced loans, but the pharaoh gave his subjects only the equivalent in kind for the deposited metals. This technically perfect reform anticipated the later Ptolemaic financial system (see Will 1960:225ff.). It is true that, contrary to the information provided by Pseudo-Aristoteles, not all segments of this reform were introduced by Tachos. For example, according to a text on a stela from Naucratis, a ten percent tax on imports and on the products of craftsmen was already in existence by 380 B.C. (see Kienitz 1953:120). In any case, Tachos succeeded in requisitioning all precious metals in Egypt, and he started to mint coins for the payment of his mercenaries (Chassinat 1907-1910: 78-86, 165-167; Hill 1927:24f.; Milne 1926:43-92; for relevant literature: Bresciani 1965:392, n. 56).

Having completed these reforms, Tachos handed over the rule of Egypt to his brother and left for Syria. While the pharaoh, however, was conducting a successful war, the Egyptians rose in revolt against him. The people were discontented with the heavy taxes, and the priests did not acquiesce in the confiscation of their goods. When the revolt became widespread, it obtained a new leader, called Nectanebo II, a nephew of Tachos and one of the generals of the Egyptian army in Syria. In 360

B.C., he turned against his uncle. Tachos asked Agesilaus and Chabrias to remain loyal to him. Chabrias, however, remained faithful to the Egyptian pharaoh only as long as there were chances of a victory. Agesilaus said that he was sent by his country to assist Egypt, and not to wage war against it. He succeeded in arranging that the Spartan leaders permitted him to go over to the side of Nectanebo II. As a result, Agesilaus and his troops remained in the Egyptian army, while Chabrias and his mercenaries returned home. The position of Tachos was hopeless, and he fled to the Persian king in Susa. If Aelianus can be believed (*Var.* V 1), Tachos died in Persia of gluttony, because he adopted the luxurious, Persian way of living to which he was not accustomed.

In the meantime another usurper rose at the town of Mendes in the Delta. The sources do not mention his name. He rebelled against Nectanebo II and called himself pharaoh. He sent messengers to Agesilaus, attempting to draw the Spartan general to his side. Agesilaus, however, remained loyal to Nectanebo, as he feared to become known as a turncoat and a traitor. At that time Nectanebo decided to return from Syria to Egypt. At one of the towns in the Delta the troops of Nectanebo and Agesilaus were besieged by the usurper, who had found many sympathisers. The besiegers started to dig a deep moat around the walls of the town in order to isolate the troops that remained loyal to the pharaoh. Agesilaus and Nectanebo, however, fell upon the rebel troops, who, finding themselves on both sides of an unfinished moat, could not use their numerical superiority and were defeated. Thereupon Nectanebo returned to a policy which was beneficial to the priesthood and the reforms by Tachos were cancelled. At the same he was forced to stop the offensive war against Persia.

Thus, the attempts by Persia to reconquer Egypt proved unsuccessful. The situation in other provinces of the Empire was not much better. Revolts had broken out in Phoenician cities and in districts of Asia Minor. Very dangerous to the king was the rapid rise to power of Datames, the son of a Carian and a Scythian woman. Datames distinguished himself in the war against the Cadusians and was subsequently appointed as commander of the bodyguards of Artaxerxes II. Around 378 B.C. he managed to become the governor of a number of districts in Cappadocia and to suppress the revolt of the Paphlagonian king Otys. Gradually he became the most powerful Persian governor in Asia Minor. The energetic activities of Datames gained the approval of the Persian king, who sent him a large army as a reward. The rapid rise to power of Datames, however, aroused the jealousy of the courtiers, who waited for the opportunity to slander him. The keeper of the royal treasury,

Pandantes, a friend of Datames, warned him via a letter that he was going to be slandered by the courtiers if he suffered a defeat in war, because the king was used to claiming victories for himself, and defeats for his generals. Datames acted very carefully and started to bring neighbouring districts under his command. These were mainly the lands of rebellious princes. He thus gradually succeeded in becoming the ruler of the many lands between the Taurus and the Black Sea. In the spring of 373 B.C. he started to show himself openly as an independent ruler. Persian-style coins have been preserved which were issued by Datames (in particular, they contain a depiction of the winged disk of Ahura Mazda).

Pericles of Limyra, a Lycian district in the eastern part of Asia Minor, also started to expand his rule, pushing back the authority of the Persian satraps. Hecatomnus, the dynast of Caria (395-377 B.C.), supporting himself on the Greek towns and mercenaries, changed his satrapy into an hereditary kingdom, although he refrained from open rebellion against Artaxerxes. Hecatomnus issued coins with a depiction of the Carian war god. During the reign of his son Mausolus (377-353 B.C.), Greek culture started to penetrate deeply into Carian society. Mausolus realized very clearly the significance of Hellenization for the prosperity of his people and he started to settle the population from the countryside in towns, the building of which was carried out in an intensive manner. As a result of the measures taken by Mausolus, the Carians became fervent carriers of Greek culture. During Mausolus' reign the capital of Caria was replaced from Mylasa to Halicarnassus. From Mylasa decrees have been preserved "from the polis of Mylasans" (from the popular assembly of the city), which are dated to the reign of the Persian kings and the satrapal rule of Mausolus. These decrees are directed against Carian conspirators who plotted against Mausolus, who is called the benefactor of the community. The popular assembly of Mylasa confiscated the property of the conspirators and used it for general purposes. Apparently, the power of Mausolus was not absolute (see Perikhanjan 1959:16-18). During Mausolus' reign a well-known building was erected at Halicarnassus, namely the temple and sepulchre of the royal dynasty, named the Mausoleum, after the ruler of that name, which in antiquity was regarded as one of the seven wonders of the world. In its plan, the Mausoleum can be traced back to the tomb of Cyrus at Pasargadae.

When Datames rebelled against the king, he was openly supported by the Phrygian satrap, Ariobarzanes. In addition, Mausolus and some other governors in Asia Minor secretly came over to Datames' side. The Lydian satrap, Autophradates, who remained loyal to Artaxerxes, received orders to suppress the revolt. He marched with his army to Cappadocia, but was repelled by Datames' forces. Ariobarzanes and Datames collected a large army and turned for assistance to Athens and Sparta. The Spartan king Agesilaus, who out of habit could not settle down to a peaceful life, put himself under the command of Ariobarzanes, hoping to collect mercenaries with funds provided by the rebellious satrap. The Athenians sent 30 war ships and 8,000 mercenaries, led by their general Timotheus, to help Ariobarzanes. The Athenian troops, however, received instructions not to infringe the treaties with the king, as if assistance to Ariobarzanes was no violation of the conditions of the Peace of Antalcidas! The revolt spread rapidly and even extended to the cities of Phoenicia. Autophradates, still loyal to the king, found himself increasingly isolated and considered going over to the other side, instead of starting a dangerous battle with Artaxerxes' opponents. Also a son-in-law of Artaxerxes came over to the side of Datames. This was the Ionian satrap, Orontes. The rebellious satraps dispatched a certain Reomithres to seek the assistance of the Egyptian Pharaoh Tachos. The latter sent money and ships to assist the rebels. The Pisidians and Lycians also supported the revolt against the Great King.

Thus, all of Asia Minor and certain adjoining districts were in state of war with Persia. The objectives of the rebels, however, were personal, and each of them was prepared to start negotiations with the king to achieve favourable conditions for himself, while betraying the others. They did not trust each other. In 363 B.C. Orontes, who should have led the army which was destined to go to Syria, went over to the side of Artaxerxes and betrayed those mercenaries who were in his service. Following Orontes, Autophradates also defected to the king's side. Finally, in 360 B.C., Ariobarzanes was betrayed by his son Mithridates and executed. The royal diplomats also succeeded in raising Datames' troops against him, and he was killed. Thus, by 359 B.C. the great satrapal revolt was over. Only Mausolus in Caria remained unpunished, because he had not openly participated in the revolt, although he had used the opportunity to extend his influence in order to realize his ambitions of becoming a completely independent monarch. In particular, he succeeded in conquering the island of Rhodes.

In 353 B.C. Mausolus died and power went to his sister and wife Artemisia. Being informed about this, and acting with disdain towards a woman's reign, the people from Rhodes sent a fleet to Halicarnassus, in an effort to occupy the city with an unexpected attack. In the eastern part of the town harbour, however, a secret arsenal had been built during the reign of Mausolus. Hearing about the impending attack by the warriors from Rhodes, Artemisia secretly moved her warships to this place. When the soldiers from Rhodes disembarked in the main harbour and left their ships moving in the direction of the city, the Carian sailors opened a canal, unexpectedly came forth in their ships into the main harbour and captured the ships that had been left behind by the sailors from Rhodes. Thereupon Artemisia manned these ships with Carians and sent them to Rhodes. The people of the island did not suspect any danger and welcomed the returning fleet. Thus the island was again conquered by the Carians. As a sign of her victory, Artemisia built a monument on the island. When finally the citizens of Rhodes regained their independence, they were unable to destroy this monument because it was dedicated to the gods. They therefore built a high wall around it, to hide it from the eyes of the public.

After the short reign of Artemisia (353-350 B.C.), the second son of Hecatomnus, called Idrieus (351-343 B.C.), became the dynast of Caria. He was succeeded by his sister Ada (343-341 B.C.). and subsequently, from 340 till 335 B.C., by the youngest son of Hecatomnus, called Pixodarus. Comparatively recently there was found a decree of Pixodarus. The text is written in Greek, Aramaic and Lycian. In the Greek text it says: "When Pixodarus, the son of Hecatomnus, became satrap of Lycia, he appointed Hieron and Apollodotus archontes of Lycia and Artemelis governor of Xanthos." Thereupon mention is made of the construction of an altar to the deity Caunus. In the Aramaic version of the text the date of the inscription is given, namely "the month of Sivan in the first year of Artaxerxes." In all probability, Artaxerxes III is here being referred to, and the decree thus dates back to the year 358 B.C. (see for the edition, ST). As stated previously, Pixodarus became satrap of Caria in 340 B.C. The question therefore arises how in 358 B.C. could he have been satrap of the neighbouring district of Lycia? The editors of the text suggested that Artaxerxes III, when he became king, was dissatisfied with Mausolus who had participated in the satrapal revolt, and Pixodarus, the youngest son of Hecatomnus, succeeded with the help of some intrigues to ascend the throne instead of his elder brother (see ST:166; cf. Childs 1981:78). This hypothesis seems to be contradicted by other sources. E. Badian, therefore, presented the suggestion that the pertinent decree was not issued in the first year of Artaxerxes III's reign, but in the first year of the rule of Arses, namely in 337 B.C. (Badian 1977). This agrees well with the traditional date of the reign of Pixodarus, but if Badian is correct it should be accepted that Arses carried the throne name of Artaxerxes (IV). It is known, for instance, that before his accession Artaxerxes II was also called Arses.

At the end of Artaxerxes II's reign, there were many tribes who lived in inaccessible places, from Arabia to Central Asia, who no longer recognized the authority of the Achaemenid king and refrained from paying tribute. Around this time Chorasmia, Sogdiana and the Saka tribes changed from being the king's subjects to being his allies.

With the continuation of intrigues at the royal court it became more and more difficult to find people who could judge the complicated political situation in a clear-headed manner, and who would attempt to bring back order into the Empire. It is true that Artaxerxes II said that everyone who wanted to discuss something with him, could do so without committing himself to any danger. Parysatis, however, the king's mother, insistently advised the dare-devils who openly wanted to disagree with the king on actual problems, to be very careful (see: Plutarch, *Mor.* 173 F–174 A).

CHAPTER THIRTY-SEVEN

TEMPORARY SUCCESSES

By his 366 wives and concubines, Artaxerxes II had 150 sons. Three of them (Darius, Ariaspes and Ochus) were sons of Queen Stateira. Darius was the eldest son. He was appointed as crown prince and received permission to wear the upright tiara, which was the royal prerogative. The reign of Artaxerxes II, however, seemed to continue for a long time, especially in the eyes of Darius, who was already past his fiftieth birthday. He decided to hasten his accession to the throne and started a conspiracy against his father. Because of treachery by one of the eunuchs the conspiracy was discovered, and Darius, together with his children, were led before the king. Artaxerxes gave the matter in the hands of a royal court and ordered the judges to register all proceedings, and afterwards to bring the records to him. The judges unanimously sentenced the accused to death. The accused was led to an adjoining room, where the executioner was waiting with a sharp knife in order to decapitate the crown prince. The judges, who were waiting in the adjoining room, demanded that the sentence should be carried out, and so the trembling executioner took the criminal by the hairs and cut off his head. According to another version, which is transmitted in Artaxerxes' biography by Plutarch, the court proceedings were carried out in the presence of the king. Darius, caught in his conspiracy, begged for grace, having fallen to his father's knees. Artaxerxes, however, incensed with anger, killed his son with his own sword. Going out of the palace and bowing deep in front of the sun, he exclaimed that the Great Oromasdes (Ahura Mazda) had punished the Lie and Disorder of the conspirators. All of Darius' sons, apart from one, were also executed.

The throne was then destined to pass on to Artaxerxes' second son, Ariaspes, but the youngest son of the king, Ochus, acting on the advice of some of the eunuchs, started to frighten Ariaspes by implying that their father suspected him of participating in the conspiracy, and planned to have him killed in a most painful and disgraceful manner. Being brought to despair, Ariaspes committed suicide. Subsequently Artaxerxes, who did not like Ochus and wanted to thwart his aspirations to the throne, appointed Arsames (*Aršāma*) as his successor. He was a bastard son by one of his concubines. Soon afterwards, however, this Arsames was killed by a Persian, on the instigation of Ochus. Thus, Ochus succeeded in eliminating all pretenders to the throne, after which he was appointed as the new crown prince.

Finally, in December 359 B.C., Artaxerxes II died at an age of 86 years, of which he had spent 45 years on the throne. His tomb at Persepolis seems to be the only monument of his at this place.

In the same year Ochus became king. He took the throne name of Artaxerxes (III). According to Aelianus (*Var.* II 17), when Ochus became king, the magi for some reason prophesied that during his reign the harvests would be bountiful and there would be cruel executions. It is difficult to say whether the predictions about the harvests proved correct, but as regards the executions the prophecies were completely fulfilled. First of all the new king killed all his nearest relatives in order to prevent any future conspiracy. On one day alone eighty of his brothers were killed.

Ochus was a man with an iron will and he held the reins of his authority tightly in his own hands. Energetically he commenced with the restoration of Achaemenid power to its former glory. Soon the opponents of Persia realized that they were confronted with a strong, adverse wind. A start was made with the suppression of the many revolts and rebellions in Asia Minor, Syria and other lands. The tribe of the Cadusians, who previously had been included into the Empire, had now turned to carrying out raids onto Persian territory. Artaxerxes III, however, forced them to surrender. According to Justinus (X 3), it was Arsames Codomannus (the future king, Darius III), who distinguished himself in close battle with the leader of the Cadusians. As a reward he was granted the satrapy of Armenia.

In 356 B.C., Artaxerxes III ordered the governors in Asia Minor, who had long since acted as independent rulers, to disband their mercenary troops. This order was followed by all, apart from Artabazus, the satrap in Phrygia and the commander of the Persian troops in Asia Minor. He rose in revolt and was joined by Orontes, the governor of Mysia. With the assistance of Athenian and Theban mercenaries the rebels defeated the force which was sent against them by Artaxerxes III. In the ensuing battles, however, they were beaten, and in 352 B.C. Orontes surrendered himself to the mercy of the king, while Artabazus fled to the Macedonian king Philip. In 345 B.C., Mentor, the son-in-law of Artabazus, succeeded in obtaining for Artabazus the king's pardon, and Artabazus returned home, to take part in the impending war with the Macedonians.

In 350 B.C. the Persians made an attempt to reconquer Egypt, which had tried to extend its influence to Palestine, Syria and Cyprus. The Egyptians, however, successfully repelled the Persian attack.

In 349 B.C., the Phoenician cities rose against the Persians. They were supported by Egypt. The force behind the revolt was Sidon and its

king, Tennes. The unrest started in Tripolis (between Arados and
Byblos), which was the centre of the confederation of Phoenician towns.
At Tripolis, at a distance of one stadium (i.e. 184.97 m) from one another, there were the separate quarters of the people from Arados, Tyre
and Sidon, and in that city the Phoenicians held their common council
and made the decisions which affected all three cities. The Persian officials who lived in the Sidonian sector behaved very arrogantly towards
the Sidonians, and so the latter decided to try to gain their independence
(Elayi 1980:26-28). The rebels destroyed a beautiful royal paradise,
located near Sidon, cutting down the trees, and burning the stocks of fodder destined for the Persian cavalry. Royal officials were also killed. The
Sidonians had built many triremes; they had made weapons and stockpiled provisions, and they had organized militia and hired mercenaries. In
addition, they sent messengers to Egypt to ask for assistance. In 346 B.C.
Pharaoh Nectanebo II sent four thousand Greek mercenaries in support
of Sidon, under the command of Mentor of Rhodes. King Tennes of
Sidon managed to defeat two Persian armies, which were commanded by
the satrap of Across-the-River, Belesys, and the Cilician governor,
Mazaeus. The rebels then spread the war to the land of their adversaries.
Rebellions broke out in Cilicia, Judah and on Cyprus. Nine Cyprian
towns, headed by their kings, united with the Phoenicians in order to
defeat the Persians.

Amid these dangers, Artaxerxes III decided to take command of the
Persian forces himself. At the beginning of 345 B.C. he collected a large
army and fleet and advanced against Sidon. According to Diodorus
(XVI 43-51), the Persian army counted 300,000 men, including 30,000
horsemen. The fleet consisted of 300 warships and 500 cargo vessels.

The Sidonians fought courageously. Tennes, however, realizing the
strength of his opponents, decided to betray his subjects to save his own
life. When the Persians assembled before laying siege to Sidon, which
was surrounded by three high walls and a moat, Tennes sent one of his
trusted slaves to Artaxerxes' camp and via him expressed his readiness
to betray his city and its population, and to participate in a campaign
against Egypt. The Persian king agreed with this proposition and promised Tennes a pardon and a generous reward. The latter involved also
Mentor in his treacherous plans, entrusting him, for appearance's sake,
with the security of an important part of the city. Tennes, together with
500 soldiers and 100 highly placed inhabitants, left the town, saying that
he was going to Tripolis for consultations with representatives from the
other Phoenician cities. Beyond the city walls, however, Tennes threw off
his mask and treacherously handed his companions over to the Persians,
who on the orders of Artaxerxes were all executed. Mentor's mercenaries

allowed the Persians to enter Sidon without any opposition. The inhabitants of the city, who had burnt their ships so that no one could escape, being deserted by their leaders, suffered a cruel fate. Artaxerxes decided to chastise Sidon in a severe manner and to break the morale of the other Phoenician cities. Many Sidonians burned their own houses, their wives, children, and themselves. Those who remained were thrown into the fire from the town walls. According to Diodorus, more than 40,000 people were killed. Artaxerxes even sold the place, where much gold and silver had accumulated as it had molten down because of the heat. King Tennes, who was of no further use to Artaxerxes, was also executed. Mentor, together with the Greek mercenaries, who previously had fought for the Egyptians and thereupon joined the Sidonian king, joined the service of Artaxerxes. The surviving part of the Sidonian population was sold into slavery and transported to Babylon and Susa. This deportation is attested by a document which was composed in Babylon in October 345 B.C: "In the fourteenth year of king Umakush[1], who is called Artaxerxes, in the month of Tashritu, captives whom the king had taken [from] Sidon, [were sent to] Babylon and Susa. On the thirteenth day of the same month a few of these soldiers entered Babylon. On the sixteenth day ... women, captives from Sidon, whom the king sent to Babylon, entered the royal palace" (ABC:114).

By 344 B.C. the remaining Phoenician cities had also ended their resistance. Phoenicia was united with Cilicia into one satrapy, and Mazaeus was appointed as governor. The Jews, who had risen in rebellion together with Sidon, were also chastised, and some of them were deported to Hyrcania along the Caspian Sea, where they still lived in the time of Orosius during the fifth century A.D. (see for sources and literature: Grosso 1958:352; Kienitz 1953:102). In 344 B.C. the rebellious cities of Cyprus were also taken by the Persians, apart from Pnytagoras, king of Salamis, who surrendered at the beginning of 343 B.C. and managed to maintain his position on the throne.

Then Persian attention turned again to Egypt. At the end of 344 B.C. ambassadors of Artaxerxes III arrived in Greece asking for Greek participation in a campaign against Egypt. Athens and Sparta treated the messengers with courtesy, promising to maintain their friendship towards Persia, but they refrained from concluding an alliance against Egypt. Thebes, however, sent 1,000 hoplites, while Argos despatched 3,000. In addition, the Greeks of Asia Minor provided 6,000 soldiers. In

---

[1] Artaxerxes III was also called Umakush (i.e. Oxus) in certain other texts from Babylonia (see Unger 1970:318, n. 3); see above, Chapter Eleven, n. 3. The correct reading of the name was first presented by R. Schmitt; previously it was read as Umasu.

the winter of 343 B.C., Artaxerxes marched off to Egypt. The Persian army was opposed by Nectanebo II at the head of his army, which consisted of 60,000 Egyptians, 20,000 Greek mercenaries and as many Libyans, let alone the strong Egyptian fleet.

When the Persian army advanced as far as the Egyptian border town of Pelusium, Egyptian preparations for the war were concluded, and the pharaoh was convinced of the invincibility of his defences. The plan of the Egyptian defences at Pelusium, however, was given to the Persians by Mentor, who used to serve the pharaoh, but at that time commanded the Greek mercenaries of the king. Artaxerxes split his army into three parts, with Greeks as their commanders, but with a Persian appointed next to each of them. The Theban contingent and part of the Persian infantry and cavalry were placed under the command of the Greek Lacrates and the satrap of Ionia and Lydia, Rosaces. The soldiers from Argos and 5,000 selected Persians were commanded by the Greek Nicostratus and the Persian general Aristazanes. They also had eighty vessels at their disposal. The third army group consisted of Mentor's mercenaries, and the Persian troops under the command of Bagoas, and the fleet. The troops of Lacrates and Rosaces attacked Pelusium, redirecting the stream of the moat to another place and constructing a dam from which the town could be bombarded with the help of siege engines. The Egyptians quickly filled the breaches in the wall with beams and repelled all further attacks. Soon the news was spread, however, that the Persian army had been seen in the rear of the Egyptian forces, in the Delta. Nectanebo withdrew to Memphis, and following several days of fierce fighting, Pelusium had to surrender. During this battle, 5,000 Egyptians were killed. The same number of Greek mercenaries, who had helped to defend Pelusium, laid down their weapons when they had been guaranteed a free return to Greece together with their property. Artaxerxes authorized Bagoas to receive the surrender of this fortress-town.

The Persians continued with their conquest of the towns in the Delta. Thereupon disagreement broke out between the Egyptians and their Greek mercenaries. Nectanebo's generals advised him to fight a decisive battle with the Persians, attacking them immediately. The pharaoh, however, refrained from taking such a decision. Persian command, using the respite, managed to conduct their fleet upstream the River Nile, and they appeared in the Egyptian rear. This forced the Egyptians to retreat to Memphis. Mentor occupied Bubastis and other Egyptian towns and let the rumour spread that those who came over to the Persian camp would be pardoned, while the towns that were taken by force would be destroyed. Mentor released captives, so that they would spread the rumour over all the land, as a result of which the Egyptians surpassed each other in their willingness to surrender their towns. Soon all the Greek mercenaries who had served the pharaoh, went over to the side of Artaxerxes III. In 342 B.C. the Persians occupied Memphis and the rest of Egypt. Nectanebo II collected his treasures and fled to Nubia, where he remained as an independent ruler until 341 B.C., as is testified by his inscriptions which were found at Edfu (Brugsch 1884, Vol. III, p. 549).

The Egyptians were severely punished for their revolt. Towns and temples were destroyed, the walls of the most important fortresses were reduced and the land was plundered. As suggested by some scholars, this is the period to which the words of the Demotic Chronicle should be attributed, when it states that in the Egyptian houses there remained no people to live in them, and that the houses themselves were occupied by the 'Medes', i.e. the Persians. In this source, composed in the form of an oracle, the prophecy included a catastrophe for Egypt and the occupation of the land by foreigners. According to the Chronicle, there would be one local pharaoh after Tachos, and thereupon Egypt would return to foreign rule, and the land would be filled with lamentation (DC:14ff.; see also Gyles 1959:46; Kienitz 1953:107; Meyer 1915:298ff.).

If credence can be given to Plutarch (*De Is.* II 6) or Aelianus (*Var.* VI 8), Artaxerxes III not only destroyed Egyptian temples, but also killed the Apis bull, hacking it into pieces and replacing it with an ass (according to another version, transmitted by Deinon, the Persian king ordered the roasting of the bull and he and his table companions ate its meat). These accounts, however, are of an anecdotal character, and cast doubt upon the objectivity of the classical writers when they report on the persecutions and pillaging of Egyptian temples and priests (cf. Ray 1987:90).

Thus, sixty years after Egypt had won its independence, it was again, in 342 B.C., incorporated into the Achaemenid empire. In this way started the 'Second Period of Persian Domination' in Egypt, which, however, lasted for only ten years. Artaxerxes III founded the 31st dynasty of pharaohs. The submission of Egypt was his greatest victory, and he returned to Persia with rich spoils. The Greek mercenaries were dismissed and sent home. The Persian Pherendates was appointed as satrap of Egypt. Mentor of Rhodes, who had distinguished himself during the submission of Egypt, was given the function of commander-in-chief of Persian forces in the western parts of Asia Minor.

Nevertheless, the position of the Persians in Egypt was not stable, because unrest and commotion did not stop and Pherendates was not able to pacify the country completely. Around 340 B.C. an Egyptian official by name of Petosiris wrote: "I spent seven years as steward of the temple of Thoth, administrating its income, and there was no shortage, although a foreign king was in full control of the land. And there was nobody who was in his former position, because battles were fought in the centre of Egypt. The south was in uproar, the north in revolt. The people travelled in fear, and there was nothing in the temple which should be at the disposal of those who were worthy of it ... The priests were too far away, and did not know what was happening ... (In the temple) no work was done, because foreigners had come and invaded Egypt'' (see Lefèbre 1921, Vol. I, pp. 3-5).

According to E. Bresciani, between 338 and 336 B.C. Egypt passed through a short period of independence under Pharaoh Khabbash (Bresciani 1965:328). Classical authors do not mention him, but he is referred to in a relatively large number of Egyptian sources. His capital was Memphis, and in one text he is called 'the son of the sun' (see Michaélidis 1943:97ff.). The Stela of Satraps indicates that during the second year of his rule Khabbash inspected the fortifications in the Delta which were built in order to repel an impending attack by the Persians. According to the same source Khabbash ordered the return to the temple of Buto of lands which had previously been confiscated by the Persian king. Apparently, Khabbash was a Nubian king from southern Egypt, who for a short time succeeded in establishing his control over all of the country.

During the reign of Artaxerxes III, the Achaemenid empire was for the last time re-instated within its former borders, and Persia once again showed its strong capability to fight for the unity of the huge Empire. It should be admitted, however, that this was done at the cost of many lives. If Artaxerxes had not been murdered in 338 B.C., it is possible that Persia would have been better prepared for the impending war with Macedonia. The Persians still had their enormous material resources and their numberless armies, but it should not be forgotten that the unity of the Empire was fought in the main with the assistance of Greek mercenaries, instead of with the Persian army, who for a long time had drawn its military quality and strength from the Greeks, both in tactics and in weaponry. It is significant that to crush the rebellion in Egypt, Artaxerxes not only used Greek mercenaries, but also appointed Greek generals as the commanders of his forces. Persian generals were only added to the staff as a precaution. In addition, during the reign of this cruel despot, the court and harem intrigues did not stop; in fact, he was to be one of their victims.

In 338 B.C. came an end to the energetic activities of Artaxerxes III. He was poisoned by his own physician at the instigation of the court eunuch Bagoas, who abused the trust of the king. He was buried at Persepolis, where in all probability he never had been during his lifetime. As far as is known, there is only one large architectural monument which was built during his reign. This is an Apadana which he built at Babylon (Unger 1970:40). A description of the multicoloured decoration of this palace is contained in the work of Diodorus (II 7).

In Persia the throne was occupied by Arses, the youngest son of the dead king. In a Babylonian text with astronomical contents, kept in the British Museum, reference is made to ''Arses, son of Umakush (namely, Ochus), who is called Artaxerxes'' (see Badian 1977:50). Two years later, however, in June 336 B.C., he also fell victim to a conspiracy by Bagoas and was killed together with all of his family.

In spite of his very short reign, Arses managed to attract the hatred of his subjects. In a Babylonian prophetic text it is said about him (although, as with other rulers, his name is not mentioned): ''This king will oppress the land ... All the lands will be forced to pay him tribute. During the time of his reign there will be no peaceful abode in Akkad. Two years [he will reign], a eunuch will kill this king'' (BHLT, II 24–III 5).

CHAPTER THIRTY-EIGHT

THE MACEDONIAN THREAT

In 336 B.C. the all-powerful eunuch Bagoas put a representative of a lateral branch of the Achaemenid family on the Persian throne. This was the satrap of Armenia, who became known as Codomannus (see Chapter 11, n. 3). The new king was forty-five years old and adopted the throne name of Darius (III). Subsequently Bagoas tried to poison his former protégé, but Darius forced him to drink the cup with poison himself.

At the very commencement of his reign, Darius suppressed an insurrection in Egypt. A demotic papyrus has survived which is dated to the second year of his rule (Gauthier 1907-1917:194). According to the Ptolemaic Canon, he ruled in Egypt for four years, while the cuneiform texts mention his five-year rule in Babylonia.

At this time Carthage was rapidly extending its power and was turning into a powerful state, which in later years could become a rival for Persia's aspirations towards Egypt.

While the top of the Persian nobility was engaged in palace intrigues and coups, a new and dangerous adversary appeared on the political horizon. From the middle of the fourth century onwards Macedonia started its rise to power, and soon this district in northern Greece was to play a dominant role in the political life of the Hellenic world.

In 360 B.C. Philip II became king of Macedonia. According to local laws he was simultaneously the army commander, the supreme priest and the highest judge. He united all of Macedonia and by 349 B.C. gradually started to subdue the Greek towns in Chalcidice, and from 342 B.C. on he began spreading his power to Thrace as well.

Macedonia was rich in all the necessities for warfare and economic growth: excellent timber, wide grazing grounds and extensive agricultural lands. Philip carried through a number of military reforms, establishing a phalanx of sixteen men in depth. The soldiers of the lines in the rear were armed with five metre long lances (the sarissa), so that the whole phalanx could participate in the fight without breaking up its ranks. Along the flanks of the phalanx, light-armed and quickly manoeuvring soldiers were placed. The army was provided with battering rams, catapults, and other siege engines.

By that time Macedonia had become the strongest military force in the north of the Balkan peninsula. At the same time Greece was as usual split up in small autonomous city-states and districts, which passed through a heavy economic and social crisis. It was clear to the Greeks that Philip would attempt to subject them, and for some time they anxiously followed his successes.

Soon a deep disagreement became apparent in the Greek states between opponents and sympathizers of Philip. Still in 341 B.C., the well-known Athenian orator and leader of the democratic party, Demosthenes, spoke out against Philip (the Philippics) for all the Greeks to conclude an alliance with Persia against Macedonia and thus to retain their freedom. Demosthenes' opponent, Isocrates, who belonged to the camp of the oligarchs, realized that the polis system would not be capable of unifying Greece, and called for the Greeks to unite themselves with Macedonia and to campaign together against Persia in order to give the landless masses of Greece a piece of land in the East. Somewhat later, when the Macedonian army was already defeating the Persians, one of the ideologues for a pan-Hellenic expedition against Persia, the Athenian Aeschines (III 132), exclaimed: "We don't live a usual life. We are born to become a miracle to our children."

The majority of the Greeks, however, following Demosthenes, did not want to give up their freedom to establish a united Greece, and they regarded Persia as a lesser evil than Macedonia. Isocrates and his adherents accused Demosthenes of wanting to turn the Greeks into Persian slaves. This was, of course, incorrect, as the ageing Achaemenid empire no longer posed a major threat to the Greeks. For instance, at that time Asia Minor consisted of a number of half-Greek monarchies, and each of the Persian satraps was prepared to declare himself an independent ruler. Only Phoenicia supported the Achaemenids, basically because of its trade competition with the Greeks. As regards the realization of the Macedonian dream of Greek unification, this would in fact lead to the liquidation of the independence of the Greek states and the enslavement of the Hellenes. For the adherents of the maintenance of freedom, there was no alternative to a resistance against a Macedonian invasion except the conclusion of a treaty with the Persian king. The enemies of Demosthenes held the opinion that he had been bribed by the Persians and had accepted their gold. This, however, was political slander.

Philip II and the Hellenized Macedonian nobility pretended that the Macedonians were Greek in origin and that they could therefore act as the defenders of Greek culture. The majority of the Greeks, however, who did not understand the Macedonian language, were not inclined to adopt these pretensions and refused to accept the Macedonians as Greeks. These disagreements continued until very recently, when linguists were able to prove that Macedonian was a Greek dialect, akin to Thessalian, which in the course of many centuries and having developed in relative isolation, adopted many idiosyncracies and foreign words (for references, see Bengtson 1965:264).

Tension between Macedonia and Persia worsened in 343 B.C. after Philip's conquest of the Thracian Chersonesus. In the same year, Argos, Messene and certain other Peloponnesian states concluded a treaty which was directed against Athens. The Macedonian kings had for long maintained friendly relations with Athens, but Philip now started to threaten its independence. In the following year, however, Achaea and Arcadia concluded an alliance with Athens. In spite of the political and social chaos, the Greeks for a time were able to struggle against Philip. Contrary to the Greeks, however, Macedonia possessed a well equipped army and large numbers of cavalry. In 338 B.C., in a decisive battle near the Boeotian town of Chaeronea, Philip defeated the united forces of the Athenians and Boeotians. This meant a victory of monarchy over the polis system, and Philip managed to bring an end to Greek independence. In 337 B.C., under Philip's command, a pan-Hellenic congress was organized at Corinth, to which all the Greek states, apart from Sparta, sent their representatives. At the congress a general peace was declared for all of the Balkan peninsula, and freedom and autonomy was granted to all Greek states. These were hollow words, however, as in reality the Hellenes had to recognize Philip as their leader. Macedonian garrisons were established at Corinth and Thebes. Thus, unity was imposed upon the Greeks without any wish from their side. Macedonia became the supreme judge of Greece, which slowly became a peripheral area. Philip received the title of 'strategos-autokrat', and was given the supreme command of the united Greek forces, although formally Macedonia did not join the allied army. A decision was also made to prepare for a campaign against Persia. Only Sparta refrained from recognizing Philip's leadership, even when it was ratified by a decision of the Corinthian League.

In 336 B.C. Philip sent an army of ten thousand Macedonians to Asia Minor, under command of the experienced general Parmenion. The pretext for this invasion was the liberation of the Greek cities of Asia Minor from Persian oppression. Some of the Greek settlements on the Hellespont received the new conquerors with enthusiasm. The towns of Cyzicus, Ephesus, and also the Carian satrap Pixodarus were prepared to cooperate with the Macedonians. In addition, the experienced general Mentor of Rhodes died unexpectedly in 336 B.C. For a number of years he had served the Persian kings.

In July, 336 B.C., at the age of forty-six years, Philip was murdered by conspirators, at the wedding of his daughter. The murderers were captured and immediately killed by the royal guards, but it remained unclear whether this crime was carried out by the conspirators from a sense of personal revenge, or whether Philip's wife Olympias, who previously had been rejected by the king, was involved.

Philip's son Alexander became the new king of Macedonia. He was at that time twenty years old. The Greeks of the Balkan peninsula were prepared to rise in revolt against the young king. He was not only opposed by the Greek democrats, but also by the aristocrats of many Greek cities. The movement was led by the old enemy of Macedonia, Thebes. The Thebans called for the Greeks to annihilate, with the help of the Persians, the Macedonian tyranny in Greece. Alexander, however, captured Thebes, destroyed it and pronounced a cruel sentence over its inhabitants. In all of the town the Macedonian soldiers hunted the children and young girls, who despairingly called for their mothers. Houses were torn down, children, women and elders who had fled into temples were massacred. The few survivors were sold as slaves. Subsequently Alexander, acting decisively, strengthened the Corinthian League. The Hellenes then finally relinquished their hope for independence. The Greek cities became part of a monarchic empire, and many political adversaries of Alexander decided to seek refuge at the court of Darius III.

Alexander realized that, in order to wage war against Persia, he needed to make many preparations and so he recalled Parmenion's army from Asia Minor. He did so because he knew that Macedonia was not yet ready for such a war. At the same time he weakened the attentiveness of the Persian leaders.

Thus, Persia received a period of respite for two years. The Persian court, however, was mainly engaged in internal intrigues, and the precious interval of time was not used to prepare for the dangerous threat that was poised towards the Persian empire. Persian commanders did not try to strengthen their armies and completely disregarded Greek advancements in the art of warfare, especially as regards siege techniques. Although the higher echelons of the Persian command realized that the Macedonians were superior to them in military matters, they nevertheless did not initiate any reforms of their forces, which consisted of various peoples who were armed with their traditional and often outdated weapons. The Persians limited themselves to hiring 30,000 Greek mercenaries, who made up the best prepared part of their army.

In the impending war, the Persians, apart from their numberless resources of manpower and funds, also surpassed the Macedonians in the number of warships at their disposal. These vessels guaranteed the Persian supremacy at sea. It is true that the Greek states and Macedonia, taken together, did not have less vessels than Persia. Alexander, however, could not rely too much on Greek support. The most powerful sea power, Athens, was not looking forward to fighting on the side of Alexander. It was also for that reason that the number of Greek troops in Alexander's army was limited and time and time again they had to prove their loyalty to the Macedonians. On the other hand, the Macedonian soldiers were equipped with the best weaponry; they were loyal to their king and they were commanded by experienced generals.

CHAPTER THIRTY-NINE

THE CAMPAIGN OF ALEXANDER

During the spring of 334 B.C., the Macedonian army started its war against Persia under the pretext of revenge for the destruction of Greek sanctuaries at the time of Xerxes' campaign against Greece, some one and a half centuries before. The army consisted of 30,000 infantry and 5,000 cavalry. The war was officially conducted on behalf of the Corinthian League, and 7,000 Greek foot soldiers, 600 Thessalian horsemen, and several hundreds of Cretan bowmen also joined the Macedonians. The nucleus of the army consisted of the heavily armed Macedonian infantry and cavalry. The army was accompanied by 160 warships, half of which were provided by unreliable Greek allies.

The campaign was thoroughly prepared. Siege engines were included in the army train to reduce towns and fortresses. There were also historians, geographers and scholars of natural history, who had to record the course of the campaign and study the places of interest in the newly to be conquered nations.

Although Darius had many more men at his disposal than Alexander, in military strength his army was far inferior to the Macedonian forces (especially as regards heavy infantry), and the most stable element of the Persian army consisted of Greek mercenaries under the command of Memnon, a brother of Mentor of Rhodes, who had died shortly before. By the beginning of Alexander's campaign, the Persians had assembled their forces in the northwest of Asia Minor. This army consisted of troops from Lydia, Phrygia and Cappadocia. They were joined by a contingent of Greek mercenaries. The commander of the Greeks, Memnon, was the only person in the Persian camp who had a definite plan of action for the impending war. He advised to avoid an open battle with Alexander and to withdraw, turning the country into a deserted waste, so that the Macedonians would not be able to advance because of a shortage of provisions for the soldiers and fodder for their animals. In addition, Memnon suggested that the war should be brought to the Balkan peninsula and that they should join forces with Macedonia's enemies in Greece. Arsites, however, the satrap of Phrygia, boastful exclaimed that he would not burn down even one house that belonged to a subject of the king.[1]

---

[1] According to P. Briant, the burning down of the king's territory could be regarded by the population as a revolt against the king (Briant 1976:188f.).

The other satraps also wished to fight a decisive battle with their Macedonian opponent. Darius was convinced that a full victory was awaiting him, and he ordered the capture of Alexander alive so that he could be led to Susa.

The first battle took place in May, 334 B.C., along the river Granicus, not far from the coast of the Sea of Marmora. In this battle the Persian infantry was numerically inferior to the Macedonian foot soldiers. According to Arrian (I 14), the Persian army at the Granicus counted 20,000 cavalry and almost as many mercenary infantry. According to Diodorus (XVII 19), the Persian cavalry counted 10,000 men, while the number of the infantry amounted to 100,000, which clearly seems greatly exaggerated. The information provided by Justinus (XI 6), to the extent that there were 600,000 men in the Persian army, is completely without foundation. The Macedonians who first crossed to the opposite side of the river were routed. Spithridates, the satrap of Lydia and Ionia, attacked Alexander and wounded him with his lance. The Macedonian cavalry for the greater part decided the outcome of the battle. When about one thousand Persian horsemen had been killed, the Persian army left the battlefield. Only the steadfast Greek soldiers, occupying the left flank and headed by Memnon, continued their resistance, although they suffered heavy losses. The Macedonians surrounded the mercenaries, captured two thousand of them and killed many. Among the Persian commanders, the satrap Spithridates and one of the sons of Darius, were killed. The remaining Persians, together with Memnon and his mercenaries, fled to Miletus.

The victory at the Granicus opened the gates to the conquest of Asia Minor. In order to defeat Persia, Alexander decided first to capture the Persian naval bases along the coasts of Asia Minor, and subsequently to advance to Syria and Phoenicia. After his victory, however, Alexander first marched to Sardis. Before he had reached the city, he was met by the garrison commander of the acropolis, Mithrines, and the noblemen in his company, so that they could formally surrender the capital of Lydia, which was surrounded by three-fold walls, together with its acropolis and treasury of the king. After this all of Lydia and Phrygia fell unopposed to the Macedonians. The Greek cities of Asia Minor also opened their gates to the new conqueror. Alexander only met strong opposition by Greek mercenaries at Miletus and at Halicarnassus. Memnon, however, was eventually forced to leave Miletus to the enemy. In the Aegean Sea the Persians had a strong fleet. Consequently the Macedonians refrained from a battle at sea. Halicarnassus, the capital of Caria, did not welcome the promised liberation by Alexander and remained loyal to the king for a long time. The defence of the city was commanded by Memnon himself, who had been appointed by Darius III as the commander of Asia Minor and the Persian fleet. The Macedonians battered the city walls with their siege engines. The beleaguered inhabitants of the city carried out sorties and set fire to the siege engines. When it became clear that the city would be impossible to defend against the many Macedonians, the people of Halicarnassus decided to set fire to the city and to withdraw to the acropolis. At Halicarnassus the Macedonians captured enormous quantities of booty, in addition to messengers from Athens, Sparta and Thebes, who had arrived there in order to try to reach the Great King for negotiations. In the Greek cities of Asia Minor a democracy was installed, and, as in the subsequently conquered districts, taxes were levied at the same rate as had been established during the time of Persian domination.

At Miletus Alexander ordered the Greek fleet, which until then had remained at his disposal, to return home. This was a decision which put all his chances on one card, as the Persian fleet was far superior to the Macedonian forces at sea. It was possible for Darius to direct his naval ships to the Greek mainland in order to attack his adversary in the rear. The Greeks, and especially Sparta, wanted this to happen. This plan of action was particularly suggested by Memnon, who had succeeded in conquering Chios and the greater part of Lesbos. The unexpected death of Memnon during the spring of 333 B.C., during the siege of Mytilene on Lesbos, freed Alexander of a dangerous adversary. The Persian army was left without its general, who in military knowledge was perhaps not inferior to Alexander. To replace Memnon, the king appointed Pharnabazus, Memnon's nephew.

After Memnon's death, plans were worked out at the king's headquarters for the further course of action. The Athenian Charidemus, who was in Persian service, advised Darius not to take command of the army himself, thereby risking his kingship, but to send instead a fleet to Greece. Charidemus argued that an army of 100,000 men, a third of which consisting of mercenaries, would be able to conquer Greece, and he was prepared to head such an army. The Persian generals, however, convinced Darius that Charidemus wanted to betray him. In his turn, the Athenian general accused them of cowardice. Darius, deeply insulted, grabbed Charidemus' belt. This was the sign which according to Persian custom meant a death sentence. When Darius' slaves carried Charidemus away, he exclaimed that the Persian kingdom would soon come to an end.

At the command of Darius, the Persian fleet was recalled from Greek waters. Thus the initiative of the war completely passed into Alexander's hands. His army continued its advance deep into enemy territory.

Arsames, the governor of Cilicia, followed the tactics which previously had been advised by Memnon, namely he withdrew while burning the land behind him. But in the summer of 333 B.C. the Macedonians conquered Cilicia, and as a result all of Asia Minor was in their hands. Meeting only limited resistance, Alexander sent part of his army as an advance guard towards Syria. In the meantime Darius collected his army in Babylonia and subsequently marched towards Cilicia. He was planning to cut off the Macedonian army by first defeating Alexander in Cilicia, before marching south towards the Macedonian advance troops which were headed by Parmenion. This plan, however, could not be executed because Darius did not manage to arrive in time in Cilicia. At first the Persians advanced through a wide valley, where Darius could spread out his whole army and where his cavalry could manoeuvre at will. The Macedonian Amyntas, who had defected from the Macedonian side and joined the Persian camp, advised him not to leave this plain. Alexander, however, had not yet been detected, and the courtiers told Darius that Alexander was probably afraid of him and that Darius would easily vanquish the Macedonian upstart. Darius therefore directed his forces to the narrow plain near the town of Issus, between Cilicia and Syria. At that place, in November 333 B.C., a great battle was fought. After their crossing of the Amanus mountains, the Persian army appeared unexpectedly in the Macedonian rear. The Persians captured the Macedonian camp and killed many of the sick and wounded soldiers. On the instruction of Darius, some captives were led through the Persian camp and allowed to escape, so that they, with their stories about the strength of the Persian army, would frighten the Macedonians. This step was severely miscalculated, for it gave Alexander the opportunity to prepare for battle.

The two armies met face to face at Issus. The right wing of the Persian army and the left wing of the Macedonians bordered upon the sea. According to Curtius Rufus (III 2.4), the Persian army counted 100,000 men, of which 30,000 were horsemen. In addition, there were about 30,000 Greek mercenaries in the Persian army, plus the various contingents from the subject peoples. According to Arrian (II 8.8), Darius' army counted 600,000 men in the aggregate. Persian command had planned that the cavalry would play a decisive role by routing the left wing of the enemy army. Alexander concentrated all of his Thessalian cavalry on his left flank in order to strengthen this area, while together with the Macedonian horsemen at the right wing he would deliver the decisive blow to the Persians. The Persian left wing was scattered, but simultaneously Alexander's centre came under heavy pressure and openings were made in the Macedonian ranks. Here the Greek mercenaries of Darius intensified their pressure, trying to push their adversaries into the sea. Alexander had to turn to the centre in order to re-establish it. At the same time the left wing of the Macedonians also found itself in danger. The soldiers of Alexander, however, advanced upon the bodyguard of Darius. Many Persian horsemen fell, while fighting around the chariot of their king. The horses of his chariot, wounded by spears, desperately tried to free themselves from their harness. Darius lost his self-control, jumped from his chariot, threw off the signs of his kingship, so that he would not be recognized, and stepped through the mountain of fallen warriors who had died in his defence, jumped on a horse and fled without awaiting the outcome of the battle. Up to this point the outcome of the fighting was not decided yet, but Darius' flight proved to be the beginning of the end, and from that moment onwards the Persians started a chaotic withdrawal. Only the Greek mercenaries maintained order and managed to withdraw in an organized manner. The Persian camp was captured by the Macedonians. The noble Persian women begged in vain for mercy from the side of their captors. Darius' mother, his wife, two daughters and an under-aged son were captured in their tent, where the victors were surprised by the abundance of golden vessels and flacons for perfume. It should be noted that, guided by political motives, Alexander showed great respect to Darius' family.

After the battle at Issus the road to Syria and Phoenicia lay open. Alexander, however, refrained from the pursuit of Darius. Instead he continued with the conquest of new territories. The governor of Damascus handed Parmenion the royal treasury (containing 2,600 talents). At Damascus three daughters of Artaxerxes III were also captured, together with the family of Mentor and Memnon and many noble Persians. The Macedonians conquered Syria and the Phoenician town of Arados, Byblos and Sidon, where they did not meet any resistance. At Sidon people well remembered their cruel fate at the hands of Artaxerxes III, and the people of the city, out of hatred for the Persians, welcomed the Macedonians. At that time the Persian fleet lost its superior position, while Alexander was provided with a strong fleet, consisting of the Phoenician and Cyprian vessels which formerly had served the Persians.

Tyre, however, the most powerful of the Phoenician towns, showed strong resistance to Alexander. Its siege was to continue for seven months, from January to July 332 B.C. The long siege changed Alexander's plans for the immediate conquest of Egypt. The Macedonian army showed itself well prepared for the difficult task of besieging Tyre. The city lay on an island about 800 metres from the coast and was surrounded on all sides by high walls. Alexander ordered the construction of a dam, thus uniting Tyre with the mainland. Subsequently he blockaded the city from the sea with Phoenician and Cyprian ships. Thereupon the Tyrians, deciding not to fight a sea battle, blockaded the approach to their town with their own ships. The beleaguered repelled several attacks, and with the help of special machines started to dump iron shields with hot red sand upon the attackers. Despite heavy losses, however, the Macedonians managed to capture the city and to destroy it. From the 13,000 captured inhabitants of Tyre, Alexander executed 6,000. Two thousand of them were impaled along the coast, while 3,000 were sold into slavery (Elayi 1980:21-22).

While the siege of Tyre continued, a Persian army headed by Nabarzanes tried to re-establish Persian control in Asia Minor. Simultaneously Darius was engaged in collecting another army in Babylonia. This was a dangerous time for Alexander, because Nabarzanes could have cut off the Macedonians from their homeland, which at that time was being threatened by Sparta. Antigonus, however, who was appointed by Alexander as satrap of Phrygia and commander of the Macedonian forces in Asia Minor, managed to defeat the Persians and to thwart the plans of their commander (Briant 1974:53f.).

Darius announced that he was prepared to present Alexander with all lands west of the Euphrates, and to give him his daughter Stateira in marriage, who was already in Macedonian captivity, and to pay 10,000 talents of silver as a ransom for his family. On these conditions Darius was prepared to conclude a peace treaty. Alexander, however, demanded that Darius would come to Alexander in person and would recognize him as king of Asia. It was impossible for Darius to accept these conditions.

In the autumn of 332 B.C., Alexander advanced on Egypt. Along the route, however, at Gaza, he met strong opposition, and the town was only captured after a siege of two months. About 10,000 Persians and local people, who had defended the town, were killed. Batis, the commander of the Gaza garrison, was tortured by the Macedonians to the amusement of Alexander. They bound him to a chariot with leather straps which had been passed through his heels, and he was thus dragged around his town. Gaza was completely destroyed and subsequently occupied by neighbouring people.

At the battle of Issus Darius had been supported by an Egyptian contingent under command of the Egyptian general Semtautefnekhet from Heracleopolis. In his inscription, which was composed after the fall of Egypt to Alexander, he writes that he saved the life of the Persian king, and thereupon fled through strange lands and across the sea, finally to reach Egypt (Kienitz 1953:111). The Egyptian satrap Sabaces fell during the battle at Issus, while the Macedonian Amyntas, who served in the Persian army, fled after the battle, with 8,000 men, to Egypt, saying that he was sent by Darius to replace Sabaces. When Amyntas arrived at Memphis, however, the new governor of Egypt, Mazaces, killed him.

At the end of 332 B.C. Alexander appeared before the walls of Pelusium. Its inhabitants welcomed him with enthusiasm. Through the whole country the Egyptians assembled in order to oust the Persian garrisons. As a result Mazaces, who had only a few Persian troops at his disposal, was forced to surrender the land to the Macedonians. Alexander went to Memphis, the old capital, where the priests placed the double crown of the pharaohs of Upper and Lower Egypt on his head. At the beginning of 331 B.C. Alexander founded, at the western end of the Delta along the Mediterranean, the city of Alexandria. A priest of Amon acclaimed Alexander as the son of Amon, which caused great enthusiasm with the newly acclaimed deity, and a simultaneous and energetic reaction by Olympias, who ordered to tell her son that she was fairly certain that he had been sired by Philip, rather than by Amon. An Egyptian legend regarded Nectanebo II, who during the reign of Artaxerxes III had fled to Nubia, as Alexander's father. Thus, long after Cambyses' conquest of Egypt when the people of the land had concocted stories about the liberation of Egypt by a descendant of a king from a local dynasty, they now held the idea that a child from one of the former pharaohs had finally liberated them from a foreign yoke. Alexander adopted the traditional titles of the pharaohs, offered sacrifices to Egyptian deities, but refrained from changing the Persian system of taxation. Having conquered Asia Minor, Phoenicia, Syria and Egypt, Alexander had changed from a ruler of the Macedonians into the king of an extensive empire.

From Egypt, Alexander returned to Syria. According to Curtius Rufus (IV 8.9-10), when Alexander was still in Egypt, the people of Samaria killed the prefect of Syria, Andromachus, who had been appointed by Alexander. As shown by archaeological excavations on the territory of ancient Samaria, during his return to Syria Alexander severely punished the people from Samaria. On being informed of the Macedonian advance, the inhabitants of Samaria fled and a great part of them hid themselves in a cave of the Wadi-Daliyeh, not far from Jericho. The Macedonians sought them out and killed them all, including the women, children and the aged (Cross 1971:48f.).

In the meantime Darius assembled his forces at the large village of Gaugamela, not far from Arbela, 35 kilometres from present-day Mosul. According to Arrian (III 8.3), Darius' army consisted, among others, of troops from India (or possibly Gandhara), Bactria and Sogdiana, who were commanded by the Bactrian satrap Bessus (see Vogelsang 1987:187f.). There were also mounted archers from the

Sakas, and Areians, Parthians, Hyrcanians, etc. The numbers of Darius' army, as presented by classical authors, are clearly exaggerated. According to Arrian (III 8.6), the Persian army included 40,000 cavalry troops, 1,000,000 infantry, 200 chariots and 15 elephants, while at that time Alexander's army counted 7,000 horsemen and approximately 40,000 infantry. According to Diodorus (XVII 53.3), Darius' army consisted of about 800,000 foot soldiers, not less than 200,000 cavalry and 200 scythe chariots. Present-day scholars are of the opinion that at the battle of Gaugamela Darius' army included some 34,000 cavalry (Marsden 1964).

Before the beginning of the battle Alexander had captured some letters in which Darius incited the Greeks in the Macedonian camp to murder Alexander. The latter planned to make these letters known in public, but Parmenion dissuaded him from doing so, fearing that these letters and Persian gold could bring some from among the Greeks into temptation.

Prior to the battle Darius invoked for his warriors their local deities, the eternal fire, the sun disk and the eternal memory of Cyrus the Great, as saviours of the Persian people and his own royal name. In order to encourage his warriors, Darius climbed a high chariot to make himself visible to all.

On October 1, 331 B. C.[2], the battle at Gaugamela took place. Essentially, this battle decided the fate of the Achaemenid empire. The centre of the Persian army was occupied by Greek mercenaries, and was opposed by the Macedonian phalanx. On the left wing there were 1,000 Bactrian horsemen, and part of the Persian infantry and cavalry. As at the battle at Issus, the Persians wanted to push along the right wing, where they had positioned Medes, Parthians, Sakas and other Iranian contingents. The right wing was commanded by Mazaeus, the former satrap of Cilicia, who carried out an attack on the Macedonian camp. At first the Sakas scattered the ranks of their opponents, and thereupon the Persians attacked with their scythe chariots. The Macedonians, however, managed to throw some of them over with long pikes, and they spread their ranks when the remaining chariots appeared. The position of the Macedonians on their left wing remained precarious, and the commander of this flank, Parmenion, asked Alexander to send immediate assistance. At the same time Alexander and his Macedonian cavalry were advancing towards the centre of the Persian army and commenced a fight with lances with the king's bodyguard. Although the outcome of the battle was still not clear, Darius, being a weak and cowardly man, fled from

---

[2] The date of the battle is known because eleven days before the event there was an eclipse of the moon.

the battlefield and went to Media. Meanwhile, the troops of Mazaeus along the right flank of the Persian army, not yet knowing about the flight of their king, continued to press upon their opponents. Gradually, however, panic started to spread amidst the Persian ranks, and the huge army was defeated.[3] According to classical authors, about 30,000 'barbarians' were killed in this battle, and only 100 Macedonians. After the battle at Gaugamela the Greek city-states gave up all hope for aid from the Persians in their struggle with Macedonia.

Via Arbela, where he found four thousand talents of silver in the royal treasury, Alexander advanced on Babylon. The Babylonian satrap Mazaeus, who had distinguished himself at Gaugamela, came out to meet Alexander and to surrender the city without resistance. Gladdened by the fact that there was no necessity to besiege such a well fortified city, Alexander maintained Mazaeus in his function of satrap. The inhabitants of Babylon, standing on the city walls, observed the entrance into the city of their new king. The commander of the citadel and the keeper of the royal treasury, Bagophanes, decorated the whole road of Alexander towards the centre of the city with flowers and wreaths. Along both sides of the road there were silver censers in which incense and other perfumes were burnt. As presents to the victor a flock of sheep was presented, together with a herd of horses. Also wild animals, in cages, were led before Alexander. The Macedonian king was also welcomed by Iranian magi, Chaldaean priests, and there were singers, dancers, etc. He entered the palace and during the whole subsequent day spent his time in inspecting the king's treasures. In October 331 B.C. he was proclaimed as King of Babylonia.[4] Alexander offered sacrifices to Marduk

---

[3] A certain Babylonian, prophetic text says that the Babylonian king, whose name, as in similar texts, is not mentioned, would rule for five years. Thereupon the 'Haneans' would attack the country and plunder it. "Thereupon the king would collect his army and take up his weapons. Ellil, Shamash and [Marduk] would be going at the side of his army (and) he would defeat the army of the Hanean" (BHLT, III, 6-9). The editor of the text, A. K. Grayson, suggested that here reference is made to Darius III, and the Hanean would be identical with Alexander of Macedonia, because at that time the name of Hanu, which during the second millennium B.C. was used to indicate one of the Aramaic peoples, was used for Thrace (*idem*:26f.). If such an hypothesis is accepted, it remains unclear how to explain the predicted victory of the king. It is also not very likely that we are here dealing with a real prophecy, because the text continues with a reference to three consecutive rules.

[4] There is some confusion in the Babylonian texts as regards the date of the rule of Alexander, because some scribes started the first year of his reign in accordance with the Babylonian custom, namely with the beginning of the new year, on April 3, 330 B.C. Other scribes date the commencement of Alexander's reign to the actual beginning of his reign in Macedonia, namely in 336 B.C.

and spent a whole month in Babylon. Before leaving the city he gave Parmenion the former house of the Persian Bagoas, in which the clothes alone were valued at a price of one thousand talents of silver.

From Babylonia Alexander marched to Elam. In the meantime he left Darius in peace. The latter had, together with the Bactrian cavalry and two thousand Greek mercenaries, fled into the Median mountains. After twenty days Alexander arrived at Susa, which in February 330 B. C. was surrendered to him without opposition. Here he could lay hold on a huge treasure, including forty thousand talents of silver and gold in ingots, in addition to nine thousand golden darics. This money constituted financial reserves for the Persian kings to be used in emergencies.

Subsequently Alexander directed his army to Persis, the homeland of the Achaemenid kings. The satrap of this land, Ariobarzanes, together with his best troops, showed energetic resistance. A Lycian shepherd, however, who sometime before had fallen into the hands of the Persians and who spoke several languages, showed the Macedonians a route which led around Ariobarzanes' army. As a result the Persian commander was forced to flee to Media, where Darius was still residing. Shortly afterwards the dynastic capitals of the Persians, namely Pasargadae and Persepolis, fell into the hands of the Macedonians. Here the main treasures of the Achaemenid empire were stockpiled. At Persepolis Alexander found treasuries full of gold and silver. There were precious metals, the value of which was estimated at about 120,000 talents in silver, and for its transport to Susa and Babylon 10,000 vehicles and 300 camels were needed. On the arrival of the conquerors, part of the population of Persepolis fled, while the remaining people suffered a cruel fate, on the special instructions of Alexander. Except for the royal palaces, the whole town was given by Alexander to his soldiers for plunder. They threw themselves upon all the gold, silver, luxury items, and clothes which were adorned with gold or decorated with purple. The costly clothes and precious vessels with highly artistic decoration were destroyed by the plunderers, and everyone took his share. As was shown by archaeological investigations, even the royal kitchens were pillaged, and the floors were covered by heaps of broken pottery. The Macedonian soldiers even killed each other while fighting for the precious items which they saw everywhere. Many Persians, seeking a quick death, hastened to thrown themselves, together with their wives and children, from the high walls of the city; others set fire to their houses and perished in the flames.

At the end of May, 330 B. C., having drunk too much, Alexander proceeded with a burning torch to the palace of Xerxes and set it afire. The fire spread over all of the city, and the royal archives, including the leather scrolls and the papyri, went for the greater part up in flames.

There were historians in the Macedonian camp, but in addition to his endless drinking parties, Alexander was only interested in his own deeds, and not in the least bit concerned with the preservation of the documents of other peoples.

Even in the classical period there were discussions about the objective of the barbaric destruction of Persepolis. Modern historians still have no unanimous explanation for the event. Cleitarchus, Diodorus, Plutarch and Curtius Rufus wrote that the burning down of the palaces was instigated by an Athenian courtesan called Thais (for references to the texts and modern literature, see Balcer 1978:120). Arrian (III 18.11) wrote that Parmenion tried to dissuade Alexander from destroying the city. Alexander, however, answered that it was necessary to punish the Persians for their campaign against Greece, 150 years previously. Some modern scholars are of the opinion that Alexander destroyed the city because of the ideological status of the place, being the religious capital of the Achaemenid empire and symbolizing the relationship between Ahura Mazda on the one hand and the Persian king and his subjects on the other (Balcer 1978:128; Briant 1980:80; Marinovic 1979:191ff.).

When in the spring of 330 B.C. Alexander marched north to Ecbatana, Darius had already left the Median capital. He fled with his closest followers through Rhagai (Raga) along the southern coast of the Caspian Sea to eastern Iran, in the hope of assembling sufficient forces from Bactria and other subject nations to turn the war in his favour. Together with the unfortunate king, there were thirty thousand Persians and Greek mercenaries. The Achaemenid empire, however, had long since turned into a colossus with clay legs, and after the battle at Gaugamela effective resistance against the invaders was no longer possible, because the western satrapies were now held by Alexander. The fate of the last Achaemenid king, who was fifty years old, was decided by the Bactrian satrap Bessus, who perfidiously murdered him. For the cowardly ruler of a huge empire this was a well-deserved end. During the last days of his life only a few thousand loyal Persians and Greeks remained with him. They, however, could not prevent the murder of their king. On the instruction of Alexander, Darius was finally buried in an incomplete tomb at Persepolis.

Bessus proclaimed himself king with the name of Artaxerxes (IV) and he established himself in Bactria. He united around him those who were determined to offer resistance to the Macedonian invaders. In 329 B.C., however, Bactria was conquered by Alexander and Bessus was captured. On the instructions of Alexander, the Macedonians cut off his nose and the tips of his ears and they led him shackled and completely naked to his execution. They bound him to the top of two trees which had been bent down. After this, as soon as they let go the trees, these sprung back and tore the body of Bessus asunder.

In Central Asia, and especially in Sogdiana, the Macedonian army was confronted with strong opposition and Alexander could only establish his authority in these regions in 327 B.C., after three years of continuous warfare.

Ever suspecting, vengeful, and without accepting any objections, Alexander resorted in Central Asia to massive executions and the ruining of whole peoples, in order to subdue the local population. His soldiers, according to Curtius Rufus (X 1.2-4), by their terror and cruel treatment of the local people, made even the name of the Macedonians widely hated throughout eastern Iran. Even in the classical period certain historians (for instance, Curtius Rufus) regarded Alexander's cruelty in these lands as senseless. This terror, however, was directed towards the elimination of the opposition by whole groups of people, not only in military matters, but also morally. In Bactria Alexander ordered the complete destruction of a town which had surrendered voluntarily and which was populated by Greeks who had been settled there during the reign of Xerxes. They were all killed, although they were defenceless and without weapons. They were accused of the crime which the Branchidae, their forefathers, had committed 150 years previously, having surrendered the treasures of their temple near Miletus to the Persians.

When Alexander was in Drangiana, he was told that a conspiracy was set up by his friend Philotas, the son of Parmenion who had rendered exceptional services to the Macedonian king for so long. It is difficult to say whether this conspiracy ever really existed. Alexander, determined to punish him, invited Philotas to his tent and talked with him in an amicable manner. Subsequently, during the night, the sleeping Philotas was arrested and fettered. After a juridical farce, the outcome of which had been determined previously, Philotas was tortured with fire and whiplashes. Thereupon Alexander sent an executioner to Parmenion with the orders to bring him back Parmenio's head.

Cleitus, another of Alexander's friends, who had twice saved his life in battle, was killed by Alexander in the darkness of night, only because Cleitus had praised the deeds of Philip by implying that Alexander's successes were inferior to his father's achievements.

Since classical times, historians have presented completely contradictory opinions about Alexander. Many modern scholars call him a great man (see, for instance, Schachermeyr 1973; Tarn 1948), but others disapprove of his conquests and regard him as a predecessor of Tamerlane (e.g. Majumdar 1951). Alexander's campaign to India, undertaken with the aim to find 'the end of the world', is regarded by a number of scholars as senseless (about this campaign, see Eggermont 1975). Alexander died at a young age, and we do not know which social-economic and political order he was planning to establish in the newly conquered lands. Most probably, he had no clear plans about this problem and it is likely that he would have maintained the Achaemenid system. P. Briant, therefore, completely correctly called him 'the last Achaemenid' (Briant 1979:1414). The greatest achievement of his conquests was the introduction of the Greek polis system in the East (see Bickerman 1966:104). Also in this respect, however, it should be noted that during the time of the Achaemenids certain important institutions which were typical of the later Hellenistic period, started to spread in the Near East (for instance, the politeumata in Babylonia).

Alexander started his Central Asian campaign with the most fantastic ideas about these lands. For instance, although Herodotus already realized that the Caspian and Hyrcanian Sea were identical, Alexander followed his teacher Aristoteles in regarding them as two different seas. The Aral Sea was at first mistaken by Alexander for the Sea of Azov. The Macedonian conquests significantly widened the geographical horizon of the Greeks, opening to them a world which stretched from the Aegean Sea to the Hindu Kush, and from the Central Asian regions to Nubia. In the wake of Alexander's soldiers there appeared Greek craftsmen and scholars, spreading Greek culture.

Alexander would not have been able to preserve his huge empire solely with the support of his Macedonians, and he therefore started to draw to his side many Persians to act as his most trusted servants, bodyguards and state officials. Starting his wars under the pretext of liberating the Greeks from Persian subjugation, he gradually accepted the customs and order of the Achaemenid court. He even accepted the deep bow to the ground, the Persian proskynesis, which he demanded to be performed by Greeks and Macedonians alike when they approached him. Having set himself the objective of uniting Iranians and Macedonians, Alexander married a daughter of Darius III, and following his example not less than 10,000 Macedonians married Persian women.

The historian who studies the classical descriptions of Alexander's campaigns, cannot escape the feeling that the Persian army should have won. The Persians fought courageously; their ranks included a large number of experienced Greek mercenaries who were loyal to their duty; they had a superior fleet, and the disposal of an enormous economic potential. Nevertheless, the fate of the Achaemenid empire had already been decided. Weakened by internecine warfare and constant revolts, ruined by heavy taxes, the subjects of the Achaemenid empire followed the course of the war without any real interest. From the old rulers they did not expect any lifting of fiscal burdens, while, as it goes in such cases (often, it is true, without foundation), they awaited the conquerors as their liberators. The circle closed itself: as the Babylonians had previously not been protected against Cyrus II by their impregnable fortifications, so now the Persians were not assisted by their gruesome scythe chariots and war elephants.

THE SOURCES AND THEIR ABBREVIATIONS

ABC   Grayson, A. K., 1975, *Assyrian and Babylonian Chronicles*, Locust Valley, New York.

ABL   Harper, R. F., 1892-1914, *Assyrian and Babylonian Letters*, Chicago.

AD   Driver, G. R., 1965, *Aramaic Documents of the Fifth Century B. C.*, Oxford.

AiWb   Chr. Bartholomae, *Altiranisches Wörterbuch*, Strassburg 1904

AP   Cowley, A., 1923, *Aramaic Papyri of the Fifth Century B. C.*, Oxford.

ASB   Streck, M., 1916, *Assurbanipal und die letzten assyrischen Könige*, 3 Vols., Leipzig.

BBS   King, L. W., 1912, *Babylonian Boundary Stones*, London.

BE   *The Babylonian Expedition of the University of Pennsylvania*, Series A: Cuneiform texts. Vol. VIII: Clay, A. T., 1908, *Legal and Commercial Transactions Dated in the Assyrian, Neo-Babylonian and Persian Periods, Chiefly from Nippur*, Philadelphia; Vol. X: Clay, A. T., 1904, *Business Documents of Murashû Sons of Nippur, Dated in the Reign of Darius II (424-404 B. C.)*, Philadelphia.

BHLT   Grayson, A. K., 1975, *Babylonian Historical-literary Texts*, Toronto and Buffalo.

BID   Voigtlander, E. N., von, 1978, *The Bisitun Inscription of Darius the Great, Babylonian Version* (Corpus Inscriptionum Iranicarum, Pt. 1, Vol. II), London.

BIDAV   Greenfield, J. C. & Porten, B., 1982, *The Bisitun Inscription of Darius the Great, Aramaic Version* (Corpus Inscriptionum Iranicarum, Pt. I, Vol. V, Texts I), London.

BIN II   *Babylonian Inscriptions in the Collection of J. B. Nies*, Vol. 2: Nies, J. B. & Keiser, C. E., 1920, *Historical, Religious and Economic Texts and Antiquities*, New Haven, Conn.

Camb.   Strassmaier, J. N., 1890, *Inschriften von Cambyses, König von Babylon (529-521 B. C.)*, Leipzig.

CDP   Griffith, F. L., 1909, *Catalogue of the Demotic Papyri in the John Rylands Library at Manchester*, Vol. III, Manchester.

CT   *Cuneiform Texts from Babylonian Tablets in the British Museum*, Vol. IV, London 1898; Vol. LVI, London 1982.

Cyr.   Strassmaier, J. N., 1890, *Inschriften von Cyrus, König von Babylon (538-529 B. C.)*, Leipzig.

DC   Spiegelberg, W., 1915, 'Die sogenannte Demotische Chronik des Papyrus 215 der Bibliothèque Nationale zu Paris', *Demothische Studien*, Heft 7, Leipzig.

EKBK   Strassmaier, J. N., 1893, 'Einige kleinere babylonische Keilschrifttexte aus dem Britischen Museum', in: *Actes du huitième congrès international des orientalistes*, Part 2, Sect. 1, Leiden (Beilage, pp. 2-35).

FGrH   Jacoby, F, 1923-1958, *Die Fragmente der griechischen Historiker*, Berlin, Leiden.

FHG   Müller, C., 1841-1870, *Fragmenta Historicorum Graecorum*, Vols. I-IV, Paris.

Friedrich   Friedrich, J., 1932, *Kleinasiatische Sprachdenkmäler*, Berlin.

GC I   *Goucher College Cuneiform Inscriptions*, Vol. I: Dougherty, R.P., 1923, *Archives from Erech, Time of Nebuchadnezzar and Nabonidus*, New Haven.

GD   Collitz, H., 1884, *Sammlung der griechischen Dialektinschriften*, Vol. 1, Göttingen.

H   Gadd, C. J., 1958, 'The Harran inscriptions of Nabonidus',
                    Anatolian Studies 8, pp. 35-92.
ICS   Masson, O., 1961, *Inscriptions chypriotes syllabiques*, Paris.
IGIDS   Solmsen, F., 1903, *Inscriptiones Graecas ad illustrandas dialectas selectae*,
                    Leipzig.
Kraeling   Kraeling, E. G., 1953, *The Brooklyn Museum Aramaic Papyri. New
                    Documents of the Fifth Century B. C. from the Jewish Colony at Elephantine*,
                    New Haven.
KZ   Berger, P.-R., 1975, 'Der Kyros-Zylinder mit dem Zusatzfragment
                    BIN II Nr. 32 und die akkadische Personennamen im Danielbuch',
                    ZA 64, pp. 192-234.
LBAT   Sachs, A. J. & Pinches, T. G. & Strassmaier, J. N., 1965, *Late Babylo-
                    nian Astronomical and Related Texts*, Providence.
Nbk   Strassmaier, J. N., 1889, *Inschriften von Nabuchodonosor, König von
                    Babylon*, Leipzig.
NKI   Langdon, S., 1912, *Die neubabylonischen Königsinschriften*, Leipzig.
NRV   San Nicolò, M. & Ungnad, A., 1929-1937, *Neubabylonische Rechts- und
                    Verwaltungsurkunden*, Vol. I, Leipzig.
OECT 10   McEwan, G. J. P., *Late Babylonian Texts in the Ashmolean Museum*
                    (= Oxford Editions of Cuneiform Texts, Vol. X), Oxford 1984.
PF   Hallock, R. T., 1969, *Persepolis Fortification Tablets*, Chicago.
Pinches,   Pinches, T. G., 1890, 'Babylonian contract-tablets with historical
   RP IV   references', *Records of the Past*, NS, Vol. IV, pp. 96-108.
PTT   Cameron, G. G., 1948, *Persepolis Treasury Tablets*, Chicago.
R II   Rawlinson, H. C., 1866, *The Cuneiform Inscriptions of Western Asia*,
                    Vol. II, London.
Schott   Schott, A., 1929, 'Die inschriftlichen Quellen zur Geschichte Ean-
                    nas', *APAW* 7.
Sm   Strassmaier, J. N., 1889, 'Inschriften von Nabopalassar und Smer-
                    dis', *ZA* 4, pp. 106-152.
Spiegelberg   Spiegelberg, W., 1928, 'Drei demotische Schreiben aus der Kor-
                    respondenz des Pherendates, des Satrapen Darius' I, mit den
                    Chnum-Priestern von Elephantine', *SPAW*, pp. 604-626.
ST   'La stèle trilingue du Létôon', *Fouilles de Xanthos* 6, Paris 1979.
Stigers   Stigers, H. G., 1976, 'Neo- and Late Babylonian business
                    documents from the John Friedrich Lewis Collection', *JCS* 28, pp.
                    3-59.
TMH II/III   *Texte und Materialen der Frau Professor Hilprecht Collection*, Band II/III:
                    Krückmann, O., 1933, *Neubabylonische Rechts- und Verwaltungstexte*,
                    Leipzig.
UCP IX/2   Lutz, H. F., 1927, *Neo-Babylonian Administrative Documents from Erech*
                    (University of California Publications in Semitic Philology, Vol. IX,
                    No. 2), Berkeley.
UET I   *Ur Excavations, Texts*. Vol. I: Gadd, C. J. & Legrain, L. & Smith, S.,
                    1928, *Royal Inscriptions*, London.
VS   *Vorderasiatische Schriftdenkmäler der Königlichen Museen zu Berlin*, Vols.
                    III-V, Leipzig 1907.
YOS   *Yale Oriental Series. Babylonian Texts*, New Haven. Vol. III: Clay,
                    A. T., 1919, *Neo-Babylonian Letters from Erech;* Vol. VI: Dougherty,
                    R. P., 1920, *Records from Erech, Time of Nabonidus*; Vol. VII: Tre-
                    mayne, A., *Records from Erech, Time of Cyrus and Cambyses;* Vol. XVII:
                    Weisberg, D. B., 1980, *Texts from the Time of Nebuchadnezzar*.

BIBLIOGRAPHY

Abbreviations:

AA	Antiqua Academiae Scientiarum Hungaricae
AcIr	Acta Iranica
AfO	Archiv für Orientforschung
AJA	American Journal of Archaeology
AJAH	American Journal of Ancient History
AJP	American Journal of Philology
AJSL	American Journal of Semitic Languages and Literatures
AMI	Archäologische Mitteilungen aus Iran
AnSt	Anatolian Studies. Journal of the British Institute of Archaeology at Ankara
APAW	Abhandlungen der Preussischen Akademie der Wissenschaften, philosophisch-historische Klasse
ArOr	Archiv Orientálni
ASAE	Annales du Service des Antiquités de l'Égypte
BIFAO	Bulletin de l'Institut Français d'Archéologie Orientale
BMQ	British Museum Quarterly
BiOr	Bibliotheca Orientalis
CAD	The Assyrian Dictionary of the University of Chicago. Glückstadt 1956-1982
DAO	Der alte Orient, Leipzig
IAN	Izvestija Akademii Nauk SSSR
Iran	Iran. Journal of the British Institute of Persian Studies in Teheran
IrAn	Iranica Antiqua
Iraq	Iraq. Journal of the British School of Archaeology in Iraq
JA	Journal Asiatique
JAOS	Journal of the American Oriental Society
JBL	Journal of Biblical Literature
JCS	Journal of Cuneiform Studies
JHS	Journal of Hellenic Studies
JNES	Journal of Near Eastern Studies
JRAS	Journal of the Royal Asiatic Society
JSOT	Journal for the Study of the Old Testament Department of Biblical Studies, University of Sheffield
Historia	Historia. Zeitschrift für alte Geschichte
KSINA	Kratkie Coobščenija Instituta Narodov Azii AN SSSR
MDOG	Mitteilungen der Deutschen Orient-Gesellschaft
MDP	Mémoires de la Délégation en Perse
MIA	Materialy i Issledovanija po Arkheologii SSSR
MIFAO	Mémoires publiés par les Membres de l'Institut Français d'Archéologie Orientale du Caire
MMAI	Mémoires de la Mission Archéologique en Iran
NC	Numismatic Chronicle
OGN	Otdelenie Gumanitarnykh Nauk AN SSSR
OLJa	Otdelenie Literatury i Jazyka AN SSSR
OLZ	Orientalistische Literaturzeitung
OR	Orientalia, Rome
PS	Palestinskij Sbornik, Leningrad
PW	Reallexicon der klassischen Wissenschaft, edited by Pauly-Wissowa, Graz
RA	Revue d'Assyriologie

SA	Sovetskaja Arkheologija
SIF	Serija Istorii i Filologii
SPA	A Survey of Persian Art, London and New York
SPAW	Sitzungsberichte der Preussischen Akademie der Wissenschaften, philosophisch-historische Klasse
TPS	Transactions of the Philological Society
UVB	Vorläufiger Bericht über die ... in Uruk- Warka unternommenen Ausgrabungen, Berlin
VDI	Vestnik Drevnej Istorii
WVDOG	Wissenschaftliche Veröffentlichungen der Deutschen Orient-Gesellschaft
ZA	Zeitschrift für Assyriologie
ZÄS	Zeitschrift für ägyptische Sprache und Altertumskunde
ZDMG	Zeitschrift der Deutschen Morgenländischen Gesellschaft
ZDPV	Zeitschrift des Deutschen Palästina-Vereins

Abaev, V.I., 1956, 'Skifskij byt i reforma Zoroastra', *ArOr* 24, pp. 23-56.
Abaev, V.I., 1967, 'K etimologii drevnepersidskikh imen', *Etimologija 1965*, Moscow (pp. 288-295).
Abaev, V.I., 1974, 'Mif i istorija v Gatakh Zoroastra', *Istoriko-filologičeskie issledovanija. Pamjati N. I. Konrad*, Moscow (pp. 310-321).
Ackroyd, P.R., 1958, 'Two Old Testament historical problems of the early Persian period', *JNES* 17, pp. 13-27.
Adams, Mc.C., 1965, *Land behind Baghdad*, Chicago and London.
Albright, W.F., 1950, *The Biblical Period*, Pittsburgh.
Alekseev, A.N., 1966, 'O tak nazyvaemoj čyme v Afinakh', *VDI* 1966, No. 3, pp. 127-142.
Aliev, I., 1960, *Istorija Midii*. Baku.
Altheim, F., 1951, review of Cameron 1948, in: *Gnomon* 23, pp. 187-193.
Altheim, F. & Stiehl, R., 1961-1962, *Die aramäische Sprache unter den Achaimeniden*, 3 parts, Frankfurt am Main.
Amusin, I.D., 1958, 'Kumranskij fragment 'molitvy' vavilonskogo tsarja Nabonida', *VDI* 1958, No. 4, pp. 104-117.
Amusin, I.D., 1971, *Teksty Kumrana*, Vol. I, Moscow.
Apffel, H., 1957, *Die Verfassungsdebatte bei Herodot*, Erlangen.
Atkinson, K. M. T., 1956, 'The legitimacy of Cambyses and Darius as kings of Egypt', *JAOS* 76, pp. 167-177.
Avery, H.C., 1972, 'Herodotus' picture of Cyrus', *AJP* 93, No. 4, pp. 529-546.

Badian, E., 1977, 'A document of Artaxerxes IV?', in: Kinzl, K.H. (ed.), *Greece and the Eastern Mediterranean in Ancient History and Prehistory*, Berlin (pp. 41-50).
Balcer, J.M., 1972a, 'Darius' Scythian expedition', *Classical Philology* 76, pp. 99-132.
Balcer, J.M., 1972b, 'The Persian occupation of Thrace 519-491 B.C.', *Actes du IIe congrès international des études du sud-est européen*, Vol. II, Athens (pp. 241-258).
Balcer, J.M., 1978, 'Alexander's burning of Persepolis', *Iran* 13, 119-133.
Balcer, J.M., 1984, *Sparda by the Bitter Sea. Imperial interaction in western Anatolia, c. 700-447 B.C.* (Brown Judaic Studies 52), Chico, California.
Balcer, J.M., 1987, *Herodotus & Bisitun. Problems in Ancient Persian Historiography* (Historia Einzelschriften, Heft 49), Stuttgart.
Balkan, K., 1959, 'Inscribed bullae from Dascyleion-Ergili', *Anatolia* 4, pp. 123-128.
Barnett, R.D., 1963, 'Xenophon and the wall of Media', *JHS* 83, pp. 1-28.
Bauer, A., 1882, *Die Kyros-Sage und Verwandtes*, Vienna.
Beloch, J., 1912-1927, *Griechische Geschichte*, 4 Vols., Berlin and Leipzig.
Bengtson, H., 1955, 'Scylax von Caryanda und Herakleides von Mysala', *Historia* 3, pp. 301-307.

Bengtson, H., 1960, *Griechische Geschichte von den Anfängen bis die römische Kaiserzeit*, Munich.

Bengtson, H., 1962, *Die Staatsverträge der griechisch-römischen Welt von 700 bis 338 v. Chr.*, Munich.

Bengtson, H., 1965, *Griechen und Perser* (Fischer Weltgeschichte, Vol. V), Frankfurt am Main.

Ben-Gurion, D., 1974, 'Cyrus, King of Persia', *AcIr* I, pp. 127-134.

Benveniste, E., 1958, 'Une bilingue gréco-araméenne d'Aśoka. Les données iraniennes', *JA* 246, pp. 36-48.

Berger, P.R., 1970, 'Das Neujahrsfest nach den Königsinschriften der ausgehenden Babylonischen Reiche', *Actes de la XVIIe Rencontre Assyriologique Internationale*, Ham-sur-Heure (pp. 155-159).

Bertin, G., 1890, 'Herodotus on the Magians', *JRAS* 22, pp. 821-822.

Bickerman, E.J., 1934, 'Notes sur la chronologie du XXXe dynastie', *MIFAO* 66, pp. 77-83.

Bickerman, E.J., 1966, 'The Seleucids and the Achaemenids', in: *La Persia e il mondo greco-romano* (Accademia Nazionale dei Lincei, Vol. LXXVI), Rome (pp. 87-117).

Bickerman, E.J., 1967, *Four Strange Books of the Bible*, New York.

Bickerman, E.J., 1976, 'The edict of Cyrus in Ezra I'', in: Bickerman, E.J., *Studies in Jewish and Christian History*, Vol. I, Leiden (pp. 72-108).

Bickerman, E.J. & Tadmor, H., 1978, 'Darius I, Pseudo-Smerdis, and the Magi', *Athenaeum*, NS, 56, pp. 239-261.

Bigwood, J.M., 1976, 'Ctesias' account of the revolt of Inarus', *Phoenix* 30, pp. 1-25.

Bivar, A.D.H., 1961, 'A "satrap" of Cyrus the Younger', *NC*, VIIth series, 1, pp. 119-127.

Bivar, A.D.H., 1969, 'The Achaemenids and the Macedonians: stability and turbulence', in: G. Hambly (ed.), *Central Asia*, London (pp. 15-26).

Boffo, L., 1977, 'Gli Ioni a Micale', *Rendiconti, Classe di Lettere* (Istituto Lombardo, Accademia di Scienze e Lettere, Milano) 3, pp. 83-90.

Boffo, L., 1979, 'Il logos di Orete in Erodoto', *Accademia Nazionale dei Lincei*, VIIIth series (Roma), 34, fasc. 4, pp. 85-104.

Boffo, L., 1983, 'La conquista persiana delle città greche d'Asia Minore', *Atti della Accademia Nazionale dei Lincei* (Memorie. Classe di Scienze morali, storiche e filologiche, Roma), VIIIth series, 26, fasc. 1.

Bogoljubov, M.N., 1969, 'K čeniju Strasburgskogo aramejskogo papirusa', *PS* 19, pp. 69-75.

Bogoljubov, M.N., 1974, 'Aramejskaja versija lidijsko-aramejskoj bilingvy', *Voprosy Jazykoznanja* 6, pp. 106-112.

Böhl, F.M.Th., 1939, 'Die Tochter des Königs Nabonid', *Symbolae ad iura orientis antiqui pertinentes P. Koschaker dedicatae*, Leiden (pp. 151-178).

Böhl, F.M.Th., 1962, 'Die babylonischen Prätendenten zur Zeit des Xerxes', *BiOr* 1962, pp. 110-112.

Böhl, F.M.Th., 1968, 'Die babylonischen Prätendenten zur Anfangszeit des Darius I', *BiOr* 1968, pp. 150-153.

Borger, R., 1972, 'Die Waffenträger des Königs Darius', *Vetus Testamentum* 22, pp. 386-398.

Borger, R., 1982, 'Die Chronologie des Darius-Denkmals am Behistun-Felsen', *Nachrichten der Akademie der Wissenschaften in Göttingen* (Philologisch-historische Klasse) 3, pp. 105-132.

Boyce, M., 1982, *A History of Zoroastrianism*, Vol. II (Handbuch der Orientalistik, Erste Abteilung, Band 8, Abschnitt 1, Lief. 2, Heft 2 A), Leiden.

Boyce, M., 1984, 'A tomb for Cassandane', *AcIr* 23, pp. 67-71.

Brannan, P.T., 1963, 'Herodotus and his history: the constitutional debate preceding Darius' accession', *Traditio* 19, pp. 427-438.

Bresciani, E., 1958, 'La satrapia d'Egitto', *SCO* 7, pp. 132-188.

Bresciani, E., 1965, 'Ägypten und das Perserreich', in: *Fischer Weltgeschichte*, Vol. V, Frankfurt am Main (pp. 311-329).
Bresciani, E., 1984, 'Egypt, Persian satrapy', in: *The Cambridge History of Judaism*, Vol. I, pp. 358-372.
Bresciani, E., 1985, 'Ugiahorresnet a Menfi', *Egitto e Vicino Oriente* 8, pp. 1-6.
Briant, P., 1974, *Alexandre le Grand*, Paris.
Briant, P., 1976, 'Brigandage: Dissidence et conquête en Asie Achéménide et Hellénistique', *Centre de recherches d'histoire ancienne* 21, pp. 163-279.
Briant, P., 1979, 'Des Achéménides aux rois Hellénistiques: continuités et ruptures', *Annali della Scuola Normale* (Classe di Lettere e Filosofia, Pisa), IIIrd series, Vol. IX, No. 4, pp. 1375-1414.
Briant, P., 1980, 'Conquête territoriale et stratégie idéologique: Alexandre le Grand et l'idéologie monarchique Achéménide', *Zeszyty naukowe Uniwersytetu Jagiellońskiego* (Prace historyczne) 63, pp. 37-83.
Briant, P. 1984, 'La Perse avant l'empire (un état de la question), *IrAn* 19, pp. 71-118.
Brugsch, H., 1878, *Reise nach der grossen Oase El Khargeh*, Leipzig.
Brugsch, H., 1884, *Thesaurus Inscriptionum Egyptiacarum*, Vol. III, Leipzig.
Brunner, G., 1959, *Der Nabuchodonosor des Buches Judith*, Berlin.
Burn, A.R., 1970, *Persia and the Greeks. The defence of the West, c. 546-478 B.C.*, London.
Burn, A.R., 1985, 'Persia and the Greeks', in: *Cambridge History of Iran*, Vol. II, pp. 292-391.
Burstein, S.M., 1978, *The Babyloniaca of Berossus*, Malibu.

Cameron, G.G., 1936, *History of Early Iran*, New York.
Cameron, G.G., 1941, 'Darius and Xerxes in Babylonia', *AJSL* 58, No. 3, pp. 314-325.
Cameron, G.G., 1943, 'Darius, Egypt and "the lands beyond the Sea"', *JNES* 2, pp. 307-313.
Cameron, G.G., 1948, *Persepolis Treasury Tablets*, Chicago.
Cameron, G.G., 1955, 'Ancient Persia', in: Dentan, R.C. (ed.), *The Idea of History in the Ancient Near East* (American Oriental Series, Vol. XXXVIII), New Haven (pp. 77-97).
Cameron, G.G., 1960, 'The Elamite version of the Bisitun inscriptions', *JCS* 14, pp. 59-68.
Cameron, G.G., 1974, 'Cyrus the "Father", and Babylonia', *AcIr* 1, pp. 45-59.
Cameron, G.G., 1975, 'Darius the Great and his Scythian (Saka) campaign. Bisutun and Herodotus', *AcIr* 4, pp. 77-88.
Capart, J.A., 1946, 'Darius' inscription from El Kab', *Bulletin of the Iranian Institute*, Vols. VI-VII, No. 1, pp. 18-19.
Cargill, J., 1977, 'The Nabonidus chronicle and the fall of Lydia', *AJAH* 2, pp. 97-116.
Carter, E. & Stolper, M., 1976, 'Middle Elamite Malyan', *Expedition* 18, No. 2, pp. 33-42.
Carter, E. & Stolper, M., 1984, *Elam. Surveys of Political History and Archaeology* (University of California Publications, Near Eastern Studies, Vol. XXV), Berkely, Los Angeles and London.
Cazelles, H., 1955, 'Nouveaux documents araméens d'Égypte', *Syria* 32, pp. 75-99.
Černenko, E.V., 1984, *Skifo-persidskaja vojna*, Kiev.
Chassinat, E., 1897-1934, *Le temple d'Edfou*, Vols. I-XIV, Paris.
Chassinat, E., 1907-1910, 'Une monnaie d'or à légendes hiéroglyphiques trouvées en Égypte', *BIFAO* 1, pp. 78-86; 7, pp. 165-167.
Childs, W.A.P., 1981, 'Lycian relations with Persians and Greeks in the fifth and fourth centuries re-examined', *AnSt* 31, pp. 55-80.
Christensen, A., 1933, *Die Iranier*, Munich.
Clay, A.T., 1921, 'Gobryas, governor of Babylonia', *JAOS* 41, pp. 466-467.
Cook, J.M., 1983, *The Persian Empire*, London, Melbourne and Toronto.
Cooke, G.A., 1903, *A Text-Book of North-Semitic Inscriptions*, Oxford.

Cross, F. M., 1971, 'Papyri of the fourth century B. C. from Dâliyeh', in: Freedman, D. N. & Greenfield, J. C. (eds.), *New Directions in Biblical Archaeology*, New York (pp. 45-69).

Dandamaev, M. A., 1960, 'K voprosu o dinastii Akhemenidov', *PS* 5, pp. 3-21.
Dandamaev, M. A., 1963a, *Iran pri pervykh Akhemenidakh'*, Moscow.
Dandamaev, M. A., 1963b, 'Pokhod Darija protiv skifskogo plemeni tigrakhauda', *KSINA* 61, pp. 175-187.
Dandamaev, M. A., 1975, review of: M. Mayrhofer, *Onomastica Persepolitana*, Vienna 1973, in: *Göttingische Gelehrte Anzeigen* 227, Heft 3/4, pp. 225-240.
Dandamaev, M. A., 1976, *Persien unter den ersten Achämeniden* (Beiträge zur Iranistik, Vol. VIII), Wiesbaden.
Dandamaev, M. A., 1984, *Slavery in Babylonia*, DeKalb.
Darmesteter, J., 1880-1883, *Le Zend Avesta*, Vols. II-III Oxford.
Debevoise, N. C., 1938, *A Political History of Parthia*, Chicago.
Demandt, A., 1972, 'Die Ohren des falschen Smerdis', *IrAn* 9, pp. 94-101.
Diakonoff, I. M., 1956, *Istorija Midii ot drevnejšikh vremen do kontsa IV v. do n.e.*, Moscow and Leningrad.
Diakonoff, I. M., 1959, 'Rabovladel'českie imenija persidskikh vel'mož', *VDI* 1959, No. 4, pp. 70-92.
Diakonoff, I. M., 1964, review of: Dandamaev 1963a, in: *VDI* 1964, No. 3, pp. 177-187.
Diakonoff, I. M., 1968, *Predystorija armjanskogo naroda*, Erevan.
Diakonoff, I. M., 1970, 'The origin of the "Old Persian" writing system and the ancient Oriental epigraphic and annalistic traditions', in: Boyce, M. & Gershevitch, I. (eds.), *W. B. Henning Memorial Volume*, London (pp. 98-124).
Diakonoff, I. M., 1971, 'Vostočnyj Iran do Kira (K vozmožnosti novykh postanovok voprosa)', in: *Istorija Iranskogo Gosudarstva i Kul'tury*, Moscow (pp. 122-154).
Diakonoff, I. M. & Neronova, V. D. & Sventsitska, I. S. (eds.), 1982, *Istorija Drevnego Mira. I. Rannjaja drevnost'*, Moscow.
Diakonoff, M. M., 1954, 'Složenie klassovogo obščestva v severnoj Baktrii', *SA* 19, pp. 121-135.
Diakonoff, M. M., 1961, *Ošerk istorii drevnego Irana*, Moscow.
Dougherty, R. P., 1929, *Nabonidus and Belshazzar. A Study of the Closing Events of the Neo-Babylonian Empire*, New Haven.
Dougherty, R. P., 1932, *The Sealand of Ancient Arabia*, New Haven.
Dovatur, A., 1957, *Povestvovatel'nyj i naučnyj stil' Gerodota*, Leningrad.
Drews, R., 1969, 'The fall of Astyages and Herodotus' chronology of the Eastern kingdoms', *Historia* 18, Heft 1, pp. 1-11.
Drews, R., 1973, *The Greek Accounts of Eastern History*, Cambridge, Mass.
Dubberstein, W. H., 1938, 'The chronology of Cyrus and Cambyses', *AJSL* 55, pp. 417-419.
Duchesne-Guillemin, J., 1948, *Zoroastre. Étude critique avec une traduction commentée des Gāthās*, Paris.
Duncker, M., 1867, *Geschichte des Alterthums*, Vols. II and IV, Leipzig.

Eph'al, I., 1978, 'The Western minorities in Babylonia in the 6th–5th centuries B. C.: maintenance and cohesion', *Or* 47, pp. 74-90.
Eggermont, P. H. L., 1975, *Alexander's Campaigns in Sind and Baluchistan and the Siege of the Brahmin Town of Harmatelia*, The Hague.
Eilers, W., 1955, 'Altpersische Miszellen', *ZA* 51, pp. 225-236.
Eilers, W., 1964, 'Kyros. Eine Namenkundliche Studie', *Beiträge zur Namenforschung* 15, pp. 180-236.
Eilers, W., 1971, 'Der Keilschrifttext des Kyros-Zylinders', in: *Festgabe Deutscher Iranisten zur 2500 Jahrfeier Irans*, Stuttgart (pp. 156-166).
Eilers, W., 1974, 'Cyrus', *Indogermanische Forschungen* 79, pp. 53-66.

Elayi, J., 1978, 'Le rôle de l'oracle Delphes dans le conflit gréco-perse d'après "Les Histoires" d'Hérodote', *IrAn* 13, pp. 93-117.
Elayi, J., 1980, 'The Phoenician Cities in the Persian Period', *The Journal of the Ancient Near Eastern Society of Columbia University* 12, pp. 13-28.
Elayi, J., 1981, 'The relations between Tyre and Carthage during the Persian period, *The Journal of the Ancient Near Eastern Society of Columbia University* 13, pp. 15-29.
Elwell-Sutton, L., 1952, *A Guide to Iranian Studies*, Ann Arbor.

Falkenstein, A., 1941, *Topographie von Uruk. I. Teil: Uruk zur Seleukidenzeit*, Leipzig.
Falkenstein, A., 1959a, 'Akiti-Fest und akiti-Festhaus', in: *Festschrift J. Friedrich zum 65. Geburtstag gewidmet*, Heidelberg (pp. 147-182).
Falkenstein, A., 1959b, 'Zwei Rituale aus seleukidischer Zeit', *UVB* 15, pp. 40-45.
Floigl, V., 1881, *Cyrus und Herodot*, Leipzig.
Francfort, H.-P., 1985, 'Note sur la mort de Cyrus et les Dardes', in: Gnoli, G. & Lanciotti, L. (eds.), *Orientalia Iosephi Tucci Memoriae Dicata* (= Serie Orientale Roma, Vol. LVI, No. 1), Rome (pp. 396-400).
Frejman, A. A., 1948, 'Plenennye vrag Darija–skif Skunkha', *IAN OLJa* 7, No. 3, pp. 235-240.
Frye, R. N., 1962, *The Heritage of Persia*, London.
Frye, R. N., 1964, 'The charisma of kingship in ancient Iran', *IrAn* 6, pp. 36-54.
Frye, R. N., 1984, *The History of Ancient Iran*, Munich.

Gall, H. von, 1972, 'Persische und medische Stämme, *AMI* NF, 5, pp. 261-283.
Galling, K., 1937, 'Syrien in der Politik der Achaemeniden bis zum Aufstand des Megabyzus, 448 v. Chr.' *DAO* 26.
Galling, K., 1954, 'Von Nabonid zu Darius. Studien zur chaldäischen und persischen Geschichte', *ZDPV* 70, pp. 4-32.
Galling, K., 1964, *Studien zur Geschichte Israels im persischen Zeitalter*, Tübingen.
Gardner, P., 1908, *The Gold Coinage of Asia before Alexander the Great*, London.
Garelli, P., 1958, 'Nabonide', *Dictionnaire de la Bible* (Supplément, fasc. 31), pp. 269-286.
Gauthier, H., 1907-1917, *Le livre des rois d'Égypte*, Vols. I-V, Cairo.
Gentili, B. & Prato, C., 1979, *Poetae Elegiaei Testimonia et Fragmenta* (*Bibliotheca Scriptorum Graecorum et Romanorum Teubneriana*), Leipzig.
Gershevitch, I., 1959, *The Avestan Hymn to Mithra*, Cambridge.
Gershevitch, I., 1969, 'Iranian nouns and names in Elamite garb', *TPS* 1969, pp. 165-200.
Gershevitch, I., 1979, 'The false Smerdis', *AA* 27, pp. 337-351.
Ghirshman, R., 1950, 'Masjid-i-Solaiman, résidence des premiers Achéménides', *Syria* 27, pp. 205-220.
Ghirshman, R., 1952, 'Cinq campagnes de fouilles à Suse (1946-1951), *RA* 46, pp. 1-18.
Ghirshman, R., 1954, 'Village Perse-Achéménide, *MMAI* 36.
Ghirshman, R., 1962, 'La civilisation achéménide et l'Urartu', in: W. B. Henning & Yarshater, E. (eds.), *A Locust's Leg. Studies in Honour of S. H. Taqizadeh*, London (pp. 85-88).
Gillis, D., 1979, 'Collaboration with the Persians', *Historia* (Einzelschriften, Heft 34), Wiesbaden (pp. 1-87).
Gnoli, G., 1980, *Zoroaster's Time and Homeland*, Naples.
Goossens, G., 1949, 'Les recherches historiques à l'époque néo-babylonienne', in: *Actes du XXIᵉ Congrès des Orientalistes*, Paris (pp. 144-145).
Goyon, G., 1957, *Nouvelles inscriptions rupestres du Uâdi Hammâmât*, Paris.
Graf, D. F., 1985, 'Greek tyrants and Achaemenid politics', in: Eadie, J. W. & Ober, J. (eds.), *The Craft of the Ancient Historian: Essays in Honor of Chester G. Starr*, Lanham, Maryland (pp. 79-123).
Gray, G. B., 1969, 'The foundation and extension of the Persian Empire', in: *The Cambridge Ancient History*, Vol. IV, Cambridge (pp. 1-25).
Greenfield, J. C., 1961, review of Brunner 1959, in: *JBL* 80, p. 298.

Griffiths, J.G., 1953, 'Basileus Basileon: Remarks on the history of a title', *Classical Philology* 48, No. 3, pp. 145-154.

Grosso, F., 1958, Gli Eretriesi deportati in Persia', *Rivista di filologia e di istruzione classica* 36, pp. 350-375.

Gschnitzer, F., 1977, *Die sieben Perser und das Königtum des Dareios*, Heidelberg.

Gunn, B., 1926, 'The inscribed sarcophagi in the Serapeum', *ASAE* 26, pp. 81-95.

Gyles, M.F., 1959, *Pharaonic policies and administration, 663 to 323 B.C.*, Chapel Hill.

Hallo, W.W., 1968-1971, s.v. 'Gutium', *RlA*, Bd. 3, pp. 708-720.

Hallock, R.T., 1960, 'The "one year" of Darius I', *JNES* 19, pp. 36-39.

Hallock, R.T., 1985, 'The evidence of the Persepolis Tablets', in: Gershevitch, I. (ed.), *The Cambridge History of Iran*, Vol. II, Cambridge (p. 588-609).

Hanfmann, G.M.A., 1978, 'Lydian relations with Ionia and Persia', in: *The Proceedings of the Xth International Congress of Classical Archaeology*, Ankara (pp. 25-35).

Hansman, J., 1972, 'Elamites, Achaemenians and Anshan', *Iran* 10, pp. 101-124.

Hansman, J., 1975, 'An Achaemenian stronghold', *AcIr* 6, pp. 289-309.

Harmatta, J., 1963, 'Das Problem der Kontinuität im frühhellinistischen Ägypten', *AA* 11, pp. 199-213.

Harmatta, J., 1971, 'The literary patterns of the Babylonian edict of Cyrus', *AA* 19, pp. 217-231.

Harmatta, J., 1979, 'Darius' expedition against the Sakā tigraxaudā', in: Harmatta, J. (ed.), *Studies in the Sources on the History of Pre-Islamic Central Asia*, Budapest (pp. 19-28).

Haussoullier, B., 1905, 'Offrande à Apollon Didyméen', *MDP*, T. VII, pp. 155-165.

Helzer, M., 1988, review of: Dandamaev, M.A., *Politišeskaja Istorija Akhemenidskoj Deržavy*, Moscow 1985, in: *Aula Orientalis* 6, pp. 125-129.

Henning, W.B., 1944, 'The murder of the Magi', *JRAS* 1944, pp. 133-144.

Henning, W.B., 1951, 'Zoroaster: Politician or witch-doctor?', Oxford.

Hermes, G., 1938, 'Zur Sociologie der Lehre Zarathustras', *Anthropos* 33, pp. 181-194; 424-444.

Hertel, J., 1924a, *Achämeniden und Kayaniden*, Leipzig.

Hertel, J., 1924b, *Die Zeit Zoroasters*, Leipzig.

Herzfeld, E., 1928, 'A new inscription of Darius from Hamadan', *Memoirs of the Archaelogical Survey of India* 34, Calcutta.

Herzfeld, E., 1929, 'Der geschichtliche Vištāspa', *AMI* 1, pp. 77-123.

Herzfeld, E., 1930a, 'Zarathustra', *AMI* 2, pp. 1ff.

Herzfeld, E., 1930b, 'Dareios Soter', *AMI* 3, pp. 1-11.

Herzfeld, E., 1931, 'Die Goldtafel des Āryārāmna', *Berliner Museen. Berichte aus den Preussischen Kunstsammlungen* 52, Heft 3, pp. 52-55.

Herzfeld, E., 1932a, 'A new inscription of Xerxes from Persepolis', *Studies in Ancient Oriental Civilization* 5, Chicago.

Herzfeld, E., 1932b, 'Dareios Abdenkung', *AMI* 4, pp. 117-125.

Herzfeld, E., 1933, 'Smerdis und Pseudosmerdis', *AMI* 5, pp. 125-142.

Herzfeld, E., 1935, *Archaeological History of Iran*, London.

Herzfeld, E., 1938, *Altpersische Inschriften*, Berlin.

Herzfeld, E., 1941, *Iran in the Ancient East*, London.

Herzfeld, E., 1947a, 'Early historical contacts between the Old-Iranian Empire and India', in: *India Antiqua. A Volume of Oriental Studies Presented to J.P. Vogel*, Leiden (pp. 180-184).

Herzfeld, E., 1947b, *Zoroaster and His World*, Princeton.

Herzfeld, E., 1968, *The Persian Empire. Studies in Geography and Ethnography of the Ancient Near East*, Wiesbaden.

Hill, G., 1927, 'Tachos, King of Egypt', *BMQ* 1, pp. 24-25.

Hinz, W., 1939, 'Zur iranischen Altertumskunde', *ZDMG* 93, pp. 363-380.

Hinz, W., 1963, 'Zu § 14 der Behistun-Inschrift', *ZDMG* 113, pp. 231-235.

Hinz, W., 1964, *Das Reich Elam*, Stuttgart.

Hinz, W., 1969, *Altiranische Funde und Forschungen*, Berlin.

Hinz, W., 1970, 'Die elamischen Buchungstäfelchen der Darius-Zeit', *Or* 39, pp. 421-440.
Hinz, W., 1971a, 'Achämenidische Hofverwaltung', *ZA* 61, pp. 260-311.
Hinz, W., 1971b, s.v. 'Persis', *PW*, Suppl. Bd. XII, cols. 1022-1038.
Hinz, W., 1972, 'Die Zusätze zur Darius-Inschrift von Behistan', *AMI* NF, 5, pp. 243-251.
Hinz, W., 1973, *Neue Wege im Altpersischen*, Wiesbaden.
Hinz, W., 1975, review of: *Istorija Iranskogo Gosudarstva i Kul'tury. K 2500-letiju Iranskogo Gosudarstva*, Moscow, in *OLZ* 1975, cols. 388-393.
Hinz, W., 1976-1979, *Darius und die Perser*, 2 Vols., Baden-Baden.
Hinz, W. Koch, H. 1987, *Elamisches Wörterbuch* (*AMI*, Ergänzungsband 17), Berlin.
Hirsch, S.W., 1985, *The Friendship of the Barbarians. Xenophon and the Persian Empire*, London.
Hodjache, S. & Berlev, O., 1977, 'Objets royaux du Musée des Beaux-Arts Pouchkine à Moscou', *Chronique d'Égypte* 52, No. 103, pp. 37-39.
Hoffmann, I. von, & Vorbichler, A., 1980, 'Das Kambysesbild bei Herodot', *AfO* 27, pp. 86-105.
Hoffmann, K., 1979, 'Das Avesta in der Persis', in: Harmatta, J. (ed.), *Prolegomena to the Sources on the History of Pre-Islamic Central Asia*, Budapest (pp. 89-93).
Hoffmann-Kutschke, A., 1907, 'Iranisches bei Griechen', *Philologus* 66, pp. 173-191.
Hofstetter, J., 1972, 'Zu den griechischen Gesandtschaften nach Persien', *Historia* (Einzelschriften, Heft 18), Wiesbaden, pp. 94-107.
How, H., & Wells, J.A., 1928, *A Commentary on Herodotus*, 2 Vols., Oxford.
Huart C., & Delaporte, L., 1952, *L'Iran antique*, Paris.
Humbach, H., 1968, 'Marathoi', in: *Pratidānam*, The Hague and Paris (pp. 154-156).
Hüsing, G., 1908, 'Die Namen der Könige von Ančan', *OLZ* 1908, cols. 318-322.
Hüsing, G., 1933, *Porušātiš und das achämenidische Lehenswesen*, Vienna.
Hutecker, W., 1885, *Über den falschen Smerdis*, Königsberg.

Istorija Turkmenskoj SSR, Vol. I, Book 1. Ashkhabad 1957.

Jansen, J., 1950, *The Coptic Story of Cambyses' Invasion of Egypt*, Oslo.
Jenni, E., 1954, 'Die Rolle des Kyros bei Deuterojesaja', *Theologische Zeitschrift* 10, Heft 4, pp. 241-256.
Junge, P.J., 1940, 'Hazarapatiš', *Klio* 33, pp. 13-38.
Junge, P.J., 1944a, 'Ākaufačiya: Ein Beitrag zur Länderkunde des alten Iran', *ZDMG* 98, pp. 369-376.
Junge, P.J., 1944b, *Darius I. König der Perser*, Leipzig.
Jusifov, Ju. B., 1958a, 'Khozjajstvennye dokumenty iz Suz i khronologija rannikh Akhemenidov', *VDI* 1958, No. 3, pp. 18-32.
Jusifov, Ju. B., 1958b, 'Tsarskoe remeslennoe khozjajstvo v Elame midijsko-persidskogo vremeni', *Trudy Instituta Istorii AN Azerbajdžanskoj SSR* 13, pp. 80-106.
Justi, F., 1879, *Geschichte des alten Persiens*, Berlin.
Justi, F., 1895, *Iranisches Namenbuch*, Marburg.

Kapantsjan, G.A., 1947, *Khajasa: Kolybel' Armjan*, Erevan.
Kapantsjan, G.A., 1956, *Istoriko-lingvističeskie raboty*, Erevan.
Kapelrud, A.S., 1949, review of: J.S. Wright, *The Date of Ezra's Coming to Jerusalem*, London 1947, in: *BiOr*, cols. 63-64.
Keiper, P., 1877, *Die Perser des Aeschylos als Quelle für altpersische Altertumskunde*, Erlangen.
Kent, R.G., 1943, 'Darius' Behistun inscription, Column V', *JNES* 2, pp. 105-114.
Kent, R.G., 1946, 'The oldest Old Persian inscriptions', *JAOS* 66, pp. 206-212.
Kent, R.G., 1953, *Old Persian. Grammar, Texts, Lexicon*, second, improved edition, New Haven.
Kienitz, F.K., 1953, *Die politische Geschichte Ägyptens von 7. bis zum 4. Jahrhundert vor der Zeitwende*, Berlin.

Kienitz, F. K., 1967, 'Die saitische Renaissance', in: *Fischer Weltgeschichte*, Vol. IV, Frankfurt am Main (pp. 256-282).

Kiessling, M. H., 1901, *Zur Geschichte der ersten Regierungsjahre des Darius Hystaspes*, Leipzig.

King, L. W., & Thompson, R. C., 1907, *The Sculptures and Inscriptions of Darius the Great on the Rock of Behistûn in Persia; A New Collation of the Persian, Susian and Babylonian Texts, with English Translations*, London.

Kleiss, W., 1971, 'Der Takht-i Rustam bei Persepolis und das Kyros-Grab in Pasargadae', *Archäologischer Anzeiger* 2, pp. 157-162.

Klíma, O., 1967, 'Gaiθāmčā māniyamčā', in: *Festschrift für Wilhelm Eilers*, Wiesbaden (pp. 37-42).

Koldewey, R., 1925, *Das wieder erstehende Babylon*, Leipzig.

Komoróczy, G., 1977, 'Ummān-manda', *AA* 25, pp. 43-67.

König, F. W., 1938a, *Der falsche Bardija: Dareios der Grosse und die Lügenkönige*, Vienna.

König, F. W., 1938b, *Relief und Inschrift des Königs Dareios I am Felsen von Bagistan*, Leiden.

König, F. W., 1972, *Die Persika des Ktesias von Knidos* (Archiv für Orientforschung, Beiheft 18), Graz.

Konow, S., 1933, 'A note on the Sakas and Zoroastrianism', in: Pavry, J. D. C. (ed.), *Oriental Studies in Honour of C. E. Pavry*, London (pp. 220-222).

Kreissig, H., 1973, *Die sozialökonomische Situation in Juda zur Achämenidenzeit*, Berlin.

Kuhrt, A., 1983, 'The Cyrus Cylinder and Achaemenid imperial policy', *JSOT* 25, pp. 83-97.

Kuyper, J. de, 1983, 'The fate of the city of Babylon during the early Achaemenids', *Akkadica* 31, p. 24.

Lambert, W. G., 1965, 'Nebuchadnezzar King of Justice', *Iraq* 27, pp. 1-11.

Landsberger, B., 1947, 'Die Basaltstele Nabonids von Eski-Harran', in: *In Memoriam Halil Edhem*, Vol. I, Ankara (pp. 115-151).

Landsberger, B. & Bauer, Th., 1927, 'Zu neuveröffentlichten Geschichtsquellen der Zeit von Assarhaddon bis Nabonid', *ZA* 37, pp. 61-98.

Leclant, J., 1967, 'Fouilles et travaux en Égypte et au Soudan, 1965-1966', *Or* 36, fasc. 2, pp. 181-220.

Lefèbre, G., 1921, *Le tombeau de Petosiris*, Vol. I, Paris.

Lehmann-Haupt, C. B., 1902, 'Gobryas und Belsazar bei Xenophon', *Klio* 2, pp. 341-345.

Lehmann-Haupt, C. B., 1933, 'Wann lebte Zaratuštra?', in: Pavry, J. D. C. (ed.), *Oriental Studies in Honour of C. E. Pavry*, London (pp. 251-280).

Lehmann-Haupt, C. B., 1921, s.v. 'Satrap', *PW*, Dritter Halbband, cols. 82-188.

Leichty, E., 1986, *Catalogue of the Babylonian Tablets in the British Museum. Vol. VI: Tablets from Sippar 1*, London.

Leichty, E. & Grayson, A. K., 1987, *Catalogue of the Babylonian Tablets in the British Museum. Vol. VII: Tablets from Sippar 2*, London.

Lenormant, F., 1870, 'Sur le campagne de Teglath Palasar II dans l'Ariane', *ZAS* 8, pp. 48-71.

Leuze, O., 1972, *Die Satrapieneinteilung in Syrien und im Zweistromlande von 520-320*, Hildesheim.

Lewis, D. M., 1977, *Sparta and Persia*, Leiden.

Lewis, D. M., 1980, 'Datis the Mede', *JHS* 100, pp. 194-195.

Lewy, H., 1949, 'The Babylonian background of the Kay Kâvus legend', *ArOr* 17, pt. 2, pp. 28-109.

Lewy, H., 1962, 'Points of comparison between Zoroastrianism and the moon-cult of Harrân', in: Henning, W. B. & Yarshater, E. (eds.), *A Locust's Leg. Studies in Honour of S. H. Taqizadeh*, London (pp. 139-161).

Littmann, E., 1916, 'Lydian inscriptions', *Sardis* 6, pt. 1.

Litvinskij, B. A., 1969, 'Saka Khaumavarga', in: *Beiträge zur Alten Geschichte und deren Nachleben. Festschrift für Franz Altheim*, Vol. I, Berlin (pp. 115-126).

Lur'e, S. Ja., 1940, *Istorija Gretsii*, Leningrad.

Lur'e, S.Ja., 1947, *Gerodot*, Moscow and Leningrad.

Majumdar, R.C., 1951, *The Age of Imperial Unity*, Bombay.
Mallowan, M., 1985, 'Cyrus the Great', in: Gershevitch, I. (ed), *The Cambridge History of Iran*, Vol. II, Cambridge (pp. 392-419).
Margules, B.B., 1960, 'Gerodot, III, 80-82 i sofističeskaja literatura', *VDI* 1960, No. 1, pp. 21-34.
Marinovič, L.P., 1958, 'Grečeskie naemniki v kontse V–načale IV v. do.n.e.', *VDI* 1958, No. 4, pp. 70-87.
Marinovič, L.P., 1979, review of: Hamilton, J.R., *Alexander the Great*, London 1973, in: *VDI* 1979, No. 2, pp. 191-195.
Markwart, J., 1891, 'Die Assyriaka des Ktesias', *Philologus*, Suppl. 6, No. 2, pp. 530-620.
Markwart, J., 1901, 'Ērānšahr nach der Geographie des Ps. Moses Xorenac'i', *Abhandlungen der Königlichen Gesellschaft der Wissenschaften zu Göttingen*, Phil.-hist. Klasse, NF, Bd. 2, No. 2, Berlin.
Marsden, E.W., 1964, *The Campaign of Gaugamela*, Liverpool.
Masson, V.M., 1959, *Drevnezemledel'českaja Kul'tura Margiany* (MIA 73), Moscow and Leningrad.
Masson, V.M., 1966, 'Arkheologičeskie pamjatniki Srednej Azii i greko-rimskie vlijanija i svjazi', *Accademia Nazionale dei Lincei* 363, No. 76, pp. 335-356.
Masson, V.M., 1967, 'Ešče raz o gerodotovoj reke Akes', in: *Ellinističeskij Bližnij Vostok, Vizantija i Iran*, Moscow (pp. 172-175).
Mazetti, K., 1978, 'Voprosy lidijskoj khronologii', *VDI* 1978, No. 2, pp. 175-178.
Mazetti, K., 1982, 'Vojna Darija II so skifami i vavilonskaja proročeskaja literatura', *VDI* 1982, No. 3, pp. 106-110.
Mayrhofer, M., 1970, *Xerxes, König der Könige*, Vienna.
McEwan, G.J.P., 1981, *Priest and Temple in Hellenistic Babylonia*, Wiesbaden.
Meillet, A., 1931, *Grammaire du vieux-perse*, Paris.
Melikišvili, G.A., 1960, *Urartskie Klinoobraznye Nadpisi*, Moscow.
Mellink, M.J., 1972, 'Excavations at Keratas-Semayük and Elmali, Lycia, 1971', *AJA* 76, pp. 257-269.
Mellink, M.J., 1974, 'Archaeology in Asia Minor', *AJA* 78, pp. 105-130.
Messina, G., 1930, *Der Ursprung der Magier und die zarathustrische Religion*, Rome.
Metzler, D., 1977, *Ziele und Formen königlicher Innenpolitik im vorislamischen Iran*, Diss., Münster.
Meuleau, M., 1965, 'Mesopotamien in der Perserzeit', *Fischer Weltgeschichte*, Vol. 5, Frankfurt am Main (pp. 330-355).
Meulenaere, H., 1951, *De Herodotos over de 26ste Dynastie (II, 147–III, 15)*, Louvain.
Meuli, K., 1954, 'Ein altpersischer Kriegsbrauch', *Westöstliche Abhandlungen, R. Tschudi gewidmet*, Wiesbaden (pp. 63-86).
Meyer, E., 1896, *Entstehung des Judentums*, Halle.
Meyer, E., 1899, *Forschungen zur alten Geschichte*, Vol. II, Halle.
Meyer, E., 1912, *Der Papyrusfund von Elephantine*, Leipzig.
Meyer, E., 1915, 'Ägyptische Documente aus der Perserzeit', *SPAW* 1915, pp. 287-311.
Meyer, E., 1923, 'König Darius I', in: E. Marcks & Müller, K.A. (eds.), *Meister der Politik*, Stuttgart and Berlin (pp. 3-35).
Meyer, E., 1939, *Geschichte des Altertums*, Stuttgart.
Meyer, R., 1962, *Das Gebet des Nabonid*, Berlin.
Michaélidis, G., 1943, 'Quelques objets inédits d'époque perse', *ASAE* 43, pp. 91-103.
Milik, J.T., 1956, 'Prière de Nabonide et autres écrits d'un cycle de Daniel', *Revue Biblique* 63, pp. 407-417.
Milne, J.G., 1926, 'The currency of Egypt', *NC* 6, pp. 43-92.
Miroschedji, P. de, 1985, 'La fin du royaume d'Anšan et de Suse et la naissance de l'Empire perse', *ZA* 75, pp. 265-306).

Nagel, W., 1975, s.v. 'Herrscher', *RlA* 4, cols. 355-367.

Nagel, W., 'Pasargadae. Ein Lagebericht zum Problem des Beginns achämenidischer Kunst und altpersischer Schrift', *MDOG* 111, pp. 75-88.

Nagel, W., 1983, 'Frada, Skuncha und der Saken-Feldzug des Darius I', *AMI*, Ergänzungsband 10, pp. 169-189.

Niebuhr, M., 1847, *Vorträge über alte Geschichte*, Vol. I, Berlin.

Nock, A. D., 1949, 'The problem of Zoroaster', *AJA* 53, pp. 272-285.

Nöldeke, Th., 1887, *Aufsätze zur persischen Geschichte*, Leipzig.

Nyberg, H. S., 1938, *Die Religionen des alten Iran*, Leipzig.

Nyberg, H. S., 1954, 'Das Reich der Achämeniden', *Historia Mundi* 3, pp. 56-115.

Nyberg, H. S., 1974, 'Histoire et religion sous Cyrus' (summary of a lecture read at the International Congress of Iranists, Shiraz, 1971), *AcIr* 1, p. 6.

Nylander, C., 1970, Ionians in Pasargadae. Studies in Old Persian Architecture, Uppsala.

Oelsner, J., 1971, 'War Nippur Sitz einer spätbabylonischen Astronomenschule?', *Wissenschaftliche Zeitschrift der Friedrich-Schiller-Universität, Gesellschafts- und sprachwissenschaftliche Reihe* 20, Heft 5, pp. 141-149.

Olmstead, A. T., 1931, *History of Palestine and Syria to the Macedonian Conquest*, New York.

Olmstead, A. T., 1933, 'A Persian Letter in Thucydides', *AJSL* 49, pp. 156-161.

Olmstead, A. T., 1938, 'Darius and his Behistun inscription', *AJSL* 55, pp. 392-416.

Olmstead, A. T., 1948, *History of the Persian Empire*, Chicago.

Oppenheim, A. L., 1974, 'A new Cambyses incident', *SPA* 15, pp. 3497-3502.

Oppenheim, A. L., 1985, 'The Babylonian evidence of Achaemenian rule in Mesopotamia', in: Gershevitch, I. (ed.), *The Cambridge History of Iran*, Vol. II, Cambridge (pp. 529-587).

Oppert, J., 1851, 'Mémoire sur les inscriptions des Achéménides', *JA* 17, pp. 255-296; 18, pp. 322-366.

Oppert, J., 1879, *Le peuple et la langue des Médes*, Paris.

Orlin, L. L., 1976, 'Athens and Persia ca. 507 B. C.: a neglected perspective', in: Orlin, L. L. (ed.), *Michigan Oriental Studies in Honor of G. G. Cameron*, Ann Arbor (pp. 255-266).

Osten, H. H. von der, 1956, *Die Welt der Perser*, Stuttgart.

Pallis, S. A., 1926, *The Babylonian akîtu Festival*, Copenhagen.

Pallis, S. A., 1954, *Early Exploration in Mesopotamia*, Copenhagen.

Paper, H. H., 1954, 'Note préliminaire sur la date des trois tablettes élamites de Suse', in: Ghirshman, R., 1954, *Village perse-achéménide* (MMAI 36), Paris (pp. 79-82).

Parker, R. A., 1941a, 'Darius and his Egyptian campaign', *AJSL* 58, pp. 373-377.

Parker, R. A., 1941b, 'Persian and Egyptian chronology', *AJSL* 58, pp. 285-301.

Parker, R. A., 1957, 'The length of reign of Amasis and the beginning of the Twenty-sixth dynasty', *Mitteilungen des Deutschen archäologischen Instituts, Abteilung Kairo* 15, pp. 208-212.

Parker, R. A. & Dubberstein, W. H., 1956, *Babylonian Chronology*, Providence.

Parpola, S., 1970, *Neo-Assyrian Toponyms*, Kevelaer, Neukirchen and Vluyn.

Patkanov, K. P., 1879-1880, 'O mnimom pokhode Taklat-Palarasa k beregam Inda', Proceedings of the Third International Congress of Orientalists, Vol. I, 33-70.

Perikhanjan, A. G., 1959, *Khramovye Ob'edinenija Maloj Azii i Armenii*, Moscow.

Petrie, W. M. F., 1886, *Naucratis*, Vol. I, London.

P'jankov, I. V., 1964, 'K voprosu o maršrute pokhoda Kira II na massagetov', *VDI* 1964, No. 3, pp. 115-130.

P'jankov, I. V., 1971a, 'Bor'ba Kira II s Astiagom po dannym antičnykh avtorov', *VDI* 1971, No. 3, pp. 16-37.

P'jankov, I. V., 1971b, 'Obrazovanie deržavy Akhemenidov po dannym antičnykh istočnikov', in: *Istorija Iranskogo Gosudarstva i Kul'tury*, Moscow (pp. 83-93).

P'jankov, I. V., 1972, 'Khorasmii Gekateja Miletskogo', *VDI* 1972, No. 2, pp. 3-21.

Poebel, A., 1938, 'Chronology of Darius' first year of reign', *AJSL* 55, pp. 142-165; 285-314.
Porten, B. & Yarden, A., 1986, *Textbook of Aramaic Documents from Ancient Egypt*. Vol. I (Letters), Jerusalem.
Posener, G., 1936, *La première domination Perse en Égypte*, Cairo.
Posener, G., 1938, 'Le canal du Nil à la Mer Rouge avant les Ptolémées', *Chronique d'Égypte* 13, pp. 259-273.
Pottier, E., 1922, *Vases antiques du Louvre*, Paris.
Prášek, J. V., 1906-1910, *Geschichte der Meder und Perser*, 2 Vols., Gotha.
Prášek, J. V., 1912, s.v. 'Kyros der Grosse', *DAO* 13, Heft 3.
Prášek, J. V., 1913, s.v. 'Kambyses', *DAO* 14, Heft 2.

Ravn, O. E., 1942, *Herodotus' Description of Babylon*, Copenhagen.
Rawlinson, G., 1875-1880, *The History of Herodotus*, 4 Vols., London.
Rawlinson, H., 1846-1847, 'The Persian cuneiform inscriptions at Behistun, decyphered and translated, with a memoir on Persian cuneiform inscriptions in general, and on that of Behistun in particular', *JRAS* 10-11.
Ray, J. D., 1987, 'Egypt: Dependence and Independence (425-343 B. C.), in: Sancisi-Weerdenburg, H. W. A. M. (ed.), *Achaemenid History I: Sources, Structures and Synthesis*, Leiden (pp. 79-95).
Reiner, E., 1977, 'The location of Anšan', *RA* 67, pp. 57-62.
Reuther, O., 1926, 'Die Innenstadt von Babylon (Merkes)', *WVDOG* 47.
Roaf, M., 1974, 'The subject peoples on the base of the statue of Darius', *Cahiers de la Délégation archéologique en Iran* 4, pp. 73-160.
Röllig, W., 1964, 'Erwägungen zu neuen Stelen König Nabonids', *ZA* 56, pp. 218-260.
Röllig, W., 1971, s.v. 'Gubaru', *RlA* 3, pp. 671-672.
Root, M. C., 1979, *The King and Kingship in Achaemenid Art* (*AcIr* 19).
Rost, P., 1897, *Untersuchungen zur altorientalischen Geschichte*, Berlin.
Rostovtzeff, M., 1918, *Ellinstvo i Iranstvo na juge Rossii*, Petrograd.
Rostovtzeff, M., 1963, *Greece*, New York.
Rowley, H. H., 1935, *Darius the Mede and the Four World Empires in the Book of Daniel*, Oxford.

Sachs, A., 1977, 'Achaemenid royal names in Babylonian astronomical texts', *AJAH* 1977, No. 2, pp. 129-147.
San Nicolò, M., 1934, 'Zur Chronologie des Bēlšîmanni und Samaš-erîba', *ArOr* 6, pp. 335-338.
San Nicolò, M., 1937, *Beiträge zu einer Prosopographie neubabylonischer Beamten der Zivil- und Tempelverwaltung*, Munich.
Sancisi-Weerdenburg, H. W. A. M., 1980, *Yaunā en Persai. Grieken en Perzen in een ander Perspectief*, Groningen.
Sancisi-Weerdenburg, H., 1985, 'The death of Cyrus: Xenophon's Cyropaedia as a source for Iranian history', in: *AcIr* 25, pp. 459-471.
Sarianidi, V. I., 1975, *Afganistan v epokhu bronzy i rannego železa* (Avtoreferat dissertatsii na soiskanie učenoj stepeni doktora istoričeskikh nauk), Moscow.
Sarre, F. & Herzfeld, E., 1910, *Iranische Felsreliefs*, Berlin.
Scala, R. von, 1898, *Die Staatsverträge des Altertums*, Vol. I, Leipzig.
Schachermeyr, F., 1973, *Alexander der Grosse. Das Problem seiner Persönlichkeit und seines Wirkens*, Vienna.
Schaeder, H. H., 1935, 'Über einige altpersische Inschriften', *SPAW* 1935, pp. 489-506.
Schaeder, H. H., 1942, 'Zwei altiranische Ortsname', *ZDMG* 96, pp. 127-138.
Scharff, A. & Moortgat, A., 1950, *Ägypten und Vorderasien im Altertum*, Munich.
Schedl, C., 1965, 'Nabuchodonosor, Arpakšad und Darius', *ZDMG* 115, pp. 242-254.
Scheil, V., 1914, 'Le Gobryas de la Cyropédie et les textes cunéiformes', *RA* 11, pp. 165-174.

Schmeija, H., 1975, 'Dareios, Xerxes, Artaxerxes. Drei persische Königsnamen in griechischer Deutung', *Die Sprache* 21, pp. 184-188.

Schmidt, E. F., 1953-1970, *Persepolis*, 3 Vols., Chicago.

Schmitt, R., 1967, 'Altpersische Minutien', *Zeitschrift für vergleichende Sprachforschung* 81, Heft 1-2, pp. 54-62.

Schmitt, R., 1977, 'Die Verfassungsdebatte bei Herodot', *Historia* 26, pp. 243-244.

Schmitt, R., 1978, *Die Iranier-Namen bei Aischylos*, Vienna.

Schmitt, R., 1980, 'Zur babylonischen Version der Bīsutūn-Inschrift', *AfO* 27, pp. 106-126.

Schmitt, R., 1981, 'Altpersische Siegel-Inschriften', *Veröffentlichungen der Iranischen Kommission* 10, Vienna.

Schmitt, R., 1982, 'Achaemenid throne-names', *Annali dell' Istituto Orientale di Napoli* 42, pp. 83-95.

Schubert, R., 1890, *Herodots Darstellung der Cyrussage*, Breslau.

Schwabacher, W., 1957, 'Satrapenbildnisse. Zum neuen Münzporträt des Tissaphernes', in: Schauenburg, K. (ed.), *Charites. Studien zur Altertumswissenschaft*, Bonn (pp. 27-32).

Schwenzner, W., 1922-1923, 'Gobryas', *Klio* 18, pp. 41-58; 226-252.

Seager, R. & Tuplin, Chr., 1980, 'The freedom of the Greeks of Asia: on the origins of a concept and the creation of a slogan', *JHS* 100, pp. 141-154.

Sealey, R., 1976, *A History of the Greek City States, ca. 700-338 B. C.*, Berkeley, Los Angeles and London.

Seidl, U., 1976, 'Ein Relief Dareios' I in Babylon', *AMI* NF, 9, pp. 125-130.

Shahbazi, A. Sh., 1982, 'Darius in Scythia and Scythians in Persepolis', *AMI* NF, 15, pp. 189-235.

Shea, W. H., 1971-1972, 'An unrecognized vassal king of Babylon in the early Achaemenid period', *Andrews University Seminary Studies*, Vol. 9 (1971), No. 1, pp. 51-67; No. 2, pp. 99-128; Vol. 10 (1972), No. 1, pp. 88-117; No. 2, pp. 147-178.

Šilejko, V., 1925, 'Pečat' tsarja Artakserksa', *Žizn' muzeja* (Bulletin of the State Museum of Fine Arts, No. 1), Moscow (pp. 17-19).

Smith, M., 1965, 'Das Judentum in Palästina während der Perserzeit', in: *Fischer Weltgeschichte*, Vol. 5, Frankfurt am Main (pp. 356-370).

Smith, S., 1924, *Babylonian Historical Texts Relating to the Capture and Downfall of Babylon*, London.

Smith, S., 1944, *Isaiah Chapters XL-LV. Literary Criticism and History*, London.

Soden, W. von, 1975, review of: Grayson, A. K., 1975, *Babylonian Historical-literary Texts*, Toronto and Buffalo, in: *ZA* 65, pp. 282-285.

Soden, W. von, 1983, 'Kyros und Nabonid. Propaganda und Gegenpropaganda', *AMI*, Ergänzungsband 10, pp. 61-68.

Spalinger, A., 1977, 'Egypt and Babylonia: a survey (c. 620 B.C.-550 B.C.)', *Studien zur altägyptischen Kultur* 5, pp. 221-244.

Spek, R. J. van der, 1982, 'Did Cyrus the Great introduce a new policy towards subdued nations? Cyrus in Assyrian perspective', *Persica* 10, pp. 273-283.

Starr, C. G., 1975-1977, 'Greeks and Persians in the fourth century B.C.', *IrAn*, Vol. 11 (1975), pp. 39-93; Vol. 12 (1977), pp. 49-115.

Stern, E., 1984, 'The Persian Empire and the Political and Social History of Palestine in the Persian Period', in: *The Cambridge History of Judaism*, Vol. I, pp. 70-87.

Stolper, M. W., 1983, 'The Death of Artaxerxes I', *AMI* NF, 16, pp. 223-236.

Stolper, M. W., 1984, 'The neo-Babylonian text from Persepolis', *JNES* 43, pp. 299-310.

Stolper, M. W., 1985, *Entrepreneurs and Empire. The Murašû Archive, the Murašû Firm and Persian Rule in Babylonia*, Leiden.

Stolper, M. W., 1987, 'Bēlšunu the satrap', in: Rochberg-Halton, F. (ed.), *Language, Literature, and History: Philological and Historical Studies Presented to Erica Reiner*, Locust Valley, New York (pp. 389-402).

Stronach, D., 1971, 'Cyrus the Great', *Bostan chenasi va honar-e Iran*, No. 7/8, pp. 4-21.

Stronach, D., 1974, 'Achaemenid Village I at Susa and the Persian migration to Fars', *Iraq* 36, pp. 239-248.

Stronach, D., 1978, *Pasargadae. A Report on the Excavations Conducted by the British Institute of Persian Studies from 1961 to 1963*, Oxford.

Struve, W., 1928, 'Zur Geschichte Ägyptens der Spätzeit', *IAN, OGN* 1928, pp. 197-212.

Struve, V.V., 1938, 'Podlinnaja pričina razrušenija iudejskogo khrama na Elefantine v 410 g. do n.e.', *VDI* 1938, No. 4, pp. 99-119.

Struve, V.V., 1943, 'Gerodot i političeskie tečenija v Persii epokhi Darija I', *VDI* 1943, No. 3, pp. 12-35.

Struve, V.V., 1946a, 'Pokhod Darija I na sakov-massagetov', *IAN* 3, No. 3, pp. 231-250.

Struve, V.V., 1946b, 'Novye dannye istorii Armenii, zasvidetel'stvovannye Bekhistunskoj nadpis'ju', *Izvestija AN Armjanskoj SSR* 8, pp. 31-38.

Struve, V.V., 1949a, 'Darij I i skify Pričernomor'ja', *VDI* 1949, No. 4, pp. 15-28.

Struve, V.V. 1949b, 'Vosstanie v Margiane pri Darii I', *VDI* 1949, No. 2, pp. 10-29.

Struve, V.V., 1951, 'Reforma pis'mennosti pri Darii I', *VDI* 1951, No. 1, pp. 186-191.

Struve, V.V., 1952, 'Datirovka Bekhistunskoj nadpisi' *VDI* 1952, No. 1, pp. 26-48.

Struve, V.V., 1954, 'Vosstanie v Egipte v pervyj god tsarstvovanija Darija I', *PS* 1, pp. 7-13.

Struve, V.V., 1968, *Etjudy po istorii Severnogo Pričernomor'ja, Kavkaza i Srednej Azii*, Leningrad.

Summer, W.M., 1974, 'Excavations at Tall-i Malyan, 1971-1972', *Iran* 12, pp. 155-180.

Sykes, P., 1921, *A History of Persia*, 2 Vols., London.

Szemerényi, O., 1966, 'Iranica II', *Die Sprache* 12, pp. 190-226.

Szemerényi, O., 1980, *Four Iranian ethnic names: Scythian-Skudra-Sogdian-Saka*, Vienna.

Tadmor, H., 1964, 'The historical background of the Edict of Cyrus', in: D. Ben Gurion Anniversary Volume, Jerusalem (pp. 450-473; in Hebrew).

Tadmor, H., 1965, 'The inscriptions of Nabunaid: historical arrangement', in: *Studies in Honor of Benno Landsberger*, Chicago (pp. 351-363).

Tarn, W.W., 1948, *Alexander the Great*, 2 Vols., Cambridge.

Thumb, A., 1902, 'Die altpersischen Keilinschriften', *Deutsche Rundschau* 112, pp. 381-393.

Tolman, H.C., 1908, *The Behistun Inscriptions of King Darius*, Nashville.

Tolstov, S.P., 1938, 'Osnovnye voprosy drevnej istorii Srednej Azii', *VDI* 1938, No. 1, pp. 176-203.

Tolstov, S.P., 1948, *Po sledam drevnekhoresmijskoj tsivilizatsii*, Moscow and Leningrad.

Tolstov, S.P., 1962, *Po drevnim del'tam Oksa i Jaksarta*, Moscow.

Torrey, Ch. C., 1917-1918, 'The bilingual inscription from Sardis', *AJSL* 34, pp. 185-198.

Torrey, Ch. C., 1928, *The Second Isaiah. A New Interpretation*, New York and Edinburgh.

Trümpelmann, L., 1967, 'Zur Entstehungsgeschichte des Monumentes Dareios' I. von Bisutun und zur Datierung der Einführung der altpersischen Schrift', *Archäologischer Anzeiger* 3, pp. 281-298.

Tozzi, P., 1975, 'Erodoto V, 106: nota preliminare sulla insurrezione ionica', *Athenaeum* NS, 53, fasc. 1-2, pp. 136-143.

Tozzi, P., 1976-1977, 'Plutarco e la rivolta ionica', *Rivista storica dell' Antichità* 6-7, pp. 75-80.

Tozzi, P., 1977, 'Erodoto e le responsabilità dell' inizio della rivolta ionica', *Athenaeum* NS, 55, fasc. 1-2, pp. 127-135.

Tozzi, P., 1978, *La rivolta ionica*, Pisa.

Turaev, B.A., 1911, 'Skifija v ieroglifičeskoj nadpisi', *Sbornik statej v čest' S. F. Platonov*, St Petersburg (pp. 358-365).

Tjurin, V.O., 1951, 'Social'noe položenie "kurtaš" po dokumentam iz "Sokroviščnitsy" Persepolja', *VDI* 1951, No. 3, pp. 21-39.

Tjurin, V.O., 1956, 'K ustanovleniju značenija social'no-ekonomičeskikh terminov Bekhistunskoj nadpisi', *Trudy Instituta Jazykoznanija AN SSSR* 6, pp. 499-525.

Unger, E., 1970, *Babylon. Die heilige Stadt nach der Beschreibung der Babylonier*, Berlin.
Ungnad, A., 1907, 'Bêl-šimanni, ein neuer König Babylons und der Länder', *OLZ* 1907, pp. 464-467.
Ungnad, A., 1960, 'Neubabylonische Privaturkunden aus der Sammlung Amherst', *AfO* 19, pp. 74-82.

Vallat, F., 1980, 'Suse et l'Elam', *Éditions Recherche sur les civilisations*, Mémoire, No. 1, Paris.
Vercoutter, J., 1962, *Textes biographiques du Sérapéum de Memphis*, Paris.
Vogelsang, W., 1985, 'Early historical Arachosia in South-East Afghanistan. A meeting-place between East and West', *IrAn* 20, pp. 55-99.
Vogelsang, W., 1986, 'Four short notes on the Bisutun text and monument', *IrAn* 21, pp. 121-140.
Vogelsang, W., 1987, 'Some remarks on Eastern Iran in the Late-Achaemenid Period', in: Sancisi-Weerdenburg, H. (ed.), *Achaemenid History. I. Sources, Structures and Synthesis* (Proceedings of the Groningen 1983 Achaemenid History Workshop), Leiden (pp. 183-189).
Vogelsang, W., 1988, 'Some observations on Achaemenid Hyrcania. A combination of sources', in: Kuhrt, A. & Sancisi-Weerdenburg, H. (eds.), *Achaemenid History. III. Method and Theory* (Proceedings of the London 1985 Achaemenid History Workshop), Leiden (pp. 121-135).

Walker, C.B.F., 1972, 'A recently identified fragment of the Cyrus Cylinder', *Iran* 10, pp. 158-159.
Wallinga, H.T., 1984, 'The Ionian Revolt', *Mnemosyne* 37, pp. 401-437.
Wallinga, H.T., 1987, 'The ancient Persian navy and its predecessors', in: Sancisi-Weerdenburg, H. (ed.), *Achaemenid History. I. Sources, Structures and Synthesis* (Proceedings of the Groningen 1983 Achaemenid History Workshop), Leiden (pp. 47-77).
Walser, G., 1983, 'Der Tod des Kambyses', *Historia* 40, pp. 8-18.
Walser, G., 1984, *Hellas und Iran*, Darmstadt.
Ward, W.H., 1910, *The Seal Cylinders of Western Asia*, Washington.
Waterman, L., 1954, 'The camouflaged purge of three Messianic conspirators', *JNES* 13, pp. 73-78.
Weidner, E.F., 1931-1932, 'Die älteste Nachricht über das persische Königshaus. Kyros I. Ein Zeitgenosse Aššurbanapalis', *AfO* 7, pp. 1-7.
Weinfeld, M., 1964, 'Cult centralization in Israel in the light of a Neo-Babylonian analogy', *JNES* 23, pp. 202-212.
Weissbach, F.H., 1908, 'Zur neubabylonischen und achämenidischen Chronologie', *ZDMG* 62, pp. 629-647.
Weissbach, F.H., 1924, s.v. 'Kyros', *PW*, Supplementband 4, cols. 1128-1166.
Weissbach, F.H., 1933, 'Zu der neuen Xerxes-Inschrift von Persepolis', *ZA* 41, pp. 318-321.
Weissbach, F.H., 1940, 'Die fünfte Kolumne der grossen Bīsutūn-Inschrift', *ZA* 46, pp. 53-82.
Wells, J., 1907, 'The Persian friends of Herodotus', *JHS* 27, pp. 37-47.
Westlake, H.D., 1981, 'Decline and fall of Tissaphernes', *Historia* 30, pp. 257-279.
Wetzel, F. & Schmidt, E. & Mallwitz, A., 1957, *Das Babylon der Spätzeit* (WVDOG 62), Berlin.
Widengren, G., 1968, 'Über einige Probleme in der altpersischen Geschichte', in: *Festschrift für Leo Brandt*, Cologne and Opladen (pp. 517-533).
Widengren, G., 1969, *Der Feudalismus im alten Iran*, Cologne and Opladen.
Widengren, G., 1974, 'La royauté de l'Iran antique', *AcIr* 1, pp. 84-89.

Wiedemann, A., 1880, *Geschichte Ägyptens von Psammetich I. bis auf Alexander den Grossen*, Leipzig.
Wiesehöfer, J., 1978, *Der Aufstand Gaumātas und die Anfänge Dareios' I*, Bonn.
Wijnen, M., 1972-1974, 'Excavations in Iran, 1967-1972', *Persica* 6, pp. 51-93.
Wilcken, U., 1942, *Über Entstehung und Zweck des Königsfriedens*, Berlin.
Wilkie, J. M., 1951, 'Nabonidus and the later Jewish exiles', *Journal of Theological Studies* NS, 2, pp. 36-44.
Will, E., 1960, 'Chabrias et les finances de Tachôs', *Revue des Études Anciennes* 62, pp. 225-275.
Winckler, H., 1889, *Untersuchungen zur altorientalischen Geschichte*, Leipzig.
Winckler, H., 1898, review of: Prášek, J., *Forschungen zur Geschichte des Altertums*, Leipzig 1897, in: *OLZ*, pp. 38-45.
Wiseman, D. J., 1974, 'Murder in Mesopotamia', *Iraq* 36, pp. 249-260.
Wiseman, D. J., 1983, *Nebuchadrezzar and Babylon*, Oxford University Press.
Woolley, L., 1955, *Excavations at Ur*, London.
Woolley, L., 1962, 'The Neo-Babylonian and Persian periods', *Ur Excavations*, Vol. IX, London.

Yoyotte, J., 1972, 'Les inscriptions hiéroglyphiques. Darius et l'Égypte', *JA* 1972, pp. 254-266.

Zadok, R., 1976, 'On the connections between Iran and Babylonia in the sixth century B.C.', *Iran* 14, pp. 61-78.
Zadok, R., 1978, 'West Semitic toponyms in Assyrian and Babylonian sources', in: *Studies in the Bible and the Ancient Near East*, Jerusalem (pp. 163-179).
Zadok, R., 1981, review of *BID*, in: *BiOr* 38, pp. 657-665.
Zadok, R., 1981-1982, 'Iranian and Babylonian Notes', *AfO* 28, pp. 135-139.

CHRONOLOGICAL TABLE

10th century B.C.	Start of Persian immigration into southwestern Iran
c. 675-640	Reign of Chishpish
c. 600-559	Reign of Cambyses I, king of the Persians
558-530	Reign of Cyrus II
553	Revolt of the Persian tribes against Median domination
550	Victory of Cyrus II over the Median king Astyages
c. 549	Persian conquest of Elam. Treaty between the Lydian king Croesus and the Egyptian pharaoh Amasis
549-548	Persian conquest of Parthia, Hyrcania and Armenia
547	Cilicia chooses the side of the Persians. Lydia conquered by Cyrus II
546	Persian conquest of all of Asia Minor
545-539	Persian conquest of eastern Iranian and Central Asian lands
Spring of 539	Persian advance against Babylonia
August 539	Persian defeat of Babylonian army at Opis
October 10, 539	Cyrus' army takes Sippar
October 12, 539	Persian occupation of Babylon
October 29, 539	Triumphant entry of Cyrus II into Babylon
539-538	Persian conquest of Syria, Palestine, Phoenicia and Samaria
538	Decree of Cyrus II concerning the rebuilding of the Jerusalem temple and the permission to the Jews to return from Babylonian captivity
538-537	Reign of Cambyses II, king of Babylon
November(?), 530	Persian war against the Massagetae, and death of Cyrus II
August 530– July 522	Reign of Cambyses II, ruler of the Achaemenid Empire
Spring 525	Battle at Pelusium between the Persian and the Egyptian armies
Summer 525	Persian conquest of Egypt
525-401	First period of Persian rule in Egypt
March 11, 522	Revolt of Gaumata
July 1, 522	Gaumata declares himself ruler of the Achaemenid empire
September 29, 522	Death of Gaumata and Darius' accession to the Persian throne
522-486	Reign of Darius I
October 3, 522	Revolt of Nebuchadnezzar III (Nidintu-bel) in Babylonia
December 13, 522	Battle along the Tigris between Darius' army and that of Nebuchadnezzar III
December 18, 522	Victory of Darius I over Nebuchadnezzar III at a battle along the Euphrates
December 29, 522	Battle at Kapishakanish between the forces of the satrap of Arachosia, Vivana, and those of the rebel Vahyazdata
December 31, 522	Battle at Izala between the forces of Vaumisa, general of Darius I, and rebellious Armenians
January 12, 521	Victory of Vidarna (Hydarnes), general of Darius I, over rebellious Medes at a battle near the town of Maru in Media
February 21, 521	Victory of Vivana, satrap of Arachosia, over Vahyazdata's troops in Gandutava in Arachosia
March 8, 521	Battle between rebellious Parthians and the forces of Vishtaspa (Hystaspes), father of Darius I, at Vishpauzatish in Parthia
March 521	Decisive victory of Vivana over the forces of Vahyazdata in Arachosia
May 7, 521	Victory of Darius I over rebellious Medes at a battle near Kunduru
May 20, 521	Battle at Zuzu in Armenia between the forces of Dadarshish, general of Darius I, and rebellious Armenians

May 24, 521	Battle at Rakha in Persia between rebellious Persians headed by Vahyazdata and the army of Artavardiya, general of Darius I
May 30, 521	Victory by Dadarshish over rebellious Armenians at a battle at Tigra, a fortress in Armenia
June 11, 521	Victory by Vaumisa, general of Darius I, over the rebellious Armenians
June, 521	Victory by Takhmaspada, general of Darius I, over the rebellious Armenians at Autiyara
June 20, 521	Victory by Dadarshish over the Armenians at a battle near the fortress of Uyama
July 11, 521	Decisive victory by Vishtaspa over the rebellious Parthians and Hyrcanians at a battle near Patigrabana
July 15, 521	Decisive victory of Artavardiya over the troops of Vahyazdata at a battle near the mountain of Parga in Persia
August 25, 521	Revolt by Nebuchadnezzar IV (Arakha) in Babylonia
October 10, 521	Victory by Darius' army over the rebellious Sagartians under Çiçantakhma
November 27, 521	Capture of Nebuchadnezzar IV by Vindafarna (Intaphernes), general of Darius I
December 28, 521	Victory of Dadarshish, satrap of Bactria, over rebellious Margians
520	Revolt in Elam headed by Atamaita
519	Darius' campaign against the *Sakā tigraxaudā*
519-515	Rebuilding of the Jerusalem temple
518	Darius' sojourn in Egypt
ca. 517	Administrative and financial reforms by Darius I. Persian conquests of northwestern India and of the islands of Samos and Chios
516-512	Persian conquests of Thrace and Macedonia. Darius' war against the Black Sea Scythians
507	Treaty between the Persians and the Athenians
Spring 499	Persian attack on Naxos
Autumn 499	Start of the Ionian Revolt
Summer 498	Defeat of the rebellious Ionians at a battle near Ephesus
497-496	Quashing by the Persians of the revolt by the Cyprian cities
End 496	Defeat of the rebellious Carians at a battle along the Marsyas river
494	Persian victory over the Ionians at the sea battle of Lade
Autumn 494	Persian conquest of rebellious Miletus
493	Quashing of the Ionian Revolt
492	Installation of democracy in the Greek cities of Asia Minor. Unsuccessful campaign by Mardonius against Greece. Arrival in Greece of Persian embassies demanding 'earth and water'
August 12, 490	Battle of Marathon
December, 486	Revolt in Egypt
November, 486	Death of Darius I. Accession to the Persian throne by Xerxes I
486-465	Reign of Xerxes I
January, 484	Quashing of the Egyptian revolt
June-July 484	Revolt in Babylon headed by Bel-Shimanni
483	Digging of a canal in eastern part of the Chalcidice peninsula August 482–March 481 Babylonian revolt under Shamash-eriba
Spring 480	Xerxes' campaign against Greece. Start of the Persian-Greek wars
August 480	Battle of Thermopylae. Sea battle at Artemisium
September 28, 480	Battle of Salamis
479	Battle of Plataea
August 479	Battle of Mycale
Spring 478	Athenian capture upon the Persians of the town of Sestos in the Thracian Chersonesus
478	Establishment of the Delian League, for the war against the Persians

466	Battle at the Eurymedon
August 465	Death of Xerxes I. Accession to the Persian throne by Artaxerxes I
465-424	Reign of Artaxerxes I
460	Revolt by Inarus in Egypt. Conquest of Memphis by the rebels. Battle at Papremis
454	Quashing of Inarus' revolt
c. 454	Revolt by the Syrian satrap Megabyzus
449	Cimon's expedition to Cyprus. Peace of Callias. End of Persian-Greek wars
431-404	Peloponnesian war
424	Death of Artaxerxes I. Murder of Xerxes II. Reign of Sekyndianos
February 423-404	Reign of Darius II
c. 413	Revolt by Pissouthnes
412-410	Treaties between Sparta and the Persian satrap Tissaphernes
411	Evagoras installed as king on Cyprus
July 410	Destruction of the Jewish temple at Elephantine
410-408	Revolts in Asia Minor and Media against Persian domination
409	Athenian victory over the Peloponnesian and Persian fleets in the harbour of Cyzicus
408	Treaty between the Persian satrap Pharnabazus and the Athenians. Appointment of Cyrus the Younger as satrap in Asia Minor
407	Appointment of Lysander as admiral of the Peloponnesian fleet, stationed in Asia Minor
c. 405	Revolt by Amyrtaeus in Egypt
March 404	Death of Darius II. Accession of the Persian throne by Artaxerxes II.
404-359	Reign of Artaxerxes II
401	Revolt of Cyrus the Younger
September 3, 401	Battle of Cunaxa
399	Deposition of Amyrtaeus, and the coming to power in Egypt of Nepherites I
397	Start of the war between Sparta and Persia
396	Spartan military campaigns in Asia Minor
395	Execution of Tissaphernes
395-377	Reign of Hecatomnus, ruler of Caria
August 10, 394	Victory of the Persian and Athenian fleets over the Spartans
393-382	Reign of Achoris, pharaoh of Egypt
392	Appointment of Autophradates as satrap of Lydia
391	Defeat of the Spartan general Thibron by the Persian army under the Ionian satrap Struthas
390	Evagoras acts independently of the Persian king
389	Treaty between Evagoras, the Athenians and Egypt against Persia
388	Appointment of Tiribazus as satrap of Ionia and Lydia
386	The 'King's Peace', or the Peace of Antalcidas, between Persia and the Greek states
381	Persian victory over Evagoras at a battle near the city of Kition
380	Treaty between Evagoras and Orontes, the Persian governor in Asia Minor
380-363	Reign of Nectanebo I, pharaoh of Egypt
378	Establishment of the Second Athenian Sea League for the war against Persia
377-340	Reign of Mausolus, ruler of Caria
373	Unsuccessful campaign of Persian army and Athenian mercenaries against Egypt. Revolt of the Cappadocian satrap Datames
367	Revolt of the Phrygian satrap Ariobarzanes. Great satrapal revolt
362-360	Reign of Tachos, pharaoh of Egypt
361	Financial reforms by Tachos

359	Quashing of the satrapal revolt
December 359	Death of Artaxerxes II. Accession to the Persian throne by Ochus (Artaxerxes III)
359-338	Reign of Artaxerxes III
356-352	Revolt by Artabazus and Orontes, Persian satraps in Asia Minor
353-350	Reign of Artemisia in Caria
350	Unsuccessful attack by Artaxerxes III on Egypt
349-344	Revolt of Phoenician cities and Cyprus against Persia
345	Artaxerxes III takes the rebellious city of Sidon
Winter 343	Campaign of Artaxerxes III against Egypt
342	Persian conquest of Memphis and quashing of the Egyptian revolt
342-332	Second period of Persian domination in Egypt
340-335	Reign of Pixodarus, ruler of Caria
338	Murder of Artaxerxes III
338-336	Reign of Arses
336-330	Reign of Darius III
Spring 334	Campaign of Alexander of Macedonia against the Achaemenid empire
May 334	Battle at the Granicus
November 333	Battle of Issus
January-July 332	Alexander's siege of Tyre
End 332	Macedonian conquest of Egypt
October 1, 331	Battle of Gaugamela
October 331	Coronation of Alexander of Macedonia as king of Babylon
330	Entrance of Macedonian troops into Susa. Fall of Persepolis and Pasargadae to Alexander. Burning of Persepolis. Occupation of Ecbatana. Fall of the Achaemenid empire.

INDEX

Sources

Modern scholars

Ancient and Early Islamic Writers

Subject index

ILLUSTRATIONS

Ill. 1. Tomb of Cyrus the Great, Pasargadae.

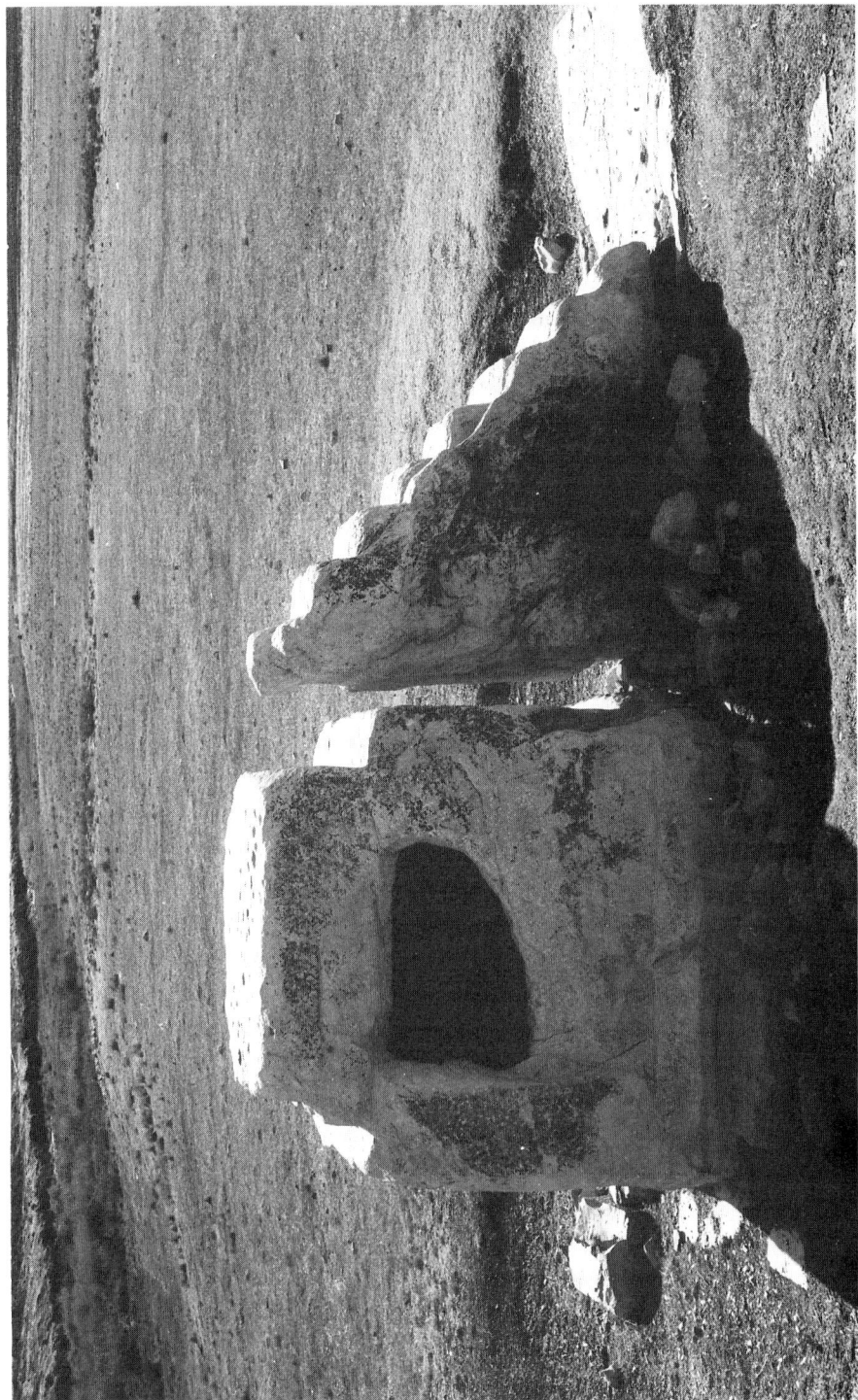

Ill. 2. Fire altar, Pasargadae.

Ill. 3. View of the Persepolis terrace.

Ill. 4. Relief depicting Darius, Perspolis.

Ill. 7. Royal Achaemenid tombs at Naqsh-i Rustam, near Persepolis.

Ill. 8. Engraving of royal tomb, in Cornelis de Bruin, Reizen over Moscovië door Persië
en Indië.

Ill. 9. The so-called Darius Statue from Susa, discovered in 1972.

inscriptions

inscriptions

inscr.

inscriptions

inscriptions

Ill. 10. Drawing of the Behistun relief of Darius, showing the row of captive rebel kings facing the king.

Ill. 11. Sculpture of Udjahorresne.

Ill. 12. The remaining walls of the Bala Hissar of Balkh, the Bactra of the Achaemenid period.

Ill. 5. The Gate of Xerxes, Persepolis, at the beginning of the eighteenth century. Engraving in Cornelis de Bruin, Reizen over Moscovië door Persië en Indië.

Ill. 6. Cylinder seal showing Darius.